American Society:
Problems & Dilemmas

ALAN WELLS

Tulane University

Goodyear Publishing Company, Inc.
Pacific Palisades, California

For S. K., M. H., and M. C. M.

Library of Congress Cataloging in Publication Data

Main entry under title:

American society: problems & dilemmas.

     Includes bibliographies.
     CONTENTS: People, politics, and government:
Harris, F. R. Let the people rule. McCloskey,
P. N., Jr. Congressional politics. Commager, H. S.
The misuse of power. Bodenheimer, T. The poverty
of the state, [etc.]
     1. United States—Social conditions—1960-
—Addresses, essays, lectures. 2. United States—
Economic conditions—1961-   —Addresses, essays,
lectures. 3. United States—Politics and govern-
ment—1969-   —Addresses, essays, lectures.
I. Wells, Alan, 1940-
HN59.A57   309.1'73'092   75-13352
ISBN 0-87620-071-4

Library of Congress Catalog Card Number: 75-13352

ISBN: 0-87620-071-4

Y-0714-9

Current printing (last number):
10 9 8 7 6 5 4 3 2 1

Printed in the United States of America

Contents

Preface

This book seeks to provide a basis for understanding the problems and changes in American society. It is concerned with the major organizational structures in America that shape much of what we do, aspire to, and think. No book, I believe, can fully describe the society in which we live, but a knowledge of social structure can be of great value for continuing analysis and awareness of what is taking place around us. The book is designed primarily for courses in American society, social problems, and social institutions. It might also be useful in an introductory sociology course that is divided between basic principles of interaction and sociological concepts on the one hand and social structural analyses on the other. The book would serve as a reading and discussion source for the latter.

The intended audience of the book consists of undergraduate students and I have tried to take their needs into account in selecting materials. The readings have therefore been chosen for their intrinsic interest and style as well as for their content. Some are not easy to understand because they deal with complex subjects, but any interested undergraduate student should be able to master them. All of the authors, I believe, avoid the worst forms of pretentious and unnecessary social science jargon. The authors of the readings range from social scientists and professional writers to politicians. I think that they share a talent for communicating to lay audiences on important issues in public affairs.

I wish to acknowledge the debt to my former teachers Bennett Berger, Irving Louis Horowitz, John F. Scott, and Kenneth Kammeyer, who have influenced my thinking about American society. I would like to thank Jeffrey Lazerow, Glennon Harrison, Robert Becker, Mary McCarthy, and Karen McLafferty for the help they have given in producing this volume.

Introduction

Few would deny that contemporary America is a highly complex and dynamic society. Such complexity and dynamism make our understanding of how America operates highly provisional, and in many ways, speculative. Indeed, nowhere is this more evident than in the different and sometimes conflicting approaches and methods used by social scientists in their efforts to understand American social structure. Some have focused on American culture—the society's major values and norms—while other investigators have emphasized the structure of inequality in America—that is, the unequal distribution of wealth, power, and prestige.

Although these are valid and useful strategies for understanding American society, an alternative approach has guided the selection of readings in the following pages. This approach examines the "organizational skeleton" of American society. The image of society embodied in this emphasis is one of people in constant and complex patterns of interaction which, over time, become organized into various types of social structures. It is recognized that we cannot get a total view of society in this way but that we are merely focusing on the identifiable parts of a complex social whole. But much interaction does give rise to social relations of various types, and the relations are the components of what we call *groups*. The groups are sometimes linked in quite stable ways to form organizations, which, in turn, are joined together in complexes that may be called institutional orders. These institutional orders may be formed with some correspondence to the basic needs and problems facing the society. But because they are real organizational complexes they cannot, for example, be purely political, economic, or religious. There are economic institutions—major corporations, banks, and so on—which make up the economic order. Such organizations, however, are by no means solely the embodiment of the society's economic problems. They have a political life of their own, they may influence military and educational decisions, and so on. Similarly, religious organizations do more than minister to the society's spiritual needs. Among other things, they manage sizable financial holdings and engage in political lobbying.

The character of the society may be derived from an examination of these institutions, their linkages, and the balance of power among them. It is usually acknowledged that economic, military and political organizations are the most important in American society, although there is considerable dispute over which is the dominant institutional order and whether or not the three are really separate (the military–industrial complex dispute). Others considered of less importance are religious, educational, and scientific organizational complexes. All interactions, groups, and organizations cannot, of course, be encompassed in this study of the major institutional orders. But these institutional orders are of central importance in the sociological task of describing how humans are shaped by society, and in turn how individuals may change society. Thinking of institutions as organizational complexes is a vital first step in understanding society, for these complexes provide crucial links between individuals, groups, and society. Thus, these complexes are the organizational skeleton of American society.

The book is divided into six sections, each with an introduction that gives an overview of the institutional area and summarizes the readings. Each section introduction ends with a list of suggested readings.

The first three sections deal with what are usually recognized as the dominant American institutions – the political, economic, and military. The linkages between them are dealt with, especially in the concluding section on the military and the military–industrial complex. The remaining sections deal with three other important institutions: science, education, and religion. Although these institutions, and the organizations that contain them, wield considerably lesser social power than the first three, they are nonetheless important in shaping social life in America.

Part I.
People, Politics, and Government

The focus of this section is on those formal political structures that formulate and carry out public policies. The first of these are political parties, which are largely concerned with election campaigning. Although a political party may attempt to devise policy guidelines in the form of a party platform, these are not binding even on the presidential candidate elected under the party's banner. Candidates for lesser offices—in the Senate, Congress, and local offices—are free to choose their own issues and answers. The next formal political structure considered is the elected body—the executive and legislative branches of federal, state, and local governments. Finally, we will examine the courts and two government bureaucracies—the civil service and police.

These organizations are not, of course, the only ones engaged in political activities, nor is all power found within their confines. Power, often defined as the ability to exert one's will over another, pervades all organizations and groups. Thus, one can study the dynamics of power in street gangs, families, churches, country clubs, and universities. One sociologist, Ralf Dahrendorf, has pointed out that power groupings form naturally in any organization.[1] At the societal level, political institutions are certainly not the sole repositories of power. Struggles go on within political institutions, and conflict occurs between political and other institutions. Thus, the church—an "other" institution—often becomes involved in legislation affecting morality, the military in defense policies, and economic or-

[1] Ralf Dahrendorf, *Class and Class Conflict in Industrial Society* (Stanford: Stanford University Press, 1969), especially Ch. 5.

1

ganizations in the many topics that affect their interests. The balance of power between these institutions is dealt with in the discussion of the military–industrial complex in Part III. The task in this section is to sketch formal political institutions without assuming that they are fully autonomous and therefore beyond the influence of other parts of society. Clearly, it takes money to run a political party and electoral campaigns, and in the absence of other forms of funding, politicians are often subservient to the economic interests that back them. For example, some of the Watergate problems that led to the resignation of President Nixon stemmed directly from the need and the ability of politicians to raise money quickly from wealthy individuals and corporations.

Political Parties

The American political scene is dominated by the Republican and Democratic parties. Both tend to be nonideological. That is, they attempt to make themselves acceptable to most of the electorate, mainly by saying little that would offend anyone. They concentrate on electing candidates acceptable to the party. The grounds for this choice are not publicly known. The national organization is mobilized primarily during presidential election years, while the fifty state organizations devote their efforts to local elections. However, once presidential candidates are nominated, they are free to select their own campaign organization. The now infamous Committee to Re-elect the President in 1972 was such an organization. Both parties have members who are conservative and others who are liberal. Switches from one party to another on ideological grounds are not considered essential. The Democratic party does seem to be becoming more liberal and the Republican more conservative. Thus, major political figures—for example, John Lindsay and John Connally—have switched to parties in which they feel ideologically more at home. The parties demand only minimal participation from their ordinary members. A citizen's political preference becomes a matter of public record when he registers to vote. This clarifies eligibility for party primaries. All taxpayers are also invited to identify their party preference to facilitate tax donation check-offs on income tax forms. Voter registration may discourage political participation, since it requires effort to register well in advance of elections. Both party registration and voting in America appear to be increasingly unstable, in part because of the nonideological nature of political campaigns. Overall, however, the Democrats are strongest in the South and among ethnic groups, Catholics, and labor union members. Republican strength is concentrated in the Midwest, in small towns and rural areas, and among white Anglo-Saxon Protestants, and they are also gaining strength in the more affluent suburban areas. Registration records and the results of gubernatorial, Senate, and House elections indicate that the Democrats are the stronger party, but Republican money— rather than a mass following—has kept that party competitive.

During the 1972 presidential campaign there was some decrease in the use of showmanship as the dominant campaigning technique. McGovern relied on celebrities to boost his image and appeal. But the nominating convention and the platform on which he ran were strongly liberal, with disastrous results. McGovern received 27.8 million votes and Nixon 44.6 million, but there was not a general Republican landslide. The conservative campaign of Republican candidate Goldwater, in 1964, ended with a landslide *against* a clear ideological position.

Minority political parties in the United States often concentrate on a few political issues or are much more strongly committed to ideologies than are either of the two major parties. The most important minority political party in national campaigns in recent years has been George Wallace's American Independent Party. Although it has some appeal in conservative and blue collar constituencies nationwide, its strength is concentrated in the South. Other parties are usually limited to one geographical region or ideology and have relatively small, sometimes miniscule, followings. They include the Conservative and Liberal Parties of New York State, the National States' Rights Party, the Socialist Labor Party, and the Socialist Workers' Party. Although the New York parties have elected candidates to statewide office (for example, Conservative Senator James Buckley), they show no signs of developing into nationwide threats. The main reason that minor parties do not thrive is that American elections are usually held for single member districts—that is, winner takes all. A system of proportionate representation (as in France and Italy), based on the percentage of the votes cast, stimulates the development of many political parties and sometimes leads to political chaos. There is some possibility that new major parties could form in the United States. An increasing number of voters are registering as independents. Another major source of political recruits would be habitual nonvoters. For example, in presidential elections, the turnout is seldom more than 60 percent of *registered* voters. Thus, even a landslide in a presidential election means that the winner attracted the votes of considerably below 50 percent of the total *eligible* population.

The Executive

The executive branch of government is considerably larger than the general public realizes. The only two elected officials in the executive branch are the president and vice-president. In addition to the White House staff and advisors, the president oversees a wide range of organizations including the Domestic Council, the National Security Council, the Council of Economic Policy, the Council of Economic Affairs, the Office of Management and Budget, the Office of Emergency Preparedness, the Office of Consumer Affairs, the Office of Economic Opportunity, the Office of Telecommunications Policy, a Special Office for Drug Abuse, the Council on Environmental Quality, the Council on International Economic Policy, and NASA. The president appoints the eleven departmental secretaries who oversee the major government departments—the federal bureaucracy. These secretaries and the vice-president form the cabinet. There are more than fifty independent government agencies in addition to these.

Table 1 gives the employment figures for the major federal government departments. The allocation of personnel within each of these departments indicates the importance and power of each. Thus, Defense, with over a million civilian employees, dwarfs all other agencies. On the basis of employment, Big Government is far more a warfare than a welfare bureaucracy. State governments of course, swell the number employed in government agencies.

Table 1
Employment in Government Departments, 1973

Defense	1,125,636	Justice	44,503
Health, Education		State	37,018
and Welfare	112,914	Commerce	32,796
Agriculture	108,500	Housing and Urban	
Treasury	98,254	Development	17,072
Transportation	68,665	Labor	12,886
Interior	66,962		

SOURCE: Allan Clements, *Taylors' Encyclopedia of Government Officials, Federal and State, 1973–74* (Dallas: Political Research, Inc., 1973).

Federal Legislative Branch

Unlike the president and his cabinet, the members of the House and Senate do not sit at the top of large bureaucracies. The knowledge and power of the legislative branch, relative to the executive branch, has been declining over the years. In a very real sense they have no institutional source of power because of this isolation from active administrative organization. Nor, as in other democracies, do they have the backing of large political party organizations. They are organized within the House and Senate into committees—twenty in the House, sixteen in the Senate, and four joint Senate-House committees. It is high rank in these committees, together with powerful backers, that give a representative or senator power.

Congress is the main public scene for lobbyists, individuals who are paid to politic on behalf of special interests. In 1973 there were eighty-three registered lobbies. Business had the largest number, thirty-five. This is one way that economic institutions influence politics. Labor had six lobbies, the power companies three, agriculture three, and professional organizations eleven. There were twenty-five miscellaneous lobbies in 1973. Among the more prominent nonbusiness lobbies are the AFL-CIO's COPE, Common Cause, National Farmers' Union, Americans for Constitutional Action (a conservative lobby), and Ralph Nader's Congress Watch.

The Court System

The federal judicial system is composed of eighty-nine district courts, ten circuit courts of appeal, and the Supreme Court. The highest court has been an object of political interests, as have the appointment and election of judges to lower courts. Note that the courts are not completely autonomous from the other branches of government as they might be, for example, if a body of distinguished lawyers chose their own most distinguished members for high court appointment. The justices of the Supreme Court are appointed by the president and must be confirmed by the Senate. As recently demonstrated, presidential nominees are not always automatically confirmed, nor do they necessarily have the approval of the leadership of the legal profession. Of the current court members, four were appointed by Nixon—Justices Berger, Blackman, Powell, and Rhenquist. These men are usually viewed as the conservative members of the court. Justices Brennan and Stewart are Eisenhower appointees, Marshall was appointed by Johnson, White by Kennedy, and Douglas by Franklin D. Roosevelt. Because Supreme Court justices are appointed for life, they are often far more independent than other federal employees. They are seldom seeking a more lucrative or prestigious position in private life, as is often true of appointees, for example, to federal regulatory commissions such as the Federal Trade Commission, Federal Communications Commission, and the Food and Drug Administration. Allied with the courts and federal government and with some coordination with the military, is a network of police and intelligence agencies. The police constitute fairly large organizations within United States society. Among these are the Federal Bureau of Investigation, the Central Intelligence Agency, the Secret Service, and local police forces. The former has 8,600 agents, and it has been estimated that 40 percent of their time is spent on political work.[2]

The first reading, by Fred R. Harris, calls for an intensification of democratic practices in American politics. His philosophy is similar to that proposed by the "new politics" and is what has come to be called *participatory democracy.* That is, many more people than at present should be informed about politics and should be actively participating in politics. To further this ideal, Harris advocates changing some of the structures of the American government. He would like to remove processes that restrict voting, and he urges that the archaic electoral college process be abolished. Harris points out that, although many barriers have been removed in recent years, the president is still not elected by the popular vote but by a complex electoral college procedure. He advocates direct election of presidents, simplified voter registration, and national holidays for federal elections. Harris' argument can be taken much further and applied to other issues. For example, some analysts argue that states are now meaningless entities and that state governments are antiquated. The Senate is inherently undemocratic since each state, irrespective of its population, has two senators. Finally, a losing vote in our winner-takes-all elections yields no representation, unless one claims that the elected candidate represents his entire constituency, foes as well as supporters.

The second selection is by Paul McCloskey, a maverick Republican congressman whose anti-Vietnam War position led him to an unsuccessful tilt for his party's 1972 presidential nomination. McCloskey analyzes the structure of congressional politics and outlines the in-

[2] See Thomas Powers, "The Government Is Watching," *Atlantic Magazine,* October 1972, pp. 51–63.

formal rules that guide a congressman's behavior. He asserts that congressmen believe that they may lose their seats if voters cast negative votes—votes against the incumbents rather than votes for the challengers. And so many congressmen do not take risks. Much the same probably applies to all political candidates. A good incumbent is one who does not offend anyone. Because of the secret way votes have been cast in the House, congressmen are often not at all accountable to their constituents. Even the *Congressional Record* is not an accurate account of what actually goes on in the House, because it may be amended by self-serving congressmen. And McCloskey points out that, even within the House, all congressmen are not equal because of the seniority system and its effects on the work of powerful committees and their chairmen.

Henry Steele Commager is concerned with the growth of power of the executive branch of government. He notes that the executive has virtually unlimited power in foreign relations today, power that it certainly did not wield in previous periods of American history. Commager's recommendations would make foreign policy more subject to popular will and might prevent the type of minor interventions that ultimately led to devastating wars in Southeast Asia.

The final article in this section, by Thomas Bodenheimer, deals with state government. He analyzes the reasons why many states are nearly bankrupt. The type of local taxation employed and Social Security payments tend to minimize the progressive nature of taxation in the United States by increasing the relative tax burden of the poor. Property taxes, which most local governments rely on for a large part of their revenue, are perhaps the most regressive. Bodenheimer believes that if the poor and middle-income populations were aware of the present distribution of wealth, they would change that distribution by political means. Only if this is done, he thinks, will state and local governments be capable of providing adequate public services without victimizing the poor.

Suggested Reading

Arendt, Hannah. *The Origins of Totalitarianism.* New York: World Publishing, 1958.

Brinton, Crane. *The Anatomy of Revolution.* Rev. ed. New York: Vintage, 1965.

Bazelon, David T. *Power in America: The Politics of the New Class.* New York: New American Library, 1971.

Dolbeare, Kenneth M., and Dolbeare, Patricia. *American Ideologies.* Chicago: Markham, 1971.

Janowitz, Morris. *Political Conflict.* Chicago: Quadrangle, 1970.

Hancock, Donald M., and Sjoberg, Gideon, eds. *Politics in the Post-Welfare State.* New York: Columbia University Press, 1972.

Horowitz, Irving Louis. *Foundations of Political Sociology.* New York: Harper and Row, 1972.

Lipset, Seymour M. *Political Man: The Social Bases of Politics.* New York: Anchor, 1963.

Mendelsohn, Harold, and Crespi, Irving. *Polls, Television and the New Politics.* Scranton, Pa.: Chandler, 1970.

Moore, Barrington, Jr. *Political Power and Social Theory.* New York: Harper and Row, 1962.

Olsen, Marvin E., ed. *Power in Societies.* New York: Macmillan, 1970.

Wolfe, Alan. *The Seamy Side of Democracy.* New York: McKay, 1973.

LET THE PEOPLE RULE

Fred R. Harris

"If liberty and equality, as is thought by some, are chiefly to be found in democracy," Aristotle wrote more than two thousand years ago, "they will be best attained when all persons alike share in the government to the utmost."

That, I believe, is still a true statement of the democratic ideal, but we are a long way yet from making it reality in America, and in some ways we are going backward. It will do no good to reform political parties unless the result is reform of the government. That is what is important.

In 1876, 82 percent of men over the age of twenty-one cast ballots in the Presidential election, but, only 60 percent of the population of voting age came to the polls in 1968. That meant that eight million more potential voters stayed away from the polls in 1968 than did four years earlier, in the 1964 Presidential election. Only thirty million people voted for Mr. Nixon in 1968; forty-seven million potential voters—seventeen million more—did not bother to vote at all.

While it may not be strictly true that "All the ills of democracy can be cured by more democracy," as Alfred E. Smith once said, that statement does point the way we must go.

In some countries the law requires that those who can read and write *must* vote. Strangely, in America, where we pay homage to the democratic ideal, we place all sorts of legal obstacles in the way of voting.

If we really believe in democracy in this country, we must assure every citizen's freedom to vote. If we really believe in citizen participation, we must knock down the unreasonable barriers which still restrict it.

If the rights of the people are to be safeguarded, we must eliminate the obvious and remaining unreasonable restrictions against popular participation in government, including the insupportable restrictions based upon age, color, and residency, as well as the undemocratic Electoral College machinery and illogical voter-registration requirements, all of which work to thwart the will of the people.

Young people today are maturing, both physically and intellectually, at far earlier ages than ever before. Through television and improved education, a young person today becomes aware at an early age of the real world and the problems of the real world; he becomes concerned about these problems and rightly wants to be involved in solving them. We must recognize this fact and respond to it.

The newest generation of Americans is the largest, best-educated, and most dedicated group of young people our nation has ever produced. In 1940, 40 percent of our population was under twenty-five. Today, the proportion is 47 percent, and by 1972 over half of the American population will be under twenty-five. The number of Americans entering college has increased by fully one-third since 1960.

In early 1970, the Congress decided that it could by statute, under the Fourteenth Amendment to the Constitution, give the right to vote in all elections—local, state, and federal—to eighteen-year-olds. In this it agreed with Professor Archibald Cox of Harvard Law School, former Solicitor General, who testified before a Senate Committee that the Supreme Court decision in the case of *Morgan* v. *Katzenbach,* which held that Congress has broad powers to legislate in regard to voting qualifications under the "equal protection" clause of the Constitution, ". . . did recognize fully the power of the Congress to make this determination with respect to voting age, and to change the age limit by statute."

President Nixon signed the bill with some publicly stated misgivings about its constitutionality, and procedures were begun for an early court test. Though the Supreme Court ruled in favor of the lower age for federal elections only, an overwhelming majority of the members of both houses of Congress had recognized the right of eighteen-year-olds to vote, and there should be no stopping of the full implementation of this right by constitutional amendment.

There has been a great change in the age at which young people take jobs, get married, and raise families. Four states—Georgia since 1943, Kentucky since 1955, and Alaska and Hawaii since they entered the Union in 1959—granted the right to persons under twenty-one to vote without any resultant difficulty— rather, indeed, with generally acclaimed success.

Many of the arguments which have been used against the right of eighteen-year-olds to vote were used in the resistance to women's suffrage more than fifty years ago; they are no longer acceptable.

As Senator Edward Kennedy of Massachusetts said in support of the statutory change which he and the Majority Leader of the Senate, Mike Mansfield of Montana, proposed, 30 percent of our forces in Vietnam and one-half of those who have died there are under twenty-one years of age. "They have earned the right to vote," he said, "and they can counsel us wisely at the polls."

America needs the energy, enthusiasm, and idealism of young people as full participants in our political system, and there is no more basic way by which that involvement can be encouraged than by opening up to them the full right of participation at the ballot box.

Historically, the greatest bar to voting in our country has been color. The Voting Rights Act of 1965 was the most effective civil rights legislation ever passed. Under its provisions, requiring the federal government to take affirmative action by sending examiners and inspectors into the Southern states, more than eight hundred thousand additional black voters were registered to vote and more than four hundred black candidates were elected to public office. Today, as Howard A. Glickstein, Staff Director of the U.S. Commission on Civil Rights, has testified, "Significant numbers of moderate white officials hold office because white and black voters have been able to turn out of office the Jim Clarks and the Bull Conners in many communities. This is what the right to vote is all about; the people have the right to determine who will govern and represent them."

The Congress in 1970, rejecting recommendations of the Nixon Administration for relaxation of this highly successful law, voted overwhelmingly for its extension, impressed by the testimony of such witnesses as Vernon E. Jordan, Jr., then Director of the Voter Education Project of the Southern Regional Council, who graphically predicted what would have resulted from failure to do so when he said: "I know as well as any man in this room that Canton and Grenada and Selma and Sandersville and hundreds of other Southern communities stand poised and ready to eliminate the burgeoning black vote in their jurisdiction. The slightest flicker of a green light from Washington is all these white-dominated communities need. When they receive the signal, they will act."

Despite the recommendations of President Nixon to the contrary, no such regressive signal came from Washington, and Congress made it clear that there was to be no retreat from the front lines in the fight for the basic right to vote to which black people had so recently advanced.

As a part of its landmark decision to extend the Voting Rights Act of 1965, the Congress decided to go two steps further and strike down residency and literacy requirements because it was felt that, in a highly mobile society and one in which television is in almost universal use, such requirements were unnecessary and improper abridgments of the right of suffrage.

Father Theodore M. Hesburgh, President of Notre Dame University and Chairman of the U.S. Commission on Civil Rights, made the case against residency requirements which, it is reliably estimated, disenfranchised more than five million people otherwise eligible to vote in the 1968 Presidential election. He stated in a letter to President Nixon: "Residency requirements seem unreasonable when applied to presidential elections, for which familiarity with local issues and personalities is irrelevant. The Commission is especially concerned because the burden of such requirements falls heavily on migrant workers, mainly Mexican-Americans from the Southwest, who are often unable to vote either in their home state or in the state in which they are working."

The Congress rightly agreed with a similar argument against literacy tests, wherever they were applied. "We found that literacy tests do have a negative effect on voter registration, and that this impact of literacy tests falls most heavily on blacks and persons of Spanish surname," Howard Glickstein of the U.S. Civil Rights Commission testified. "Particularly persons for whom English is not a native language are intimidated by the prospect of the test and fear the embarrassment of failing it or, where the test consists of reading a text aloud, of mispronouncing words."

It is time to move also against the outmoded Electoral College. In 1907, at statehood, Thomas P. Gore and Robert L. Owen were elected as the first United States Senators to represent the newly recognized State of Oklahoma. Actually, Thomas P. Gore had received only the *third* highest number of votes cast in the preceding statewide Senatorial referendum, but a gentleman's agreement had been made at the Oklahoma Constitutional Convention by which the two halves of the new state, east and west, would each have one of the first two Senators. This gentleman's agreement could be, and was, carried into effect because the statewide referendum had no legal standing, since in that day U.S. Senators were elected not by the people but by the state legislature. This procedure, instituted by those who mistrusted popular rule, seems foreign to us now. It would never be countenanced today and would be denounced, were it advocated, as outrageously undemocratic.

Yet American citizens still do not have the right to elect their own President and Vice-President. Instead, citizens of each state are allowed by their votes to select electors, and these electors are permitted then to cast the votes of each state, not even being required in most states to vote in accordance with the majority will. Worse, if there is no majority of Electoral College votes in the country, the selection of the President is decided by the U.S. House of Representatives.

Once it became clear in the wee hours following Election Day 1968 that Vice-President Humphrey would not be chosen President by a majority vote of the Electoral College, I recall with what dread many of us contemplated the constitutional crisis which seemed in prospect if the selection were thrown into the House of Representatives. One member of the Vice-President's staff immediately began to draw up voting lists purporting to predict the House votes which could be counted upon to be cast for Mr. Humphrey. "If we can just get one more popular vote than Nixon gets, we can make a stronger race in the House," this zealous staffer had already been heard to say. "But I believe we can win in the House in any event." The thought was chilling.

The long evolution of popular democracy in America has finally brought the nation to another important time of decision: whether or not to abolish the Electoral College and give the people the full power directly to elect the President of the United States. There is common agreement that the present Electoral College system is full of inequities and dangers to our political stability.

The facts are unarguable. Three times the *runner-up* in the popular vote has been elected President. Using the 1960 census, it takes 392,930 citizens of California to equal the voting power of 75,389 citizens of Alaska in the Electoral College. Under the present "winner-take-all" system, the citizen who votes for the losing candidate in a given state is not only disenfranchised, but also finds his dissenting vote being cast for the winning candidate in the Electoral College. As

Thomas Hart Benton said of this archaic system over a century ago, "To lose their votes is the fate of all minorities, and it is their duty to submit; but this is not a case of votes lost, but of votes taken away, added to those of the majority and given to a person to whom the minority is opposed."

In the 1968 election, Vice-President Humphrey was awarded the eight electoral votes of Connecticut by receiving the votes of 616,000 people, while Mr. Nixon picked up an offsetting eight electoral votes in South Carolina when only 261,000 people there voted for him. Where is the justice in that?

Where indeed? The article of our Constitution which sets forth the method by which a President is elected has at long last, through time and radically changed circumstances, finally come into conflict with the fundamental principles upon which our entire system of popular government rests. Direct election of the President is the only method which meets all of the requisite tests. It is the only method which eliminates all inequities.

Some have spoken out against the popular election of Presidents because they say it would destroy the two-party system. I do not agree. The plan advocated by Senator Birch Bayh of Indiana would require a 40 percent plurality for election, thus encouraging, as Senator Bayh has stated, "potential splinter groups to continue to operate within the framework of the two-party system, since no minor party could reasonably hope to win forty percent of the total popular vote." Neither am I moved by the argument of some urban spokesmen that direct election would lessen the influence of urban states. Rural opponents of the plan have argued just the opposite. The truth is that, with direct popular election, each person's vote would count the same, and communities of the same size would have the same influence, whether in a large state or a small one, and, as Senator Bayh has made clear, "We ought never to have a privileged class of voters—and certainly not in the election of the President."

The responsibility and the power of the modern American President, nationally as well as internationally, are so awesome, when compared with those when the Electoral College was devised, that it should come as no surprise that the method of choosing a President to govern a slightly populated nation of competing states in the eighteenth century simply will not do today. The President of the United States must now have an electoral mandate that is clearly evident to and understood by people all over the earth. Times have changed, and if we expect to live up to our basic principles, we must eliminate the present constitutional distortion of the popular vote for President and insure beyond reasonable doubt the sovereign power of the people to elect. "If the President is to be the man of the people, if all the people are to stand on the same footing, equal masses of people must be given equal votes, equal bargaining power," noted political economist Lucius Wilmerding, Jr., has correctly said.

Ours is a democratic system of government in which the government derives its powers from the consent of the governed. The people of America know what this means; that is why both the Gallup and Harris polls show that 81 percent of them favor outright abolition of the Electoral College.

"The federal system is not strengthened through an antiquated device which has not worked as it was intended to work when it was included in the Constitution and which, if anything, has become a divisive force in the federal system by pitting groups of states against groups of states," Senator Mike Mansfield of Montana has wisely commented. "The Presidency has evolved, out of necessity, into the principal political office, as the courts have become the principal legal bulwark beyond districts, beyond states, for safeguarding the interests of all the people in all the states. And since such is the case, in my opinion, the Presidency should be subject to the direct and equal control of all the people."

Otis H. Shao, Dean of the Graduate School of the University of the Pacific, put his finger on another important reason for changing our system for electing Presidents, the difference between what we profess and what we practice, when he said that "those of us who explain the ways of our government to oncoming generations of students and voters find that we become artful dodgers as we attempt to justify the Electoral College.

"To insure the rights of all eligible Americans—young and old, majority and minority groups, urban and rural residents—to have their voting wishes count, we need a direct election of the man who will hold the highest office in the land."

It is outrageous that the archaic filibuster rule of the Senate was used to prevent a 1970 vote on this issue in that body. The fight for this reform is a fundamental one, and it must be continued with renewed determination.

State voter-registration requirements are also undemocratic. Whether or not Senator Ralph Yarborough of Texas could possibly be reelected in November 1970 was actually first determined many months earlier, in January of that year, when every Texan who expected to take part in the decision had to go to a certain place on a certain day and reregister, as is required annually in that state.

Long before citizen interest in distant elections has been stirred, each prospective voter in Texas must be sufficiently motivated to register to vote, or else he will be ineligible to take part in the vital decisions to be made in the elections which are to follow many months later. Obviously, this kind of legal device especially bars poor whites and Mexican-American, black, and other minority voters in Texas from exerting their full electoral strength in the state. In many other states, the registration laws are almost equally undemocratic.

Organizing and promoting drives to get people registered has always been an extremely costly and wasteful aspect of Democratic campaigns. This essential activity was sadly neglected in the poorly financed 1968 Presidential campaign of Vice-President Humphrey, especially because the registration drive in some states would have had to have been launched and financed even before Mr. Humphrey had secured the nomination of the Convention. These unnecessarily restrictive state laws can and should be liberalized by state legislatures, but uniform national action is what is needed most.

It was because of this particular problem that I appointed the Freedom To Vote Task Force of the Democratic National Committee in 1969 and named as its Chairman and Vice-Chairman former Attorney General Ramsey Clark and

Mrs. Mildred Robbins, Honorary President of the National Council of Women. Their job was summed up well in the beginning statement Mr. Clark made: "If you believe in our system of government, you want everybody to participate, and you'll take your chances with the decision."

The Universal Voter Enrollment plan, which the Ramsey Clark task force recommended, would shift the initial burden of registration from the individual to the federal government. The United States is virtually the only advanced democratic nation in the world which does not have such a plan. The idea is not new and has been found successful in Canada as well as in several of the states. Where used, it has resulted in voter registration of more than 90 percent of the voting-age population. It is an inexpensive and effective means of shoring up the foundations of our democratic institutions.

Under this plan, in the weeks immediately preceding an election, enrollment officers would visit every residence in the land and enroll to vote every qualified person who does not refuse, much like the taking of the census—and for a far more fundamental purpose.

No citizen would be barred from voting because of failure to enroll before election day, or because of loss of enrollment certificate or absence from his district or from the country. Nor would he be disqualified from voting for President if he changed his place of residence, even on the day before the election. He would in that case simply have to complete an affidavit identifying himself, following a procedure no more complicated than that required to cash a check.

The recommendations of the Ramsey Clark task force would be administered by a National Election Commission and would cost only five million dollars in non-Presidential election years and fifty million in Presidential election years—or less than fifty cents per eligible voter, a small price to pay to allow the involvement of all our citizens in the electoral process.

Elections would be much more fair, because they would be less dependent upon which candidate or party was able to register the greatest number of supporters, as well as turn them out to vote. The public, rather than individual candidates or parties with axes to grind, would pay for the registration of voters—a less costly, because more consolidated, process.

The task force also recommended the establishment of a National Elections holiday on the date of every Presidential election "to assure full opportunity for voter participation and to solemnize this as the most important occasion for the exercise of a citizen's obligations in a free society."

The Congress must become more responsive to the people. Majority caucuses in the Senate and House should meet regularly and publicly, committee chairmen and conference committee members must be made more responsible to the majority, and the seniority rule must cease to work against the public will.

Since the founding of our country, we have amended the Constitution six times to extend the voting power of the people: The Fourteenth and Fifteenth Amendments granted black people the right to vote; the Seventeenth Amendment provided for the direct election of United States Senators; the Nineteenth

Amendment allowed women to vote; the Twenty-third Amendment extended voting rights to residents of the District of Columbia; and the Twenty-fourth Amendment made the poll tax illegal. The movement in America has been progressively and inexorably toward more popular control of the government. It is time now to move further in the people's interest.

"This country, with its institutions, belongs to the people who inhabit it," Abraham Lincoln declared. "Why should there not be a patient confidence in the ultimate justice of the people? Is there any better or equal hope in the world?"

There is, indeed, no better or equal hope than a patient confidence in the ultimate justice of the people, if we will remove the remaining and unreasonable barriers to the free expression of their will.

CONGRESSIONAL POLITICS: SECRECY, SENILITY, AND SENIORITY

Paul N. McCloskey, Jr.

[Public] disinterest and apathy have helped to create and preserve a new type of profession: that of the practicing elected Congressman. Success in this profession, unfortunately, has come to mean success in being reelected rather than success in serving the national interest.

Bernard Shaw once had one of his characters say something to the effect that all professions are a conspiracy against the public. Why? Because the members of a profession are prone to establish a closely knit, unspoken relationship among themselves, considering their primary professional obligation to be that of enhancing and promoting their *profession,* even to the extent of concealing from the public their individual professional failings.

Lawyers dislike suing one another for breach of trust to a client; doctors are universally reluctant to testify that a fellow doctor may have been negligent in leaving a surgical sponge in his patient's stomach; judges are reluctant to come forward to discuss a fellow jurist's alcoholism. To do so would be to cast discredit on their profession — to raise doubts in the mind of the public about the profession generally, and inevitably to dim a little of their own luster as members of that profession. Likewise, to candidly lay bare the unsavory aspects of a fellow professional's conduct is to attract the antagonism of other members of the profession with whom one deals on a daily basis, those whose cooperation can be of extreme benefit and whose hostility can cause extreme difficulties in one's practice of his profession.

This is a fact of life and human nature, along with the good and bad instincts that lie just beneath the surface of all of us.

The true mark of a profession is courage in disciplining itself and its members for unprofessional conduct *before* an outraged public insists on punitive action.

Thus, bar associations that disbar and suspend their erring members, medical societies that terminate the licenses of negligent practitioners, the religious order
that defrocks its wayward priests – these are deserving of high praise because of
the inevitable awakening which follows public disclosure. Professional self-
discipline or self-policing and the resultant publicity run counter to the shared
desire of members of the profession that they as a group enjoy public respect and
veneration.

The second problem with self-discipline is that those who find their fellow
professionals guilty of misconduct have made enemies of both the guilty individual and his friends. The loss of future cooperation from these new enemies is
easily understood. Thus it has always been an act of high courage when one
member of a profession comes forward to lay bare the grossly negligent or un-
conscionable conduct of another. This just "isn't done" in professional circles,
and while the exposer of fraud and incompetence may have the temporary respect
of the public at large, he may be fairly sure of receiving the private hostility and
recriminations of many of his brother professionals who feel justified in concealing the imperfections of a few in order to promote the profession as a whole.
The search for truth about professional competence and the behavior of individual practitioners, consequently, is not always assisted by the members of the
profession itself.

So it is with politics.

Consider the House of Representatives. There are 435 elected representatives – of widely diverse viewpoints, probably an extremely accurate mirror of
the diverse views of Americans generally, though not in the proportion of such
views held at any given time. A few rules of the profession of being a Congressman have developed, and again it should be stressed that these rules directly result from that hard fact of life of American politics, the apathy of the great silent
majority of voters. The first result of that fact of life is to impel the applicant
for public office to stir the voters' apathy: to build a constituency on some
ideological base or emotion. Unfortunately, it is easier to stir apathy while
preaching fear, hate, and anger than it is to seek to inspire people to faith in a
given cause.

Surfeited with television and radio entertainment, athletic contests, movies,
and the opportunity for travel, the average American citizen has more than
enough to do to earn a living, communicate with his family and pursue the various chances at happiness available on all sides. It is indeed difficult to obtain his
enthusiastic commitment to political involvement. To even obtain the attention
of a sufficient percentage of the electorate, the candidate is stimulated either to
espouse sensational causes or to campaign eighteen hours a day for many months.
My friend Lou Frey of Florida took this latter route by ringing 40,000 doorbells
in a six-month congressional campaign.

In my own initial campaign, I was accustomed to getting up at 6 A.M. and
campaigning steadily until midnight for a period of some four months. Nevertheless, at the end of that period I had managed to shake hands personally with no
more than 10,000 potential voters and to address perhaps another 10,000 in

audiences. Considering that I needed at least 100,000 votes to guarantee a victory in the final election, the problem of informing the electorate immediately becomes apparent.

This introduces the second evil result of citizen apathy. Lacking the time to go to all the citizenry personally, the candidate must resort to roadside signs, mailing materials, and media advertising. Road signs certainly create name recognition, but is there a citizen in America who has ever been enlightened by one as to a candidate's qualifications and views? My predecessor in Congress used the slogan "He is doing a good job for you" in conjunction with a picture of his smiling and benevolent face. This procedure worked exceedingly well for eight straight terms in the Congress, although most citizens had no real way of knowing whether the sign spoke the truth.

A mailing to my own San Mateo County's 240,000 voters costs at least $15,000 today; a full-page newspaper ad in the five major daily papers which serve the county will cost more than $10,000. In metropolitan areas the cost of radio and television advertising is almost prohibitive, since a congressional candidate must pay for coverage of areas other than his own district. The television stations of the San Francisco Bay area, for example, cover ten congressional districts. Consequently, the congressional candidate in San Mateo County gets about fourteen cents in value for every dollar he pays in television advertising costs. The inevitable result in both newspaper and radio/television advertising is to condense the candidate's efforts to a simple slogan consuming a minimum of space and time, and thus requiring a minimum expenditure. It is difficult to get across one's abilities, experience, and qualifications in simple slogans such as "He is doing a good job for you" or "No hokum with Slocum."

Once elected, the incumbent benefits greatly from this same apathy which originally caused his despair. Now *he* has the advantage of the frank, a means by which mail can be sent directly to each constituent, postage free, and at an expense limited solely to the cost of the paper and the printing of the self-serving document he sends out. A "newsletter" or "report from Washington" can be sent to all of my 180,000 postal patrons in San Mateo County at a cost of about $1,500, as opposed to the $15,000 or more which would be required of a nonincumbent, who must pay for his postage. True, I cannot properly or legally include political campaign materials in such a newsletter or report, but the document itself performs the service of placing my name periodically before the electorate, many of whom will never know or care how I am representing them, how hard I work or how I am voting on issues crucial to their lives, liberty, and pursuit of happiness.

The name-recognition factor alone, coupled with the apathy and disinterest of most voters, should be sufficient to insure the incumbent Congressman's reelection year after year—with one important exception. Here lies the rub. The exception to success in my profession occurs when an incumbent takes a position or casts a vote which a competent opponent can use to stir public apathy by creating strong feelings *against* the incumbent.

As several elderly Congressmen are wont to tell newly elected colleagues, "No

man has ever been defeated on the basis of what he *didn't* say." The penalties in
the profession of politics are applied to those who attempt to lead, take controversial positions and, most of all, allow those controversial positions to become
known to their constituents.

A number of private rules have been developed in the House of Representatives to protect the incumbent against the occurrence of these unfortunate difficulties. These rules might be characterized as follows.

*1. Never take a position on a controversial question unless and until you
have to.*

A Republican colleague from an adjoining district once told me he never took
a position on a controversial issue if he could help it. Constituent inquiries as to
his position on a pending bill would be responded to with "I am still studying
the matter" or "There is considerable merit in your suggestion and I will give it
every consideration before making up my mind on the final vote."

To illustrate that such deceptions cut across partisan lines—and need not
hinder one's career—consider that Lyndon B. Johnson, as a United States Senator, followed a rule of responding to almost all issue mail by profusely thanking
his correspondents for their contribution to his study of the matter at hand.
While this may have flattered his constituents, it certainly gave them no clue to
his thought processes or how he expected to vote.

*2. When you take a position, try to couch it in language which will lead
people on all sides of the issue to respect your views or to be confused as to
where you actually stand and as to the precise steps you plan to implement to
follow that position.*

Thus, when asked by an antiwar advocate how he intends to vote on the defense appropriation bill, a Congressman will respond, "I feel it was a mistake that
we ever went into Vietnam. I strongly favor getting out at the earliest practicable
date, but don't wish to hamstring President Nixon in his efforts to get us out as
soon as possible." To a prowar inquiry the same Congressman might respond,
"I am glad to vote for the defense appropriation bill, which will enable the President to achieve peace with honor. I regret the fact that we have never permitted
our fine young men in the armed service to achieve the victory you suggest is
necessary." The Congressman will then proceed to vote for the defense appropriation bill, knowing that he has maximized the chance that both pro- and antiwar
advocates will understand his interest on their behalf.

*3. If possible, on controversial issues, seek to have the vote secret or
unrecorded.*

The House of Representatives has always surrounded its proceedings with
secrecy, and until the passage of the Congressional Reform Act of 1970 most
major controversial issues could be disposed of without disclosing a Congressman's position. This was accomplished through the practice of meeting as a
"committee of the whole House" for the purpose of amending bills. Thus, when
a bill is reported to the floor the House adopts a rule limiting the debate on the
bill and then goes into the "committee of the whole House" to debate those pro-

visions for one hour, two hours, four hours, etcetera, depending on the rule. At the end of the debate the rule generally permits the offering of amendments. There may be relatively few members on the floor at the time, and adoption or rejection of amendments is determined first by voice vote. If the chair is in doubt, or if 20 percent of those present request it, a standing vote is ordered by the chair. This involves a head count of those standing in favor of the amendment and those against it, and if the vote is close, again 20 percent of those present can request a "teller vote." Until 1970 the teller votes—which consisted of those in favor walking past two tellers in one aisle and those opposing walking past two other tellers in the opposite aisle—were unrecorded, and then as now the clerk and the doorkeeper of the House pursued an iron-clad rule of preventing individuals in the gallery from having pencil and paper in hand in order to note how individual Congressmen voted.

A great number of controversial issues were thus disposed of without a record vote, since if an amendment was defeated it could not be offered later under the rules of the House, even though the Constitution itself specifies that votes shall be recorded on application of 20 percent of those present. Thus, for years issues such as the SST, the ABM, even the funding of the Vietnam War itself, were never able to achieve record votes. A constituent back home who wondered what his Congressmen's position was on the SST, for example, could never find out unless the Congressman was willing to tell him.

This may have had some bearing on why the SST was approved during 1969 and 1970, before teller votes became public. Most Congressmen were pretty well aware that a majority of their constituents opposed the SST, but there was no need to stir a hornet's nest as long as voting on the amendment to delete funding for the SST was unrecorded.

In 1971, when the Congressional Reform Act caused the teller vote to be recorded upon application of 20 percent of the members, the SST proposal was finally defeated in the House by a vote of 217 to 208. Less than a year earlier it had been tacitly approved when, by a vote of 86 to 102, an amendment to delete SST funding had been defeated. Not only did the new roll-call rule reverse the earlier SST vote, but it provided a much higher rate of voting participation among the people's representatives, because they knew that their actions—or lack of them—would be revealed to the public. The growing number of Congressmen who are finally seeing the light on Vietnam has undoubtedly been enhanced by the knowledge that now a member of Congress can no longer say he is for peace and then vote to continue the funding of war.

Though enactment of the Congressional Reform Act has forced some honesty on the institution, other forms of deception remain. These will not be easily rooted out, for they have more to do with custom and human nature than with formal rules.

Each congressional office is autonomous, each an individual principality subject to the rules, whims, or mores inflicted by its reigning monarch. Among Congressmen there is a grand reluctance to intervene in any way with the operations of their colleagues. One may junket, juice, philander, or cavort to excess with lobbyists without risking even the mildest internal rebuke, so long as proper form is observed—which is to say so long as the offending member does not flaunt his sins. Despite his well-known transgressions, former Representative Adam Clayton Powell of New York angered his colleagues only after publicly proclaiming, "I haven't done anything more than other Congressmen." When he added, "Nor, by the grace of God, do I intend to do anything *less*," he was stripped of his seniority, his committee chairmanship and ultimately his House seat.

A year or so ago it was discovered that a Republican colleague had mysteriously received credit for voting on a number of occasions when actually he had been absent from the House proceedings. After the hullabaloo in the press died down, and lame excuses were offered all around, the offender was unanimously elected by his colleagues to raise funds for his party's congressional campaigns.

Some members are notoriously lax in reporting their campaign contributions; the blank envelope stuffed with greenbacks is not unknown. One Congressman who a few years ago reported all contributions and expenditures, as the law requires, received a call from an official of the House who told him his report must be submitted "in more acceptable form" because he had violated certain ancient—and unrealistic—spending limitations. Then the official proceeded to tell the Congressman how to shift expenditure A to line B and so forth, until the report became acceptable. Acceptable it may have been, but it was not an accurate and honest reflection of the Congressman's campaign finances.

We are simply full of too many professional deceptions, if not outright dishonest ones. How many of us complained when the Government Operations Committee, whose Freedom of Information Subcommittee is charged with investigating and exposing official censorship, voted to bar the press from its organizational meeting last year? As a rule of custom, almost any Congressman encountering a colleague in the presence of the latter's constituents will—no matter what their differences or the colleague's competence—remark something to the effect that he is "one of the best Congressmen here."

The *Congressional Record,* which purports to be a true rendering of congressional proceedings, is not that at all. Each Congressman and Senator is allowed to "revise and extend" his remarks at the end of each legislative day after having seen his actual spoken words in print. It is not uncommon for members to have second thoughts on their original utterances and thus to eliminate them or rewrite their role in actual House or Senate proceedings. Through seeking permission at the beginning of each day's legislative business "to revise and extend my remarks and to include extraneous matter," a legislator may later insert page after page of material leaving the impression that he made an impassioned speech on one burning issue or another when in truth he has not. If he wishes to carry his deception to the nth degree, he may then mail—postage free—that nonspeech to his constituency.

Although legislative matters theoretically consume most of a Congressman's time, this is rarely true in practice. The energies of a great many of us are spent primarily in feathering the elective nests. Many members of Congress use their official facilities and staff help for various forms of constant campaigning. Infant-care booklets, provided free, may be mailed to all new mothers along with rhapsodical notes on the subject of motherhood. Home-district newspapers may be so carefully clipped that no new Tenderfoot Boy Scout, bathing beauty, or bake-off contest winner goes unremarked by the Congressman. Banks of automatic typewriters may pound out congratulatory notes to thousands of students at graduation time. There are agricultural yearbooks, gardening pamphlets, special House of Representatives calendars, and hundreds of other documents with which to flatter or campaign. Sometimes there is no rest even for the dead: their survivors may be sent weepy letters of condolence.

Perhaps all this is good in the cause of accumulating seniority, but it accomplishes little in the public interest. Indeed, such trivia may be detrimental to the public interest or good, because they consume time and energies which might be better spent.

The net result of these deceptions and practices—and the public apathy permitting them—is that the Congress belatedly responds to public opinion rather than courageously leading the way toward reform, modernization, and progress. A member knows, for example, that he has not benefited by speaking out on controversial issues or attempting to educate his constituency too often to new concepts. It is one of life's disappointing facts that the apathetic voter, knowing little of and uninterested in the work done by his Congressman, can be impelled to vote against him by a single vote with which that constituent disagrees.

Thus, a speech or vote favoring liberalized abortion will perhaps draw the permanent antagonism of many of the Catholics in a Congressman's district. It may be that the voters would agree with 95 percent of his positions if they knew of them, but their attention is drawn to that issue on which he has voted in opposition to their beliefs. Granted that the Catholic vote may be no more than 5 percent of the total necessary to defeat the incumbent. Another 2 percent, however, can be added should he indicate a position against providing coverage for chiropractic services. Every chiropractor and his patients can clearly understand that this vote is against *their* interests, and those who are uninvolved in the other issues of our time may well vote against the incumbent solely because of this single position. Lockheed employees may tend to vote against the Congressman who votes against the Lockheed loan. And so it goes. The politician, knowing that the 5-percent, 2-percent and 1-percent segments of his constituency will ultimately add up to a base sufficient to defeat him, tries to cloak himself in anonymity as to both his position on issues and his voting record. Small wonder, then, that our young people feel Congress to be unresponsive to rapidly changing circumstances and rapidly changing human needs.

There is one final great evil of public apathy. When once elected to the House of Representatives, many members will probably continue to serve until their death if they, in the words of the famous Speaker Sam Rayburn of Texas, "go along and get along." The Democratic dean of our California delegation, Chet Holifield, put it very well in a recent letter to another California Congressman who questioned the system: "I was here for twenty-eight years before election as Chairman of the House Committee on Government Operations. For twenty-four of those years I served next to and below William Dawson. For the past six years I have carried the load of Chairman without the title or power of the Chairmanship. If anyone knows the faults of seniority, I believe I do." (Dawson was incapacitated by a stroke several years before his death, and was unable to preside over the Committee, which was therefore almost paralyzed for several years.) "When I first came to D. C. in 1943, Sam Rayburn told the class of newly elected Congressmen, 'Boys, if you want to get along, go along.' As the years have passed by I have repeated that admonition to myself many times when frustration was about to overwhelm me."

Under the system of seniority which has prevailed in the House since 1911 (when the House revolted against a dictatorial Speaker and amended its operating rules), continued reelection assures an individual of ultimate power either as a committee chairman or as the ranking minority member of a committee. The power of chairmen and ranking members is immense. They control what legislation will be held by the committee, the dates and times of committee hearings, the selection and calling of witnesses, and the appointment of subcommittee chairmen. In short, these powerful old men run the show.

If a corporation selected its chief executive officer on the basis of who had been employed by the corporation the longest, the stockholders would speedily elect new management. Yet this is the custom of the House of Representatives— a body that the framers of our Constitution saw as closest to the people of all their national public men. The senior member is automatically a committee chairman, regardless of his leadership qualities, his ability, or his physical health. During my first two years in the House, the chairman of my primary committee was in his eighties and incapable of presiding over a productive agenda. In 1970 the average age of the ten most powerful committee chairmen in the House was seventy-four; three were in their eighties. It is said of Congressmen, "Few die and none retire." Why should they? Their power is assured so long as they remain in Congress; their reelection is assured so long as they do not provide grounds for antagonism among their constituency or interrupt prevailing constituent apathy.

In view of this situation, I wrote to our Minority Leader, Gerald R. Ford, on January 29, 1970, suggesting that the Republican minority in the House (we have been a minority for thirty-six of the last forty years) raise the issue of the seniority system as a party issue. My letter said, in part:

> I would propose that the Republican Members of the House and Senate agree that in the event the Republicans achieve a majority in either House, we will adopt a rule whereby Committee Chairmen are selected on the basis of administrative and management skill, rather than on seniority alone.

The average age of the presidents of the twenty-five largest corporations in America is fifty-seven. The average age of the most powerful Committee Chairmen in the House is well over seventy, and three Committee Chairmen will be in their eighties this year. In many cases, the most senior Member may also be the ablest manager in the hard work of pushing bills through the legislative process. It is indefensible, however, that we be *required* to accept as Chairman an individual who is *not* the ablest leader, merely because he has served the longest period of time on the Committee involved. No profit-making organization in the free enterprise system could satisfy its stockholders on this point, and the Republican Party, after all, is supposedly the Party which provides and insists upon management excellence in the conduct of the complex problems of government.

I further proposed that the Republicans work out a method of election of committee chairmen promising to impose the new procedures should we be elected to a majority in the Congress in 1971.

Following receipt of this, Ford appointed a Republican task force to revise the seniority system. By the end of 1970, we had worked out a method of election of chairmen or ranking members, and the political implications of our doing so assisted in causing the Democrats to do likewise. Thus, in January 1971, with the convening of the Ninety-second Congress, both parties adopted rules providing for the election of chairmen and ranking members.

Was the seniority system ended, however? Unfortunately, no. Both parties turned around and elected the twenty-one most senior members of their respective committees as chairmen or ranking members! In only one of the forty-two elections was a question even raised as to the fitness of the senior member. I believe the situation would be improved if congressional pensions were cut back 10 or 20 percent for each year a member chooses to serve past age seventy, and I have prepared legislation to this end.

The secrecy, senility, and seniority which Congress pursues is, of course, only too apparent to the executive departments which deal with Congress. Those departments therefore can feel some encouragement should they in turn wish to be secretive with members of Congress.

THE MISUSE OF POWER

Henry Steele Commager

In the historic steel seizure case of 1952 Justice Jackson said that, "what is at stake is the equilibrium of our constitutional system." Now, after twenty years marked by repeated, and almost routine, invasions by the executive of the war-making powers assigned by the Constitution to Congress, we can see that more is at stake even than the constitutional principle of the separation of powers. At stake is the age-long effort of men to fix effective limits to government, the reconciliation of the claims of freedom and of security, the fateful issue of peace or war, an issue fateful not for the American people alone, nor alone for the stricken peoples of southeast Asia but for the entire world.

It is not sufficiently realized that the kind of military intervention we have witnessed in the past quarter century is, if not wholly unprecedented, clearly a departure from a long and deeply rooted tradition. Since the Neutrality Proclamation of 1793 that tradition has been one of nonintervention. Washington, and his cabinet, refused to intervene in the wars between France and her enemies even though the United States was far more deeply "committed" to come to the aid of France by the terms of the Treaty of Alliance of 1778 than she was to intervene in Vietnam by the terms of the SEATO Treaty. Notwithstanding almost universal sympathy for the peoples of Latin America who sought to throw off Spanish rule, we did not intervene militarily in that conflict. The ideas of "Manifest Destiny" and "Young America" dictated support to peoples everywhere struggling to throw off ancient tyrannies, but no President intervened militarily in the Greek struggle for independence from Turkey, the Italian uprisings against Austria, the Hungarian revolution of 1848 or other internal revolutions of that fateful year, Garibaldi's fight for Italian independence, the many Irish uprisings against Britain, in Ireland and even in Canada—close to home, that—or even *mirabile dictu,* the ten-year war of the Cubans against their Spanish overlords from 1868–1878. Nor, in more modern times, did Presidents see fit to intervene on behalf of Jewish victims of pogroms, Turkish genocide against Armenians, or Franco's overthrow of the Loyalist regime in Spain. Whether such abstention was always wise is a question we need not raise here. The point here

Reprinted by permission of *The New Republic,* ©1971 Harrison-Blaine of New Jersey, Inc.

is that in none of these situations did the Executive think it proper, or legal, to use his powers as Commander-in-Chief or as chief organ of foreign relations to commit the United States to military intervention in distant lands. With the sole exception of McKinley's unnecessary participation in the Boxer Expedition, that concept of executive powers belongs to the past quarter century. And if it should be asked why the United States should refrain from intervention in the internal struggles of other nations, even when her sympathies are deeply involved and her interests enlisted, it is perhaps sufficient to say that few of us would be prepared to endorse a principle that would have justified the intervention of Britain and France in the American Civil War—on behalf of the Confederacy of course—and that in international law you cannot really have it both ways.

The unlimited power of the Executive in foreign relations is no longer justified as an emergency power, but asserted to be a normal and almost routine exercise of executive authority. Lincoln pushed his authority to the outward limits of what was constitutionally permissible, but confessed, with characteristic humility, that the emergency required him to do what he did, and asked Congress to give retroactive sanction to his acts. No such humility characterizes what we may call The Johnson-Nixon Theory of Executive Authority. Thus President Johnson asserted that he did not need the authority of the Tonkin Gulf Resolution to justify his bombardment of North Vietnam, for he already had that: thus President Nixon's assistant attorney general asserted that the President's authority to invade Cambodia "*must* be conceded by even those who read executive authority narrowly" (June 16, 1970). Why must it be? Certainly not because of the persuasive character of the arguments advanced by this distinguished counsel, for that character is wanting.

The new commitments are not, as generally in the past, ad hoc and even fortuitous, but calculated and ideological. Thus we do not drop bombs on Vietnam or Laos because "American blood has been shed on American soil"—Polk's excuse. Nor does the President respond to an imperative like the attack on Fort Sumter or even to U-boat warfare. Nor do recent Presidents presume to act—like President Truman—in response to a United Nations decision. Now Presidents act to "contain communism" or to protect "vital interests" nine thousand miles away, or to fulfill "commitments" that are never made clear and that other nations (pledged to them just as solemnly) do not think require military fulfillment (e.g., the SEATO "commitments" that bind Britain, France, Pakistan, etcetera). And they do so by programs that are by their very nature open-ended and tenacious. Thus Secretary Rusk's assertion in 1966 that 'no would-be aggressor should suppose that the absence of a defense treaty, congressional declaration, or United States military presence, grants immunity to aggression"; the key words, for our purposes, are "absence of treaty" and "absence of congressional declaration." For this left only the alternative of the application of the executive power, unilaterally in the international arena, unilaterally in the constitutional arena too.

As power corrupts, the possession of great power encourages and even creates conditions in which it seems imperative to use it, and the concentration of that power vastly increases the risks of misuse. We had one example of that as early as 1846: what began as a simple vindication of a boundary line ended up as a war in which we tore Mexico in two.

Now the original assumption of our Constitution framers, that Presidents could not engage in war on their own, was greatly strengthened by the elementary fact that they could not if they wanted to, because there were no armies or navies with which to war. At the time of the ratification of the Constitution the United States Army consisted of 719 officers and men. Our armed forces increased to some 20,000 by 1840, to 28,000 on the eve of The Civil War and to 38,000 by 1890. Even in 1915, with the world locked in mortal combat, the armed forces of the United States were less than 175,000. With the worst will, there was little that Presidents could do with these forces. Now we have a wholly new situation. Not only do we keep some three million men under arms at all times—since 1951 the number has rarely fallen below that—but we have the greatest and most formidable armaments that any nation ever commanded.

The problem is complicated by a new terminology, the obsolescence of older terms that once had clear legal meaning, and the emergence of new terms, some of them (like "combat," meaning only ground troops, or "protective reaction") designed to deceive. Thus it is conceded that the President has authority to "repel" attacks, but the term has been drained of meaning. When we launch or support invasions of Cambodia and Laos not to defeat the enemy or to conquer territory but to enable us to withdraw, anything can be called a protective reaction. Besides, it has become a truism that all wars are defensive. Hitler claimed that his assaults on Denmark and Norway were "defensive."

Even the constitutional concept of a declaration of war has been drained of meaning by the presidential interpretation of the Tonkin Bay Resolution. Thus in congressional testimony in 1967, it was formally asserted that that resolution, together with the SEATO treaty, constituted a "functional declaration of war"—thus combining an original contribution to international law with repeal of an important provision of the Constitution.

There is a final consideration of importance: the growing role of the Executive Agreement—a method for bypassing the requirements of treaty-making. Unknown to article II of the Constitution, this emerged early as a useful method of disposing of routine business that did not rise to the dignity of a treaty. Until very recent times it was customarily used only for such routine business as tariff agreements, postal conventions, patent arrangements and so forth, the great majority of which were negotiated in pursuance of congressional authorization. As late as 1930 the United States concluded 25 treaties and only 9 executive agreements. But in 1968 it concluded 16 treaties and 266 executive agreements. As of January 1, 1969 the United States had a total of 909 treaties and 3973 executive agreements. And while the great majority of these were still concerned with routine matters, a substantial number dealt with problems that in the past had been considered proper subjects of the treaty-making power.

In 1940 Attorney General Jackson spelled out the permissible and impermissible limits of the use of executive agreements in foreign affairs: "The President's power over foreign relations, while delicate, plenary and exclusive, is not unlimited. Some negotiations involve commitments as to the future which would carry an obligation to exercise powers vested in the Congress. Such presidential arrangements are customarily submitted for ratification . . . of the Senate before the future legislative power of the country is committed."

And he made a distinction between what was proper and what was improper relevant to the current scene: "The transaction now proposed represents only an exchange with no statutory requirement for the embodiment thereof in any treaty and *involving no promises or undertakings* by the United States that might raise the question of the propriety of incorporation in a treaty." It is superfluous to point out that the use of executive agreements in such areas as joint use of air bases and joint defense of them in Spain, repudiates these carefully drawn limitations. For these, and similar agreements, do "carry promises and undertakings of future action." They *are* properly the subject for treaties.

Great questions of constitutional law are great not because they are complicated legal or technical questions, but because they embody issues of high policy, of public good, of morality. We should therefore consider the problem of the presidential authority to make war not merely in the light of constitutional precedents, but in the light of wisdom and justice.

In 1967 Under Secretary of State Nicholas Katzenbach asserted that "history has surely vindicated the wisdom of the flexibility of the conduct of our foreign affairs." Two years later Senator McGee stated that, "the decision-making process may be reduced by events to a single day, or even hours. On more than one occasion the time allotted by crisis incidents to those who must make the decisions has been less than the time it would take to assemble a quorum of the Congress." Is that true? Have Presidents been well advised, in the light of history, to bypass Congress in using American armed forces overseas? Would consultation with the Congress, would even second thoughts and delay, have made a difference detrimental to national, or world, interests? Was it really of vital importance that General Jackson pursue the Seminoles and hang Arbuthnot and Ambrister? Would the fate of Texas have been different had Polk consulted the Congress before launching a war? Had he done so he might have escaped the name that has clung to him through history—"Polk the Mendacious." Was it essential to bombard Greytown on the Mosquito coast in 1854—would we do that now? Grant himself learned what a mistake it was to send troops to the Dominican Republic in 1869, for a Senate, perhaps more strong minded than later Senates, refused to back him up or to allow him to go through with his plans for annexation. Was McKinley wise to commit five thousand troops to the invasion of China in 1900, and would we do this today in a comparable situation? Our commitment to the provisions of the constitution of the Organization of American States is perhaps sufficient commentary on the wisdom of our many military interventions in the Caribbean, and President Wilson's resort to an international conference – that rescued us from an ugly situation in Mexico – sufficient commentary on the wisdom of the Pershing expedition into Mexico. Would any President launch such an expedition today? In 1919 the hapless Jacob Abrams was sentenced to jail for twenty years for distributing leaflets criticizing the Archangel and Siberian expeditions: at the time he had only the consolation of being the occasion for one of the greatest of all Justice Holmes's opinions. If he were living now he might have the dubious consolation of knowing that almost everyone agrees with his argument. We have paid a high price in the long-range enmity of the Russians for that particular folly. A strong case can be made out for FDR's destroyer bases exchange and for extending protection to Greenland and Iceland, but is it conceivable that the Congress would have denied him the right to carry through these programs?

If we turn to the many examples of presidential war-making in the past twenty years we are, I submit, impressed by the fact that in almost every instance the Congress was actually in session and available for consultation: the Korean intervention, the landing of troops in Lebanon, the Bay of Pigs, the occupation of the Dominican Republic by President Johnson, and the successive series of forays into Vietnam, Cambodia and Laos.

There is one further observation that may be instructive. Almost every instance of the use of presidential force in the past has been against small, backward, and distraught peoples. Call the role of the victims of presidential application of force in the past: Spanish Florida, Honduras, Santo Domingo, Nicaragua, Panama, Haiti, Guatemala, a China torn by civil war, a Mexico plagued by civil war, a Russia and a Vietnam likewise plagued. It is a sobering fact that Presidents do not thus rush in with the weapons of war to bring Britain, France, Italy, Russia, or Japan to heel. Would we have bombarded Southampton to collect a debt? Would we have sent an expedition into Rome to protect Americans against a threat from a fascist government? Would we have precipitated a war with Britain over a boundary dispute in Maine? Would we land marines in France if customs collectors did not behave themselves? Would we bomb Russia for years if shots were fired – without any hits – at an American vessel? And does it comport with the honor and dignity of a great nation to indulge its Chief Executive in one standard of conduct for the strong and another for the weak?

This record does not justify Mr. Katzenbach's rosy view of the use of presidential authority, nor is there a single instance that bears out Senator McGee's assertion that "on more than one occasion the time allotted by crisis . . . has been less than the time it would take to assemble a quorum of the Congress."

"Reason may mislead us, experience must be our guide," said James Madison at the constitutional convention. By "reason" he meant theory or doctrine. Experience must indeed be our guide, and on the basis of a century-and-three-quarters of experience, confirmed by a quarter century of intensive modern experience, we can say with some confidence that: with the exception of the

Civil War — a special case — and perhaps of the Korean War where the President acted in conformity to the decision of the UN Security Council — there are no instances in our history where the use of war-making powers by the Executive without authority of Congress was clearly and incontrovertibly required by the nature of the emergency that the nation faced. On the contrary, in almost every instance the long-run interests of the nation would have been better promoted by consultation and delay. We can also say that great principles of government are not to be decided on the basis of the *argumentum ad horrendum* — by conjuring up hypothetical dangers and insisting that the structure and operations of government must be based on the chance of these rather than on experience. It was to this kind of argument that Thomas Jefferson said, "Shake not your raw-head and bloody-bones at me."

Is it possible to mitigate the dangers of the misuse of the executive power in the war-making arena? I think it is, and venture a few recommendations.

What Justice Jackson said in the steel seizure case is relevant now as then. "Power to legislate for emergencies belongs in the hands of Congress, but only Congress itself can prevent power from slipping through its fingers." That power has been slipping from the hands of Congress. That Congress has the power to reverse this trend should be clear. It can pass the Javits Bill designed to limit the use of armed forces in the absence of a declaration of war or affirmative authority from the Congress; this together with the Fulbright resolution on national commitments and the Cooper-Church amendment might provide an effective curb on presidential war-making.

I suggest also that the Senate meet the argument of emergency, hypothetical as it is, by creating a permanent committee, a quorum of whose members would remain permanently in Washington, with authority to require that the President consult with the Senate or the Congress before taking any action that might involve the nation in armed conflict. Such a committee could be counted on to respond to a genuine emergency just as promptly as would the President, and counted on, too, to present the case for caution.

The Senate should create a standing committee to consult with the President on all executive agreements, and with authority to designate those of sufficient importance to require submission to the Senate as treaties.

And finally, the Congress should reinvigorate the power of the purse, that power which, as James Madison said, "may be regarded as the most complete and effectual weapon with which any Constitution can arm the immediate representatives of the people." It should use with more particularity than in the past the power to limit the place and the manner of the introduction of American arms and armed forces.

The problems that confront us cannot be solved by debates over precedents, by appeals to constitutional probity, or by confronting presidential power with congressional. These may mitigate but will not resolve our crisis. For all of these gestures address themselves to symptoms rather than to the fundamental disease. That disease is the psychology of the cold war, our obsession with power, our assumption that the great problems that glare upon us so hideously from every corner of the horizon can be solved by force.

Abuse of power by Presidents is a reflection, and perhaps a consequence, of abuse of power by the American people and nation. For two decades now we have misused our prodigious power. We misused our economic power, not least in associating economic with military assistance, and in imposing economic sanctions against nations who did not see eye to eye with us about trade with our "enemies." We misused our political power by trying to force neutrals onto our side in the cold war by bringing pressure on the nations of Latin America to support our shortsighted policy of excluding China from the United Nations — surely the most egregious blunder in the history of modern diplomacy. We misused our political power by planting the CIA in some sixty countries to carry on what we chose to regard as national defense but what was in the eyes of its victims the work of subversion. We misused our military power in forcing our weapons on scores of nations, maintaining military alliances like NATO and SEATO and imposing our will upon these where we were able. We misused our international power by flouting the sovereign rights of neighboring countries like Cuba and Guatemala and the Dominican Republic and violating our obligations under the OAS treaty and the United Nations. And we are even now engaged in a monstrous misuse of power in waging war on a distant people that does not accept our ideology or our determination of its future. Is it any wonder that against this almost lurid background, Presidents misuse their power?

As we have greater power than any other nation, so we should display greater moderation in using it, greater humility in justifying it, and greater magnanimity in withholding it. In the long run the abuse of the executive power cannot be divorced from the abuse of national power. If we subvert world order and threaten world peace, we must inevitably subvert and threaten our own political institutions first. This we are in the process of doing.

THE POVERTY OF THE STATE

Thomas Bodenheimer

State and local governments entered the 1970s in a state of deep crisis. All states made or considered welfare cuts in 1971. At least twenty state welfare departments began 1971 with deficits. Twenty-four state Medicaid programs were in the red, and many are denying health services to the poor. San Francisco county welfare recipients were cut back to $88 per month. Twenty-six city recreation halls in Cleveland were closed, and 85 percent of recreation department employees were removed from the payroll. Mayor Lindsay laid off thousands of New York City employees, crippling welfare, health, lead-poisoning, and rat-control programs. In California, Connecticut, and other states, freezes went into effect on state hiring. In California, state employees were denied cost-of-living wage increases.

What is happening? Widespread cutbacks in state and local public services. Decreases in numbers of public employees. Freezes in public employee wages. What is the reaction to these cutbacks and freezes? Los Angeles teachers struck for one month in 1970 to fight against inadequate school funding. New York City's Brownsville broke out into riots in 1971 to protest 10 percent welfare cuts. Welfare-rights groups sued the state of California for cutting health services. Public employee strikes for higher wages swept the country in 1970–1971: city workers in Atlanta and San Francisco; police in Pittsburgh, New York, and Milwaukee; sanitation workers in Seattle; postal workers across the country; teachers in Woburn, Scranton, Stamford, Newark, Philadelphia, Muskogee, Chicago, Gary, Toledo, Butte, and many other cities and towns.

The number of work stoppages in the government sector has increased tenfold in four years. Public employees are demanding decent wages. Employees and users of public services are protesting cutbacks.

The answer of state and local governments to these protests and strikes? The Governor of Connecticut stated that his state is "wallowing in debt." The Governor of Pennsylvania pushed for new taxes to avert bankruptcy. California and Michigan faced large budget deficits. Massachusetts expects a $100 to $200 million deficit in its Medicaid program. In city after city, state after state, the same answer: there is no money.

How do taxpayers respond to this crisis of their governments? In Youngstown, Ohio, and in suburbs of St. Louis, schools were closed for weeks because voters refused to approve tax levies to operate them. In Cleveland, voters turned down a city income-tax increase. In California, a medical-school bond issue was defeated. A virtual tax revolt is upon us—people are refusing to pay. More than 2,300 well-organized tax protest groups exist around the country with two million members.

People's lives are increasingly dependent upon the state (the public sector). Eleven million public workers are now employed at federal, state, and local levels. In addition, tens of millions of people rely on the government for educational and social welfare services: students needing an education, welfare recipients, and users of public hospitals and health facilities. This group is expanding with rising public school and college enrollments, a 22.5 percent increase in welfare recipients in 1970, and a growing governmental share of health-care financing. Thus we have uncounted millions of public clients—people receiving services from the state.

The cutbacks and freezes show that governments have been less and less able to meet the needs of public workers and public clients. In order to maintain or improve services and to raise wages, taxes must be increased. Yet taxpayers are refusing to pay. These two trends—the rising demands of public workers and public clients, and the refusal of taxpayers to pay more—have placed the state in profound crisis. This crisis reflects a paradox of modern American society: in the richest country of the world the public-welfare sector is stricken by poverty.

To explain the poverty of the public-welfare sector, we must examine the relation between the government and the corporate rich. This relation is two-fold. First, the state collects relatively few taxes from the corporate rich, placing the major tax burden on working people and the poor; and these taxpayers are rightfully refusing to pay more. Second, the government provides huge subsidies to corporations, thereby using up a considerable portion of its budget in a way that does not benefit the general public. Public workers and clients are striking and protesting against the government's refusal to appropriate decent amounts for health, welfare, education, and recreation services.

Let us look at some details of this tax-and-subsidy system which impoverishes the public-welfare sector.

Taxation in America

Taxes can be classified as regressive, proportional, or progressive, according to how they are shared by different income groups. A regressive tax hits the poor harder than the rich; if families with income under $5,000 pay 10 percent of that income in a certain tax, whereas families over $15,000 pay 5 percent of their income in the same tax, then that tax is regressive. A tax is proportional if all are taxed the same percentage of their incomes, e.g., a 10 percent across-the-board tax. A progressive tax makes rich people pay, for example, 25 percent of their income while poor people might pay 10 percent.

Equitable taxation makes people pay according to their ability. Rich people normally save a sizable part of their incomes, and thus a 50 percent tax does not cut into the amount of necessities they can buy. Poor people spend all or most of their incomes on food, shelter, clothing, and transportation; and even a 5 percent tax becomes an enormous burden. Thus proportional taxation—such as a 10 percent tax for everyone—is not just; it hits the poor family very hard, yet is of little consequence to the rich. Only progressive taxation, with a substantial increase in tax rate as income rises, is truly equitable.

In fiscal year 1968–1969, federal, state, and local governments collected $312.6 billion. These revenues include $222.7 billion in taxes, $46.6 billion in social insurance payments (such as social security), and $42 billion in miscellaneous charges (such as state liquor sales, fines, etcetera). The federal government collected $199.6 billion of the total revenues. State and local governments collected $59.8 billion and $53.2 billion respectively. State governments also received $17.8 billion in intergovernmental transfers from the federal government, and localities received $26.1 billion in transfers.[1]

The *individual income tax* accounted for 36 percent of all tax revenues in 1968–1969.[2] The great bulk of income tax payments—$87 billion in that year—goes to the federal government. People generally believe that this tax is truly progressive, with the rich paying significantly more than the poor. This belief is a myth. In fact, most people pay at approximately the same tax rate. And the super-rich frequently pay very little.

According to Brookings Institution economist Joseph Pechman, individuals or families earning between $4,000 and $5,000 pay an average of 5 percent of their incomes in federal income taxes.[3] Those making between $6,000 and $7,000 pay an average income tax of 7 percent; from $8,000 to $9,000 the average is 8 percent; the $12,000 to $13,000 bracket pays 10 percent; and the $15,000 to $20,000 category pays 12 percent. Pechman contends that rates rise from 23.5 percent on incomes between $50,000 and $75,000 to 34 percent on incomes over $1 million. However, he fails to take into account that a large portion of capital gains to the rich is never reported as income. Thus the actual average tax rate for earners over $50,000 is closer to 20 percent.[4]

Thus the federal income tax is progressive only to a very slight degree. And many wealthy people take advantage of enormous tax loopholes to pay little or no tax. In 1969, fifty-six people with incomes over $1 million paid no federal income tax at all. The total amount of revenue lost to the federal government through loopholes to the rich is estimated at a staggering $50 billion per year.[5] And the Tax Reform Act of 1969 did very little to correct these injustices.

The income tax is minimally progressive because it rests on the principle that some incomes are more taxable than others. Wages are taxed fully, income from stocks and other investments is taxed less, and income from municipal bonds is not taxed at all. Stern gives the following examples in *The Great Treasury Raid:* "Albert's $7,000 was earned over a year's time in a steel mill. Albert pays $1,282 in taxes. . . . Charles merely picked up the telephone, told his broker to

sell some stock, and netted a $7,000 profit. Charles's tax: $526."[6] And Mrs.
Horace Dodge, with $1.5 million in yearly income from municipal bonds, paid
no taxes at all. Thus the income tax structure invariably hurts working people,
who get most of their income from wages.

Social security payments amounted to $44 billion in 1968-1969, thus consti-
tuting 16 percent of total tax revenues. In describing social security, Pechman
writes: "The payroll tax is the most burdensome tax levied by the federal government on the poor in the United States."[7] The following figures show why.
A family with an income of $3,000 to $4,000 pays an average of 11.3 percent of
this income in social security payments. Families with incomes between $5,000
and $7,500 pay 6.8 percent in social security. Between $7,500 and $10,000,
families pay 4.2 percent. From $10,000 to $15,000 the tax is only 2.1 percent.
Over $15,000 the rate is less than 1 percent.

Why is social security so regressive? First, it taxes only wages. Low-income
people earn money only from wages, all of which are subject to the payroll tax.
People with higher incomes may have non-wage sources of money which are not
taxed. Second, there is a cutoff point at $7,800; wages above $7,800 are not
taxed. A person earning $7,800 might pay $390 in social security payments,
while someone making $15,600 also pays $390. The first person pays a 5 percent
tax whereas the second pays only 2.5 percent.

Third, the employer's portion of social security is actually paid by the employee. Social security deducts a certain percentage of the employee's income,
and also collects money from the employer for each person on the payroll. However, the employer does not really pay his share. He generally shifts his portion
of the payroll tax to the employee by keeping wages down. According to Pechman, most economists believe that "a major share of a payroll tax is borne by the
wage earner, and some believe that all of it rests on him. . . . While they
[employers] very likely are unable to reduce wages immediately after imposition
of the tax, they can do so effectively over time by not increasing wages as much
as they would have if the tax had not been introduced." The only exception
might be a strongly unionized plant where "unions may succeed in inducing management to grant a larger wage increase after imposition (or increase) of the payroll tax. In such circumstances, part or all of the payroll tax may be shifted to
the consumer." Thus the employer does not pay social security taxes. Usually
the worker is taxed by receiving lower wages, and occasionally the consumer
bears the burden through higher prices.

The *corporate income tax* accounts for 14 percent of total tax revenue, most
going to the federal government. The federal corporate tax revenue in 1968-
1969 was $36.7 billion, with corporate profits before taxes totaling $136 billion.
Thus the corporations appear to be taxed at a 27 percent rate. However, economists generally believe that corporate stockholders do not pay this entire tax
themselves. As in the case of social security, corporations shift part of the tax to
workers by keeping wages down, and part to consumers by raising prices.

How do corporations do this? Let us suppose that there were no corporate tax, and that corporate profits were $100 billion. Let us then suppose that the government imposes a corporate tax approximating $40 billion. The corporations manage to increase their pre-tax profits to $140 billion by raising prices and keeping wages down. In that case, after-tax corporate profits are still $100 billion. The corporations have paid no taxes but have shifted the burden to workers and consumers.

Suppose, however, that the corporations earn $120 billion in pre-tax profits, a $40 billion tax is imposed, and the corporations are able to raise their pre-tax profits only to $140 billion. Net profit, then, is $100 billion, and the corporations have lost $20 billion in taxes. In this case, the corporations managed to shift only 50 percent of their taxes and must pay the remainder themselves.

In reality, it is not known exactly what percent of corporate taxes are shifted, but the figure can be conservatively estimated to be 50 percent. Corporations, then, are actually taxed not at a 27 percent rate, but closer to 15 percent.

Some corporations find ways to successfully avoid the corporate tax. Oil companies are a good example. In 1967, Texaco was taxed at 1.9 percent of its income, Standard Oil of California at 1.2 percent, and Atlantic-Richfield paid no tax at all. Between 1960 and 1968, corporate profits increased 91 percent, whereas corporate taxes dropped by $5 billion.[8]

Sales and excise taxes brought in $39 billion to all levels of government in 1968-1969. For state governments, these taxes make up 48 percent of tax revenue. Sales taxes hit people in proportion to the percentage of their income spent on the taxed items. A sales tax on bread or milk is extremely regressive since everyone must buy basic foods, and for the poor, food is a high proportion of the family budget. A sales tax on caviar, French champagne, or diamond rings is not regressive since poor people are not interested in such items. Some state sales taxes are approximately proportional, since food, gas, and electricity are not taxed. (Any proportional tax, remember, is not equitable since the poor are less able to afford the payments.) Other states, however, place a sales tax on all items, resulting in very regressive taxation.

Most unjust of all is the *property tax*. This levy brings in $30 billion, making up 11 percent of all taxes. For local governments it becomes very important, accounting for 82 percent of tax revenues. (If one counts total local revenues, including transfer payments from federal and state governments, property taxes make up 38 percent.) Almost all property taxes are paid by tenants and homeowners. The property tax on business establishments is generally assessed on amounts far lower than the real value of the property, and can be shifted to consumers. In apartment buildings the property tax is totally shifted to tenants in the form of higher rents. The extraordinary regressivity of the property tax is shown by these figures from Rostvold's study of California financing: families earning $1,000 per year pay 13 percent of their income in property taxes; those making $4,000 to $5,000 pay 5 percent in property taxes; and families with incomes over $15,000 pay only 2 percent in property taxes.[9] The richer the family, the lower the percentage of taxation. It is no surprise that local governments, financed heavily by property taxes, are facing a tax revolt from millions of tax-exploited, lower-middle-income homeowners.

What is the overall effect of taxation in America? One authoritative estimate is shown in the following table.

As the table shows, taxes hit the poor far harder than the rich. Up to $10,000 income, taxes are actually regressive. From $10,000 to $50,000 the rate is essentially proportional. Only the very rich appear to pay a substantially higher rate; however, the 45 percent figure may be far above the true figure because of already noted large amounts of unreported capital-gains income. In any case, the very rich pay at a lower rate than the very poor.

Money Income Levels[10]	Overall Percentage Tax Rate
Under $2,000	50.0
$ 2,000 – 3,999	34.6
$ 4,000 – 5,999	31.0
$ 6,000 – 7,999	30.1
$ 8,000 – 9,999	29.2
$10,000 – 14,999	29.8
$15,000 – 24,999	30.0
$25,000 – 49,999	32.8
Over $50,000	45.0

Government Subsidies to the Rich

A sizable portion of the federal budget is spent to help private corporations increase their profits. These corporate subsidies total well over $30 billion per year, according to a 1971 Associated Press survey.[11] The exact amount is hard to determine, since it depends on the definition of subsidy. The $30 billion figure refers only to payments giving special advantages to business; if one includes all money passing from the government to private industry, the figure is far higher. In addition, governmental laws and regulations assist the corporate rich through franchises, licensing, contracts, etcetera. Without question, federal aid to private enterprise is more than twice what the government spends for all its welfare programs.

A significant portion of the $75 billion defense budget goes to private corporations. Some $20 billion is spent on procurement of supplies—buying bombs, tanks, and planes from private companies. Defense research and development cost $7 billion, which is also paid largely to private business.

Research and development in general is an important government subsidy; in 1969 the federal R&D expenditure topped $17 billion, one-tenth of the entire budget. Corporations are reluctant to spend their money for R&D, which is an expensive and risky undertaking. Thus the government pays, yet the profits deriving from newly developed products belong to the companies.

Large subsidies go to certain sectors of the economy which are "in trouble."

Agriculture is the best known: farmers received between $6 and $9 billion in 1970. Not surprisingly, a large part of this money was paid to big corporate farms which were never in trouble to start with. In 1970 two huge California growers alone received $4.4 million and $3.3 million in subsidies, and four hundred farmers were each paid over $100,000. A recent limitation on subsidy payments is being successfully evaded by dividing large farms into smaller sections.

The purpose of the $3 to $4 billion foreign aid program is not, as many Americans believe, to aid foreign countries; rather it serves to aid United States business to gain a foothold in those countries. The Agency for International Development (AID) lends money to underdeveloped countries, but that money is mostly used to buy American products. If AID finances a telephone network or potable water system in Peru, the telephone poles, wires, transformers, and water pipeline must be bought from American, not Peruvian, companies. Often United States construction firms actually build the projects. In these and other ways, foreign aid is a mechanism for transferring money from taxpayers to United States business.

Pollution control is another corporate subsidy. Government pays to mop up after industries have destroyed the environment and gives financial incentives to encourage industries to stop polluting. Again, the cost of controlling pollution rests on the taxpayer rather than on the corporate polluter. And numerous other subsidies benefit the corporate rich: half a billion dollars to the shipping industry, millions for airlines and railroads, government training programs for corporate employees, loan guarantees, construction contracts, and so on.

In these and countless other ways, governments help private corporations to lower their costs and maximize their profits. Higher profits result in increased stockholders' dividends. And these dividends do not go to average Americans. The richest 1 percent of families in the country own over 80 percent of the stock. So corporate subsidies almost exclusively benefit the very rich.

Corporate subsidies, then, compete with health, education, and welfare services and with public workers' salaries for the scarce tax dollars. Coupled with a tax system that favors the rich and lays its major burden on working, poor, and middle-class people, corporate subsidies become just another reason why the "impoverished" government cannot meet the needs of its workers and its clients.

The tax and subsidy system, then, tends to transfer money from the average taxpayer to a handful of wealthy corporate stockholders. It is precisely this system that helps to perpetuate a radically lopsided distribution of income in the United States. In 1967, the highest 10 percent of the population received 28 percent of total national income, whereas the lowest 10 percent received less than 2 percent.[12] This inequality has not changed since 1910.[13] The distribution of wealth (income, plus assets such as real estate, stocks, bonds, savings, etcetera) is much more favorable for the rich. The top 10 percent of the population owns 60 percent of the country's wealth, with the super-rich 1.6 percent owning 32 percent of all assets.[14] One-half of the population, on the other hand, owns virtually nothing.

As Kolko puts it in *Wealth and Power in America,* "We have not taxed the rich to give to the poor; we have taxed both the rich and the poor and . . . contributed only a small fraction of the proceeds to the welfare of the poor."[15]

Implications for Local Organizing

If all poor, working-class, and middle-class people were united and aware of the government's role in perpetuating the maldistribution of wealth in society, the inequality would not be allowed to continue. But these groups have defined themselves narrowly as workers, clients, or taxpayers and are frequently pitted against each other.

Competition is particularly evident on local issues. In municipal hospitals, for example, employees may strike for wage increases. The strike threatens patients, whose health care — a life-and-death matter — is temporarily halted. Likewise, taxpayers are angered, since higher wages mean higher taxes. Teachers' strikes create similar feelings in parents and taxpayers.

Disunity among workers, clients, and taxpayers also springs up when public clients demand improved services. Night and weekend clinics at a health center mean night and weekend work, which is not desired by most employees. Workers are afraid that client demands might mean speeded-up working conditions, since no new workers might be hired. Community control over hiring becomes a major threat to workers who fear the loss of their jobs. And taxpayers regard demands for increased services as equivalent to tax increases.

Again and again, the triad of public worker, public client, and taxpayer finds the members at odds with one another. However, this competition is not necessary. It is caused by the poverty of the state. Worker, client, and taxpayer fight over the few crumbs begrudgingly dropped into the public sector by the corporate giants, who greedily consume their multibillion dollar fare of subsidies and tax breaks. Were the exploited triad to combine and demand its share, there would be plenty of money and services to go around.

Groups engaged in local struggle must understand the potential conflicts and must develop demands that encourage unity. Every wage battle by public workers should include a demand for financing increased wages by progressive taxation. Every drive for increased services spearheaded by the community should include demands for more employees to carry out the services and a proposal for tax reform to pay for them. Workers' demands must include provisions for improved services. Clients' demands must speak for better wages and working conditions for workers. Demands must always include tax-reform proposals, especially at the local level where the regressive property tax finances many programs.

Unity among workers, clients, and taxpayers requires an understanding of why the public-welfare sector is so poor. The reason, of course, is the regressive character of the tax system and the payment of large corporate subsidies. With this understanding, the three groups can unite around programs that call for more and better services, improved wages and working conditions, paid for in a manner that more equitably taxes the rich and the corporations.

NOTES

1. U.S. Bureau of the Census, *Governmental Finances in 1968–1969* (Washington: Government Printing Office, 1970).
2. "Total tax revenues" will be taken to mean taxes plus social insurance payments. This total in 1968–1969 was $269.3 billion.
3. Pechman, J., *Federal Tax Policy* (Washington: Brookings Institution, 1971).
4. Gurley, J. G., "Federal Tax Policy," *National Tax Journal*, 20:319, September 1967.
5. House Ways and Means Committee, "Tax Reform, 1969" (Washington: Government Printing Office), pp. 1788 and 4199.
6. Stern, P., *The Great Treasury Raid* (New York: Random House, 1964).
7. Pechman, J. et al., *Social Security: Perspectives for Reform* (Washington: Brookings Institution, 1968).
8. House Ways and Means Committee, "Tax Reform, 1969," pp. 4194, 4315.
9. Rostvold, G., *Financing California Government* (Dickenson Publishing Co., 1967).
10. Herriot, R. and Miller, H., "The Taxes We Pay," *The Conference Board Record*, 8:31, May 1971.
11. *San Francisco Chronicle*, August 1, 1971.
12. Budd, E. C., "Postwar Changes in the Size Distribution of Income in the United States," *American Economic Review*, 60:247, May 1970.
13. Kolko, G., *Wealth and Power in America* (New York: Praeger, 1962).
14. Lundberg, F., *The Rich and the Super-Rich* (New York: Bantam Books, 1968).
15. Kolko, *Wealth and Power*.

Part II.
Economics,
Political Economy,
and the Welfare State

Although an individual can choose to minimize his participation in other institutions in American society, it is almost impossible to withdraw from all forms of economic activity. With the volunteer army, one can avoid direct military involvement. Politics can be avoided, as is demonstrated by the very large number of nonvoters in the United States. And the individual can use educational, religious, and scientific institutions as he needs them. All but the most isolated farm residents, however, are in some contact with economic organizations, at least as consumers.

The major sociological interest in the economy has focused on the stratification system—the unequal distribution of wealth and prestige. The main economic variables studied by sociologists have consequently been income, property, and occupation. Most of the studies have been in the domain of social psychology. That is, they have been concerned with the placement of individuals in society and with the social and psychological impact of their relative standing on these dimensions. Further sociological interest has centered on the structure and operation of organizations and the characteristics of various types of work.

The first concern of this section is the overall structure of the larger economic units, the corporations, and their interaction and coordination. This topic has been largely ignored by both sociologists and economists, but it is now beginning to arouse considerable interest in the social sciences. This is illustrated by the selections in this chapter,

by sessions devoted to the topic at recent national sociological association meetings, and by such popular social science magazines as
Society.[1] While there has been considerable congressional debate,
and there have been committee hearings on banks and the giant corporations, these have had little political impact. This may be because
the United States has no authentic political party untainted by corporate money and interests that can demand a national hearing. Unlike
some countries, the United States has no labor party or labor press
that can voice criticism of corporations and reach a large segment of
the public.

The opening selection by Andrew Hacker sketches the basic United
States economy. Contrary to conventional wisdom, he no longer sees
a free enterprise economy characterized by numerous competing
firms. True, there are many firms; small companies are continuously
being formed and going out of business, but they do not set the tone
of the economy as a whole. They tend, rather, to be marginal operations. Hacker believes that understanding the large corporation is the
key to understanding what he terms corporate America.

In the next article, Peter Drucker continues the argument of corporate domination. He describes the new type of corporate takeover
and the establishment of conglomerates, a new form of giant diversified corporation. In addition to domestic expansion of this type,
most of the major United States corporations have extended their
interests overseas to a degree that makes them virtually stateless, that
is, they do not belong to any single country. The interests of the
new multinational corporations, as Drucker outlines them, could well
conflict with those of individual nation-states, the United States
included.

The concentration in selective industries is given in Table 1. For
many industries, over half of the output is produced by four or fewer
corporations, many of which are closely linked by conglomerate and
banking ties to other industries. Recent experience has shown that in
some, if not all, of these industries, cartel-like arrangements in pricing
are quite open. Although evidence of conspiracy is usually only cir-
cumstantial, these corporations work in concert, usually by price
leadership. One raises its prices and the others follow. This appears
to be true in the petroleum industry, which holds many other industries in its grasp. In 1971, for example, the largest share (44.2

[1] See *Society*, vol. 11:2 (January/February 1974), which is devoted to the American
economy.

Table 1
Concentration in Selected Industries, 1967

Industry	Percentage of shipments accounted for by industry leaders	
	Four largest	Eight largest
Blast furnaces and steel mills	48	66
Motor vehicles	92	98
Aircraft	69	89
Petroleum refining	33	57
Paper mills	26	43
Construction machinery	41	53
Farm machinery	44	56
Telephone and telegraph apparatus	92	96
Motors and generators	48	60
Shipbuilding and repair	48	63
Radio and television receiving sets	59	69
Organic fibers, noncellulosic	84	94
Cellulosic man-made fibers	86	100

SOURCE: U.S. Bureau of the Census. Annual Survey of Manufacturers: 1971, "Industry Profiles," M71(AS)-10. Washington, D.C.: Government Printing Office, 1973.

percent) of United States power consumption was from petroleum, 32.9 percent was from natural gas, and 18.2 percent from coal.[2] The largest industrial corporations wield immense financial power. The largest two in sales and assets, General Motors and Exxon, are financially stronger than the total economies of most countries. The former had about $35.8 billion in sales and $20.3 billion in assets in 1973[3] and employed more than 800,000 people. Exxon grossed about $25.7 billion in sales on $25.1 billion assets. It employs 137,000 people. Both companies had earnings over $2 billion. Other corporations in the top twenty sales ranking include the other automobile majors—Ford ranked third and Chrysler fourth. Oil companies are also prominent. Texaco and Mobil were sixth and seventh respectively, Gulf tenth, Standard Oil of California eleventh, Standard

[2] See Congressional Quarterly Guide to Current American Government, April 1974 (Washington, D.C.: Congressional Quarterly, Inc., 1974).
[3] Information in this paragraph is derived from the Fortune magazine's listing of the five hundred largest industrial corporations. See Fortune, May 1974, pp. 32ff.

Oil of Indiana fifteenth, and Shell eighteenth. (There are three oil companies in the next ten corporations as ranked by sales.) Others in the top twenty are: General Electric, fifth; International Business Machines, eighth (but third in earnings); International Telephone and Telegraph, ninth (third in employment); Western Electric, twelfth; U.S. Steel, thirteenth; Westinghouse, fourteenth; DuPont, sixteenth; General Telephone and Electric, seventeenth; Goodyear, nineteenth; and Radio Corporation of America, twentieth. The ten largest employers among these employed over 3.4 million workers, and the sales of the top twenty compose more than one third of the national economy (Gross National Product).

The major corporations are not isolated entities, but are indeed coordinated and interrelated to form a full-fledged institutional order. Cross-ownership and joint board members constitute real ties. Other ties are provided by banks. The House Committee on Banking and Currency has investigated the part played by commercial banks in the United States economy. The committee report notes that the banks now own large blocks of stock in the major corporations. Thus, it is reported that "of the total of slightly over one trillion dollars in assets held by all institutional investors in the United States in 1967, $607 billion or approximately 60 percent is held by commercial banks."[4] The committee held that ownership of 5 percent of a corporation's stock was a substantial holding. According to some economists, 5 percent is close to a controlling interest if the remainder of the corporation's stock is widely dispersed. The report notes that "seventeen of the fifty largest merchandising companies and seventeen of the fifty largest transportation companies have one or more of the surveyed banks each holding 5 percent of their common stock."[5] Some of the committee's findings on bank ownership in some well-known corporations are summarized in Table 2.

The committee report also considers interlocking directorship as part of the banks' influence. It notes that "The interlocking relationships, such as stockholding and director interlocks between this small group [forty-nine of the largest] of banks and the fifty largest merchandising, transportation, utility, and life insurance companies, are . . . substantial."[6]

[4] U.S. Congress, House, Subcommittee on Domestic Finance, Committee on Banking and Currency, *Commercial Banks and Their Trust Activities: Emerging Influence on the American Economy*, 90th Congress, 2nd Session, 1968, vol. I, p. 1.
[5] Ibid.
[6] U.S. Congress, House, Subcommittee on Domestic Finance, Committee on Banking and Currency, *Commercial Banks and Their Trust Activities*.

Table 2
Bank Trust Holding in Selected Corporations

Corporation	Percentage of Common Stock	Bank
TransWorld Airlines	15.2	Chase Manhattan
Northwest Airlines	18.4	Chase Manhattan, Bank of N.Y.
United Airlines	8.2	Morgan
American Airlines	7.5	American
Pan American	6.7	Chase Manhattan
Eastern	6.4	Chase Manhattan
Alcoa	25.3	Mellon National
Reynolds	5.5	Chase Manhattan
Kaiser	6.6	Morgan
Kennecott Copper	17.5	Morgan
American Smelting and Refining	15.5	Morgan
Boeing	8.7	Chase Manhattan
Burlington Industries	14.4	Morgan
Celanese Corporation of America	7.7	Morgan
Crown Zellerbach	5.1	Bankers' Trust
	5.9	Fidelity Bank

SOURCE: U.S. Congress, House, Subcommittee on Domestic Finance, Committee on Banking and Currency, *Commercial Banks and Their Trust Activities: Emerging Influence on the American Economy*, 90th Congress, 2nd Session, 1968, vol. I.

Thus the Committee reports that

> 73 interlocking directorships with 27 of the 50 largest transportation companies were discovered to exist between the banks surveyed and these major transportation companies. These 49 banks also hold 86 interlocking directorships with 22 of the 50 largest United States utilities. Examining the 50 largest insurance companies, which are in direct competition with commercial banks for savings and the granting of loans, these 49 banks hold a very large 146 interlocking directorships with 29 of the 50 largest life insurance companies in the United States. This is an average of 5 directorships per insurance company on whose boards these banks are represented.[7]

There is, therefore, more coordination and less free enterprise than the general public imagines.

[7] Ibid.

The United States economy, of course, embraces more than the activities of major corporations. It involves all consumers and the gainfully employed, and the production of all goods and services. Since 1968 it has exceeded $1,000 billion (trillion) when measured as GNP (Gross National Product). According to government statistics, about 63 percent of this is personal consumption (goods and services), 15 percent goes to private investment, and 22 percent is government expenditure. The largest component groups of the private sector are manufacturing and trade (wholesale and retail), followed by finance, insurance and real estate; and power, transport and communication. The labor force exceeded eighty-five million in 1973. Table 3 gives the breakdown of the labor force by occupational group. It shows that the United States economy is increasingly characterized as white

Table 3
Distribution of Employment by Major Occupational Groups

	1960 (%)	1972 (%)
White-Collar	43.1	47.8
Professional and Technical	11.0	14.0
Managers and Administrators	11.2	9.8
Sales	6.4	6.6
Clerical	14.5	17.4
Blue-Collar	36.3	35.0
Craftsmen	13.3	13.2
Operatives	17.3	16.6
Non-Farm	5.7	5.2
Service Work	12.7	13.4
Private Household	3.0	1.8
Other	9.7	11.6
Farm	7.9	3.8
TOTAL	100	100

SOURCE: U.S. Department of Labor, Bureau of Labor Statistics, *Monthly Labor Review*, vol. 96, no. 12, December 1973.

collar. Despite the country's rural past, few people today are employed in agriculture. Over 50 percent of women and 90 percent of men between the ages of twenty and fifty-four years were actively employed in 1972.

Knowles and Prewitt deal with the position of blacks in the American economy. Blacks are concentrated in the financially unrewarding sectors. Few own their own small businesses, and when they do the enterprises are usually marginal. Like women of all races, blacks suffer discrimination when seeking employment and credit. Black capitalism may not offer much hope for blacks as a group in today's corporate economy. Knowles and Prewitt note that blacks are largely excluded from the most lucrative jobs. They suffer more unemployment and underemployment than whites, and they are underrepresented in skilled manual (as well as white-collar and managerial and professional) occupations. Some steps have been taken to remedy this situation, but we are still far from an equitable solution. The black population is likely to remain a vocal force calling for the restructuring of the economy.

Due to the emergence of conglomerates and multinational corporations, the overall economic system in the United States is no longer easily defined. Certainly our system does not resemble socialism. That would imply government ownership and control of basic industries. Nor does it remotely resemble communist systems, with their extensive state control and ownership throughout the economy and the absence of all but purely personal private property. Certainly the United States does not approach the model of capitalism, which stresses individualism and is characterized by private ownership of productive plants and widespread competition. The United States economy is a new phenomenon. It might be called something like "postindustrial corporatism," if this is used to describe a highly technological economy dominated by giant interlocking corporate units with limited private property and considerable government coordination, rather than ownership, of the economy.

While the economy affects everyone in the society, it also clearly has reciprocal effects on the other major institutions in society. Leading businessmen in the United States (like Karl Marx before them) make the assumption that the economy is and should be the most important institution. Decisions made by politicans now have a considerable impact on the economy. The government is expected to intervene to keep overall economic performance on the rise, but it is also expected to heed the advice of and to work with the consent of the major corporate leaders. The government is charged with regulatory responsibilities—such as the operation of the Securities and Exchange Commission, the Federal Reserve Bank, and so on—but its power is circumscribed by corporate inputs. It is not unreasonable to claim that economic organizations influence political institutions more than they are influenced by those institutions. Both political parties have a largely corporate ideology, despite the recent statements of such prominent (although perhaps marginally powerful) liberal politicians as economist John Kenneth Galbraith in his somewhat belated advocacy of socialism. Money, and especially corporate wealth, most decidedly leads to political influence through lobbying, and also through bribery. We know, as a result of Watergate, that corporate leaders play an influential role in determining which candidates run for election and how much money those candidates have for campaigning. Clearly, in the absence of effective campaign reform, politicians will continue to need considerable sums of money (more than ever before because of escalating television and media campaign costs) to get elected. Obviously corporations will continue to give to politicians who advocate policies that benefit corporations. These influences remain, especially in foreign policy, where there are few competing domestic interests to counteract the desires of the few multinational corporations.

Like political structures, educational institutions tend to be subservient to economic interests, although they have some autonomy. One of their main purposes is clearly to prepare persons for positions in the economy. In return, corporations support and thereby gain some influence over institutions of higher education. While corporate representatives often sit on the governing boards of universities, much of their influence is not in the day-to-day operation, but rather in overall strategic decisions. Thus, if the economy needs more engineers, business is likely to endow more engineering departments or to urge the government to subsidize areas in which business needs are greatest.

The last two articles in this section assess the welfare state aspects of the United States economy and government. Claus Offe claims that welfare measures in the United States and in Western Europe have not altered the balance between the poverty and affluence generated by the economy. The evolution of the welfare state, he adds, does not indicate structural change in society, only reformism, and large corporations benefit from it more than the poor. To Offe, welfarism is *not* a move towards "creeping socialism," but a push for corporate capitalism.

Robert Lampman is much more optimistic than Offe in his evaluation of welfare programs in America. He notes that the measurement of poverty and the aims of the government were never very clear, so it is difficult to judge how effective the government programs have been. Expenditures for welfare, however, increased dramatically between 1960 and 1972. Two goals, Lampman believes, have been achieved—welfare benefits reaching the poor have increased, and the number of statistically poor has been reduced. Nonetheless, income in the United States has not become drastically more equalitarian. Overall, Lampman sees a benign liberal government acting effectively against poverty in a continuing process of developing a welfare state.

Suggested Readings

Chasin, Barbara H., and Chasin, Gerald. *Power and Ideology.* Cambridge, Mass.: Schenkman, 1974.

Galbraith, John K. *The New Industrial State.* Boston: Houghton Mifflin, 1967.

Gans, Herbert J. *More Equality.* New York: Vintage, 1974.

Green, Mark J., et al. *The Closed Enterprise System.* New York: Bantam, 1972.

Kapp, K. William. *The Social Costs of Private Enterprise.* New York: Schocken, 1971.

Lopreato, Joseph, and Lewis, Lionel S., eds. *Social Stratification: A Reader.* New York: Harper and Row, 1974.

Mintz, Morton, and Cohen, Jerry S. *America, Inc.* New York: Dial Press, 1971.

Mouzelis, Nicos P. *Organization and Bureaucracies.* Chicago: Aldine, 1967.

Moynihan, Daniel P. *The Politics of a Guaranteed Income.* New York: Vintage, 1973.

Phelan, James, and Pozen, Robert. *The Company State.* New York: Grossman, 1973.

Pilisuk, Marc, and Pilisuk, Phyllis, eds. *How We Lost the War on Poverty.* New Brunswick: Transaction Books, 1973.

Seligman, Ben B. *Permanent Poverty.* New York: Quadrangle, 1970.

Sexton, Patricia Cayo, and Sexton, Brendon. *Blue Collars and Hard Hats.* New York: Random House, 1971.

Stern, Philip M. *The Rape of the Taxpayer.* New York: Vintage, 1974.

Sweezy, Paul M., and Magdoff, Harry. *The Dynamics of U.S. Capitalism.* New York: Monthly Review Press, 1972.

Tiffany, Donald W.; Cowan, James R.; and Tiffany, Phyllis M. *The Unemployed.* Englewood Cliffs, N. J.: Prentice-Hall, 1970.

White, William H., Jr. *The Organization Man.* New York: Doubleday, 1957.

CORPORATE AMERICA

Andrew Hacker

Since the end of the second World War the corporate form has emerged as the characteristic institution of American society. Its rise has made time-honored theories of politics and economics irrelevant, and its explosive growth has created new breeds of men whose behavior can no longer be accounted for by traditional rules of conduct.

America is not yet dominated by the corporate way of life, but the corporation is central to the nation's economy. The one hundred fifty largest firms produce more than half of our country's manufactured goods, and the five hundred largest own over two-thirds of the productive assets of the nation.

There remains, of course, a substantial part of the economy which cannot be called corporate. The small-business community still embraces most of the working and entrepreneurial population. Yet all signs indicate that the future lies with the great corporate institution, and no one seriously contends that there will be a rebirth of small business or a reduction of corporate growth. If not presently typical of our economic or social institutions, the corporation is "prototypical"—typical not of what exists now but rather of that which will be at some future time. To study the corporate form, therefore, is to speculate on a future America.[1] From contemporary reality must be extrapolated the trends.

Unlike the religious and guild structures of earlier centuries, the large firm of today has no theoretical rationale linking power, purpose, and responsibility. Indeed, the dilemma is even more fundamental. For there is no satisfactory answer to the first question of all: What is a corporation?

The question centers on the problem of who is represented in the exercise of corporate power, and whether that power is evidenced in politics or any other segment of society. Most Americans believe that power should be representative, that the ability to control resources should act in the name of human beings if it is to be legitimate. The corporation, however, is power—the power of productive assets—without a human constituency. It has interests to promote and defend, but they are the interests of a machine more than those of the people who guide, and profit from, the machine's workings. The managers who sit astride the corporate complexes do indeed have power; but it is the power bestowed on them by the resources of the enterprises they tend. Executives come and go, and their terms of office in the top positions are surprisingly short. But the productive assets remain, continually developing new interests to be safeguarded and new demands to be fulfilled.

The increasing irrelevance of people may be illustrated by the role of the stockholder. Approximately a third of all stock purchases are held for less than six months. Thus, an appreciable fraction of those who are the legal owners of corporate America are not ongoing constituents of the firms in which they happen to hold shares but rather transient investors with no sustained interests in the fortunes of the companies bearing the names on their stock certificates.

Nor can it be claimed that a corporation represents its stockholders. This proposition needs little explanation. Legal ownership and effective management have little or nothing to do with one another at the present stage of corporate development. Management recruits its own members with no interference from stockholders, and company policy is made by the men who will carry it out. A large corporation will have over one hundred million shares of stock outstanding, and upward of a million owners. Such a dispersion of ownership means that power gravitates to the full-time executives who not only run the company but also make up the agendas for the board of directors' and stockholders' meetings. Furthermore, the individual stockholder attending the annual meeting has power only in proportion to the number of shares he holds. In addition, almost half of the stockholdings in American corporations are held not by people but by other corporate entities. According to a survey taken by the New York Stock Exchange, about half of the outstanding shares were held by fiduciaries, stockbrokers, security dealers, nominees, and institutions. This means that when a vote is taken at an annual meeting, the ballots of the myriad Smiths and Joneses and Browns are joined by those of Merrill Lynch and Metropolitan Life and Ford Foundation. Individual stockholders support the existing management out of habit or inertia, while institutional stockholders do so as a matter of considered policy. The upshot is that the acquiescence of individual stockholders combines with the interest of institutional stockholders to give management a free hand.

That power may be rendered legitimate by demonstrating its representative quality has always been one of the foundations of democratic theory. Where power is exercised by—and within—voluntary associations, it can usually be argued that officials are elected by constituents who have consented to the uses of authority and cast equal votes in determining personnel and policies. Authority may be assigned rather than direct, and consent may be tacit rather than active, but the presumption remains that power in public and in private life will have a representative base.

Correlative to this theory is the familiar pluralist model: a society composed of a multiplicity of groups, and a citizenry actively engaged in the associational life. The sociology of democracy adumbrated by James Madison and reiterated

by Alexis de Tocqueville is firmly rooted in our thinking. This model presupposes a wide dispersion of power among many interacting and overlapping
groups in both society and the political system. Some measure of equilibrium
among forces is assumed, and if there is conflict, it results in compromises that
do not oppress any of the participants. And the groups with which we are dealing are presumed to be voluntary associations, consisting of individual citizens
who join together to further their common interests. Well suited to this scheme
are the myriad professional, occupational, religious, and other groups that speak
in their members' names. Were groups such as the American Medical Association,
the United Automobile Workers, the National Association for the Advancement
of Colored People, and the American Legion the only participants in the struggle
for political and economic preferment, then the sociology of democracy would
continue as a viable theory. For it may still be assumed that, despite tendencies
toward bureaucratization, the power of these associations is simply an extension
of the interests and wills of their constituent members.

But when General Electric, American Telephone and Telegraph, and Standard
Oil of New Jersey enter the pluralist arena, we have elephants dancing among the
chickens. For corporate institutions are not voluntary associations of individuals
but rather associations of assets, and no theory yet propounded has declared that
machines are entitled to a voice in the democratic process. A corporate institution cannot easily claim to have "members." It may profess to speak for its employees, but there is often evidence that not a few on its payroll are quite out of
sympathy with the management's policies. It may profess to speak for its stockholders. But many of these are not human beings; and of those who are, a vote
is cast for each share owned and not by the conventional democratic standard of
one ballot per individual. Neither our constitutional law nor our political theory
is able to account for the corporate presence in the arena of social power. Indeed, it is not at all clear by what right the corporation is entitled to power at all.
It may well be that discourse will follow reality, that we will find some painless
way of rationalizing the arrangements in our midst. But as yet no philosophy
has been created which mingles men and machines as joint participants, nor is it
clear that American inventive genius will be able to adjust the vocabulary of
democracy so as to allow corporate institutions to assume the role of just plain
folks.

Corporate Power

Discussions of corporate power tend to be vague, and not a few commentators
seem to assume a general agreement that corporate institutions exercise great influence in society. But what, precisely, is the power of the corporation? Power
to do what?

The conventional view is that the businessman is far from a free agent. Any
executive will wax eloquent on how he is hemmed in on all sides. He will point
to a plethora of government agencies, all of which regulate his conduct. There is
the Federal Trade Commission, the National Labor Relations Board, the Antitrust

Division of the Justice Department, and, of course, the Internal Revenue Service. And then there are labor unions, further limiting his freedom of action. He has customers and suppliers telling him what they want and what he can get; and he has stockholders waiting for dividends, capital gains, and efficient management. And of course there is the ubiquitous consumer who must be satisfied at all stages lest bankruptcy be the consequence. However, the question is not whether businessmen feel hamstrung, for they have objected to their powerlessness since they were first told to buy safety devices for their dangerous machines. The point is whether these limiting factors take on much significance when weighed against the areas of unrestricted freedom of action.

It should be noted at the outset that large corporations do not go bankrupt. They can, as the steel companies have demonstrated, be inefficient, and still be profitable. Their relative share of the market can rise or fall, and their rank in the industry may change slightly over the years, but mergers and reorganizations keep the assets and production facilities intact. To be sure, a corporation must make its decisions with an eye on profit. But in the highest circles the concern is with the growth of the enterprise over several decades, and profits are but a means to this end. The real issue is how autonomous these enterprises are and what are the consequences of their decisions for society as a whole. What, in short, can corporations do with the power they are alleged to have?

Despite an occasional outburst from the White House, corporate managers can administer prices as they see fit. They are not required to submit proposed increases to any government agency for approval. They may ask what the market will bear, and, generally speaking, the market will pay what is asked. Stockholders have accustomed themselves to a modest dividend, and this is usually passed on to them without discussion. Top management maintains a suitable level of earnings by its ability to set prices. In addition, it decides what proportion of the earnings will go to the stockholders and what proportion is to be retained by the company. Wages are, of course, subject to collective bargaining. But this process simply maintains the status quo. For wage increases just about keep pace with increases in productivity, and the share of a corporation's income which goes to wages remains about the same over the years. Management has even more freedom in determining salaries. Here it can determine who is to become wealthy and how great this wealth is to be. Decisions on executive compensation, in particular, go far toward determining aspirations for an entire society. The purchasing power bestowed on the men at and near the top makes for a style of life which becomes a goal for those lower down on the pyramid.

The large corporations shape the material contours of the nation's life. While original ideas for new products may come from a variety of sources, it is the big companies that have the resources to bring these goods to the public. The argument that the consumer has "free will," deciding what he will and will not buy, can be taken just so far. For in actual fact we *do* buy much or even most of what the large corporations put on the shelves or in the showrooms for us.

Companies are not unsophisticated, and they have a fair idea of what the consumer will be willing to purchase. But the general rule, with fewer exceptions than we would like to think, is that if they make it, we will buy it. Thus, we air-condition our bedrooms, watch color television in our living rooms, brush our teeth electrically in the bathroom, and cook at eye level in the kitchen. It is time for frankness on this score: the American consumer is not notable for imagination and does not know what he "wants." Thus, he waits for corporate America to develop new products and, on hearing of them, discovers a long-felt "need" he never knew he had. What should be noted is that the number and character of a man's possessions have a singular impact on the personality of their owner. Materialism is not uniquely American, nor is the high valuation placed on material possessions entirely the result of management decisions. However, the perpetuation of this system of values, with its stress on tangible possessions and labor-saving devices, is due to corporate judgment about what sales are needed if rates and turnover of production are to be kept at the optimum level.

And more than any other single force in society, the large corporations govern the character and quality of the nation's labor market. The most visible example of this prowess has been the decision of companies to introduce computers into the world of work, bringing an unmistakable message to those who must earn a living. Millions of Americans are being told what skills they will have to possess if they are to fill the jobs that will be available. A company, whether its product happens to be power mowers or life insurance or air transportation, has the freedom to decide *how* it will produce its goods and services. And having made this decision, it establishes its recruiting patterns accordingly. Individuals must tailor themselves to the job if they want to work at all. Most of us and all of our children will find ourselves adjusting to new styles of work whether we want to or not.

The impact of corporate organization and technology on the American educational system deserves far closer attention than it has been given. Whether we are talking of a vocational high school in Los Angeles or an engineering college in Milwaukee or a law school in New Haven, the curriculum is largely determined by the job needs of our corporate enterprises. The message goes out that certain kinds of people having certain kinds of knowledge are needed. All American education, in a significant sense, is vocational. Liberal-arts students may enjoy a period of insulation, but they are well aware that eventually they will have to find niches for themselves in offices or laboratories.

Corporate managements are free to decide where they will locate their plants and offices. This power has also contributed, probably more than anything else, to the suburban explosion, for the white-collar class must have a place to live. A handful of executives decides which parts of the country are to prosper and which are to stagnate. If over half the counties in the United States lose population each decade, this is largely because corporate managements are unwilling to locate facilities in areas they consider unsuitable. On the other hand, regions the corporations do favor experience a radical transformation. New citizens move in and old values must adjust themselves to new influences. Cities and towns, while welcoming branch plants as sources of jobs and revenue, find that what were once local decisions are now made from the outside and by outsiders. Moreover, as corporations expand across the nation, they turn many of their white-collar employees into transients who are prepared to leave as management beckons them to new job opportunities. The nomadic life has consequences for family and personality which are not without disturbing qualities.

The regions that have not prospered in postwar years have been those where corporations have opted not to situate. Too much can be made of the New England "ghost towns." Actually, corporations have "pulled out" of very few places; more critical has been their failure to establish or expand facilities in alternative parts of the country. Thus, patterns of migration—from the countryside to the city and from the city to the suburb—are reflections of corporate decisions on plant and office location.

Related to this have been the corporate decisions to locate their firms' headquarters in the center of our largest cities, especially the East Side of New York. Leaving aside the architectural transformation with which we will have to live for many years, the very existence of these prestige palaces has drawn hundreds of thousands of people into metropolitan areas not equipped to handle them. Thus have come not only the traffic snarls and the commuter crush, but also the pyramiding of suburbs for the young-marrieds of management and the thin-walled city apartments for others in their twenties, fifties, and sixties.

Perhaps it has been said too often that ours is an age of "organization men." Yet there is more than a germ of truth in this depiction of the new white-collar class that is rapidly becoming the largest segment of the American population. The great corporations molded this type of individual, and the habits and style of life of corporate employment continue to play a key role in setting values and aspirations for the population as a whole. Working for a large organization has a subtle effect on a person's character. It calls for the virtues of adaptability, sociability, and that certain caution necessary when one knows one is forever being judged.

The type of success represented by a senior engineer at Western Electric or a branch manager for Metropolitan Life is now the model for millions. Not only does the prestige of the corporation rub off on the employee, but he seems to be riding an escalator that can only move upward. Too much can be made of the alleged "repudiation" of business and corporate life by the current generation of college students. This may be the case at Swarthmore, Oberlin, and in certain ivied circles. But the great majority of undergraduates—who are, after all, at places like Penn State and Purdue—would like nothing better than a good berth in Ford or Texaco. Indeed, they are even now priming themselves to become the sort of person those companies will want them to be.

The pervasive influence of the large corporations derives less from how many people they employ than from their great wealth. Our largest firms have a good deal of spare cash to spend where they like. These companies make profits almost automatically every year, and they find it necessary to give only a fraction of those earnings to their stockholders in the form of dividends.[2]

Thus, the big firms have had the money to create millions of new white-collar jobs. Department heads in the large companies ask for and are assigned additional assistants, coordinators, planners, and programmers who fill up new acres of office space every year. And everyone appears to keep busy: attending meetings and conferences, flying around the country, and writing and reading and amending memoranda.

That a large proportion of these employees are not necessary was illustrated when, due to a long labor dispute, one large corporation took the unprecedented step of firing one-third of its white-collar force. The wholesale departure of these clerks and executives had no effect on the company's production and sales. Nevertheless, the company was not one to show that an empire could function half-clothed, and it hired back the office workers it did not need just as soon as the cash was again available.

If all this sounds a bit like Alice in Wonderland, it would be well to ponder on what the consequences would be if all our major corporations cut their white-collar staffs to only those who were actually needed. Could the nation bear the resulting unemployment, especially involving so many people who have been conditioned to believe that they possess special talents and qualities of character?

Corporate wealth, then, is spent as a corporation wishes. If General Motors wants to tear down the Savoy-Plaza Hotel in New York City and erect a headquarters for itself at Fifth Avenue and 59th Street, it will go ahead and do so. An office building could, at a quarter of the cost, have been located at Eleventh Avenue and 17th Street. But why should cost be the prime consideration? After all, the stockholders have received their dividends, new production facilities have been put into operation, and there is still plenty of money left over. Nor is such a superfluity of spare cash limited to the very largest concerns. Ford, which is generally thought of as General Motors' poor sister, was sufficiently well heeled to drop a quarter of a billion dollars on its Edsel design and still not miss a dividend.

Management alone decides when to invest—in new capital equipment, in new locations, in new processes, products, and personnel. It need not receive the approval of any governmental agency, and no such agency can compel a corporation to go ahead with an investment program if it feels like retrenching. While top executives will be attuned to expectations of the public's buying, it can just as well shape these expectations by announcing a buoyant expansion program. The goodwill of investors need not be courted, as large corporations can use their retained earnings for investment purposes. And there is increasing reliance on the huge investing institutions—insurance companies, pension funds, banks, brokerage houses—for funds. Representatives of these institutions sit on or are close to the boards of the large corporations and are really part of the corporate circle. Together they decide how and in what amounts capital will be invested over the decades to come. The power to make investment decisions is concentrated in a few hands, and it is this power which will decide what kind of a nation America will be. Instead of government planning there is boardroom planning that is accountable to no outside agency: and these plans set the order of priorities on national growth, technological innovation, and, ultimately, the values and behavior of human beings. Investment decisions are sweeping in their ramifications—no one is unaffected by their consequences. Yet this is an area where neither the public nor its government is able to participate. If the contours of the economy and the society are being shaped in a few score boardrooms, these decisions, so far as the average citizen is concerned, are in the laps of the gods.

The Corporate Elite

From these observations at least one conclusion is possible: an "elite" presides over corporate America. Yet it must be understood that the "elite" in question consists not so much of identifiable personalities (how many of the presidents of our twenty largest corporations can any of us name?) but rather of the chairs in the top offices.

The typical corporation head stays at his desk for less than ten years. The power he exercises is less discretionary than we would like to believe, and the range of decisions that can be called uniquely his own is severely limited. (It is only in the small companies on the way up that the top men impress their personalities on the enterprise.) When a corporation president retires and his successor is named, the price of the company's stock, presumably a barometer of informed opinion, does not change perceptibly.

The top managers of the largest companies do not gather at scheduled intervals to make their key decisions in concert. At the same time, it is clear that they know what is on one another's minds. Whether they come together casually at their clubs or hunting lodges, or slightly more formally at the Business Council or the Committee for Economic Development or the Foreign Policy Association, they are definitely not isolated from each other. Informal conversation elicits plans, hopes, expectations. There is a community of interest and sentiment among this elite, and any thought of a "conspiracy" is both invalid and irrelevant. Moreover, the critical investment decisions bring together many members of the elite—executives, bankers, brokers—and the decision to expand or retrench is clearly based on consultation and agreement. Such decisions are made with the knowledge of what others are doing or plan to do. The lines of communication are built into the system.

Nor is the corporate elite a "class," any more than the corporate world is "capitalist" in the classical sense. The members of the elite come from a variety of backgrounds, or at least from every segment of the middle class. Birth and upbringing are of negligible importance, and promotion to the highest corporate circles is based on talent more than on manners or connections. Those in the elite group are simply the men who sit in particular chairs at any particular time; the chairs, rather than their occupants, have the power. Thus, there is little point in discussing "who" has the power unless one explores the sources of that power. This needs to be stressed because there is strong reason to believe that the institutional structure determines the behavior of the men who hold positions in it and that it does not really matter who the officeholders are as individuals.

The top men in the top companies are symbolic of a new breed of American. Their distinction lies in having passed the stringent tests by which our society determines who will rise to its heights and who will be left behind. Every modern organization has multiple hurdles, and the route to the top for an archbishop, a four-star general, or a university chancellor has a great deal in common with that traveled by a corporation president. Career success today is based on talent, and what is especially rewarded is ability and willingness to devote one's talents to goals chosen not by oneself but by others.

The future corporation president can emerge from anywhere in the generous bosom of the American middle class. All that companies ask, in their initial recruitment of potential executives, is that a young man possess a college diploma. It doesn't matter where he went to school, and in most cases no one cares who his father was or what he did for a living. Among the top executives of today there are more products of the Big Ten than of the Ivy League, and in the corporate circles of the future it is clear that graduates of Purdue will far outnumber those from Princeton.

The president of one large corporation was born in Lolo, Montana (population 235), and went on to Montana State University. Itasca, Texas; Walton, Kentucky; Hattiesburg, Mississippi; and Shelby, Nebraska produced local boys who made it to the top ranks of Gulf Oil, North American Aviation, Texaco, and the Ford Motor Company. Very few of today's top executives went to private preparatory schools, and hardly more than three or four out of a hundred are listed in the metropolitan Social Registers.

The open-eyed young man, first taken on as a technician of one sort or another, soon discovers what is wanted if he is to distinguish himself from his classmates. This is the comprehension that he is, above all else, working in and for a business. The up-and-comer soon learns to think first in business terms: the specialized skills he was taught at college are useful only if they can be applied to augmenting the firm's earnings. At a certain point he may have to compromise with professional standards in making or promoting a profitable but less-than-quality product. How he reacts to this challenge will be noted by his superiors.

By the time he is in his early thirties, the man-on-the-way-up will have left his old friends behind at their account books and drafting boards. He is now manager of a large department or perhaps a branch plant. The best indication of his early success is that he now has as subordinates men older than himself; not only has he passed his peers but he has bypassed some who were once ahead of him. What is required now is the top-management look, usually achieved by emulating the appearance and outlook of one's immediate and remote superiors. It is generally an air of taciturn tough-mindedness, an impression of deliberate decisiveness. Those who undergo such a transformation do so not deliberately but as an unconscious adaptation.

The executive personality can probably be mastered more easily by the boy from Itasca than by the graduate of Groton. The corporate graces are, on the whole, those of middle-class life in Detroit or Chicago. In contrast to his European counterparts, the American executive does not have to know wines and is actually a step ahead if he prefers his steak without sauce Béarnaise. What is needed most in these years is ambition, drive, willingness to make company business the center of his life. The difficulty is that this test comes at just the wrong time. His children are in high school and faced with all the problems of adolescense; his wife is beginning to feel the passing of the years and starts to wonder just where she stands in his diffused affections. But at this period he must bring work home every night—except those nights when he is traveling to a trade-association meeting in San Francisco, to a commission hearing in Washington, to merger negotiations in Chicago, or simply to see what has gone wrong at the assembly plant in Shreveport.

No one can assert with complete confidence that the fourteen-hour day is absolutely necessary for high-quality executive performance. Walter Bagehot once observed that businessmen work much too hard for their own good, with the result that they make a lot of money in the morning and then, instead of stopping when they're ahead, proceed to lose half of it in the afternoon. However, if the sheep are to be separated from the goats, certain rituals must be enforced and observed. One corporation chairman calls frequent Sunday-morning meetings just to see which of his vice-presidents grumble.

During this period, also, a presidential contender will have to become something of a philosopher. Thus the need to affirm that the economy is the central institution of the society, that business profit is the prime mover in the nation's life. He will, moreover, come to believe that whatever it is his company produces is absolutely necessary for the well-being of the American citizen-consumer. He must take the view—and this attitude cannot be faked—that the six-sided frozen French-fried potato is an asset to the nation's dinner table; that automobile exhaust is not really responsible for air pollution; that his firm is doing all it can to give jobs to blacks and school drop-outs. For only if such sentiments are uttered with a ring of inner conviction will he be adjudged a true company man.

A man's fate can be shaped by whether the special area of interest he developed many years ago turns out to be a critical one for the corporation at the time when the penultimate promotions are being made. There appears, then, to be a semi-deterministic "Law of Strategic Talents," accelerating the rise of individuals who have skills that unexpectedly take on central significance. Nevertheless, it would be a mistake to counsel an ambitious young man, now entering college, on how to equip himself for the semi-finals of 1995. Advice that he prepare himself for computerized investment programming or psychoanalytic labor relations could well be an act of misguidance. For just when he is ready for the final round, the company may discover that consumer resistance has returned and the top job may be given to an old-fashioned sales type who has the unscientific knack of making people want to take out their checkbooks. There are, as the sages keep telling us, some things that just can't be planned.

All things considered, the American corporation has become a self-selecting, self-contained civil service. The men at the top of corporate America undergo far less criticism than the average senator or governor, in part because they don't have to face popular elections and in part because the ideology of private ownership insulates them from public scrutiny. It may well be that the time has come to alter outdated assumptions about the presumed "private" character of our major corporations. By any reasonable measure AT&T is as important an institution in American society as the state of Alabama, and the presiding officer of that company deserves as much attention as the governor of that state. Corporation executives are not very interesting people, however, and not the least reason is that they have had to become bland in order to get where they are.

It would be wrong to call these men conservatives, for once again the conventional language of ideology does not apply here. Many of the decisions they make, whether so intended or not, have revolutionary consequences for all of society. The technological and marketing transformations they have effected have given a new shape to postwar America, and the plans they are making for the remainder of the century may alter the face of the nation beyond recognition.[3]

The men who preside over American corporations are chiefly of unpretentious origins, and they have won a race where there is room at the finish line for only a few. At no time in their trials were they expected to display humane learning, any more than a philosophy professor is asked to show a profit for his department. The job of an employee is to protect the interests of his employer, even if that employer is an abstract combination of assets called a corporation. Most corporation presidents would not even belabor the theory that what is good for General Electric or General Dynamics is good for the country. Their job is to look out for the good of their company.

This should not be taken as criticism. Most of these men have invested their energy and ardor in a particular line of endeavor. To expect that our corporations will somehow produce an aristocratic order is to misunderstand important conditions that have accompanied recent changes in the structure of American life. It is futile, then, to wish that our corporate managers underwent more instruction in moral philosophy or modern sociology. During most of their formative years, the exigencies of the climb force them to think of themselves rather than for themselves. This is an inevitable consequence of opening careers to the talented, of breaking down the barriers that once prevented men of inauspicious background from rising to the top.

Not only corporations but universities and medical centers, foundations and research institutes, government agencies and the military establishment are recruiting and shaping individuals to serve their needs and eventually fill their top positions. The making of the nation's corporate elite is more than a success story. Its greater significance is as part of the natural history of our time, wherein men perceive what is wanted of them and then pattern their lives to meet these specifications.

Corporate Capitalism

If our large corporations are using their power to reshape American society, the general public's thinking about such concentrated influence still remains ambiguous. There persist, for example, the ideology of antitrust and the fond place in American hearts still occupied by small business. Thus, politicians can count on striking a resonant chord when they call for more vigorous prosecutions under the Sherman Law and for greater appropriations for the Small Business Administration. Most Americans do agree, from time to time, that our largest companies are too big and should somehow be broken up into smaller units. But just how strong or enduring this sentiment is is hard to say. No one really expects that Mobil Oil or Bethlehem Steel can or will be "busted" into ten or a dozen entirely new and independent companies. Thus, if the ideology that bigness equals badness lingers on, there is no serious impetus to translate that outlook into action.

Part of the problem is that if Americans are suspicious of bigness, they do not really know what it is about large corporations which troubles them. Despite the periodic exposures of defective brake cylinders or profiteering on polio vaccine, the big story is not really one of callous exploitation or irresponsibility. Given the American system of values, it is difficult to mount a thoroughgoing examination of capitalism or to be "anti-business" in an unequivocal way. The result is that our commentaries in this area are piecemeal and sporadic. We have the vocabularies for criticizing "big government" and "big labor," but the image of the large corporation is a hazy one, and despite its everyday presence in our midst, our reaction to its very existence is uncertain.

The American corporate system continues, in major outlines, to be capitalist in structure. Talk of a welfare state, of a mixed economy, even of a managerial revolution is of limited utility, for the fact remains that major decisions in the economy are private. They are made within closed circles, and public agencies cannot intrude in any effective way. Corporate capitalism of course differs from classical capitalism, but the transformation has been only in the adjective—not the noun. This is why reform is so difficult. Can the private managers of corporate capital be made institutionally responsible to the public? Accountability seems impossible in the American framework. Experience has thus far shown that public agencies set up to regulate private enterprise are soon brought to a close sympathy with the industries they are supposed to be regulating. This should occasion no great surprise. Corporations are powerful, and they will use their resources to maintain a climate favorable to themselves. While in the realm of pure logic a Federal Power Commission in Washington might tell Standard Oil of California what it might or might not do, in actual fact such an agency is less powerful than the corporation. Similarly, our ideology permits us to rest happy in the thought that the Antitrust Division of the Justice Department could "break up" General Dynamics or International Business Machines into collections of separate companies. The fact of power, however, is that this has not been done and cannot be done because government is weaker than the corporate institutions purportedly subordinate to it. This is the politics of capitalism. It is expressive not of a conspiracy but rather of a harmony of political forms and economic interests on a plane determined by the ongoing needs of corporate institutions.

Are there alternatives to corporate capitalism? Few voices are heard suggesting the public ownership of major industries, and it is just as well, for the odds are that nationalization would end in disillusion. The problem is that there is no real middle ground. This was known to both Adam Smith and Karl Marx, but it is a fact hard to swallow in an age that seeks reason along the course of moderation. Suppose that America followed the British pattern and nationalized a few industries such as railroads, electricity, and the coal mines. Instead of becoming agencies of the public interest, these industries would soon enter service as handmaidens of the private sector of the economy. For the preponderance of economic power remaining in corporate hands would ensure that the industries in the public sector were suitably docile and did not serve as vehicles for serious planning that might jeopardize corporate interests. In short, partial nationalization would not make economic decisions accountable to the public but would create yet another set of official agencies to be captured by corporate enterprise.

On the other hand, the state could nationalize all industry, thus once and for all destroying private economic power. This was and is the Marxian prescription, offered with the full understanding that the old order must be felled with one stroke if the new is to rise from its ashes. But the problems of irresponsibility in corporate America are minor compared with those of totalitarianism, and the Marxist alternative to capitalism is hardly one that those who have known a free society will embrace with enthusiasm.

Hence the frustrations that mark any search for a middle ground. We hear much of regulation, of intervention, of planning on the part of government. But who, for example, are to be the planners? What is to be their source of power, as against their legal authority, and who will give force to their decisions? And is it possible to prevent corporate institutions from seducing, capturing, and otherwise infiltrating those who are mandated to plan the economy in the public interest? Until such questions are answered, the power of corporate America will continue to grow, and in directions of its own choosing.

Unincorporated Americans

There are losers as well as winners in the growth of corporate organization and technology. Not all who work for corporations have secure, let alone ascending, careers. The unskilled and the untrained continue to be hired at hourly wages, and then only for those hours when their services are required. Many of the unemployed are, indeed, corporate unemployed: they have been laid off from jobs they once had with corporations or have not been hired for jobs that corporate technology has been able to abolish. By the same token, trade unions are in a relative stage of decline, a development at least partly to be attributed to technological innovations that have swelled the proportion of white-collar workers in the employed population. Indirectly, and to some extent directly, corporate decisions have, therefore, both increased unemployment and diminished the role of unions. The latter consequence is a serious blow to the doctrine of social pluralism, for organized labor has been traditionally counted upon as a source of countervailing force against the strength of corporate management. The weakening of the unions deprives society of another check to the power of the corporation.

It may well be that two Americas are emerging, one a society protected by the corporate umbrella and the other a society whose members have failed to affiliate themselves with the dominant institutions. This second America will in part consist of small businessmen and other independent spirits who manage to do well without corporate attachments. But, more importantly, it will be comprised of superfluous Americans: the unemployed, the ill-educated, the entire residue of human beings who are not needed by the corporate machine. Little thought has been given to these people. How are they to earn their living? How will they maintain their sense of self-esteem? If this pool grows to substantial proportions, if it finds effective leadership, if it gives vent to its resentments – then, and perhaps then only, will a force arise to challenge the great corporate institutions. For then will power meet power, the power of a mass movement confronting the power of the machine. The discard heap that the machine created may arise to devour its progenitor.

This revolution—with or without violence, whether from the left or from the right—will be averted only if corporate America can make room in its environs for those who demand entry. Has it the jobs, the resources, the will, and the imagination to achieve this? Thus far, corporate America has escaped open attack because the victims of new technology do not yet outnumber its beneficiaries. But technology advances according to rules of its own, and loyalty to now-dominant institutions may diminish if accelerated automation or economic reverses reduce the corporate constituency. In this event, this second America, the society of losers, may grow in numbers and power with increasing rapidity. The resolution will not be a pleasant one.

NOTES

1. This chapter will consider the business corporation, chiefly because it is the chief instrument of economic power and the prime agency for technological development in American society. In fact, the nation's largest firms employ only a minor proportion of the country's labor force. However, the five hundred biggest industrial companies provided jobs for about fourteen million Americans, or 70 percent of the population working in that sector of the economy in 1969. Moreover, that figure is a substantial advance over a dozen years ago and is actually 1.35 times higher than it was in 1955, when only half were on the top five hundred payrolls.

    The fastest-growing segment of the work force is in non-business employment: not only agencies at all levels of government but also in a surfeit of non-profit enterprises funded from public and private sources. Many of these organizations are also corporate in structure—universities, foundations, medical centers, research institutes—and thus many of the observations made here apply to them as well as to business firms.

2. Quite clearly, the biggest corporations stand no risk of going out of business. Of the firms ranking among the top 40 a dozen years ago, all but two are still in pre-eminent positions. And the pair that slipped continue to remain in the top 100.

3. While it is amusing to reflect on the horse-and-buggy values of a man like Henry Ford, his real role was to hurtle the nation into an era that would be incapable of adhering to earlier standards. The philosophical pronouncements of businessmen receive far too much attention; the decisions they make while doing their jobs are the important catalysts of social change.

THE NEW MARKETS
AND THE NEW CAPITALISM

Peter F. Drucker

The "Takeover Merger"

"Diversification mergers," though continuing right through the 1960s passed their peak around 1964 or 1965. From then on, until the end of 1969, the mergers that made the headlines were something quite different, "merger by takeover." This merger is forced upon a reluctant, and often loudly resisting, management by organizing a stockholders' revolt against it. And the one who "takes over" is almost invariably a very much smaller company, a total outsider—indeed, typically a brash newcomer who did not even exist a few years earlier. In the "diversification mergers," both parties plighted their troth with the promise of "synergism" which would somehow make the combined business more productive than the two had been alone. But in the "takeover," the justifying slogan is "asset management," that is, the maximization of the value of the shareholders' equity through financial management. In effect, the "takeover" is far less a merger of business than a *coup d'état*. A guerrilla leader, himself owning practically no part of the company he acquires, gets the outside shareholders of large publicly owned companies to oust their own "professional business management" and put him into the saddle. The more successful of these new corporate guerrilla captains went from one "takeover" to another. Starting with nothing, they built "conglomerates" showing total revenues in the billions.

Among the "takeover" victims have been some of the oldest and best-known companies in the country, companies run by entrenched "professional management." They include two of the world's largest steel companies, Jones & Laughlin and Youngstown Sheet & Tube, both with sales around the billion dollar mark. They were taken over respectively by Ling-Temco-Vought, built by James Ling in a few years from a small electronics shop into a medium-sized aerospace company with sales around $160 million, and by Lykes Brothers Steamship, a New Orleans-based shipping line which never in all its forty years of history had had sales of more than $70 million.

Reprinted with permission from *Man, Ideas, and Politics* by Peter F. Drucker (Harper and Row, New York, 1971); first published in *The Public Interest*, September 1970.

In another bitterly fought takeover, AMK, a company of whom a few years earlier nobody had even heard, took over the old United Fruit Company in Boston—a company with over $400 million in assets and almost $400 million in sales. (This was AMK's second leap—in the first one a year earlier, it had taken over one of the oldest meat-packers, Morrell.) AMK's base had been a small company making industrial machinery. The United Fruit shareholders sided with the raider, not because their management had failed, but because it had been so successful in its attempt to turn around and save an old and ailing enterprise that it had accumulated a large amount of cash. The most spectacular of these takeovers would have been (it never came off) the takeover of the country's sixth-largest bank, Chemical New York—with assets of $9 billion—by a company, called Leasco, that was not even mentioned in the financial handbooks of 1966. It had started out, a few years earlier, as a small computer leasing operation without any capital to speak of and with fewer than a dozen employees.

There thus came into being a whole new group of entrepreneurs. They are not "owners," but they know how to mobilize the vast multitude of shareholders of big publicly owned companies against management. They have been able again and again to unseat "professional management" in the name of "asset management," that is, by promising to maximize financial returns. And their aim is not the "synergism" (whatever that may mean) of "diversification." It is the "conglomerate" built by financial manipulation and based on financial control.

The New "Growth" Companies

Perhaps even more significant, however, is another development, and one that never before coincided with a wave of mergers. It is the emergence of yet another group of new entrepreneurs, far more numerous than the "asset managers" and perhaps a good deal sounder, though neither as colorful nor as spectacular. These are the men who have been building new "growth" businesses in very large numbers. New businesses are, of course, being started all the time. But these new businesses have been started as "growth" businesses, and from the beginning were supported by large investments from the capital market. In every year from 1965 to 1969, eight to ten thousand brand-new "growth" businesses got going. These entrepreneurs went to the capital market for anything up to $1 million before their business had even been started, produced its first product, or made its first sale. A year or two later most came back for another substantial sum of money, ranging from $1 million to $10 million apiece. These companies were still sufficiently small and their investors sufficiently few in number—and were also what the securities laws call "sophisticated investors" (that is, primarily investment institutions)—not to have to register their securities with the Securities Exchange Commission. Yet they were sufficiently large already to have to apprise the Commission of their existence. All told, these new businesses raised about $5 billion to $10 billion annually from the "sophisticated investors" during the last five years.

"Science-based" companies, most nonfinancial readers will instantly think.

And indeed the "science-based" companies that sprang up in the 1950s around Boston on Route 128 or on the Peninsula south of San Francisco were the forerunners. But though "science-based" industries (such as "learning" or computer application) are to be found among the new "growth" ventures of the 1960s, they constitute a small fraction of the total. Among the "glamour" stocks for which the "sophisticated investors" bid were franchise restaurants, magazine and book publishers, nursing homes and hospitals, prefabricated housing and mobile homes, manufacturing, and others.

Some of these new "growth" companies are even to be found in finance, both on Wall Street and as managers of investment trusts. The first of these financial growth ventures—and the most successful one to date—Donaldson, Lufkin & Jenrette, was started ten years ago by a group of young business school graduates. It had become by 1969 the seventh largest Stock Exchange firm. Then it singlehandedly achieved what Franklin D. Roosevelt, with all the power of the United States government behind him, had failed to bring about thirty years earlier: to force the Stock Exchange out of being a "private club." When Donaldson, Lufkin & Jenrette outgrew its capital base in 1969 and threatened to quit the Exchange unless permitted to sell shares to the public—something always strictly forbidden by the rules which, in effect, limited investment in Stock Exchange firms to wealthy individuals—it had become so important that the Stock Exchange had to give way. Donaldson, Lufkin & Jenrette raised $12 million by selling shares to the public last April.

Very few of these new companies can be compared with Xerox, the growth company *par excellence* of the American economy in post-World War II—a company having barely $1 million in sales as recently as 1950, still having less than $15 million in sales in 1960, and, in 1969, reporting sales of $1½ billion. But a good many of these new companies grew, within a short period, to respectable middle size—$50 million, $60 million, $70 million, sometimes even $100 million in sales. An even larger number grew to the point where their founders could sell them at a considerable capital gain to older, staid and less "dynamic" companies bent on "diversification," or could, in a few cases, become "takeover entrepreneurs" in their own right. Not since the railroad and banking ventures of the Age of Jackson has there been any comparable explosion of new ventures getting, from the start, broad financial support in large amounts.

What "Could Not Have Happened"

Neither the "takeover merger" nor the new "growth" ventures could really have happened, according to "what everybody knows" about the structure of the American economy. This is brought out clearly by the cleavage between the actual developments and the magisterial announcements regarding what could happen—just when the actual developments were approaching their peak.

Nineteen sixty-seven was the year in which takeovers exploded and in which also the largest number of new "growth" businesses appeared on the capital market. It was also the year which produced the all-time best seller by an American academic economist, John Kenneth Galbraith's *The New Industrial State*. This book has two fundamental theses. One, professional management in the big corporation is so firmly entrenched that it cannot be challenged, let alone be overthrown, from inside or outside. The dispersed "public" stockholder is completely disenfranchised, to the point where management need not, and indeed does not, aim at maximizing profitability, but can run the business comfortably to perpetuate itself in power. Secondly, *The New Industrial State* asserted that new businesses simply cannot come into existence in this economy of large corporations which manipulate the market, both that of goods and of capital. And such small new businesses as did manage to get born certainly could not possibly grow.

What makes the contrast between the theses of this best-selling book and the reality of the very moment when it appeared particularly significant is, however, that Galbraith in this book was not the innovator and iconoclast and the exploder of the "conventional wisdom" that he had been in his earlier books. The two theses of *The New Industrial State*, however provocatively phrased by Galbraith, were the most conventional and most widely accepted theses regarding American economic structure. They go back indeed to the years before World War I, when John R. Commons, the father of American institutional economics, first propounded them. They underlay, of course, Veblen's work in the years of World War I. They were given full documentation in the classic on American corporate structure, Berle and Means' *The Modern Corporation and Private Property*, which came out in 1932. They were restated in the three books which initiated, one way or another, the tremendous interest in and study of the American business corporation in the last twenty-five years; James Burnham's *The Managerial Revolution* (1941) and my own books, *The Concept of the Corporation* (1946) and *The New Society* (1950). For once, in other words, Galbraith in *The New Industrial State* was the very voice of the "conventional wisdom." But this makes it all the more apparent that something significant must have happened in the very structure of the American economy in these last few years.

Indeed, not even the "diversification merger" is truly compatible with the prevailing and generally accepted doctrine of "managerialism." The doctrine preaches that entrenched management in the large publicly owned company does not need the outside financial market. Large, well-established companies, so said the received wisdom of the last forty years, are capable of financing themselves through "retained earnings." But if this was indeed correct, the "diversification mergers" would not, indeed could not, have happened. The accepted doctrine also preaches that such a company does not have to compete for management. Management can perpetuate itself and can offer competent mediocrities safe careers. Yet in these mergers, one top management voluntarily abdicated— for of course the new, merged company needed only one top management. No top management would commit suicide if immune to stockholder control in the first place, and capable of providing itself with the resources for its own security of tenure. And indeed none has ever done so, under these conditions. It is just that these conditions are not—or are no longer—those of the real world.

Unlike the "defensive" mergers of yesterday, the "diversification mergers" do not strengthen a company in the markets for its products or in manufacturing efficiency. The only explanation why managements in companies that are apparently doing quite well—as in the case of Commercial Credit and Control Data, Montgomery Ward and Container Corporation, Sheraton Hotels, American Radiator and Westinghouse Air Brake—might be willing and often eager to merge, is that they find themselves under pressures they cannot neglect. They are unable to attract resources they must have to survive and which they cannot generate just by being big and established. The "diversification merger," like the "take-over" and the new "growth entrepreneurship," was a seismic disturbance that argues some major structural shift someplace deep below the economy's surface.

The Multinational Company

One more, equally significant, development occurred in economic structure during these last few years—and it too "could not have happened." Fifteen years ago all but a handful of the major American businesses were entirely "American" (or at least "North American," i.e., with a subsidiary in Canada) in their geographic distribution. Today the great majority of major manufacturing companies are "multinational," with 20 percent to 50 percent of their output produced outside the United States. Indeed, as Jean-Jacques Servan-Schreiber pointed out in his book, *The American Challenge* (which followed Galbraith's *The New Industrial State* as the international economics best seller for 1968), the American companies producing in Europe are the world's third largest industrial power, out-produced only by the United States and Russia, and in turn out-producing even Japan and Germany. Nor is "multinationalism" confined to manufacturing companies. Large American banks—the Bank of America, the First National City Bank, and the Chase Manhattan—have today an even larger proportion of their business outside the United States than have most multinational manufacturing companies. Several Stock Exchange houses are also—White Weld, for instance—truly "multinational" and have become leading underwriters in the European capital markets. And then there are the "off shore" investment trusts, American-managed but domiciled outside the country and confined by law to doing business exclusively with non-Americans. One of them, Investors Overseas Service, started only in 1956 by a former social worker from Philadelphia, Bernard Cornfeld, had, by the end of 1969, amassed almost $2½ billion in assets and had become the leading asset-manager in many European and Latin American countries.

This development began in the United States, and for the first few years "multinational" was synonymous with "U.S.-based." Around 1965, however, the move to "multinationalism" became truly "multinational." The fastest growers these last few years have been the Swedes. Today, three out of every ten men working for Swedish-owned manufacturing plants work outside Sweden—a few short years ago, the figure was one out of ten! Then the Japanese, around 1968, began to move. Every issue of the *Oriental Economist*, Japan's counterpart of the *Wall Street Journal*, reports a new manufacturing plant, built by a Japanese company abroad, a new joint-venture with a non-Japanese company to produce abroad, a new Japanese manufacturing subsidiary abroad. The development has been so sweeping that one student, Judd Polk, an economist at the International Chamber of Commerce, argues that we should replace the old theory of international trade, which deals with the "international distribution of the fruits of production," with a new theory of the international allocation of the factors of production. Another observer, Howard Perlmutter of the University of Pennsylvania, predicts that, by 1985 or so, the bulk of the world's supply of manufactured goods will come from three hundred worldwide companies, producing in all the major countries, managed multinationally, and owned by shareholders from all the major countries.

More than half of the production of the U.S.-based multinationals outside the United States has been added in the last five years. Yet five years ago, every economist "knew" that American multinational expansion had been stopped, that indeed the American multinational company was in for a sharp contraction. For in 1965 the United States government banned further investment of United States funds in American multinational businesses abroad, especially in the developed countries (other than Canada and Japan). The ostensible reason was concern for the balance of payments—though a major reason was surely also the desire to placate our European allies, especially de Gaulle, who were complaining loudly that we were buying up too many European economies. The ban has been strictly policed and is faithfully observed. Yet every year since 1965, the multinationals have invested more in Europe. The explanation is simply that America never financed the European acquisitions and new business abroad of the "multinationals"; the Europeans did it all along. They exchanged their holdings in their own national companies, trading in a restricted national market for holdings in a multinational company that was worldwide in scope and management. During these last ten years Europe actually invested quite a bit more—a billion or two— in shares of U.S.-based companies than U.S.-based companies invested in production in Europe (whether through starting a European business or through acquisition of an existing one). The result of this is that Europeans, in the aggregate, now probably own as much of leading American businesses—up to 20 percent in some cases—as American businesses own of major industries in Europe. So far, no one has paid much attention to this. But predictably we will one day soon discover it; and then "foreign domination of American industry" is likely to become as much of a political slogan in this country as "American domination of French (German, British, Italian, Dutch, etc.) industry" has become a political slogan abroad.

The Swedish and Japanese examples are even more amazing. In both countries the government has all along exercised the tightest control over investment abroad. In both countries investment in manufacturing plants abroad was officially banned and currency for it was simply not available. The "multinational-ism" of industry in these two countries is, in other words, also being financed by the "multinational" investor—especially the investor in the countries in which investment is being made—who exchanges his ownership of a local business against a share in the ownership of a multinational one.

But this is as incompatible with the "verities" of international economic theory as the "takeover" wave or the emergence of the new entrepreneurs is incompatible with the received wisdom of the doctrine of "managerialism." It is not only Keynesian theory that assumes the fiscal and financial sovereignty of the national state—all economic theory these last fifty years has done that. But no sooner did the most powerful state, the United States, exercise this sover-eignty, than—totally unplanned—the "Euro-dollar market" sprang up through which Europeans channeled their capital into American-based multinational companies, thus defeating the intentions of both the United States and their own governments as well.

It can be argued that the new mergers, whether "diversification" or "take-overs," are "temporary phenomena," and also that many of these were neither sound nor desirable. It can be argued that the new entrepreneurs were simply the froth on a stock market boom that is now over. It can be argued—as Gen-eral de Gaulle did—that the "multinational" company is an abomination and a flagrant violation of the immutable laws of politics and history. These arguments are not without substance. There is indeed little doubt that a good many of the conglomerates were jerry-built, the result of financial sleight of hand and "asset exploitation" rather than "asset management." A good many of the new busi-nesses, the shares of which were eagerly bought up by "sophisticated investors," were certainly fad and folly, and little else. And one need not be an ultra-nationalist to see some real problems in multinational companies that have revenues larger than the national income of some of the countries they operate in, and who make their decisions in headquarters that are far away from the countries that depend on them and far beyond the reach of these countries' governments.

But that these developments of the last ten years may not be to everybody's liking; that they may not all have been desirable or sound; and that not all their results may be enduring, does not alter two facts. They happened; and they have fundamentally affected economic structure, domestically (in every devel-oped country) and internationally. Whether one likes them or not—and I per-sonally have great reservations—one must ask the question: what explains them? One must assume that such far-reaching changes, which fly in the face of so much we considered "knowledge" in the field, must have their causes in major shifts in the structure of the economy.

And the New Problems

These new markets will predictably generate new problems of public policy. Three in particular are already clearly visible—and for none do we have an an-swer. Indeed, with respect to none have we even tackled our homework.

The first and most *novel* of these problems will be the role and responsibility of the new financial powers, the "fiduciaries" of the financial mass consumer who are the real "owners" of today.

Majority ownership of America's (and Europe's) businesses will increasingly be controlled by people who are neither owners nor managers, but trustees. What should their role be? It can be argued (in fact it has been argued by some of the most thoughtful fund managers) that being trustees they cannot and must not interfere in the management of the companies they invest in. If they do not like a management, they can sell their shares in the company; but they have no authority from anyone to exercise control. But if these institutions do not exercise control, who does—or can? Management either is uncontrolled and uncontrollable, or the policing function falls to the "takeover" entrepreneur. Clearly neither solution is acceptable. Yet no new one is in sight.

But the problem can also no longer be avoided. Indeed it has already been raised—though in the least expected form. "Nader's Raiders"—the young lawyers who work under and with Ralph Nader of automotive-safety fame—raised it when they asked, in the spring of 1970, that foundations, endowments, and other trustees withhold their proxies from General Motors management and vote their shares instead for a series of changes in the company's board, changes in policies and management which "Nader's Raiders" hold to be in the public interest. Almost at the same time, though of course in a totally unrelated development, the Antitrust Division of the Department of Justice filed suit against a very large fiduciary manager, the Continental Illinois Bank in Chicago. What the Antitrust Division charged was that the bank's practice—and every major bank engages in it—of having different officers of the bank sit on the boards of directors of competing companies was in violation of antitrust even though these directors did not represent "ownership" but simply the shares held by the bank in trust for very large numbers of individual beneficiaries. That, in effect, Antitrust attacks as illegal precisely the very exercise of control—and the same interference—the absence of which "Nader's Raiders" castigate, does not affect the importance and seriousness of the issue, nor does the fact that nothing in our economic experience is much help deciding it. But it will have to be tackled—and soon. It will, indeed should, become a major issue of public policy.

Multinational Company vs. National State

The second and most *important* problem—important in terms of its impact—will be that of the multinational business.

Professor Perlmutter's prediction that, in another fifteen or twenty years, the world's manufacturing production will be in the hands of three hundred mammoth multinational companies, while widely quoted, represents an extreme rather than the most probable trend. But it is not rash to predict that, within every developed noncommunist country, a fifth or a quarter of total manufacturing output will be produced by companies that are "multinational" in their operations. Indeed, this is reality rather than forecast in ten of these countries (the

United States, Great Britain, Canada, Germany, Italy, Holland, Belgium, Switzerland, Norway, and Sweden), is fast becoming reality in an eleventh (Japan), and is some distance from accomplished fact in only two (France and Brazil).[1]

This means that in the developed countries a very big part of the economy is subject to decisions made beyond the reach of the national government. But it also means, conversely, that governmental decisions in most developed countries—France and Canada being the only important exceptions—have impact far beyond the country's own borders through the effect they have on the multinationals headquartered in that country. American antitrust regulations, tax laws, and restrictions on trade with Communist powers are held by government authorities to bind the subsidiaries and affiliates of United States-based companies everywhere. No other country is quite so openly nationalistic. But other governments, too—especially those of the big countries such as France, Germany, and Japan—like to look upon "their" multinationals as instruments of their own economic policies in the world, while at the same time bitterly resenting that the subsidiaries of "foreign" multinationals on their soil are, in some measure, beyond their complete control.

This is not a problem of "capitalism." Indeed, the same ambivalence characterizes economic relations within the Soviet bloc. Quite clearly the multinationals which the Russians have been trying to build throughout Eastern Europe are primarily resisted for political reasons. They remove a part of the Polish, Czech, or East German economy from the decision and control of the Polish, Czech, or East German governments. Multinationals, whether "capitalist" or "Communist," put economic rationality ahead of political sovereignty.

De Gaulle's opposition to the "multinationals" was therefore not "anti-American." He also opposed non-American multinational attempts—for example, that of the Italian Fiat company to merge with Citroen, France's ailing automobile manufacturer—as vigorously as he opposed the Americans coming in. He forbade French companies to become multinational themselves and to move beyond France. Indeed, de Gaulle's insistence on the congruence of political and economic sovereignty was completely consistent and was the only rational policy for the problem worked out so far any place by anyone.

It was also a total, resounding failure. A larger part of the advanced sectors of French industry—computers or pharmaceuticals, for instance—is controlled by foreign multinationals than is the case in any of the large developed countries other than Canada. French capital is more lavishly invested in multinationals than the capital of any other of the "majors." *Not* in French-based multinationals making their decisions in Paris—there are none, thanks to de Gaulle—but in the shares of foreign-based, that is, American, Swiss, Dutch, and Swedish multinationals. And at the same time, there is no country where so many of the ablest young executives, researchers, and managers work for foreign-based companies. What defeated de Gaulle, in other words, were the pressures and preferences of the two new mass markets, especially perhaps that of the new "consumers" of the career market, the young, educated knowledge people.

Yet de Gaulle, with his usual clarity, at least saw the problem. The multi-national corporation is by far our most effective economic instrument today, and probably the one organ of economic development that actually develops. It is the one non-nationalist institution in a world shaken by nationalist delirium. It is not a political institution itself and must not be allowed to become one. Yet it puts economic decisions beyond the effective reach of the political process and its decision-makers, the national governments. This may well be exactly what we need to de-fang the nationalist monster. But national governments and their organs, whether legislative or executive, are unlikely to see it this way. And how we accommodate this tension between economic rationality and political sovereignty in the next few years will have a tremendous impact on both the economy and the working of government.

When Concentration Is Competition

The third and most *difficult* problem posed by the emergence of the new markets and the new entrepreneurs is that of concentration and competition. In the other two areas we have to find new answers. In respect to concentration and competition, we have to unlearn old ones. And that is far more difficult, especially as the old ones have been held with almost religious fervor and have almost become sacred chants for large groups of economists, politicians, lawyers, and businessmen.

Two concepts have guided our approaches to the problems of concentration and competition for many years: "concentration of manufacturing assets" and "concentration of market power." The measurements developed for these two aspects of economic concentration are widely accepted as giving us in conjunction both an X-ray photograph of the bony structure of our economy and reliable guides to diagnosis and treatment. But the first measurement is becoming unreliable, while the second one has become misleading.

For a long time "concentration of manufacturing assets" remained fairly constant. But according to the antitrusters, it took a tremendous jump upward in the last twenty years. In 1950, the two hundred largest "manufacturing companies" controlled 40 percent of the country's manufacturing assets. In 1970, the top two hundred control 60 percent—the biggest increase in economic concentration ever recorded in this or any other country.

The odd thing, however, is that this tremendous concentration has not been accompanied by any increase in concentration in economic power in any single market for goods, that is, in any single market in which manufacturing companies operate. In most of these markets, concentration has probably gone *down* during the last twenty years. In market after market, new companies have challenged the big old companies and have taken away from them a piece here or a piece there of their traditional business. This is true whether we speak of book publishing or of pharmaceuticals, of building materials or of retail sales.

"Manufacturing assets" no longer define the concentration in the American producing economy. What is counted in this rubric includes assets shown in the balance sheets of American-domiciled businesses wherever the assets may actually be, whether within or without the United States. In 1950 these assets were almost exclusively within the United States. Today, however, most major American companies are multinational, with at least 20 to 30 percent of their production and assets outside the United States. Therefore, at least one quarter of these 60 percent—that is, 15 percentage points—should be subtracted from the official figure, which would bring the rate of concentration in American manufacturing down to 45 percent.

At the same time, however, what counted as "manufacturing companies" in 1950 were largely companies that were actually manufacturing. To be sure, General Motors even then owned one of the largest finance companies, the General Motors Acceptance Corporation; but its assets were a very small fraction of total GM. Today, as a result of "diversification" and "takeover" mergers, a very substantial number of companies which are still counted as "manufacturing companies," actually have very large assets—in some cases the majority—outside of manufacturing, in service businesses, and above all in finance. And in finance, "assets" are not really assets but are essentially "liabilities," that is, money borrowed to be lent out immediately. During these past twenty years, whenever a manufacturing company merged with a financial company it acquired on its balance sheet financial assets very much larger than its own "manufacturing assets" had been—even though in terms of profitability, let alone of economic power, the manufacturing company may well have been the bigger one. These financial assets are, however, from then on considered "manufacturing assets" in the figures. When Control Data acquired Commercial Credit on December 31, 1967, it had manufacturing assets of $470 million. Commercial Credit had assets of $3 billion—the total of both is, however, now considered "manufacturing assets," since Control Data was legally the acquiring company. If the biggest of all attempted "takeovers" had gone through—that is if Leasco, a computer service company, had succeeded in taking over Chemical Bank–New York Trust Company—Leasco assets of less than $800 million would have been augmented by Chemical Bank assets of $9 billion, with the combined total of almost $10 billion all counted as "manufacturing assets." We have therefore to deflate the official figure for "manufacturing assets" by at least another 10 percentage points to take out assets that should not have been counted as "manufacturing assets" at all. In other words, in terms of true "manufacturing assets" in the country, the two hundred largest companies today almost certainly have a smaller share of manufacturing industry than they had twenty years ago.

This would bring the two sets of figures—manufacturing assets and concentration of market power—back into alignment. Yet, clearly, the conclusion that there has been no "concentration" is not plausible. For while there has been neither greater concentration of American manufacturing assets nor greater market-concentration, the diversification and takeover mergers—and the multinational expansion—*have* clearly produced a considerable concentration in decision-making power. They have led to very large businesses, acting in many areas and countries but nonetheless incorporated in one legal entity and directed by one top management.

The result, however, is often *increased* competition, even in the goods and services economy. And the result is almost always increased competition—indeed deconcentration—in the capital and investment economy and in the work and careers economy.

The Control Data–Commercial Credit merger increased concentration in neither the computer nor the installment-paper market. On the contrary, it made these markets more competitive by strengthening what had been the "underdogs" in both. An even more telling example is the acquisition a few years back of Folger, a rather small regional coffee blender, by Procter & Gamble. This clearly added to Procter & Gamble's bigness. Since P&G is also a leader in processed foods, the new acquisition also added, albeit not greatly, to its market share in the "processed foods" industry and thereby to industrial concentration. But with the resources of Procter & Gamble behind it, Folger could reach out for national distribution in the coffee market. Because the national coffee market had, for years, been dominated by a few brands in a typical "oligopoly" pattern, Folger's acquisition by Procter & Gamble therefore also meant significant *deconcentration* in one important market. What then were the "real" consequences— concentration or deconcentration?

We may well be drifting toward a situation in which leadership and concentration in one market—that of goods, of capital, or careers—is the "countervailing force" for competition and deconcentration in one or both of the other markets. Surely it is not without relevance that the most common criticism of "multinationals," whether the Americans in Europe or the Europeans and Japanese in the United States, has been that their size enables them to indulge in "excessive competition."

The pressures towards this kind of concentration, which is so very different from what the term has implied traditionally, will increase rather than decrease. Technology is pushing in that direction, especially in the materials and chemicals industries. Technology is forcing Du Pont, traditionally primarily a producer of chemicals for the textile industry (e.g., synthetic fibers), to go into pharmaceuticals on the one hand and composite materials including new combination metals on the other. Technology has already forced the two big can companies, twenty years ago producers of a single product, the tin can, to become manufacturers of "packaging" which includes plastics, glass, paper products, and so on. And this, in turn, forced the largest manufacturer of paper-based packaging, Container Corporation of America, as said before, to merge with a retail and mail order chain, Montgomery Ward, to obtain enough financial and management muscle to stand up to the new packaging giants. Another powerful force moving business toward concentration will be concern with the environment. Purity of heart by itself will not clean up the environment, whether we talk of air, water, the open spaces, or the city. It will require massive "systems" effort in every area, that is, companies that can mobilize major technological and economic resources across a wide variety of skills, disciplines, technologies, and markets.

But above all, the pressures of the new mass markets, the mass markets for capital and investment, and for jobs and careers, should push for continuous concentration along the new lines—that is, along the line of diversification in industry and diversification in geography.

We will, therefore, have to think through what kind of "diversification" is desirable, productive, and rational, and what is simply financial manipulation and empire-building. What kind makes the economy more open, more flexible, more competitive, and what kind furthers concentration and monopoly? Which one creates enterprises that are more manageable and perform better, and which one creates managerial monstrosities?

What we should want is reasonably clear. We want diversification rather than diffusion. We want federalism rather than either centralized tyranny or dispersion. We want "asset management" rather than financial manipulation. But into which of these categories a given structure falls is by no means clear. Indeed it is not even clear to the antitrusters, who are sharply split between those who accept and indeed welcome "conglomerates" as leading to increased competition, and those who bitterly oppose them as producing increased concentration. This issue predictably will be one of the main concerns of the next ten years, in the United States as well as abroad. That there is no "right" decision is not so important—there rarely is for problems of this kind. But that the old and accepted concepts and measurements are no longer appropriate is going to make the going rough. And that we will have to learn to "trade off"—that is, to balance concentration in one economic dimension with competition in another—goes against the grain of decision-makers, whether economists or politicians, businessmen or bureaucrats; they all, understandably, resent and resist such complexity.

A New Reality

The economic developments of the last ten years signify more than a change in economic structure. They changed economic reality. This will require new thinking and the sloughing off of a great many traditional concepts, ideas, and policies in respect to "monopoly," "concentration," and "competition," for instance, and in respect to the relationship between the world economy and the nation-state. It will require the development both of new theoretical understanding and new policy concepts. For so far we have no economic theory that embraces or even connects the three dimensions of the economy and thus integrates the new "mass markets" of capital and investment and of careers with the old mass market of goods and services, prices and productivity. The specific developments that characterized the 1960s may well have been temporary phenomena, never to recur. The developments of which they were the first expression and the visible symptom have only begun.

NOTES

1. Of these, incidentally, the United States, Holland, Switzerland, and Sweden are "headquarters countries." In Germany, ownership of industry by companies based abroad—mainly United States, Dutch, and Swiss—and ownership of businesses abroad by German companies roughly balance. In Japan, where the "joint-venture" predominated—i.e., a partly foreign-owned company doing business in Japan in partnership with a Japanese company—ownership or co-ownership of businesses abroad by Japanese companies is growing so fast that Japan may soon also be in "ownership balance." Great Britain, Canada, Italy, Belgium, France, and Brazil are far more "owned" than "owning."

RACIAL PRACTICES IN ECONOMIC LIFE

Louis L. Knowles and Kenneth Prewitt

The United States has built the strongest, most productive economy known to man. The abundance is spread among not only the entrepreneurial class but also the laborers. It is safe to say that no people has ever enjoyed a standard of living as high as that found in white America. Yet black America remains bound in a poverty resembling that found in underdeveloped nations. The discrepancy between unprecedented white affluence and black poverty is the result of the almost total exclusion of black Americans from entrepreneurial activity and the market. The vast majority of blacks have functioned only as menial workers and exploited consumers. The present division of the economy along racial lines is the result of both intentional and unintentional institutional racism.

The Exclusion of Black People From Free Enterprise

Ownership of capital and the right to invest it in profit-making enterprises has always been associated with the American concept of freedom. Yet the white business world has consistently denied to black people the opportunity to control substantial financial resources. The total number of black-owned businesses in the United States is estimated at no more than 50,000. If black people owned businesses in proportion to their representation in the population, there would be ten times as many black businesses, or 500,000.[1] The discrepancy is actually greater than these figures indicate; many of the 50,000 enterprises listed as black-owned are proprietorships which can best be described as marginal in nature.

At the end of 1963, blacks owned or controlled only thirteen banks, fifty life insurance companies, and thirty-four federally insured savings and loan associations, with combined assets totaling $764 million or only 0.12 percent of the total assets of financial institutions in the country.[2]

The National Association of Market Development, an association of businesses which serve predominantly black communities, has only 131 black-owned firms

Louis L. Knowles and Kenneth Prewitt, Eds., *Institutional Racism in America,* ©1969. Reprinted by permission of Prentice-Hall, Inc., Englewood Cliffs, New Jersey.

out of a total of 407 members.[3] The most startling fact of all is that the situation is deteriorating rather than improving. Between 1950 and 1960, the number of black businesses decreased by more than one-fifth of its original total.[4]

There are many problems within the ghetto itself which limit the development of black enterprise. The educational background of most black people effectively cripples them for highly skilled positions. Years of experiencing white prejudice and personal failure have created a chasm of despair in the ghetto, which works against ambition and participation in business ventures. But major responsibility for the *de facto* racist situation continues to rest with the white business world.

The greatest difficulty the black would-be businessman faces is the lack of available credit. Aside from overt discrimination among financiers, the black entrepreneur is at a sharp disadvantage in the face of credit standards designed to measure the reliability of white applicants. A financial institution considering a loan application examines the credit history of the applicant, the collateral to be held against the loan, the prospects for business success, and other related criteria. The black man is more likely than the white man to have a poor credit record due to the loan sharks and exploitative merchants that feed off ghetto residents. Black people usually have no property or investments that could be used as collateral. And finally, the black businessman who wishes to locate in his own community, where the income level is at or near the poverty line, will have poorer prospects for success than the white merchant in the white middle-class community. *The present standards, when applied without regard to race, will lead to more white ownership of enterprises and less black participation in the economy.*

There are strong indications that the standards for assessing credit risk are not good measures of a black man's reliability. During the years 1954–1963, the Federal Small Business Administration made a total of 432 loans. Of this number only seven loans went to black businesses despite the fact that the organization was ostensibly following nondiscriminatory policies.[5] Then, in 1964, the Small Business Administration launched its 6 X 6 plan: $6,000 for six years. The SBA evaluated applicants for this program on criteria other than credit history or collateral. Of 219 loans made, 98 went to black people. Only eight of the 219 were delinquent and none were liquidated. These statistics cast doubt on the idea that black businesses are a high credit risk.

The black businessman is also plagued by insurance costs which are as much as three times higher than those that most whites pay. Insurance companies are hesitant to cover ghetto property due to the danger of possible damage in civil disturbances; only very high premiums will draw them back into the black community.

Black entrepreneurs, along with other small businessmen in the nation, face growing pressure from the large corporations that increasingly dominate the economy. The trend is symbolized by the disappearance of the corner grocery store and the proliferation of chain supermarkets. The "little man" will eventually disappear from the American business scene if conditions do not change in some unforeseen way. The efficient corporate giants already control major segments of both the retail and industrial sectors of the economy. This development can only mean less black participation in business since there is virtually no black representation at the level of national corporation management.

The fact is that the lack of black-owned businesses reinforces the dependency of black people upon the economic interests of the white economic community. White businesses share in the responsibility to dissolve this relationship of economic dependency. Although small in magnitude, the SBA's 6 X 6 plan, mentioned above, is a step in this direction. Such programs represent a significant start in that they lay the groundwork for bigger, more inclusive programs. After the recent rebellions, New York began the nation's first mandatory high-risk pool to provide insurance for businessmen in the ghetto. The bill provides for a joint underwriting fund to share losses among the leading insurance companies. Programs like this will hopefully make insurance for black economic ventures cheaper and easier to obtain. Philadelphia's First Banking and Trust Company agreed in September of 1966 to funnel loans into the ghetto through an all-black organization. Steps are being taken, but they are not coordinated, planned, or really encouraged.

Of primary importance is the supplying of financial resources to the black community. The SBA has shown that loans to blacks can be safe and profitable. The organization of new black banks would be instrumental in persuading other financial organizations to invest in the ghetto. The competition from the black-owned banks would make the other institutions more sensitive to the needs of black customers. There is evidence for this, especially in Atlanta, Georgia, and Durham, North Carolina.

There are other steps that private enterprise and the government could take. Chain stores or industries could franchise black-owned and operated units within the ghettos. This type of endeavor speaks directly to the deprivation of the ghetto, which is lack of capital power. Such a project was developed in south-central Los Angeles by Aerojet General, a West Coast subsidiary of General Tire and Rubber Company. Aerojet General has invested $1,333,000 to set up an independent, black-run plant. Also, there are other construction programs which could be offered to black contractors: FHA's 3 percent insured loans for low-income housing developments, the new two-thirds grant program for small public facilities, and public housing units.

It should be kept in mind that economic assistance of any form should not be imposed on the black community without its consent, nor should whites follow any preference for one economic form over another in giving financial aid to the ghettos. Much of the above discussion could be misconstrued as a defense of "black capitalism." It is probable that many black communities across the nation will decide to use the model of private entrepreneurial activity as a means to the end of economic security. But it is also quite possible that groups of black people will lead the way in the development of new cooperative and community-owned forms of production and marketing. Financial resources should be made available for these experiments, and not just to "safe" black businessmen who have adopted all the mores and values of the dominant white economic system.

The Black Worker

The black population of the United States has not only been excluded from the business world, but it has also been relegated to the lowest level of the laboring class. Although token efforts have been made to hire and promote blacks to a greater extent during the last decade, there has been no measurable improvement in the status of the black worker relative to the general population.

The lack of high-income, skilled jobs among black workers largely accounts for the fact that black median family income was only 58 percent of white median income in 1966.[6] It is even more discouraging to note that the purchasing power of the black family relative to the white family has declined over the past twenty years. In constant 1965 dollars, median nonwhite family income in 1947 was $2,174 lower than median white income. By 1966, the gap has grown to $3,036.[7]

The subordinate economic status of black workers can be traced to unemployment and underemployment. Black unemployment has remained throughout the postwar period at a rate double that for whites. Since 1954, despite the unprecedented period of sustained economic growth, the black unemployment rate has been continuously above the 6 percent "recession" level which is used as a signal of serious economic difficulties when it is prevalent for the entire work force.[8]

More serious than unemployment is the vast amount of *underemployment.* The Riot Commission reports (using 1966 data) that if nonwhite employment were upgraded proportionately to the level of white employment, about $4.8 billion in additional income would be produced. This is significantly greater than the $1.5 billion in additional income that would be gained if nonwhite unemployment were to be reduced to the level of white unemployment.[9]

Behind these figures lies a record of overt racial discrimination in hiring and promotions that persists into the present. Firms have refused to hire black people or they have assigned black workers to menial positions below their capabilities. Discriminatory practices have persisted through the civil rights era despite government actions and the proclamations of concern by business leaders. Commenting about the disparity in wage levels, the Kerner Commission states, "However, the differentials are so large and so universal at all educational levels that they clearly reflect the patterns of discrimination which characterize hiring and promotion practices in many segments of the economy."[10]

Beyond blatant racism, there are a variety of structural factors that are working against black workers who already occupy the bottom of the economic ladder. In the past the American economy successfully absorbed huge masses of unskilled laborers. But the postwar urban scene into which black people have moved is very different from nineteenth-century America, which found room for the European immigrant groups. The demand for unskilled labor was much greater in the last century and the early part of the twentieth than it is now. The steady advance of automation has raised the skill-level required to obtain steady employment. Furthermore, no American institution has taken sufficient steps to insure that black people gain the skills necessary for entry into the modern job market.

Industry once flourished in the central cities, but much of it in recent decades has followed the pattern of white emigration to the suburbs. The "white flight" to the suburbs is itself motivated by prejudice and myths about falling property values. That business and industry would follow the "money, management, and workers" out of the city is not surprising. But the ghetto resident is left without the means to reach most jobs. Many metropolitan centers are woefully deficient in providing low-cost public transportation between outlying industries and the inner city.

The soaring technological economy and the job opportunities for blacks are drawing farther apart rather than closer. To stem this growing gap, businessmen of a liberal cast talk now of the business world taking a backward step in an effort to draw the black community along. But this plan asks business to behave in an unbusinesslike way, something it has rarely been known to do. The fundamental rule by which all American enterprises live is to make a profit. A business that does not earn a profit is not a business very long. Managers seek the lowest possible production costs and maximum efficiency. Therefore, personnel are hired according to their productivity and efficiency. The average white man will be much more likely to have the training, references, and cultural background needed to convince an employer that he will contribute to the productivity and efficiency of the business. Often a firm will use a written test to assist in rating applicants. These tests are almost always designed to test ability in the context of white society, and therefore they discriminate against black people, as do IQ and aptitude tests in public schools.

Interviews are used by employers to gauge the personality of a prospective worker. Especially in white-collar positions, the ability of an individual to fit into the operation without causing psychological disruption among the other workers is a crucial factor in the evaluation. The applicant should conform to accepted standards of dress, speech, and manners. The employer evaluates the job-seeker from the ghetto by means of a code of appearance and behavior that is very different from that which is considered acceptable in the black community. Too often a black person must act "white" in order to obtain a job, although his ability to conform to white culture may have little to do with whether he can perform the task for which he is hired. The black worker faces the same battery of problems with respect to promotion that he did when he originally sought employment. In addition, in many cases the worker will lose all seniority if he accepts a promotion. One study indicates that black workers more often than whites will choose to retain their seniority rather than accept promotion.[11]

This behavior reflects the understanding of the black worker that if he should lose his job it is much more difficult for him to find new employment than for a white man to relocate.

The attitudes and policies of management are not the only source of racial discrimination in the job market. Labor unions have closed themselves tightly in the face of the black request for more and better jobs. The black people arrived on the urban scene after the unions had solidified into strong power groups. Consequently they were not able to join hands with other segments of the labor force as the great waves of European immigrants had done in previous decades. Now the labor unions are agencies that protect their mostly white membership from potential workers, many of whom are black. Unions are an obstacle for black people rather than an institutional channel by which they can gain access to American affluence.

The AFL-CIO and other national labor organizations have stated their opposition to racial discrimination over and over again during the past two decades, yet the good intentions have not penetrated to the level of the union locals. A. Philip Randolph, president of the Brotherhood of Sleeping Car Porters, stated in 1962 that black workers are discriminated against "in apprenticeship training, hiring policies, seniority lists, pay scales, and job assignments in many locals, especially the building trades."[12] The statistics show that Randolph was correct. In 1962, out of a labor force of 10.5 million black workers, only 1.5 million were members of trade unions.[13] The refusal to admit black men to union apprenticeship programs has done much to create this inequity. Both the NAACP and the U.S. Civil Rights Commission in the early 1960s attacked the problem of discrimination in apprenticeships. The commission investigation produced some detailed examples within trade unions:

a. In St. Louis, out of 1,667 apprentices in craft programs in the building, metals, and printing trades, only seven were black.
b. In Atlanta, the construction industry had twenty black apprentices out of a total of 700 positions. All of the blacks were in the dirtier trowel trades— bricklaying, plastering, lathing, and cement finishing.
c. In Baltimore, out of 750 building trade apprentices, only twenty were black.
d. In both Atlanta and Baltimore, there were no black apprentices in the Iron Workers, the Plumbers, the Brotherhood of Electrical Workers, the Sheet and Metal Workers, and the Painters Union.
e. In Detroit less than 2 percent of all craft union apprentices were black.[14]

The situation within the giant industrial unions such as the UAW is slightly different. General union membership is easy to obtain for those black people in unskilled assembly-line positions. However, the apprenticeships that could lead to higher paying, skilled positions are for the most part reserved for whites. For example, one Detroit manufacturing company had a labor force that was 23 per-

cent black; but out of 289 apprenticeships, only one was held by a black man.
In a joint apprenticeship program of the UAW and the Automotive Tool and Die
Makers Association in Detroit, one out of 370 positions was occupied by a black
man.[15]

Labor organizations responded to the charges of the NAACP and Civil Rights
Commission by pointing to the removal of discriminatory clauses from their con-
stitutions, but racist policies remain unmitigated at the local level. There have
also been a few attempts to integrate the union hierarchy, but these have amounted to little more than token efforts. For example, that George M. Harrison, president of the Brotherhood of Railway and Steamship Clerks, is a member of the
Civil Rights Committee of the AFL–CIO while his own union has discriminated
against blacks indicates the type of effort being taken by labor unions to offer
equal opportunity to blacks.[16] This form of noncompliance with directives from
the central office of the AFL–CIO is rampant, and it is a clear indication that the
labor movement is in a poor position to uphold and respect its own policies.

No effective pressure to change discriminatory practices has been brought to
bear on the unions from outside. Labor leaders voice the rhetoric of integration,
but they have not found an effective way of changing grass-roots attitudes. The
federal government has barely begun to grapple with the problem. The National
Labor Relations Board, which is constituted totally of white men, has been ineffective. The Department of Labor has been unable to enforce Sec. 703(d) of
the 1964 Civil Rights Act, which forbids discrimination in apprenticeship programs. In Philadelphia, for example, not one of the four important craft unions
in the building trades has a program that meets the legal regulations of the Bureau
of Apprenticeship and Training.

It will be surprising if government agencies seriously attack union racism, for
the labor force constitutes a powerful portion of the electorate, which can destroy an administration that does not meet the favor of the workers. A campaign
to eradicate grass-roots union racism, if it had any substance at all, would probably signal the end of many political careers. It is interesting to note that although the President's Commission on Civil Disorders contains a relatively thor-
ough discussion of racist business practices, it includes only one sentence refer-
ring to union discrimination.

The Exploited Black Consumer

The black person who is fortunate enough to be employed has not yet
achieved the financial security of the white wage earner. The black urban communities are filled with stores and businesses that are geared to extract the maximum profit from a clientele that is trapped in the ghetto by prejudice and poor
public transportation. Most of these stores are owned by white merchants, so
the proceeds return to the white community rather than staying in the ghetto
where they are needed.

Ghetto residents pay more for all kinds of goods and services than do people
living in white neighborhoods. According to testimony by Paul Rand Dixon,

chairman of the FTC, an item selling wholesale at $100 would retail on the average for $165 in a general merchandise store and for $250 in a low-income specialty store.[17] Thus the customers of these outlets are paying a premium of about 52 percent.

Television, radio, billboards and other advertising media constantly encourage black Americans to acquire the symbols of the affluent society. Since good housing is difficult for black people to find or to finance, they invest in less expensive durable goods such as cars, stereo sets, televisions, and clothing. These items would be beyond the reach of most black wage earners if it were not for the ghetto merchants who conveniently extend credit to anyone, at exorbitant rates.

All the states require by law that installment contracts state specifically how much the buyer is paying for credit. But a study made by David Caplovitz in New York demonstrated that many merchants in low-income areas ignore installment contracts altogether, or if they do use them, the merchants intentionally do not differentiate between the cost of credit and the cost of the product. Merchants often emphasize the small down payment and the low monthly installments without informing the buyer about the length of the contract. The ghetto businessman compensates for extending credit to high-risk buyers by selling inferior merchandise whose price has been marked up 200 to 300 percent.[18]

The local merchants are not the only parties guilty of consumer exploitation. Many of the unscrupulous practices could not exist were it not for the finance companies and banks that buy up unpaid installment contracts from merchants. These institutions know by the very terms and form of the contract that they are purchasing dishonest and exploitative contracts, yet they continue to do so.

Frequently merchants will not place price tags on items in ghetto stores. This practice allows the salesman to guage the naiveté of the customer and consequently how much he can charge without causing suspicion.[19]

Perhaps the most serious form of consumer exploitation directed at black people is found in the housing market. Realtors, government housing agencies, and financial institutions have together managed to create almost total residential separation of the races. The black family that has accumulated sufficient resources has great difficulty purchasing or renting a house in a white community. Available housing in the ghetto tends to be overpriced and suffering from inadequate maintenance. The Kerner Commission reported that, based on a study of Newark, New Jersey, "nonwhites were paying a definite 'color tax' of apparently well over 10 percent on housing. *This condition prevails in most racial ghettos.*"[20]

Real estate agencies play the largest role in maintaining segregated communities. The Washington lobby of the National Association of Real Estate Boards testified against the acceptance of the fair housing provision of the 1966 civil rights bill. The association represents 83,000 realtors in every state of the Union. If the national organization is so blatant in its opposition to fair housing, it can be imagined how local agencies operate.[21]

A common realty practice is known as "blockbusting." In this operation, the realtor persuades a black family to move into an all-white neighborhood. The realtor then does everything in his power to foster anxiety over falling property prices among the white homeowners. The agent then capitalizes on the psychological insecurity of the whites by buying their homes at prices below market value and then reselling the property at a handsome profit to minority families. A Philadelphia study by two real estate economists, Chester Rapkin and William G. Gimby, revealed the profitability of such speculative activities. On the average, blockbusters double their investment in less than two years.[22]

The blockbusting racket is based on a myth, according to an urban sociologist, Sherwood Ross, and economist Luigi Laurenti. A study of over 1.3 million homes in forty-seven major cities led to the conclusion that property values do not decline when black families move into a neighborhood. The authors state: "White homeowners talked into selling short by crooked real estate swindlers and panic-peddlers would find their homes rising steadily in value if they would only hold on to them."[23] Laurenti, who studied one thousand integrated neighborhoods, found that prices rose in 44 percent of the cases when blacks entered, remained stable in 41 percent, and declined in only 15 percent relative to closely matched white neighborhoods.[24]

Federal housing programs have also contributed to racial separation and inadequate housing for black people. The Federal Housing Administration from its inception in 1934 has favored racially homogeneous neighborhoods. The FHA manual stated: "If a neighborhood is to retain stability, it is necessary that properties shall continue to be occupied by the same society and race group." The FHA sometimes refused altogether to provide mortgage insurance for integrated housing. More often, it employed delaying tactics which effectively stalled such projects until they failed financially or accepted segregation. After the Supreme Court in 1948 ruled against racially restrictive covenants in housing codes, the FHA dropped the discriminatory phrases in its charter but continued to insure mortgages with restrictive covenants.

Not only has the FHA historically supported segregation as financially sound policy, but it has established credit requirements for housing loans that discriminate against the black populace. FHA requires a minimum present income, good prospects for future income, and evidence of faithful repayment of past obligations. It has been shown earlier that black people are systematically excluded by criteria of this nature due to their position at the bottom of the economy. The result has been that although the FHA loan program has become the backbone of white suburban housing, it has not appreciably changed the housing situation for black people.

The massive urban renewal programs of recent years were designed to eliminate much slum housing and thereby beautify the core section of the major cities. But most slums have been replaced with public facilities and high-income housing. The black people that are evicted by the bulldozers cannot return to live in the area, but must seek out other areas of low-rent housing. Urban renewal may beautify the cities, but it *adds* to the housing problems of minority citizens.

In addition to real estate interests and federal housing programs, the credit institutions of the country share the responsibility for segregated housing. Banks, savings and loan associations, and insurance companies finance 70 percent of all mortgages. They invest where they believe the risk is least and the property is most marketable. Investment directors continue to regard areas that are becoming integrated as poor risks despite studies which indicate that prices remain stable or rise in most integrated communities. Moreover, investors continue to display a racial bias that regards black people even with the proper credentials as poorer credit risks than whites.

The difficulty of obtaining loans from established firms means that many black people are forced to deal with independent speculators. This type of arrangement usually entails interest rates of 19 percent or more, and families can be dispossessed after five days for failure to make a payment (by comparison, the FHA interest rate is between 5 and 7 percent).

In recent years a number of laws have been passed at the federal level that are aimed at stopping racial discrimination in housing. A Supreme Court decision of 1968 extends the concept of open housing to all forms of residence including single family dwellings. But laws can do very little to correct an injustice that is rooted deeply in the nation's economic pattern. Open housing laws, despite their intent, are limited in beneficial impact since they must be superimposed on a housing market and housing programs which are racist in their structure. Given the present structure and method of federal intervention in the area of housing, even complete nondiscrimination in regard to federal benefits would not greatly affect the continuing expansion of segregated patterns of residence. Residential segregation is a fact in this country. It will persist until there is massive action for its curtailment. Financial institutions must be willing to extend credit to many more minority applicants. If necessary, the federal government can insure their loans. The conservative life insurance industry has committed itself to a profitable investment of $1 billion of its $17 billion in the ghettos. This is a step in the right direction. The Rent Supplement Act, which provides federal rent subsidies to low-income families, is also a step. But each of these programs just cures the symptoms; they do not reach the disease. To solve the housing problem, a stop must be put to all economic forces which perpetuate residential segregation. Realtors must be forced to change their ways. Mortgages must be made easier to get. But, above all, jobs and black credit institutions must be made accessible to the un- and under-employed in the ghetto so that the normal avenues of institutional financing are open to them.

Ending the exploitative system of black economic dependence will be a task of overwhelming magnitude. There is no single answer to the three-fold oppression described in this section. Even a massive job program only touches at a single issue of secondary importance; if all black unemployment were wiped out, the problems of underemployment, lack of black capital, and consumer exploitation would persist.

Many of the issues cannot be touched by legislation. Laws cannot change credit criteria in a way that will allow large amounts of capital to flow into black hands nor can legal action force unions to admit black laborers. Progress will be made only as the black community organizes to exert pressure on white structures and as white people become aware that major sacrifices must be made at all levels. To right the wrongs of the past will be a long and costly process involving profound changes in the definition of self-interest for the American economy.

The critical issue is control. Reforms in the areas of employment, union practices, consumer exploitation and ownership, and so forth promote effective change only insofar as they enable black people to move toward control of substantial economic resources. Only then will it be possible for blacks to end their dependency on white America and to develop economic institutions to meet their needs.

NOTES

1. "The Ordeal of the Black Businessman," *Newsweek,* March 4, 1968, p. 72.
2. Andrew Brimmer, "The Negro in the National Economy," in *The American Negro Reference Book,* ed. John P. David (Englewood Cliffs, N.J.: Prentice-Hall, Inc., 1966), p. 297.
3. Ibid., pp. 290–91.
4. Ibid., p. 295.
5. Eugene Foley, "The Negro Businessman: In Search of a Tradition," in *The Negro American,* ed. T. Parsons and K. B. Clark (Boston: Beacon Press, 1966), p. 575.
6. *Report of the National Advisory Commission on Civil Disorders* (New York: Bantam Books, 1968), p. 251.
7. Ibid., p. 251.
8. Ibid., p. 253.
9. Ibid., p. 255.
10. Ibid., p. 256.
11. James R. Wetzel and Susan Holland, "Poverty Areas of Our Major Cities," *Monthly Labor Review,* 89, October 1966, 1105–1110.
12. Labor Research Association, *Labor Fact Book* (New York: International Publishers, 1963), p. 83.
13. Ibid.
14. Arthur Roos and Herbert Hill, *Employment, Race and Poverty* (New York: Harcourt, Brace & World, Inc., 1967), p. 409.
15. Ibid., p. 410.
16. *Labor Fact Book,* p. 83.
17. *Advisory Commission on Civil Disorders,* p. 276.
18. David Caplovitz, *The Poor Pay More* (New York: The Free Press of Glencoe, 1967), Chaps. 2 and 6.
19. Ibid., p. 17.
20. *Advisory Commission on Civil Disorders,* p. 252. (Italics added.)

21. Hearings Before Subcommittee No. 5 of the Committee on the Judiciary, House of Representatives, 89th Congress, Second Session, "Statement of Alan L. Emlen, Chairman, Realtor's Washington Committee, National Association of Real Estate Boards," pp. 1585–1603.
22. George Grier, *Equality and Beyond* (Chicago: Quadrangle Books, 1966), p. 35.
23. Hearings Before Subcommittee No. 5 of the Committee on the Judiciary, House of Representatives, 89th Congress, Second Session, Statement by Attorney General Katzenbach, Exhibit No. 6, pp. 1228–1230, No. 6, pp. 1219–1224.
24. Grier, p. 34.

ADVANCED CAPITALISM AND THE WELFARE STATE

Claus Offe

The concept of the "welfare state" is perhaps vague enough to allow everyone his own definition of it, but all—conservatives, liberals, and socialists alike—seem to agree that Western capitalism has already moved into this orbit. The poor and the unemployed may see the welfare state as promising security or even affluence. The professional administrator, however, usually conceives of it as a safety valve for potential social problems or as an efficient instrument to control economic and social problems which regularly erupt in capitalist society.[1] By this time even the taxpaying man on the street has accepted most features of the welfare state as at least necessary evils.[2] I should like to offer some observations on what I consider to be the logic of development towards the welfare state.

During a recent extended stay in the United States, I was amazed at the unusual mutuality of admiration between America and Western European countries. Europeans in general are led to believe that the States are far ahead of us in almost every area of life—scientific and technological achievement, affluence and economic success, and political freedom. Of course, some of our conditioning is simply the residue of the post-fascist period of "reeducation," but it is still very prevalent. Books such as J. J. Servan-Schreiber's *The American Challenge* are successful because they capitalize on this belief. Therefore, when a European visitor to the United States encounters dozens of articles, books, and statements which glorify the achievements of West European welfare states like England, Holland, West Germany, and the Scandinavian countries, he is justifiably surprised. Even American academic experts in social policy studies seem to assume that their country is quite backward compared to certain Western European countries. Robert Heilbroner indicated this in a recent *Transaction* article.[3] If Europeans and Americans share anything at all, it is a profound feeling of their own relative failure and great admiration for what is going on across the Atlantic.

The historical genesis and contemporary quality of these apparent differences

This chapter is a revised version of a lecture given at the New School for Social Research in 1971. Reprinted from *Politics and Society*, Summer, 1972, pp. 479–488. ©by Geron-X, Inc. Used by permission.

provide hundreds of researchers and commentators with material for endless speculation. Will the differences dissolve, maintain themselves, deepen, and so forth? Heilbroner focuses on the "differences in basic institutions, attitudes, or responses that we call 'national character.' "[4] Rather than join the discussion of what the national differences are on both sides of the Atlantic, I prefer to describe the similarities of both systems and indicate how these systems are simply different manifestations of the same institutional structure—i.e., the economic, social, and political mechanism of advanced capitalism. My approach, then, begins with *unifying factors* and *similarities* rather than *differences* and *comparative* performance. Such an approach might be frustrating to those who would hope for more mutual imitation of each other's achievements—more features of the European welfare state in the United States and more advanced technologies and management techniques in Europe—but I can see few advantages to the traditional approach.

There are, to be sure, *quantitative* national differences worth mentioning. In the field of social security, for example, and other current transfer payments, the United States ranks behind France, West Germany, Austria, Italy, Belgium, Canada, the Netherlands, and the United Kingdom; only Portugal performs worse than the United States. Although this data comes from the late fifties, recent statistics indicate that "social welfare" has not been significantly improved since the Eisenhower years.[5] Similar comparisons could be made with regard to health, life expectancy, infant mortality, urban unrest, poverty, and a number of other indicators.

However, I find this preoccupation with quantitative comparisons and ranking scales somewhat misleading. Of course, it is true that the proportion of people who starve or suffer from other unmet needs can vary considerably. But two essential details are overlooked by this kind of statistical ranking: (1) the fact that such cases actually do occur in the wealthiest countries of the world, which, incidentally, have explicitly and without exception committed themselves to the *political* goal of universal welfare; and (2) the fact that *all* advanced capitalist societies with their own structural mechanisms *create* endemic systemic problems and large-scale unmet needs, regardless of their extent. The common denominator of the most advanced and of the most backward welfare state is the coexistence of poverty and affluence, or in more precise terms, the coexistence of the logic of industrial production for profit and the logic of human need. This contradiction, which is a basic characteristic of every capitalist society, has in no way been resolved by the arrival of the welfare state. The contradiction has been simply tempered or modified in a few aspects. The welfare state in no way represents a *structural change* of capitalistic society. It does not direct itself primarily toward those classes and groups which are the most obvious *victims* of the capitalist process of industrialization; nor does it care for *old societal needs.* Instead, the welfare state tries to compensate for *new problems* which are the by-products of industrial growth in a private economy. Finally, its development has followed few of the ideological dogmas of the various political parties of capitalist societies. I should like to discuss briefly each of these negative characteristics of the welfare state.

1. *The welfare state bears no resemblance to what Marxist theorists would call a revolutionary process, that is, basic structural change.* What appears in the welfare state are new elements *within* advanced capitalist societies, but no basic change of these societies. That is, the welfare state has not changed political and economic power relationships. It has not changed the private mode of production for profit into public work directed to the solution of human need. It is even a moot question whether or not the welfare state was in any way responsible for recent general incomes improvement, relatively undramatic in any case. The English economist Meade has suggested that the welfare state cannot redistribute income to a very great extent because of the constraints built into the economic system. He concluded that only extremely progressive taxation in the welfare state could lead to a more equal distribution of income, but such taxation would "be bound to affect adversely incentives to work, save, innovate and take risks."[6] It is not likely that the powers that be in any capitalist society, welfare or not, would desire either this form of taxation or its consequences.

Although there is some evidence which indicates that countries with strong Social Democratic or Labor parties adopt welfare state measures more quickly and easily than countries with Conservatives in power, this has nothing to do with structural change. The proposal in the 1972 American federal budget that roughly 55 out of 229 billion dollars be spent for welfare and social policy purposes should not be interpreted as a shift to the Far Left. It should be pointed out that it was Bismarck who introduced the first general social insurance scheme in Germany—in order to buy off some of the nineteenth-century revolutionary Social Democrats.

2. *Although the term "welfare" connotes a paternalistic solicitude by the state in behalf of the lower classes, corporate business enterprises derive far greater proportionate benefits.* Even a superficial glance at direct and indirect state subsidies reveals that defense and space industries, corporate agribusiness, the industrial users of government-guaranteed foreign loans, and publicly financed research and development capture the lion's share of state "welfare." Weidenbaum shows the emergence of a new semipublic sector of the economy, which almost exclusively depends on the state for its survival but which at the same time operates according to the principles of profitability.[7]

It is clear, then that the definitions of the welfare state given in most social science textbooks are weighted toward a proportionately small number of "welfare" recipients: e.g., "government-protected minimum standards of income, nutrition, health, housing, and education for every citizen, assured to him as a political right, not as charity."[8] They rarely mention government-protected minimum floors of defense research and development expenditures, or the maximum ceilings of taxation or pollution control regulation—all of which aid business enterprises and corporate executives to save costs or gain profits far beyond what anyone would consider mere charity.

The writers who apply the "Who benefits?" criterion often arrive at the conclusion that the welfare state is more accurately defined as "capitalism for the poor and socialism for the rich." Regardless of who benefits most from the welfare state, it should be understood that the welfare state in a capitalist society is by no means restricted to a defined area of problems or a narrow range of "welfare" problems. Rather than "creeping socialism," it is the most generous underwriter of large business enterprises in capitalism's short but glorious history.

3. *The welfare state cannot deal with primary human needs directly; it can only attempt to compensate for the new problems which are created in the wake of industrial growth.* Examples of this phenomenon abound. For instance, in the area of housing, when it became strategically important for corporate capitalism to take over the inner city for managerial headquarters, banking, and communication centers, the balance of urban life was disturbed, and it was necessary for the state to assume the "welfare" function of new public housing for those who were displaced from the inner city. Rapid capitalist development necessitated large-scale internal migration and immigration from foreign countries in a short period of time, multiplying the social problems of the city and once again causing the state to care for the problems which capitalism created.

Another consequence of industrial growth and subsequent urban development was disappearance of the three-generation family. Mobile isolated units are more functional in a capitalist economy, thus the ascendancy of the nuclear family and the destruction of the social framework of intrafamilial "social security." A whole new range of welfare problems—from social security and aging to health and education—sprang into being. The state had to assume the burden of these new "welfare" problems.

Of course, industrial growth presupposes hazards and risks—not only the greater possibility of accidents at work or on the highways and a steadily high rate of unemployment, but also the hundreds of diseases and health or ecological problems tied in with industrial work and urban life. Public and private insurance of all kinds attempted to compensate for the chaotic living conditions in the city, which at best became an unhealthy but necessary gamble.

Finally, changing industrial technology demanded new kinds of skills and training—that is to say, more public expenditure for education. And when more industries became automated, educational requirements became stricter, education took on the additional task of occupying the time of large numbers of youth who would otherwise be unemployed. Since adolescents could no longer be counted on to help support their families, more welfare funds were needed for their mothers and fathers.

All of this means that the long and complicated process of capitalist industrial growth destroyed or altered the fabric of *every* social institution, not just the work-related ones. In other words, the services of the welfare state are not major social accomplishments, as some commentators would have it, but, rather, are meager compensations for the price of industrial development. In this perspective, most of the measures commonly associated with the welfare state fail to live up to their expectations as generous improvements of the quality of human life. They appear to be designed as stopgap mechanisms to offset the process of rapid and often permanent deterioration of social life caused by the capitalist pattern of industrialization. If the welfare state in its historical development has been following the path of "compensation" and "offset" rather than the path of improvement and the widening of life chances, there is a further aspect of its logic of development which I should like to touch on briefly.

4. *The development of the welfare state took place in relative independence from political controversy and ideological debate.* In order to support this point, one could quote from both the "End of ideology" and the "Does politics make a difference?" literature. There is considerable evidence that, as far as government and corporate interests are concerned, the ideological level of "welfare state" discussion lags behind actual changes rather than providing normative guidelines for their implementation: "While the argument about the welfare state has long since been resolved at the operational level . . . , it most definitely *has not* been resolved at the ideological level."[9] The lip service that is being paid to old liberal stereotypes and myths has little influence on the actual operation of governments. The lack of choices made on principle is also acknowledged by authors who place "top priority" on "renovating out ideology."[10]

On the other hand, some authors have recently raised the question of whether politics is relevant at all: Is it the conscious will of voters and legislators, or is it the complete interrelationship of social and economic conditions which determines policy outcomes?[11] The latter would mean that ideological standards are not only absent, but would be inapplicable even if they existed, because the margin of "feasible" policy alternatives is too small to allow for principled choice. It is exactly this situation that best describes the development of the welfare state. Party platforms and election results seem to have no influence on the percentage of the state budget that is spent for welfare purposes or the new welfare programs that are inaugurated. Far more important policy determinants are economic and social variables such as the growth of productivity, the extent of social mobility, the technological level of basic industries, the size and composition of the work force, the age structure of the population, and other macroeconomic and macrosociological indicators.

This is as true in Great Britain and West Germany as it is in the United States. In Great Britain, for example, consider the large number of important reforms and policies which survived the last change of government: economic planning, incomes policy, the socialized health system. And in West Germany a Social Democratic government followed a Conservative one without any major change in domestic policy. Far from being the outcome of an ideological struggle, the development of the welfare state seems to be immune to ideological chatter.

Political decision-making in the welfare state is bound to be quite narrow. On the one hand, in the words of Richard Titmuss, no Western democracy "whatever its political color, is today publicly committed to an official policy of more unemployment, less education, no social security provisions for the needy and no tax deductions for the needs of dependents."[12] On the other hand, no government can afford to expand welfare services beyond a certain limit without being punished by inflation, unemployment, or both. The margin of decision thus becomes so slight in a capitalist system as to be barely visible. The conservatives then are partly correct in their assessment of the welfare state as "creeping socialism," not because it is socialism but because it creeps. The welfare state is developing step by step, reluctantly and involuntarily. It is not kept in motion by the "pull" of a conscious political will, but rather by the "push" of emergent risks, dangers, or bottlenecks, and newly created insecurities or potential conflicts which demand immediate measures that avoid the socially destabilizing problem of the moment. The logic of the welfare state is not the realization of some intrinsically valuable human goal but rather the prevention of a potentially disastrous social problem. Therefore, welfare states everywhere demonstrate that the tendency of being transformed is less a matter of politics than a matter of technocratic calculus. Or to use the somewhat nobler phrase of Professor Moynihan, they indicate a tendency towards the "professionalization of reform"[13] and the concomitant "benign neglect" of those groups of the population whose demands the professionalized reformers consider less than urgent.

This technocratic and quite apolitical manner of reacting to emerging social pressures dooms the welfare state to an endless and aimless process of self-adaptation. Very simply, *the welfare state tends to generate as many problems as it is able to solve.* Once again, we need not delve deeply into social politics to find an abundance of examples of the self-contradictory effects of welfare state intervention.

Milton Friedman gives a good illustration of the problem in a biting criticism of a particular public housing project.[14] The project initiated the following chain of events: (1) Only a limited amount of funds was available; (2) therefore, an income limitation had to be imposed for occupancy; (3) this limitation had a selective effect in favor of "broken" families; (4) the predictable result was a high density of problem children and an exceptionally high rate of juvenile delinquency; (5) other social problems were generated from the high rate of crime among the youth of the area. Although the net effect of the welfare project is difficult to assess, it can hardly be called wholly successful. Instead, the welfare bureaucracy, placed under budgetary constraints, shifted the problem from one area (housing) to another (delinquency).

A similar case is analyzed by Barbara Ehrenreich and John Ehrenreich.[15] They point out the relationship between health costs for the average American and federal expenditures for health, which leaped from five to twelve billion dollars between 1965 and 1967. During this time "hospitals took the lid off their reported 'costs' and doctors began to redefine 'reasonable' fees as the highest they could get away with. Between 1964 and 1969, physicians' fees rose by 33 percent, and hospital charges by 77 percent. By 1970 the average consumer . . . was worse off medically than he had been in 1964."

Professional social scientists are accustomed to reacting in one of two ways to this type of vicious circle. They either analyze it in highly jargonistic terms like "unanticipated consequences of purposive social action" or "pathologies of bureaucracy" and attempt to design organizational remedies, which are by and large an exercise in futility. Or they resign themselves nostalgically to the desirability of inaction, arguing with Bernard Rosenberg that "all political problems can be reduced to one of two categories: those that solve themselves and those for which there is no solution. . . . We go on fatuously defining, and thereby creating, problems beyond our capacity to solve except by generating even greater problems."[16] I should like to suggest another interpretation: Neither the dynamics of bureaucracy *itself* nor human impotency vis-à-vis political problems lies at the root of welfare problems. Rather the inherent, institutional constraints of a capitalist economy confound every effort of the welfare state to solve its internal difficulties.

At least one problem looms large if we assume that "inaction" is not a valid answer to our question. Increasing authoritarianism seems to be the only remaining remedy to control the problems which spawn ever new problems. In its initial state, authoritarianism does not necessarily mean open repression. The populace need only be exposed to a wave of diffuse propaganda against "permissiveness" along with dramatized reports of welfare fraud and corruption to justify stiffer rules of eligibility and closer controls on welfare recipients.[17] Until very recently California marital law "made social workers function literally as detectives," as Wilensky observes.[18] In Connecticut, legislation is proposed to prevent welfare mothers from having illegitimate children. Legislation is also before the California Assembly to force "able-bodied" welfare recipients to work in a public work force. And not long ago Vice-President Agnew cautiously discussed the possibilities of separating illegitimate children from welfare mothers. These are only a few unsystematic impressions which confirm a much larger body of empirical evidence indicating the direction in which the welfare state is heading.

This is not a unique American experience. In Germany adolescent workers are exploited in public "apprentice homes." West Germany also suffers from scandalous living conditions in its low-income public housing projects. Great Britain is only beginning to see the magnitude of its racial strife. Every welfare state has its problems and most point toward some kind of "welfare paternalism" or authoritarianism. It is not enough to speak of "American facism," which is overt and visible in the black ghettos of United States cities, as a kind of popular catchword. The syndrome can be observed in Western Europe as well, and in areas outside the ghettos. Alvin Gouldner and Bertram Gross predict a rapid growth and interpenetration of the welfare and police bureaucracies.[19] They see a policeman behind every welfare worker, physician, and teacher, ready to control the disadvantaged efficiently and effectively.

In the wake of this welfare authoritarianism has come an awakening interest in the Marxist concept of the "Lumpenproletariat."[20] O'Connor refers to it as the "postindustrial" proletariat,[21] comprising those strata which (a) do not participate in the productive process and (b) are not competing for jobs with those who do. The latter differentiates them from the classical unemployed, who were called the "industrial reserve army" by Marx. In economic terms, technologically advanced production has caused a decrease in the quantitative manpower requirements and an increase in the qualitative manpower requirements of advanced capitalism. A growing amount of surplus labor power is generated by this process, made up of the unemployed, the marginally employed, the part-time employed, the racially discriminated segments, the unskilled groups, the members of welfare families, segments of the elderly and of the college populations, perhaps also parts of a future professional army. The state supports this growing body of the population on a level close to subsistence: "Thus a new class is generated, consisting mostly of unskilled unemployed who have lost their competitive link to the labor market and who consist of a permanent welfare class."[22]

The future development of the welfare state will depend on its capability to absorb this segment of the population into social and economic roles, that is, to make them participants in society. The only way this group can participate in our society legitimately is to be "productive" within the institutional framework of the labor market and capitalist industry—a solution which neither the economy alone nor the educational system seems to be able to provide. The more likely developments will no doubt include large-scale "anomie," retreatism or symbolic emigration—to communes, drugs, and dozens of subcultures. So long as the welfare state cannot find a place for this group in its society, it has to suppress, control, or fragment it, for it cannot allow it to become an independent, organized political force.

Given this structural dilemma of the welfare state, it seems to be more of a transitional phase in the development of Western post-World War II societies than an ultimate, stable sociopolitical arrangement. The concept itself fails to be convincing. It cannot live up to its promise and stimulate feelings of trust, loyalty, and hope. Though academic social policy experts as well as policymakers are not in agreement on the most likely and most desirable alternative course of action, a negative agreement seems to develop as to the limits of the welfare state. Either its promise of equality and security for all has to be openly rejected, or this promise will be fulfilled at the price of truly revolutionary changes in both the economic and the political system.

NOTES

1. Frances F. Piven and Richard A. Cloward, *Regulating the Poor: The Function of Public Welfare* (New York: Pantheon Books, 1971).
2. Lloyd H. Free and Hadley Cantril, *The Political Beliefs of Americans* (New York: Simon & Schuster, 1968).
3. Robert Heilbroner, "Benign Neglect in the United States," *Transaction* 7:12, Oct. 1970.
4. Ibid., p. 17.
5. Ibid., p. 16.
6. J. E. Meade, *Efficiency, Equality, and the Ownership of Property* (Cambridge, Mass.: Harvard University Press, 1964).
7. M. Weidenbaum, *The Modern Public Sector* (New York: Basic Books, 1969).
8. Harold Wilensky and Charles N. Lebeaux, *Industrial Society and Social Welfare* (New York: Free Press, 1965), p. xii.
9. Free and Cantril, p. 40; cf. Chaim I. Waxman, ed., *The End of Ideology Debate,* 1969.
10. George Cabot Lodge, "Top Priority: Renovating Our Ideology," *Harvard Business Review* (September/October 1970).
11. Thomas Dye, *Politics, Economics, and the Public* (Chicago: Rand McNally, 1966). The most recent contribution to this ongoing debate is by Stuart H. Rakoff and Guenther F. Schaefer in *Politics and Society* 1:1 (November 1970): 51–77. A parallel though unrelated debate in France and Germany has been centered on the concept of "technocracy": cf. C. Koch, D. Senghaas, eds., *Texte zur Technokratiediskussion.* Frankfurt, Europäische Verlagsanstalt, 1970.
12. R. M. Titmuss, "The Welfare State: Images and Realities," ed., Charles I. Schottland, *The Welfare State* (New York: Harper & Row, 1967), p. 103.
13. D. Patrick Moynihan, "The Professionalization of Reform," *Public Interest* (Fall 1965).
14. M. Friedman, *Capitalism and Freedom* (Chicago: University of Chicago Press, 1962).
15. B. Ehrenreich and J. Ehrenreich, "The Medical–Industrial Complex," *The New York Review of Books,* vol. XV, no. 11 (December 1970), p. 14.
16. B. Rosenberg, Foreword to *Societal Guidance, A New Approach to Social Problems,* S. Heidt, A. Etzioni, eds. New York, 1969, p. v, vi.
17. This situation is vividly described in S. M. Miller and P. Roby, *The Future of Inequality* (New York: Basic Books, 1970).
18. Wilensky, *Industrial Society.*
19. Cf. B. M. Gross, "Friendly Fascism, A Model for America," *Social Policy* (November/December 1970), pp. 44–52.
20. B. Franklin, "Lumpenproletariat and Revolutionary Youth," *Monthly Review* 21:8 (January 1970).
21. J. O'Connor, "Some Contradictions of Advanced U.S. Capitalism," *Social Theory and Practice* 1 (Spring 1970): 1–11.
22. M. Nicolaus, "Proletariat and Middle Class in Marx," *Studies on the Left* 7 (January/February 1967).

SOCIAL WELFARE
AND POVERTY IN AMERICA

Robert J. Lampman

John F. Kennedy's slogan was, "Let's get the country moving again." He sought to reduce unemployment and increase the rate of economic growth without causing inflation or a deficit in the balance of payments. His emphasis was on efficiency and, although he did press for such New Deal–Fair Deal measures as civil rights, health insurance, and aid to education, his Administration placed higher priority on an investment tax credit, research and development outlays, and, above all, a Keynesian tax cut designed to spur economic recovery.

Lyndon B. Johnson's vision of a "Great Society" emphasized equity. He foresaw a nation where no one would have to live in poverty and all would have sufficient money income, public services, and civil rights to enable them to participate with dignity as full citizens. It would be an affluent society, but also a compassionate one, one that called for sacrifice by the majority to bring out the talents and willing cooperation of previously submerged and disadvantaged minorities.

It is right to call the war on poverty—first enunciated in President Johnson's State of the Union message and promptly endorsed by Congress in the Economic Opportunity Act of 1964—a logical extension of Franklin D. Roosevelt's Social Security Act and Harry S. Truman's Employment Act. It is also correct to identify it as in the general pattern laid down by the more advanced welfare states of Western Europe. But no other president and no other nation had set out a performance goal so explicit with regard to "the poor." No one else had elevated the question "What does it do for the poor?" to a test for judging government interventions and for orienting national policy.

This question served as a flag for the great onrush of social welfare legislation commencing in 1965 and the consequent expansion in the role of the federal government. When poverty became a matter of national interest, Washington moved into fields where state and local governments had held dominant if not exclusive sway up to that time. This movement was manifested by the enactment

Reprinted from *The Public Interest*, No. 34 (Winter 1974), pp. 66–82. Copyright © by National Affairs, Inc., 1974.

of such measures as Medicare and Medicaid, and aid to elementary and secondary education. It led to uniform national minimum guarantees in the food stamp program, in cash assistance to the aged, blind, and disabled (under the title of Supplemental Security Income), and in stipends for college students in the form of Basic Educational Opportunity Grants—all adopted in the first Administration of President Richard M. Nixon. Other interventions—notably equal opportunity legislation, the provision of legal services for and on behalf of the poor, and "community action"—made little impact on the budget, but reflected new efforts by the federal government to be an integrative force in national life.

Measuring Poverty

The scope of the American poverty problem and ways to measure progress against it were originally stated in terms of income. "Poverty" was quite arbitrarily defined as pre-tax money income below $3,000 in 1962 prices ($4,300 in 1973 prices) for a non-farm family of four. Perhaps this is no more arbitrary or unreasonable than the official definition of "unemployment," and like the latter, it enabled a quantification—in this case, of the changing number of poor people and hence of progress toward the goal of eliminating poverty. No target date was ever set for reaching this goal.

In the late 1940s, over 45 million persons, almost a third of the population, had incomes below the poverty line. This number was reduced in the period 1950-1956 by about one million per year. It stood, then, at about 39 million through the late 1950s and early 1960s. After that period of recurring recession, the more favorable developments of 1962-1969 brought the number in poverty down by almost two million per year to under 25 million persons (about 12 percent of the total population), where it stands today. The typical family in poverty has a "poverty income gap" of $1,000 (i.e., its cash income falls about $1,000 below the poverty line); the gaps of all poor families add up to $9 billion, which is less than 1 percent of the gross national product.

Some neo-conservative critics have faulted the anti-poverty theme as committing the government to an unattainable goal. As Aaron Wildavsky phrases it in a recent article in *Commentary,* "Part of the secret of winning, as any football coach knows, lies in arranging an appropriate schedule. Governmental performance depends not only on ability to solve problems, but on selecting problems government knows how to solve." However, eliminating income poverty, as defined, may be rated a "set up" on the schedule, since it was reasonable to believe in 1964 that increases in per capital real income, stable unemployment, and an evolving set of cash transfer programs would all contribute to the goal. As of 1973, the goal is virtually achieved. The "poverty income gap" will be reduced by the Supplemental Security Income plan, which goes into effect in January, and could be further cut by merely "cashing out" the $2 billion worth of food stamp benefits that are in the current budget.

Unfortunately, the measure of poverty employed was not well articulated with the larger vision of a Great Society and the several components of policy directed toward its building. There is a hiatus between the measure and the policy in that expenditures targeted to the poor, but taking the form of non-cash or in-kind benefits (e.g., food stamps, health care, or education benefits), do not show up in family money income. It is more unfortunate that the goal with respect to these in-kind benefits was never made precise. Was it simply more for the poor than they had been receiving, or was it access to (or consumption of) a per capita quantity of selected goods and services equal to the national average? Or was it—and here the goal would be most expansive—the achievement by the poor of health (as indicated by morbidity and mortality experience) and educational attainment (as indicated by school test scores) in line with norms for the non-poor population? We will comment later on the fact that such goals—which would require compensatory expenditures and new and untried methods—were read into the several programs by both proponents and opponents. We will also return later to a third anti-poverty goal, namely increased political participation by the poor. But more to the point here is the failure to establish definitions of "health care poverty" and "education poverty" and the like in any way comparable to the income poverty definition.

The Rise in Social Welfare Spending

We can say that if the import of the anti-poverty theme was to expand the broad set of "social welfare expenditures under public programs" and to get more cash and in-kind benefits for the poor, then it must be identified as a huge success. Social welfare expenditures are defined by the Social Security Administration as those for health, education, welfare services, and income maintenance. Such expenditures by the federal, state, and local governments went up almost fourfold between 1960 and 1972—from $52 billion to $193 billion (see Table 1). They were 10.6 percent of GNP in 1960 and 17.6 percent in 1972. By far the greater part of this rise happened after 1965. The average annual increase in real terms was only 5 percent between 1960 and 1965. Since 1965 that rate of increase has been 9 percent. To keep this in perspective, it should be noted that social welfare expenditures have risen more rapidly than GNP in every decade. The post-1965 record is one of unusually sharp transition toward a "mature" welfare state. Perhaps the full measure of this trend is that public *and* private spending now devote 9.0 percent of GNP to income maintenance, 7.6 percent to health care, 6.8 percent to education, and 1.4 percent to welfare and other services—a grand total of about 25 percent of GNP. (This contrasts with about 8 percent for the military.) A rising share—now 40 percent—of all public and private social welfare expenditures is funded via the federal government, and a considerable part of the private spending is encouraged by income tax exclusions (e.g., employer contributions to health insurance) and deductions.

It is, of course, impossible to say what part of the acceleration of social welfare expenditures would have occurred without the marking out of the poor as a target for federal attention. The declaration of war on poverty coincided with the realization that federal budget revenues were rising faster than projected expen-

Table 1
Social Welfare Expenditures Under Public Programs
(Federal, State, and Local)

	1960	1965	1970	1972
	(In Billions of Dollars)			
Total	52.3	77.2	146.0	192.7
Social insurance	19.3	28.1	54.8	75.1
Public aid	4.1	6.3	16.5	25.6
Health and medical programs	4.5	6.2	9.8	12.4
Veterans programs	5.5	6.0	9.0	11.5
Education	17.6	28.1	50.8	61.1
Housing	.2	.3	.7	1.4
Other social welfare	1.1	2.1	4.4	5.7

Source: Alfred M. Skolnik and Sophie R. Dales, "Social Welfare Expenditures, 1971-1972," *Social Security Bulletin,* December 1972, Table 1.

ditures for ongoing programs. So there were annual "fiscal dividends" to be claimed for tax cuts, general revenue sharing with the states, or new programs. In the event, some of these dividends were claimed by the military; some went to federal tax cuts (particularly in 1964, 1965, 1969, and 1971); but the great bulk of them went to social welfare programs. Yearly federal outlays for older income maintenance programs went up from $28 billion in 1963 to $75 billion in 1973, while spending on new Great Society programs went up from $2 billion to $36 billion. Of the latter total, $20 billion provided goods and services directly to people and $16 billion was in the form of grants to state and local governments and non-profit institutions. These increases came in large part out of forgone tax cuts, although Social Security payroll tax rates and state and local tax rates were raised. This meant that overall the nation's tax system became somewhat less progressive. The new federal programs claimed only part of rising incomes and few families experienced direct cuts in their standard of living because of them. Almost everybody was better off and almost nobody was worse off—truly, a Great Society!

By no means all of these increased expenditures went to families in income poverty, or even to families who would be poor without receipt of benefits. Out of the 1972 total public social welfare expenditures of $193 billion, only $25 billion was income-tested in a way designed to confine it to poor families. Many of the non-income-tested benefits, however, go to poor families. Eighty billion dollars of the total was in the form of cash transfers to persons. A rough guess, based on a 1967 survey, is that about $35 billion of this $80 billion went to the pre-transfer poor. In the earlier year, cash transfers went to 40 percent of all households and took 6.1 million households out of income poverty. The pre-transfer poverty income gap was $24.3 billion; post-transfer it was $9.7 billion.

These cash transfers are heavily weighted, of course, toward the aged and disabled and do little for the poverty of families headed by able-bodied men under 65.

Of the $193 billion of social welfare expenditures, $113 billion takes the form of goods and services. If 10 percent of the education services, half of the health services, half of veterans services, and most of a wide range (totaling $14 billion) of housing, social services, and food stamps go to the poor, then about $32 billion of non-cash benefits can be credited to the poor. As we noted earlier, none of these non-cash benefits are counted in the income measure of poverty, and no increases in them or in direct taxes to pay for them figure directly in the recorded reduction of poverty. It is of at least related interest that the pre-transfer poor have about 3 percent of "original" income, but after all social welfare expenditures and offsetting taxes are taken into account, they have about 8 percent of "post-tax money and in-kind income."

Poverty and Income Inequality

We have asserted that two anti-poverty goals have been accomplished. The number of people in income poverty has been reduced, and public social welfare expenditures carrying disproportionate benefits for the poor have been substantially increased. Numerous critics claim, however, that these two achievements are relatively insignificant and that a "real" war on poverty would aim for far greater victories. Let us consider two of these claims: first, that inequality of income should be substantially narrowed; and second, that benefits for the poor must be not simply large but also "effective" in meeting the needs of the poor.

Some economists and others have wanted to set the poverty line equal to a constant fraction (say, one-half) of the national median of family incomes. By that standard there has been virtually no reduction of poverty in recent decades. Setting such a standard is essentially the same as saying the goal should have been to increase the share of total money income received by the lowest fifth of households—which is about 5 percent—and thereby to narrow the overall inequality of income. By this measure, inequality has failed to decline in the United States since the end of World War II and is higher than in several Western European nations.

To change the lowest fifth's share of income from 5 to, say, 10 percent of total income is a demanding goal and would require strong measures. Senator George S. McGovern's $1,000 per person refundable tax credit, which called for a thoroughgoing change of the income tax base with all income subject to a 33 percent tax rate, would only have changed the share of the lowest fifth by about 2 percentage points. Those points would, of course, have had to be offset by reducing the post-tax income share of the top 80 percent of families from 95 to 93 percent. Increasing governmental outlays for the poor and assuring them new rights to jobs and political participation mean that some of the non-poor have to give something up, and many discussions of the poverty program are flawed by not being explicit about this. In practice, some violations of vertical and horizontal equity do occur. Some of the pre-transfer poor have more combined money income and in-kind benefits than do some of the non-poor. This kind of leap-frogging of poor over non-poor in income ranking—and some unhappiness with poverty programs because of it—might not have happened if the total income distribution had been more clearly in view.

However, comprehending the distribution of money income and its dynamics' is a bewildering challenge. It is remarkable that this distribution shows little change over the decades (see Table 2), in spite of staggering changes in the size and composition and geographic location of the population: the size and role of the family (with the decline of the three-generation extended family); the pattern of participation in the labor force (with men starting to work later and retiring earlier and more women working away from home); the decline of farming and self-employment and the rise of service industries, government employment, and professional and technical occupations; a rise in the median income of black, relative to white, families; the increase in taxes and government spending; the growth of fringe benefits; and the conversion of ordinary income into capital gains. The explanation must be that some of these changes offset others in such a way as to sustain a constancy in the shares of the several fifths, but we have no good explanation as to why the offsetting changes should balance out so neatly.

Table 2
Shares of "Total Money Income" Received by Fifths
of Families, Ranked by Income

Families	1950	1970
Lowest fifth	4.5	5.5
Second fifth	12.0	12.0
Third fifth	17.4	17.4
Fourth fifth	23.5	23.5
Highest fifth	42.6	41.6

The Intricacies of Income Distribution

One matter confusing to many people is that, although there has been no shift in the distribution over time, there is a considerable amount of redistribution every year. That is, there is a spread between the lowest fifth's share of earnings and property and their share of total income after taxes and transfers. Ben Okner at the Brookings Institution calculates that federal income and payroll taxes and cash transfers alone raise the share of the lowest fifth from 1.7 percent of "original" income to 6.3 percent of "income after redistribution." In spite of—and to a certain extent because of—this rather extensive redistribution in one year, inequality has not lessened over time. We say *because of* since there can be no doubt that social security and public assistance benefits have enabled old people and women heading families to withdraw from the labor force and to live and be counted separately as low-income households.

It is not clear that the percentage shares of "total money income" going to fifths of "families" measure faithfully whatever changes in economic inequality may have taken place. Consider all the things left out of account—home production, imputed rent from owner-occupied housing and consumer durables, non-money benefits from employers and governments, realized and unrealized capital gains and losses, leisure, direct taxes paid, work expenses such as child care costs, and disamenities experienced as a worker and as a consumer. Numerous adjustments to the crude income data would have to be made to get a true ranking of "richer to poorer" persons. These might include adjustment for family size, number of workers, part-year workers, variability of income, and net worth. Tax and welfare policies are often keyed to highly refined and adjusted definitions of "income" and "family," which take account of legislative determination of "reasonable classification" in ways that the crude income rankings do not.

The 12 percent of the population now counted as being in income poverty are quite different in composition from the persons in the lowest fifth of families. The latter group now includes all those with incomes under $5,500. As an example of the difference, aged couples with $3,000 or more of income are not below the poverty line, but many of them are, of course, in the lowest fifth. A large family with $6,000 is not in the lowest fifth but is below the poverty line. It is a matter for judgment as to whether the poverty ranking, which makes adjustments for family size and holds to a constant market-basket of goods in setting the income cut-off, yields a more acceptable target group for governmental policy than does the lowest fifth. In any event, it would not be easy to get a consensus among experts on how best to measure overall income inequality and what targets should be set for changing it. The income poverty measure and goal doubtless have more public support than would any particular measure and goal which start from the thought that government should "manage" the whole income distribution.

Perhaps some of the difficulty arises from lack of awareness of the facts of income distribution. Few people seem to realize or accept their actual ranking in the income distribution. How many people with combined family incomes of $30,000 realize that they are not "middle class," but are actually in the top five percent of the distribution? Although economists are wont to look to an index of inequality of income shares in comparing the fairness of result of one political economy with that of another, this particular measure has never had any standing among political leaders. None has rallied political troops with a plan to change the shares of the several fifths in a stated way. Concern with income inequality has been more indirect; the focus has been on "fairness" in taxation, relief for those "unable" to work, replacement of income lost without fault, sharing the cost of extraordinary expense, and helping people get a minimum provision of "essentials" in order to assure "equality of opportunity." It is interesting to note that advocates of such schemes as progressive income taxes and social security often deny that they are concerned with income redistribution. These have been more acceptable political approaches to equity questions than have wide sweeps to "correct" the distribution of income as such. The goal of eliminating poverty is a modest addition to the array of apparently politically useful rationales for redistribution.

Economic inequality among persons is immensely complicated. This explains why it is possible for people to reach contradictory conclusions about what is happening on the inequality front in America. In the last ten years there was no significant change in the distribution of "total money income" as it is conventionally measured, but there *was* a great drop in the percentage of people living in "income poverty." There was no increase in the progressivity of the overall tax system, but there *was* a considerable increase in public money for the poor. Further, there *was* some narrowing of inequality in the consumption of food and medical care, and perhaps of housing, educational services, and public recreational facilities as well.

Thus, many critics have contributed to the feeling that the anti-poverty goal and programs in pursuit of it have been unworthy because they did not seek a more fundamental change in the distribution of income. Another group has fed the belief that poverty programs have failed because they did not meet new standards of "program effectiveness" that were introduced after 1964. The poverty theme and program-planning methodology both came into the social programs part of the federal budget at the same time—and both with the enthusiastic support of the same high-level appointees of President Johnson. It is ironic that the evaluations and cost-effectiveness studies and experiments started under the Johnson administration have been used with some success by President Nixon to support his decision to cut back on certain parts of the poverty program.

The Escalation of Standards

It can be argued that a poverty program is "effective" if it simply channels more money or standardized goods or services to the poor, and thereby brings the level of income and consumption of the poor up to some stated minimums. To the extent that this was the goal of the President and the Congress that enacted the set of related measures, the budget shows considerable success in reaching the goal. But as individual programs came up for budget review they were judged against quite different goals.

Any program will, of course, get a low score on a cost-effectiveness basis if the goals are set high enough and the constraints (or side effects to be avoided) are numerous enough. So the key to understanding what a low score means is to look at the goals and where they come from. Charles L. Schultze, Edward R. Fried, Alice M. Rivlin, and Nancy H. Teeters comment on this topic in their Brookings publication, *Setting National Priorities: The 1973 Budget:*

> It is no longer enough for politicians and federal officials to show that they have spent the taxpayers' money for approved purposes; they are now being asked to give evidence that the programs are producing results. . . . In the 1960s . . . people began asking more of the federal

government. First, a variety of new programs were enacted, many of them designed to provide direct services to people, especially poor people. Poverty was to be reduced not just by giving people cash income but by providing medical care, pre-school programs, job training, legal services, compensatory education, and opportunities for community action. . . . Along with the new activities came the gradual development of new and far more ambitious standards for judging federal programs. For the first time, federal officials—indeed all government officials—were being asked to produce "performance measures" as evidence that their efforts were achieving results. Administrators of education programs were asked, not just to show that money was spent for teachers' salaries or books or equipment, but for evidence that children were learning more. . . . Even transfer programs were judged in a new light. It was not enough to distribute food stamps to a specified number of people. Attention was focused on measurement of nutrition or malnutrition. It was not enough that Medicare and Medicaid paid medical bills for the poor and the aged. Attention was focused on the quality of care and the effect of the federal programs on the price of care for the rest of the population (pp. 449, 451).[1]

This is an intriguing statement by key members of the Johnson Administration. Schultze was Director of the Bureau of the Budget and Rivlin was Assistant Secretary of Health, Education, and Welfare. In those roles they were foremost among those asking for "performance measures" as evidence that the programs were "achieving results." "Results" meant not simply that the poor were getting the same quality of educational and health services as the non-poor, but that these services were meeting some new tests of effectiveness that had never before been applied. In this exercise, the poor served as pawns in contests to reform all governmental policies, contests in which the best became the enemy of the good. Appraisals of the budget against poverty became entangled with discoveries that the links between educational spending and learning, and between medical care outlays and health, are not too clear.

Special circumstances in the development of the war on poverty may explain some of this escalation of standards. At the outset the policy was one of "let many flowers bloom," since there was no firm methodology as to what poverty—other than income poverty—was, and no consensus on preferred methods for dealing with it. The Office of Economic Opportunity (OEO) was charged with responsibility for evaluating the role of existing anti-poverty programs, devising alternatives, encouraging innovation, demonstrating and experimenting with previously untried schemes, and advising the President how best to allocate given levels of anti-poverty funds. This meant that more programs were initiated on a tentative, pilot, and small-scale basis than could be funded nationwide. Hence some programs had to be shot down.

The statement of rigorous goals and new methods for evaluating performance specified by the Program Planning Budgeting System were built into the new governmental programs more readily than into the old ones. R. Sargent Shriver manned many key OEO positions with experts from the Department of Defense and its satellite Rand Corporation, where program-planning budgeting had flowered. Furthermore, as time went on, the evaluators developed their own preferences for inclusion in the anti-poverty budget and were comparing a range of rival programs against a perhaps untried ideal. Thus some reached the conclusion that the Aid to Families with Dependent Children program was a "failure" because a negative income tax was a better alternative. Aids to existing schools were found to be unsatisfactory because a radical transformation of education via a voucher system was envisioned as more desirable. This kind of competition, which was built into the operation, no doubt encouraged the public to view anti-poverty programs as uniquely questionable. Perhaps the verdict would have been more favorable if a new set of non-tentative programs could have been established at one blow and put into operation—as was the case with the Social Security Act of 1935—before program-planning budgeting was brought in, so that critical evaluations could have been produced more even handedly across the complete range of government operation.

It is important to make the distinction between "effective" programs and "efficiently managed" programs. An effective program is one which achieves a stated purpose, sometimes in spite of a degree of mismanagement. Some efficiently managed programs fail to achieve a stated purpose (i.e., to be effective) because they are not well designed or because no design would achieve the purpose. Nothing we have said above is meant to condone corrupt, sloppy, slow, or misguided execution of government programs. The introduction of a considerable number of separate programs with novel purposes—some of which involved several federal departments, state and local governments, and private contractors—stretched the skills and powers of managers. Some observers see the problem as more fundamental than lack of management skills. They conclude that the federal government cannot satisfactorily reach poor families via such cumbersome intermediaries. If poverty is a national problem, does not its amelioration require direct federal administration? Alternatively, if a particular anti-poverty purpose cannot be efficiently managed via federal guidelines to state and local governments, should that purpose be abandoned to the vagaries of general and special revenue sharing? These are not easy questions. The Nixon administration has proposed to virtually federalize public assistance and at the same time to de-federalize manpower training.

Perhaps we should regard these issues not as signs of failure of the poverty program, but as indications of the problems of success. The goal of reducing poverty has been established, substantial resources have been committed (and more are likely to be); the problem now is how to rationalize and manage the use of these resources, by dealing with overlaps of programs and integrating programs for the poor with those for the non-poor.

Equity and Economy

In addition to the program-by-program analysis of effectiveness and management efficiency referred to before, the evolution of the federal government's role against poverty has forced two other critical issues forward. Both are potentially explosive as equity issues and as "budget busters." One issue arises out of congressional willingness to emphasize new in-kind benefits for the poor, to establish high standards for them, and then to *underfund* them so that few of those potentially eligible can in fact get such benefits. Consider what would happen if Congress managed tax laws in a similar manner! For example, child care standards are set at over $2,000 per year per child, which is more than most non-poor working mothers are willing to pay for such care; part-subsidy for child care may extend to families well above the poverty line, but the benefits are in fact distributed almost randomly. Currently, about $1.5 billion is allocated to day care, but many who are eligible cannot find places, and some who are poor consume more of the service than do most of those who are not poor. To straighten these equity issues out will require either a great deal of extra money—perhaps as much as $15 billion a year—or a sharp reduction in the cost of each child care place. Similar problems are to be found in housing—public low-rent housing may cost the government more than most near-poor families spend on housing and it is available for only a small fraction of all the poor. Rent assistance and rent supplements tied to specifically approved new construction are not much more equitable. About $2 billion now goes to these three programs. Again, to design a replacement that would produce an equitable result poses the choice between expanding the number of beneficiaries and cutting back on the level of maximum benefit per family. Problems akin to this are found in public job creation, medical care, food stamps, and college scholarships.

The second issue arising out of the achievement of anti-poverty goals as stated ten years ago is: How many income-conditioned cash and in-kind benefits can we offer simultaneously? If Medicaid and child day care and housing and food stamps and college scholarships and cash public assistance are each made more equitable—that is, fully funded at a uniform national level—and if all eligible persons below some moderate cut-off income level (say, twice the poverty line) take advantage of all of them, then the current federal, state, and local outlays for income-conditioned benefits, which now total $25 billion, will rise by several times that amount. In such a situation, a family headed by a non-worker might have combined benefits of Medicaid with an insurance value of $1,000, a housing allowance worth $1,000, a food stamp bonus worth $1,300, a college scholarship for one youngster worth $1,400, and a cash income of $2,400 (to select the figure offered by Nixon's Family Assistance Plan). This means a combined guarantee of $7,100. But each of the benefits has a take-back rate or a rate at which the benefit falls to zero as earnings or other income rises. This is sometimes called an implicit tax rate. In Aid to Families with Dependent Children it amounts to 67 percent; in the Basic Educational Opportunity Grant it is 20 percent; in the food stamp program it is 30 percent. These tax rates have a way of combining and building a "dependency trap." Hence, even if each of the revised and more equitable benefit programs were to have what is now thought of as a reasonable tax rate, a family might well lose 50 cents in cash benefits, 30 cents in food stamps, 25 cents in housing allowance, 25 cents in health insurance, and 20 cents in college scholarship for every extra dollar earned. In this hypothetical example, the combined tax rate is 150 percent. This confiscatory rate of take-back of benefits means that a family would have to earn an amount substantially greater than $7,100 before it is really any better off than it would be without work, even if child care subsidies come into play. The fact that a number of benefits in our example are payable to people at twice the poverty line ($8,600 for a family of four) makes millions of non-poor families subject to high cumulative tax rates. If tax rates are lowered on each program, then additional families, who are subject to both payroll tax and income tax, are added to the benefit rolls.

There appear to be only a few ways out of this dilemma. One is to eliminate all but one or two of the enumerated programs and keep the combined guarantee and tax rates low. The other is to convert some of the income-conditioned benefits into non-income-conditioned ones. Thus, to combine these ways, we could trade off food stamps and housing allowances for a higher cash guarantee, and convert Medicaid into universal health insurance. But there seem to be powerful forces at work to expand rather than to contract income-conditioning of benefits, and the separate federal departments and separate congressional committees tend to respond in an uncoordinated manner to these forces. A subcommittee of the Joint Economic Committee, chaired by Representative Martha Griffiths, is currently studying this problem and may come up with recommendations on how to improve legislative consideration of income-conditioning of benefits.

Participation by the Poor

Thus far we have argued that the war on poverty is best interpreted as a logical extension of the liberal welfare state. It was based on a confidence that the poor—especially the well-educated young blacks among the poor—would benefit from a stronger economy. It was also grounded in the belief that the rapidly growing set of health, education, and income maintenance institutions could be extended and adapted to improve the well-being of the poor. Hence, income poverty and poverty in key goods and services could be reduced.

However, a third type of poverty was also recognized, namely, lack of participation, and the remedies for this were not so clear. Indeed, it was not spelled out what participation poverty is, any more than it was detailed what education poverty or health care poverty might be. Some seemed to assume that it was confined to those in income poverty and would be overcome as a by-product of the elimination of the latter. Some argued quite the other way around, that only with the participation of the poor in the planning and execution of anti-poverty programs would the other aspects of poverty be overcome. Like general revenue sharing, participation is advocated as both a preferred means and a desired end.

It was known, of course, that the poor voted less frequently than the non-poor. Voting rights legislation would help on that. Few among the poor were members of unions, cooperatives, or voluntary associations of any kind. Many of them felt they had little influence over what went on in their own neighborhood, to say nothing about policy determination at the national level. Numerous remedies for participation poverty and the feelings of powerlessness were offered. Voluntary organizations, including churches, the Boy Scouts, and community charities, should be encouraged to include the poor not only as "clients" but as full participants. Poor people should be helped to organize as workers, consumers, and clients. New types of unions, tenant associations, and "welfare rights" organizations were to be formed to help people "gain control of their own destinies." But the most unique invention to reduce the powerlessness of the poor was the "community action agency," which was to have a hand in administering some federally funded social welfare efforts at the neighborhood level. These agencies were to facilitate "maximum feasible participation" by members of target neighborhoods, not all of whom were necessarily in income poverty. They were, in effect, a fourth level of government, distinct from state and local units. They were encouraged by OEO to design their own anti-poverty strategies, to adapt standard programs to their own local situations, and to employ and otherwise to involve as many local individuals as they possibly could.

The community action or participation strand of the war on poverty may be evaluated on several levels. One has to do with the effectiveness or efficiency of specific social services delivered in the participatory framework. These differed widely from place to place and year to year. They included such diverse activities as family planning, pre-school education, legal services, recreation, vocational training, and ombudsman services. In some instances, the purposes were inspired by OEO officials, who saw community action as a way to go around established federal, state, and local administrations and to try out various "non-bureaucratic" approaches to the delivery of services.

In a detached scientific vein, one must acknowledge that even a discovery of what fails to work against poverty is valuable. The flexibility of this variant of the revenue sharing technique makes it attractive, but the variability of projects defies a summary evaluation. Some critics allege that community action was counterproductive in some instances because it promised more than it could deliver, thus setting up expectations that were later frustrated. Others, most notably Edward C. Banfield in his provocative book *The Unheavenly City,* fault community action along with other anti-poverty techniques for failing to change the life style of the chronic poor or to stop the antisocial behavior of urban youth who riot, as Banfield puts it, "for fun and profit."

Another question for evaluating community action is whether it improves participation levels for the poor and lessens feelings of powerlessness. There are examples to support any conclusion, but no good scales for measuring how these important variables may have changed over time. Local community action agencies did provide valuable work and leadership experience for many from impoverished backgrounds. Such techniques as demonstrations, rent strikes, and class action lawsuits were used to protect the rights of some groups. On the other hand, some found that the troubles and risks of taking part in the "politics of the poor" outweighed the gains, and they became even more cynical than they were before about participation.

On a still different level, one can ask whether the community action approach attracted support from the general public for the major programs against poverty. It did dramatize in human terms what poverty was like in affluent America. It appealed to conservatives on the grounds that welfare services should be tailored to the specific situation and confined to the poor, rather than centralized and universalized. (President Nixon found kind things to say about community action in 1969 only to withdraw his support in 1973.) It offered ways for non-poor volunteers to follow their charitable impulses and to learn about poverty at the grass-roots level. At the same time, some community action leaders or their rivals may have undermined public support for anti-poverty programs by their radical critiques of the "real" causes of poverty and the "crisis of a sick society" which it supposedly represented. Perhaps it was inevitable in such troubled times that anti-poverty action groups would serve as a forum for a heady brew of social criticism. The fact that community action seemed at times to be working at cross purposes with prevailing institutions and attitudes undoubtedly contributed to confusion and doubt in the minds of many voters.

"What Does It Do for the Poor?"

The efforts of the last ten years to achieve a society in which no one has to live below a poverty level, in which access to a minimum of certain key goods and services is assured, and in which government invites the political participation of all have been at best partly successful. We have noted, however, that even the successes have been called failures by reference to newer and higher goals which have tended to emerge almost before the ink is dry on the old ones. Eliminating income poverty is not enough; income inequality must be modified. Improving expenditures for goods and services going to the poor is not enough; they must be effective, efficiently managed, and equitable. Allowing the poor to participate in decisions about how to allocate a small part of the nation's anti-poverty budget is not enough; they must be assured full participation in all matters that affect them, and rivals for leadership of the poor must have a chance to be heard.

We have asserted that some of this escalation of goals is evidence not of failure but of the problems of success. But some part of this tendency may be put down to failure to make the goals more specific and limited at the outset. A target date for the elimination of income poverty could have been set. Definitions and measures of poverty with regard to key goods and services and participation could have been offered. Failure to count in-kind benefits in the measure of income poverty and lack of coordination of the target populations for the several programs may have contributed to a feeling of less accomplishment than would otherwise have been the case. In our pluralistic system, goals seldom hold as originally enunciated. The President may announce them only to see Congress modify them in one way, and state and local governments, administrators, courts, outside experts, and participating groups in yet other ways. Goals are likely to run on ahead not only of achievement, but of knowledge of how to achieve them. There is a tendency for planners at the presidential level to set wide goals and to embrace a variety of sometimes contradictory methods in order to rally a wide spectrum of support. This tendency may explain why anti-poverty efforts have not been confined to a limited set of carefully targeted measures, and why they have not emerged at the expense of—but rather in addition to—other social welfare expenditures.

There is still much unfinished business on the anti-poverty agenda—particularly with regard to families with children. Thus it is still relevant to address new policy with the rude and restrictive challenge, "What does it do for the poor?" What started out under the anti-poverty flag as an emphasis on social welfare expenditures for the poor is now enmeshed in efficiency and equity issues involving much of the population. That flag is not wide enough to symbolize, for example, the new range of issues associated with congressional willingness to set high benefit levels in a series of separate in-kind programs such as those having to do with food, housing, health care, job creation, and college scholarships. It seems likely that these programs will pay out the greater part of their benefits to non-poor people, but will not exclude the remaining poor. Knowledge gained in the war on poverty should be applied to establishing new priorities and constraints for the next stage in the development of the American welfare state.

NOTE
1. © 1972 by the Brookings Institution, Washington, D.C.

Part III.
Military Institutions and the Military-Industrial Complex

The military—Army, Navy, Air Force, and Marine Corps—is the largest centrally organized complex of institutions in the United States. The four branches are organized in well-defined hierarchies of command, and they are coordinated by the Joint Chiefs of Staff and the Department of Defense. Uniforms and a separate judicial system clearly set them apart from the rest of society, although, as we shall see, this does not mean that they operate in isolation. Through the massive *civilian* department of defense and as consumers of civilian and military material, the military has strong links to other institutions.

Military institutions have not been widely studied by American social scientists and so there is little information about them in most textbooks. The armed services are usually mentioned in the context of social psychological studies of military personnel, of organizational (bureaucratic) dynamics, or of professionalism. This lack of attention to the impact of the military on society is perhaps due to the relative unimportance of the military in the recent American past. That is, there has been a lag between the growth of the military and the development of sociological interest. The days of unquestioned civilian supremacy, however, are over, and researchers and the public must recognize the military as an important component of society if they are to grasp reality. It might be well to keep in mind the preeminence of the military owners of the means of violence in many societies in the past and in the present—there are more military governments in the world today than liberal democracies or communist regimes. When a state degenerates into an arena for naked force, the military comes to power.

The sizes of the armed services are presented in Table 1. They have declined since the Vietnam war peak, but the more than two million uniformed personnel and one million civilians employed by the military still constitute a substantial part of the workforce (more than 5 percent). Table 2 indicates military financial outlays. Because of inflation, defense expenditures are expected to rise to $926 billion in fiscal year 1975, despite small personnel cuts. We are still spending vast amounts of money on defense in *peacetime*.

The basic facts and figures of the military establishment are outlined by Adam Yarmolinsky. The military is a very substantial portion of the general economy, and further defense expenditures are

Table 1
Defense Employment (in thousands), Fiscal Years 1964–1975

	1964	1968	1973	1974[1]	1975
Military					
Army	972	1,570	801	782	785
Navy	667	765	564	551	541
Marine Corps	190	307	196	196	196
Air Force	856	905	691	645	630
Total Military	2,685	3,547	2,252	2,174	2,152
Civilian					
Army	360	462	333	356	359
Navy	332	419	322	326	324
Air Force	305	331	271	271	270
Defense Agencies/OSD	38	75	72	76	75
Total Civil Service	1,035	1,287	998	1,029	1,028
Total Military and Civil Service	3,720	4,834	3,250	3,203	3,180
Defense-Related Industry	2,280	3,173	1,693	1,742	1,752
Total Defense Manpower	6,000	8,007	4,943	4,945	4,932

[1] Estimates
SOURCE: Department of Defense, *Commander's Digest*, 15:10 (March 7, 1974).

Table 2
Defense Expenditures (in billions of dollars), Fiscal Years 1964-1975

Appropriation Title	1964	1968	1974	Current Dollars Total Obligational Authority 1975
Military Personnel	13.0	19.9	24.4	25.9
Retired Pay	1.2	2.1	5.2	6.0
Operation and Maintenance	11.7	20.9	24.2	26.6
Procurement	15.0	22.6	18.7	19.9
RDT & E	7.1	7.3	8.3	9.4
Military Construction	1.0	1.5	1.8	2.1
Family Housing	.6	.6	1.1	1.3
Civil Defense	.1	.1	.1	.1
Military Assistance	1.0	.6	3.3	1.3
Total	50.7	75.6	87.1	92.6

SOURCE: Department of Defense, *Commander's Digest*, 15:10 (March 7, 1974).

hidden in NASA and AEC (as well as CIA) expenditures. About 60 percent of the military budget is spent on material and plant bought from civilian suppliers. Thus, the military is the largest single customer in the country. This expenditure generates some four million civilian jobs and is crucial to the economies of states that have large military installations and industries. Yarmolinsky concludes by describing past feuds within the military and the steps that have been taken to remedy them. This includes a discussion of the way the command structure is now organized.

Morris Janowitz discusses the impact and implications of the all-volunteer military that, since the end of the draft, has become a reality. A fully professional force, he claims, could become isolated unless major changes are made. To recruit good personnel, some form of post-military career security must be devised. Military personnel should be moved from one geographical area to another less often to permit more stable family life than is now possible. Internal education should be modified to reflect new military realities, discipline should be modernized, and the services should be "civilianized" to a degree. Janowitz sees a need for a redefinition of the military career and a need for new responsibilities for the armed forces in civilian life. They could, for example, serve in times of natural and man-made disaster and in environmental control.

Since the low point of morale during the Vietnam war—when fraggings (assassination of officers), race relations, and drug abuse caused the officer corps some concern—the situation has apparently improved. Although the armed services are still authoritarian "total institutions" and are relatively low paying, they do provide security. Some would claim they are the nearest an American can get to the conditions of socialism (in regimentation and in guaranteed health care, housing, food and clothing, and pensions). Perhaps because of rising unemployment, the military has been able to recruit enough volunteers without drastically lowering standards. The main change has been a substantial increase in the proportion of black enlisted personnel (to 20 percent of the Army and 18 percent of the Marine Corps in 1973).

The range of tasks that the military must be prepared for are highly diversified and are worldwide in scope. The forces are equipped with an almost unbelievable array of weapons for fighting in any type of engagement, from brush fire skirmishes through the so-called conventional (World War II style) war to tactical and all-out nuclear conflict. This range of weaponry has led to an excessive reliance on technology (as in Vietnam) and a confused recognition by senior officers that they can no longer win the "big wars."

There are now thousands of nuclear weapons in the Soviet Union and the United States aimed at their targets and waiting. Each one, in the words of a former United Nations secretary general, "has a destructive power greater than that of all the conventional explosive that has ever been used in warfare since the day gunpowder was discovered." The United States has one thousand Minuteman ICBMs, fifty-four Titan IIs, six hundred fifty-six Polaris-Poseidon submarine missiles, twenty-seven squadrons of strategic bombers, and thousands of lower yield tactical nuclear weapons. In an all-out attack on the Soviet Union, the Department of Defense has estimated that these weapons would inflict between 70 and 120 million Soviet fatalities from the initial blasts alone. Radioactivity would add to this total later. Meanwhile, Soviet warheads would cause an initial 100 to 120 million fatalities in the United States. Hence, the "no win" attitude. After such devastation, Mexico, Brazil, and perhaps India—if they were undamaged in the conflict—would emerge as superpowers. Instead of such certain suicide, military strategists have proposed more measured and flexible—but probably no more rational—nuclear exchanges.[1] For "brush fires," the military now has the massive C-5A transport, helicopter gun ships, a wide array of Vietnam-tested weapons, and probably many more to come.[2]

The remaining part of this section deals with the relationship between the military and other institutions, and with what has come to be called the military-industrial complex. H. L. Nieburg (cited in Suggested Readings) has described how these ties came about. After World War II, the government wanted sophisticated weaponry in order to keep its lead in the arms race with the Soviet Union—the so-called Cold War. The government had production and research and development installations (for example, the Army's Redstone plant, which developed the first missiles) but began to contract work out to business. The rush was on, and the best scientists and technicians flocked to high-paying jobs with private contractors. This weakened the government's research capacity, so more and more money was channeled to the corporations. They operated on a cost-plus basis—they were guaranteed full expenses and a profit margin, irrespective of the original contract bid. Defense work was highly lucrative and risk-free. Even with some contract modifications, it still is.

The new defense boom greatly expanded the business of many contractors and even created new ones. Between 1960 and 1967, nineteen companies had Department of Defense contracts totaling more than $2 billion. Five companies—Lockheed, General Dynamics, McDonnell-Douglas, Boeing, and General Electric—had contracts totaling more than $7 billion. Some companies (ten of the top fifteen contractors) did most of their business with the Department of Defense. Thus, 88 percent of Lockheed's sales were for defense. Money also flowed into universities. The Massachusetts Institute of Technology and Johns Hopkins University made the top one hundred contractors in 1967 with $95 and $71 million respectively, and many others had research and development grants in the millions. Thus, Nieburg says, the United States has become a "contract state." The economy is no longer a free enterprise system. Instead, because of defense spending, it is now a "government-subsidized private-profit system."

The article by Seymour Melman claims that we have now gone beyond the contract state with its relatively weak ties between con-

[1] For a debate on this issue between, among others, Secretary of Defense James R. Schlesinger and Senator Edmund S. Muskie, see *Sane World*, May 1974.
[2] For details, see Michael T. Klare, *War Without End* (New York: Vintage, 1972).

tractors and the military. Now a new industrial (state) management, centered in the Department of Defense, presides over the country's largest industries. It is the most important management group in the country, and perhaps the world's biggest industrial administrative office. Melman claims that the cost of this military machine has been very high. While money has poured into defense, our health has declined and our cities have decayed. While scientific effort has been directed into military and space channels, civilian industry has stagnated and fallen behind foreign competitors. Melman's examination of the characteristics of the state-management leads him to conclude that much that appears irrational in military policy (for example, nuclear overkill) can be explained by the interests of the defense managers. They have extended their control over industries and increased their decision-making power and budget, *without* noticeably increasing their efficiency. Expanding defense has been encouraged by the myth that the United States was rich enough to support it along with civilian affluence. Melman's diagnosis that we cannot have both guns and butter seems to have been substantiated by inflation and recession in 1975.

In the next article, Michael Reich introduces a different view of the military–industrial complex. He believes the government discovered defense expenditure as an important means to support capitalism—a means that is easily justified and offends few powerful economic interests. There is, he concludes, no other alternative to military spending as a stimulant to the economy. The corporate world is unlikely to attempt welfare expenditure or to produce the social goods suggested by Melman.

The final article by Pilisuk and Hayden asks if there is an inherently aggressive military–industrial complex preventing peace. They review the literature and note that the definition of military–industrial complex varies from writer to writer. Their analysis circumvents the issue of whether the military, political, or economic institution is dominant, for the leaders of each have a common perspective on world affairs. Pilisuk and Hayden believe that American society *is* a military–industrial complex and that there is little hope for lasting peace while it is so constituted.

Suggested Readings

Andreski, Stanislav. *Military Organization and Society.* Berkeley and Los Angeles: University of California Press, 1968.

Barnet, Richard J. *The Economy of Death.* New York: Antheum, 1971.
Clotfelter, James. *The Military in American Politics.* New York: Harper and Row, 1973.
Donovan, James A. *Militarism, U.S.A.* New York: Charles Scribner's Sons, 1970.
Fulbright, J. William. *The Pentagon Propaganda Machine.* New York: Vintage, 1971.
Huntington, Samuel P. *The Soldier and the State.* New York: Vintage, 1958.
Houser, William L. *America's Army in Crisis.* Baltimore: Johns Hopkins University Press, 1973.
Janowitz, Morris. *The Professional Soldier.* New York: Free Press, 1960, 1971.
Klare, Michael T. *War Without End.* New York: Vintage, 1972.
McGarvey, Patrick J. *C.I.A.: The Myth and the Madness.* Baltimore: Penguin, 1973.
Melman, Seymour. *Pentagon Capitalism.* New York: McGraw-Hill, 1970.
Moskos, Charles C., Jr. *The American Enlisted Man.* New York: Russell Sage, 1970.
_____, ed. *Public Opinion and the Military Establishment.* New York: Russell Sage, 1971.
Nieburg, H. L. *In the Name of Science.* New York: Quadrangle, 1970.
Pilisuk, Marc. *International Conflict and Social Policy.* Englewood Cliffs, N. J.: Prentice-Hall, 1972.
Rose, Steven, ed. *Chemical and Biological Warfare.* Boston: Beacon, 1969.
Russett, Bruce M., and Stepan, Alfred, eds. *Military Force and American Society.* New York: Harper and Row, 1973.
Yarmolinsky, Adam. *The Military Establishment.* New York: Harper and Row, 1971.

THE SIZE, SCOPE, AND COST OF THE ESTABLISHMENT

Adam Yarmolinsky

The size and scope of the military establishment have major impacts on American society, not only on the obvious quantifiable dimensions but on the qualitative dimensions of that society as well. Indeed, the quality of life in the United States is markedly affected by the pervasive outreach of the establishment. The military until recently absorbed three-quarters of federal expenditures (as distinct from total federal outlays), and close to 9 percent of the gross national product; military spending has been declining, but it still amounts to more than two-thirds of the federal government's purchases of goods and services. It has called on at least one American male in four for military service, and it provides a livelihood for one in ten members of the nation's labor force. One in four American men who served in the military is a veteran of American wars.

The military establishment as a segment of the economy can be described with considerable precision. As Table 1 shows, expenditures by the Department of Defense for the last eight fiscal years, in constant dollars, and as a percentage of gross national product, have been very substantial. Vietnam expenditures are broken out, so that the reader may make his own judgments about the future expenditures by applying his own assumptions about the future of the war in Vietnam—and the prospect of more Vietnams in the future.[1]

To the extent that the sources of funding for the military establishment extend beyond the Department of Defense, they are included in Table 2. We have assumed that half of the Atomic Energy Commission's activities are for military purposes. The cost of medical care, disability payments, and low-cost insurance for veterans of past wars, provided by the Veterans Administration, are listed as national security expenses, although it can be argued that many VA services are a substitute for welfare payments by other public authorities.

The Supporting Assistance program of the Agency for International Development is designed to improve the military and police forces of countries whose

Table 1
Department of Defense Expenditures, Fiscal Years 1961–1970

Fiscal Year	Actual Expenditures			In Constant 1958 $[1]			As % of GNP		
	For Vietnam	All other	Total	For Vietnam	All other	Total	For Vietnam	All other	Total
1961	—	$44,676,000,000	$44,676,000,000	—	$42,419,000,000	$42,419,000,000	—	8.8%	8.8%
1962	—	48,205,000,000	48,205,000,000	—	45,900,000,000	45,900,000,000	—	8.9%	8.9%
1963	—	49,973,000,000	49,973,000,000	—	46,050,000,000	46,050,000,000	—	8.7%	8.7%
1964	—	51,245,000,000	51,245,000,000	—	46,595,000,000	46,595,000,000	—	8.4%	8.4%
1965	$ 103,000,000	47,298,000,000	47,401,000,000	$ 91,000,000	41,562,000,000	41,653,000,000	*	7.2%	7.3%
1966	5,812,000,000	49,565,000,000	55,377,000,000	4,961,000,000	42,309,000,000	42,270,000,000	.8%	6.9%	7.7%
1967	20,133,000,000	48,198,000,000	68,331,000,000	16,789,000,000	40,192,000,000	56,981,000,000	2.6%	6.2%	8.7%
1968	26,547,000,000	50,826,000,000	77,373,000,000	19,879,000,000	40,266,000,000	60,145,000,000	2.9%	6.2%	9.1%
1969[2]	28,800,000,000	49,600,000,000	78,400,000,000	22,500,000,000	38,700,000,000	61,200,000,000	3.0%	5.3%	8.3%
1970[2]	24,900,000,000	53,000,000,000	77,900,000,000	18,700,000,000	39,700,000,000	58,400,000,000	2.6%	5.5%	8.1%

[1] Actual figures deflated by Dept. of Commerce deflator for federal purchase of goods and services.

*Less than .1%

[2] Figures for 1969 and 1970 are presented to the nearest hundred-million only.

Note: Excludes DOD civil functions such as rivers and harbors work of the Corps of Engineers.

SOURCE: *Budget of the United States Government*, Fiscal Year 1969, *Survey of Current Business*, August 1968; Releases of the U.S. Dept. of Defenses. See also Testimony of Robert C. Moot in *The Military Budget and National Economic Priorities*, Hearings before the Subcommittee on Economy in Government of the Joint Economic Committee, 91 Cong. 1 Sess. (1969), Part 1, p. 320. Mr. Moot, Assistant Secretary of Defense (Comptroller), argues in support of the official figures for Vietnam expenditures given here. These figures are challenged as substantial overestimates in Chapter 2, "Defense" in Charles Schultze, *Setting National Priorities: The 1971 Budget* (The Brookings Institution, 1970). For a more extended discussion of these and related issues, see Parts 1 and 2 of the referenced Hearings.

Table 2
National Security Expenditures, Fiscal Years 1961–1970

Fiscal Year	Department of Defense	Atomic Energy Commission[1]	Veterans Administration	Selective Service System	Total
1961	$44,676,000,000	$1,356,000,000	$5,376,000,000	$33,000,000	$51,441,000,000
1962	48,205,000,000	1,403,000,000	5,378,000,000	35,000,000	55,021,000,000
1963	49,973,000,000	1,379,000,000	5,666,000,000	35,000,000	57,053,000,000
1964	51,245,000,000	1,382,000,000	5,552,000,000	41,000,000	58,220,000,000
1965	47,401,000,000	1,312,000,000	5,634,000,000	43,000,000	54,390,000,000
1966	55,377,000,000	1,202,000,000	5,707,000,000	54,000,000	62,340,000,000
1967	68,331,000,000	1,132,000,000	6,366,000,000	58,000,000	75,887,000,000
1968	78,840,000,000	1,232,000,000	6,858,000,000	61,000,000	86,991,000,000
1969	77,877,000,000	1,225,000,000	7,263,000,000	65,000,000	86,430,000,000
1970[2]	76,504,000,000	1,230,000,000	8,196,000,000	74,000,000	86,004,000,000

[1]National security related portion assumed to = ½ of total.
[2]Figures for 1970 are estimates. The total for 1971 is estimated at about $81,000,000,000.

Note: In addition to the above figures, several federal subsidy programs are justified wholly or partially on military grounds. Examples include the maritime subsidy, the minerals stockpile, the federal Interstate Highway Program of 1956, the National Defense Education Act, the federal Program for Support of Airport Construction, and oil depletion allowance. Some portions of foreign economic aid and the space program are justified partially on national security grounds.

SOURCE: Federal Budget documents; U.S. Department of Defense releases.

stability is deemed vital to American security, but the money comes from the State Department rather than the Defense Department, and is not included in Table 2.

The Kennedy and Johnson administrations went to considerable lengths to distinguish between the military space program of the Department of Defense and the program of the National Aeronautics and Space Administration, but many major industrial entities that do business with NASA also depend on the Defense Department as their only other important customer in the aerospace industry. And since NASA pays its share of fixed costs, as well as helping to balance out the peaks and valleys in defense production, there is some justification for including some portion of the NASA budget as part of defense costs. Because of the uncertainty of the calculation, however, it is excluded. Similarly, there is no item for the Central Intelligence Agency, because its overall budget and the proportion devoted to clearly military purposes are both secret.

Of the total expenditures by the military establishment, 60 percent goes for the purchase of plant, equipment, and supplies, as distinguished from compensation for military and civilian personnel. And of this percentage, about 60 percent goes for material for which there is no significant commercial market: it consists exclusively of guns rather than butter. A tabulation for the fiscal years 1961–1970 appears in Table 3, showing that the military establishment is clearly the largest single customer in the United States and, by a wide margin, the largest single purchaser of goods for which there is no other market. For these unique goods, it represents in a sense a uniquely protected market, where continuing relationships are particularly important, since the unsuccessful seller cannot seek out other buyers.

The people who work in the military establishment themselves constitute a market for food, clothing and shelter, for automobiles and television sets and, later, for retirement cottages. As a group, their needs may be indistinguishable from those of the rest of the population, but in particular communities, and in some larger areas—southern California, tidewater Virginia—they dominate the economic landscape because of their sheer mass, a dominance that is most vividly apparent when a military base is abandoned or a big defense plant loses contracts. The comparative importance of the military establishment in each state is shown in Chart 1, which provides the percentage of total employment that is defense-generated. The kinds of organizations that figure in the list of defense contractors range from General Electric and General Motors to small machine shops. They are all parts of the military establishment.

For most of the people to whom defense dollars are paid, those dollars are their primary connection with the military establishment. But for some of the most important members of the establishment—civilian political appointees, key senior officers—the cash nexus is their least significant connection with it (as is the case with draftees as well). And some of the people who receive significant amounts of defense dollars—stockholders in businesses with mixed defense and commercial markets, academic administrators whose budgets include substantial

Table 3
Department of Defense Expenditures, by Category, Fiscal Years 1961–1970

Fiscal Year	Military-Oriented[1]	Capital Outlays and Supplies		Pay and Allowances	Total
		Common to Military and Civilian use[2]	Subtotal		
1961	$19,200,000,000	$ 8,900,000,000	$28,100,000,000	$16,600,000,000	$44,700,000,000
1962	20,900,000,000	9,500,000,000	30,400,000,000	17,800,000,000	48,200,000,000
1963	23,000,000,000	9,000,000,000	32,000,000,000	18,000,000,000	50,000,000,000
1964	22,400,000,000	9,700,000,000	32,100,000,000	19,100,000,000	51,200,000,000
1965	18,100,000,000	9,600,000,000	27,700,000,000	19,700,000,000	47,400,000,000
1966	20,600,000,000	12,700,000,000	33,300,000,000	22,100,000,000	55,400,000,000
1967	26,200,000,000	16,400,000,000	42,600,000,000	25,700,000,000	68,300,000,000
1968	31,000,000,000	25,000,000,000	56,000,000,000	22,000,000,000	78,000,000,000
1969	31,500,000,000	25,000,000,000	56,500,000,000	21,400,000,000	77,900,000,000
1970[3]	28,800,000,000	25,400,000,000	54,200,000,000	22,300,000,000	76,500,000,000

[1]Consists of procurement and RDT & E expenditures for weapons systems and related hard goods.
[2]Consists of all other purchases, including construction, services, and soft goods.
[3]Figures for 1970 are estimates. The estimate for the fiscal 1971 total is $71,200,000,000.

SOURCE: U.S. Department of Defense.

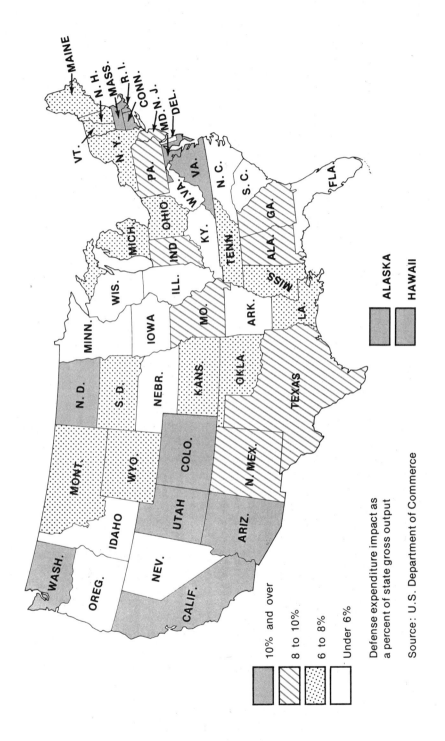

Defense expenditure impact as
a percent of state gross output

10% and over

8 to 10%

6 to 8%

Under 6%

ALASKA

HAWAII

Source: U.S. Department of Commerce

129

defense contracts—may not think of themselves as part of the military establishment at all.

The major population elements in the military establishment are military personnel, direct-hire civilians, and employees of defense contractors. There is a fourth large category of persons primarily dependent on members of the first three groups: wives and dependent children; tradesmen, from the military tailor to the lunchroom proprietor around the corner from the defense plant, whose customers are members of the military establishment; the professional men—lawyers and accountants, bankers and brokers, public relations counselors and trade journalists—who serve defense contractors; the retired military men for whom the establishment provides a second income, and often the basis for their postmilitary retirement occupation;[2] and others various degrees removed.

A former Pentagon reporter for the *New York Times,* Jack Raymond, noted that the reach of the military budget is larger than generally imagined. As he observed, "It provides, for example, $6,000 for flowers for American battle monuments. Flower growers, too, can be a part of the military–industrial complex." And so can the many other peripheral groups that contribute, whether overtly or covertly, to the furthering of the military–industrial image in the public consciousness.[3]

How far should such a list extend? Should it include the labor leaders of defense plant unions? The editors and publishers of newspapers in communities with substantial defense plants or military bases? The ministers of the principal churches in such communities? The members and staffs of the Armed Services Committees and military appropriations subcommittees of the House and Senate? The congressmen from districts with substantial defense business? The president of a university seeking to retain (or to attract) faculty whose research interests are dependent (to a greater or lesser extent) on defense research assistance? While it seems possible to define and measure the population of the military establishment, the fact is that the list of persons ultimately connected with the military is almost infinitely extensible.

Nevertheless, several conclusions about the population of the military establishment appear from Tables 4 and 5. About 40 percent of the people are not directly employed by the government; most who are so employed are probably not career employees, at least among the rank and file of military personnel. (The line between career and noncareer is harder to draw among civilian employees since the civilian retirement system does not create the inducements to career commitment after the first few years of service that the military retirement system does.)

The military establishment as an organization is usually visualized as a monolith, but in reality it is more like a modern structure of prestressed concrete, held together by the tensions between opposing forces. From 1947 until 1961, the Department of Defense was a loose confederation of independent fiefdoms, uneasily presided over by the Secretary of Defense. The Army, the Navy, the Marine Corps, and the Air Force controlled their own budgets and determined

Table 4

Defense-Generated Employment, Fiscal Years 1965-1967

Category	1965	1967
Armed services	2,716,000	3,350,000
Civilian employees of the federal government	919,000	1,088,000
Employees of state and local governments	13,000	19,000
Employees of defense contractors, subcontractors, and their suppliers	2,101,000	2,972,000
Total:	5,749,000	7,429,000
Occupational group of civilian employees included above:		
Professional workers	495,000	635,000
Managers, officials, and proprietors	255,000	333,000
Salesworkers	66,000	95,000
Clerical and kindred workers	567,000	745,000
Craftsmen, foremen, and kindred workers	615,000	860,000
Operatives (semi-skilled)	710,000	990,000
Service workers	135,000	165,000
Laborers and farm workers	190,000	255,000
Total:	3,033,000	4,078,000

SOURCE: Monthly Labor Review, September 1967, pp. 10, 18.

their own force structures, with a minimum of coordination among them, although the President and the Secretary of Defense did determine totals. Discussion had taken place on how the Department of Defense should be organized as a department, to deal with the problem of strategic nuclear war, or with the development of new weapons systems, but the controversies that engaged their protagonists most intensely were those that turned on the quasi-theological question of roles and missions. Were missiles a new form of artillery, and therefore within the proper domain of the Army, or a new kind of airplane and, therefore, the preserve of the Air Force? Could the Army properly use close support aircraft painted Army color and flown by pilots in Army uniforms, or should these planes be painted Air Force color and flown by pilots in Air Force uniforms? How far should the Marines carry amphibious warfare beyond the beachhead?

At its inception, the new Defense Department was still adjusting to the shrinkage of Army manpower from a World War II high of 8,226,373 men in 1945 to a low of 591,487 in 1950, just before the Korean War. The most violent controversies arose over scarce congressional appropriations, as in the 1949 fight between the carrier admirals and the Air Force proponents of strategic bombing, when the fight was carried into the press and rival columnists were enlisted by the opposing sides.

These controversies extended to intraservice rivalry as well. Within the Army,

Table 5
Department of Defense Employment by Category, 1961–1968, as of June 30 of each year.

			Military Manpower[1]				
Year	Career Officers	Non-Career Officers[2]	Sub-Total, Officers	Career Enlisted Men	Non-Career Enlisted Men[3]	Sub-Total, Enlisted Men	Total Military Manpower
1961	246,000	69,000	315,000[5]	1,030,000	1,129,000	2,159,000	2,473,000
1962	271,000	72,000	343,000	1,047,000	1,406,000	2,452,000	2,796,000
1963	257,000	77,000	334,000	1,014,000	1,341,000	2,355,000	2,689,000
1964	255,000	83,000	338,000	993,000	1,345,000	2,338,000	2,676,000
1965	251,000	88,000	339,000	998,000	1,307,000	2,305,000	2,644,000
1966	257,000	92,000	349,000	996,000	1,736,000	2,733,000	3,082,000
1967	264,000	120,000	384,000	996,000[6]	1,985,000[6]	2,981,000	3,365,000
1968[6]	278,000	118,000	396,000	996,000	2,020,000	3,016,000	3,412,000

			Civilian and Total Manpower			
	GS-1 through GS-7	GS-8 through GS-18[4]	Subtotal, Classified Employees	Wage Board Employees	Total Civilian Manpower	Total Department of Defense Manpower
1961	316,000	178,000	506,000	536,000	1,042,000	3,515,000
1962	326,000	191,000	525,000	544,000	1,070,000	3,866,000
1963	313,000	203,000	528,000	522,000	1,050,000	3,739,000
1964	308,000	217,000	536,000	494,000	1,030,000	3,706,000
1965	305,000	226,000	547,000	487,000	1,034,000	3,678,000
1966	341,000	237,000	594,000	544,000	1,138,000	4,220,000
1967	374,000	249,000	654,000	648,000	1,303,000	4,668,000
1968	NA	NA	675,000	642,000	1,317,000	4,729,000

[1] Excludes officer candidates such as academy cadets and midshipmen, aviation cadets, etc.
[2] Less than four years of service.
[3] Four years or less of service, except Army (three years or less).
[4] Includes P.L. 313 and other salaried employees. GS-1 through GS-7 are primarily clerical and secretarial positions. GS-8 through GS-18 are primarily managerial and professional positions. PL. 313 covers high-level scientific and technical positions.
[5] Approximated from sample and inventory data.
[6] Estimated.
NA = Not available
Note: Details may not add to totals due to rounding.
SOURCE: U.S. Department of Defense.

the "technical services"[4] had for decades successfully resisted efforts to streamline and integrate their operations. In the Navy, the old-line bureaus presented the same problem. Even the newest service, the Air Force, suffered from the efforts, often successful, of the Strategic Air Command (SAC) to dominate the entire organization.

    Some small beginnings to resolve these conflicts into a unitary, orderly process had been made in the 1949, 1953, and 1958 amendments to the National Security Act, which established the legal basis for a single Department of Defense, and Secretary of Defense Thomas S. Gates had taken a firmer hand than his predecessors in reducing rivalries. But during 1961 and 1962, under Secretary Robert S. McNamara, essential new machinery was created, particularly the "five-year program and force structure," to begin to resolve the conflicts in more orderly fashion. The Systems Analysis shop was created within the Office of the Secretary of Defense to give the Secretary the analytical tools to evaluate proposals from the individual services . . . and the services themselves were reorganized, substantially overhauling the Army technical service and Navy bureau structures.

What has emerged is still by no means monolithic. As Chart 2 makes clear, the line of operational command of forces in the field goes from the President and the Secretary of Defense through the Joint Chiefs of Staff to the commanders in chief of the eight field commands.[5] The military departments—Army, Navy, Air Force—train and supply the men, and develop and procure the equipment for the operating commands, but there are no units under the direct operational authority of any military department. While this is an accurate description of existing arrangements, it is not the whole truth. If Chart 2 was shown to field-grade officers—colonels and majors—now on active duty, many of them would deny that it represented the formal command arrangements, and would insist that the military services do control their own troops in the field. For these officers, the Department of Defense is not an overarching organization of which their service is a part. When they speak colloquially of the department, or "DOD," they do not customarily include their own organizations, but only the Secretary of Defense and his staff (technically the Office of the Secretary of Defense, or OSD), a separate and alien entity with which their organization is forced occasionally to deal, rather like a foreign power.

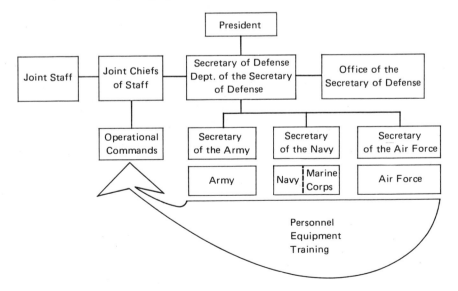

Their belief about the lines of command is partly true. The people who do the work for the Joint Chiefs are the four hundred officers of the Joint Staff—with several appendages which swell their numbers to perhaps twice that figure. These officers prepare the memoranda on proposed policy issues, take them through the various stages of evolution—first the blue, then the buff, then the green, then the purple (if the Joint Chiefs disagree), and finally the white memorandum, which goes to the Secretary. But the Joint Staff doesn't do the real work. That is done by the staffs in each military department, who prepare the service position on every issue, and these positions are then negotiated out, if possible, within the Joint Staff. The primary role of each member of the Joint Chiefs, except the chairman, is to serve as chief of his own service, and he is briefed for the weekly Chiefs' session not by the Joint Staff, but by his own service staff.

This arrangement is what the Congress had in mind when it amended the military unification legislation in 1958 to include a specific prohibition against the creation of a single general staff, and the numerical restrictions on the size of the Joint Staff are intended to carry out this explicit policy. Congress feared the power of a fully militarized Department of Defense, and sought to perpetuate interservice competition, or, as it has been put more cynically, a situation in which one service could be played off against the others. This competition may be an important tool in preserving civilian control.

In this process, the services provide a powerful assist. In 1961, for example, the Secretary of Defense transferred the strategic intelligence staffs out of the military departments, to form the Defense Intelligence Agency, reporting to the Secretary of Defense through the Joint Chiefs. This was done in part on the ground that strategic intelligence was a function of the operating commands and should be placed in operations, rather than with training and supply. When the intelligence staffs were transferred out of the military departments, the departments began to build up their staffs in areas called, euphemistically, "foreign technology," so that they were able to compete, to some extent at least, with the new interservice agency.

By the same token, the legislative liaison staffs of the individual services vastly outnumbered the legislative liaison staff of the Secretary of Defense—and his efforts to reduce their numbers have thus far been unavailing. Tampering with these staffs means intervening directly in long-established relationships with key legislators and congressional committees; in an organization the size of a military department, the organization can compensate internally for externally imposed reductions. Service links with the Congress, and particularly with the Armed Services Committees and their senior members and staff, are closer than the links between the Secretary of Defense and his staff and the Congress and congressional staff. The controversy over these relationships resulted in the disbanding in 1965 of the Capitol Hill active Reserve units, including the famous 999th Air Force Reserve Squadron commanded by Major General Barry M. Goldwater, USAF, which permitted eighty-three Congressmen and Senators to spend short periods of active duty in such prime military observation posts as London and Paris. But the 999th was only a surface manifestation of a more deep-seated and persistent phenomenon.

In the field, the joint operational commands exercise more authority in form than they do in fact over their separate service components. Until recently, the principal staff officers of the service components of a joint command—for example, the Assistant Chief of Staff for Operations, U.S. Army, Pacific—would outrank their opposite numbers for the entire joint command itself. Even in Vietnam, the complaint has frequently been made, and not infrequently well documented, that service interests have not been subordinated to common concerns. While civilians have been agonizingly conscious of the Vietnam war's needs and demands dominating the political landscape, military observers complain bitterly that the Pentagon practices business as usual—that the military departments do not give the war priority over the internal needs of the military organization; that command rotation policies, for example, were designed to give everyone a turn, rather than to achieve the most efficient level of operations, and that departmental research and development programs have not been sufficiently oriented to the needs of the war.

Beyond the Department of Defense itself, the organizational picture is even less monolithic. The Atomic Energy Commission, for example, determines with the advice of the Defense Department the amount of weapons-grade nuclear material to be produced, subject only to White House review. The serpentine wall between the military and civilian space programs has been difficult to trace, and is likely to shift significantly depending on the perspective from which it is viewed. The management of clandestine and covert operations of a military or quasi-military nature has reportedly been a bone of contention between the CIA and the Department of Defense for some time. And defense contractors involved in the development of new weapons systems not infrequently find that they must choose between the service staff position and the position of the Secretary of Defense's own staff—and they choose at their peril.

In the TFX (tactical fighter, experimental) competition, for example, the essential difference between the Boeing and the General Dynamics proposals was that General Dynamics bet that the Secretary of Defense meant what he said about producing a common Air Force-Navy airplane, and Boeing bet that the services would persuade the Secretary to forget it. Boeing lost. In the same vein, a major international incident was precipitated when the Royal Air Force, listening only to its opposite numbers in the U.S. Air Force, and ignoring the analysts in the Office of the Secretary of Defense, as well as those on the President's Science Advisory Committee, assured their superiors that America's Skybolt missile program, on which Britain hoped to build an essential element of its strategic air power, would not be abandoned.

Each of the services has its own link with its major industrial suppliers through a kind of alumni association—the Association of the United States Army, the Navy League, the Marine Corps League, and the Air Force Association. These associations relate retired military personnel to the more active elements in the Reserves, with financial support from major defense contractors. Each association, not surprisingly, takes a generally expansionist view of its alma mater. But this view may bring it into conflict with the other associations, or even with the civilian hierarchy of the military department, as in 1963, when the Air Force Association opposed the administration's policy of nuclear restraint, and Secretary of the Air Force Eugene Zuckert refused to attend the Association's reception in his honor.

The military establishment, then, is no simple pyramid of power. But its base is more than broad enough to accommodate a good deal of internal bureaucratic conflict without diminishing significantly its overall impact on American society.

NOTES

1. To place these figures in a longer historical perspective, President Harry S. Truman in 1949 put a $14.4 billion ceiling on defense expenditures (5.4 percent of the GNP for that year). The combined budgets of the War and Navy departments were $792,037,000 for 1929 and $6,202,435,000 for 1939. For an important analysis of the role of defense in future federal budgets, see Chapter 2, "Defense," in *Setting National Priorities: The 1971 Budget*, Charles Schultze, ed., The Brookings Institution, 1970.

2. By 1980, expenditures for retirement pay are projected to be roughly one-fifth of the total budget for military personnel, and by 2020, almost 30 percent.

3. Jack Raymond, "The Growing Threat of Our Military–Industrial Complex," *Harvard Business Review*, Vol. 46, No. 3 (May–June 1968), p. 53.

4. Adjutant General, Army Medical Service, Chemical Warfare, Finance, Military Police, Ordnance, Quartermaster, Transportation. (The Signal Corps is considered partly combat and partly service.)

5. These are currently the Alaskan, Atlantic, Continental Air Defense, European, Pacific, Southern, Strategic Air, and Strike commands. The last is an emergency fire-fighting force around the world. As an indication of how rapidly bureaucracies become stratified, the United States command in Vietnam, by far the largest of the commands, does not report directly to the Joint Chiefs, but through the commander in chief of the Pacific command.

TOWARD AN
ALL-VOLUNTEER MILITARY

Morris Janowitz

For over twenty-five years, the United States relied on Selective Service as the means of obtaining military manpower. By July 1973, this system is scheduled to be terminated by Congress. Military authorities have set January 1, 1973 as the target date for the transition to an all-volunteer system, hoping to achieve "zero-level" draft calls by that time.

Thus far the chief means of realizing an all-volunteer armed force has been an economic incentive. The revised schedules will raise the basic pay of a recruit to $268 a month and, if we add allowances, the effective total comes to $4,872 a year, or close to the symbolic $5,000 pay that many analysts thought necessary to achieve an all-volunteer armed force. But a substantial pay raise without a more thorough-going reorganization of the armed forces and, indeed, a rethinking of the entire meaning of the military profession, may leave us far from the intended objective.

So far, the steps to adapt the armed forces to an all-volunteer system have been limited. There has been some improvement in the physical character of barracks facilities for enlisted personnel, a wider latitude in the rules about personal appearance, and an alteration of the daily routine of garrison life. In the area of race relations, there have been extensive training programs and group discussions, which take into account the new self-consciousness of black personnel. But on the crucial question of the relationship of the military to a *career* pattern, a relationship which links the military to later civilian life, there has been little thought, particularly as it affects officers. Many of the younger military are committed to the success of the all-volunteer system, which they see as an opportunity to institute needed reforms, but the exodus of some of the most intelligent and innovative officers from the ground forces—in part because of the reduction of the military total—squeezes out some of the men who could have taken the lead in the necessary rethinking and reorganization.

Reprinted from *The Public Interest*, No. 27 (Spring 1972), pp. 104–117. Copyright © by National Affairs, Inc., 1972.

On balance, it appears that the United States military will be reduced, by 1975, to an overall total of 1,750,000 men;[1] in fact, the possibility of a force of 1,500,000 men thereafter cannot be ruled out. The reduction in personnel re-flects national policy to limit the overall size of the armed forces and the number of troops stationed abroad. The cost of military equipment will rise at a steady rate because of the new machinery that military authorities believe they require; so will personnel costs. To keep the military budget within limits, the trend will be to reduce the size of active-duty personnel. Following the experience of Great Britain, the United States forces will most likely fail (but by a lesser margin) to meet the authorized requirements. An American equivalent of that most descriptive British term, "shortfall," will come into vogue. No doubt a range of factors will account for the failure of the military to meet their recruit-ment quotas: low prestige of the military profession, family dissatisfaction, ex-cessive job rotation, underemployment during early assignments. However, it is clear that the decline in career prospects will operate as the most powerful nega-tive incentive. Why enter a profession whose career and promotion opportunities are highly uncertain and declining? A powerful element of a self-fulfilling prophecy is already at work; each reduction in forces serves only to dampen new recruitment, especially officer recruitment. Paradoxically, the faster the initial reduction to a long-run troop level the more readily the adaptation can be made to a volunteer force.

But all of this obscures the fact that an all-volunteer force for the first time will be a professional force and the United States will have to confront an issue which it has not had to face before—how a full-time professional military fits into the larger framework of a democratic society. Until now, under Selective Service, there was an admixture of civilians for whom military service was an excursus in their lives; because of this large leavening the army was not walled off from the society. At the same time, the armed services always thought of the officers as a cadre which could be quickly expanded, on the outbreak of war, to include large numbers of reservists and newly inducted officers from civilian life. But given our present doctrine of deterrence, the army that is being created will be a "force-in-being," a self-contained, technically-trained force which presum-ably will be adequate to maintain the "balance of terror" in nuclear war.

The problem before us, then, is what *kind* of armed forces does a modern democratic society need, and how does professional service in the army, for officers and enlisted men, mesh with civilian life? In short, the military is no longer the distinctive, isolated, "heroic" *calling* of the past, maintaining the "honor" of the society, but is now a *profession* and *occupation* subject to all the vicissitudes which life is hazard to in a bureaucratic setting. Given this change-over, major reorganizations are necessary in the areas of education, career system, deployment, and participation of the military in civilian life, if the men of the quality that is necessary are to be attracted to the service and if the military is to be compatible with the standards of a democratic society. It is to these problems that this essay addresses itself.

The Redefinition of Career

The all-volunteer service requires a fundamental redefinition of the content and duration of the military career. A significant number of both officers and enlisted men will continue to serve for six years or less; for them, military experience is an interlude in an essentially civilian existence. But for another segment, military service will cover an expanded period of time, often up to twenty years. But where do they go after that? For this group, military service must be redefined as one stage in a two-step career in public service, military service being the first step and entry into the civil service the second. In this way the idea of a career can be shaped.

For enlisted men and women the successful completion of a specified period of service, such as two or three periods of enlistment, would constitute effective entrance into civil service employment. The United States Civil Service or the Department of Labor would have the responsibility for placing these people in the federal service or, by negotiation, with state or local governments. Such an approach would make recruitment manageable and insure a higher quality of personnel. It would also make possible reform of the pension system and reduce costs. When an enlisted man transferred to the civil establishment, his pension benefits would be incorporated in his new job and paid upon retirement from civil employment. Or he could, if he wished, opt for private employment and take a military-type pension. Such a system is operating today in the Federal Republic of Germany with considerable effectiveness.

The pattern of the officer career would be restructured to permit a more flexible system of exit from active duty. Today, most officers leave either after short-term duty (two to five years of obligatory service) or after twenty years of service. But an exit with appropriate pension protection after ten to twelve years is essential for the flow of personnel which takes advantage of the newer skills of the younger men. As in the case of enlisted personnel, after a specified number of years of service officers should have the option of joining the civilian government establishment or have some vested, transferable pension rights. While such an approach can be fully applied only after the present reduction in the size of the officer corps is accomplished, it could be implemented immediately for new officers entering the system.

The armed forces today face the trauma of reduction in force and at the same time the need to retain the most able personnel during a period of contracting opportunities. The impact falls most heavily on the Army and particularly on its officers, the young captains and majors who must anticipate a slow and limited rate of advancement. This is the so-called "hump in rank" which develops during a contraction after a period of rapid expansion. The negative effects are already being felt in the high proportion of able young officers who are planning to leave after their short-term obligatory service.

A system which permits retirement after ten to twelve years of service is an essential step to enable the armed forces to retire with dignity those of less competence and, at the same time, to reduce the hump-in-rank problem.

However, it is equally essential to deal with the more serious problems posed by the presently expanded number of general officers. The ratio of general officers to total military personnel has grown steadily since the mid-1950s, yet, despite the overall reduction of personnel, the Pentagon is reluctant to force out general officers. The excessive number of such officers has a very negative effect as the military struggles to adapt to a new environment. The ground force, in particular, is sharply divided between its junior and midcareer officers who actually fought in Vietnam, and the cadre of senior officers who flew over the battlefield or were in command management positions.

The incorporation of men in their forties into the general officer group is essential to heal the breach and to offer an incentive for able midcareer officers to remain in the service. But existing retirement procedures are only partially adequate to deal with this problem because of the large numbers involved. A special commission of the Secretary of Defense is necessary to handle the major reduction (as much as 50 or 60 percent) in the number of active-duty general officers.

Providing a Home

Over the years the United States armed forces have evolved a deployment system which reassigns manpower through the continuous movement of personnel. The pattern is justified in the name of preventing stagnation, training personnel for higher command, and adapting the organization to change. During the period between World War I and World War II, the necessity of training a small cadre which could be expanded readily during wartime gave validity to such a service-wide reassignment system. In the post-Vietnam period, as we move toward an all-volunteer force of less than two million, these procedures are outmoded.

The practice is needlessly expensive, it is disruptive of military effectiveness and solidarity, and it serves as one of the major sources of discontent with the conditions of military life. The frequent fluctuations of manpower strength since 1945 to some extent made these patterns of rotation necessary, but the all-volunteer force will have a more stable level of manpower, thus making possible a more stable system of personnel deployment.

In the case of the Army a modified version of the British regimental structure is required. Each enlisted man and each officer would be attached to a basic unit, and a significant portion of his military career would be spent within that brigade, and in rotation of assignments within the brigade. When he is rotated out of his basic unit for staff duty and advanced schooling, he could be expected to return to his original unit. Overseas assignments and rotation home would be within the brigade system. For the Navy a home port concept, and for the Air Force a home base, would be the equivalent of an Army brigade. These are not novelties but regular practices in other armies.

One of the most powerful sources of negative attitudes toward career military service, especially among young officers, is the feeling that their talents are underutilized. In the past, military personnel were less sensitive to their immediate assignment, since there was always the assumption that some future war would "break out" and they would be effectively engaged. But in the present political context, officers want to establish a linkage between their immediate assignment and the military purpose. The reliance of the military on short-term officers and the emergence of the concept of deterrence make the issue of boredom and the day-to-day job especially relevant.

One of the changes urgently required is that operational units be given some degree of responsibility for military training. The current practice is to centralize training in specialized training units, a practice which was justified during a period of rapid mobilization and expansion. The allocation of training functions to operational units would make it possible for personnel, especially junior officers, to be more fully engaged; it would also produce important fiscal savings. In many support, technical, and even educational units, underutilization is less a matter of inadequate daily work loads. Here the morale problem derives from the failure of military personnel to be incorporated into the life of the larger military establishment; they feel excluded from the basic mission and purpose. In such units personnel could be organized into the equivalent of fully-alerted reserve units with monthly evening assignments and annual field training operations.

The armed forces have developed extensive educational programs as means of upgrading their personnel, such as programs of basic literacy and the completion of high school and even college-level work. These programs generally make use of civilian personnel and civilian institutions. While such arrangements are generally appropriate, there is considerable room for the employment of qualified active-duty military personnel. Such assignments would not interfere with regular active-duty tasks since they would be secondary and after-duty assignments.

A New Kind of Education

In all the services, an officer's career is linked to an elaborate system of professional education—initial academy or ROTC schooling plus a three-stage, professional, in-service educational step ladder, to which is added specialized courses. For an important minority, there is also an advanced degree at a civilian institution. The successful officer following the prescribed career will spend as much as 25 to 30 percent of his career in a classroom. Military officers require extensive education; moreover, some of this education is a fringe benefit in that it assists them in the transition to civilian employment after retirement. But the present system is wasteful: It is often mechanical and repetitious, and it involves costly logistical support and a change of duty station. Also, it is generally true that the higher the level of in-service schooling, the more the training becomes merely a form of indoctrination in official policy. Consequently, much military education is resented by military officers as a waste of time of effective portions of their professional career.

Military education, like the reassignment system, is based on the traditional notion of the "outbreak" of war and the need for rapid mobilization of a mass armed force. The services believe that they require a large pool of highly trained professional officers who have been exposed to higher professional schools, so that if the military had to expand rapidly, enough trained officers would be available for rapid promotion. But with the advent of nuclear weapons and the doctrine of deterrence, the military has become more a force-in-being and less a cadre for mobilization; consequently, the existing notions of military education need to be revised.

With the termination of Selective Service, the number of officer recruits who will enter the active service will decline, their academic quality will be lower, and they will be much less representative of the nation as a whole, being drawn largely from the South and Southwest and from rural and small-town areas. In order to maintain the number, quality, representativeness, and vitality of short-term, active-duty reserve officers, two basic changes are required.

First, the military services need to place a stronger emphasis on Officer Candidate Schools for recruitment and training of new officers. Young men who have successfully completed two years of college should be eligible. Many men in the middle of their college careers seek a break in their education, and can be expected to return to college after two to four years of military service; others will be expected to work toward the completion of their college degree while on active duty.

Second, any college student in the United States—either on entrance into college, or when he becomes a junior—should have access to a collegiate ROTC program. In addition to the existing and modified ROTC programs in each of the ten major metropolitan areas, there should be a composite ROTC program which would enroll students from any accredited college in the vicinity. In a particular metropolitan area, one of the existing ROTC units should be responsible for the administration and conduct of the program, but the program should be available to all colleges in the area. In many metropolitan centers, this arrangement is being carried out informally; but it needs to be formalized and publicized.

Basic changes in the nature of officer education are required. First, the format of service academy training needs to be modified in order to insure the maximum integration of the new officer into civilian society. Two paths (or a combination of the two) are possible. One would be to permit all or a portion of the junior class to study at a civilian university in the United States or abroad. Another would be to extend the academy program to five years, one of which would be devoted to a work experience with the Peace Corps or Vista or to some other form of community or business employment.

Second, the three-step, in-service schooling system needs to be consolidated. At a minimum, it should be converted into a two-level system. The most direct approach would be to eliminate the National War College and increase the *inter-service* component of the colleges of the three services. Much of the National War College curriculum repeats that of the service war colleges; its atmosphere is doctrinaire and, since it is located in Washington, it places an undue emphasis on current events. The services should make more use of intensive short courses of one or two weeks to deal with new organizational and strategic doctrine. These courses would not involve costly logistical support or change of station, and they would be more flexible as to content and timing. Equally, there should be more alternatives to attendance at the service schools, and their importance in the system of promotion should be reduced. Instead of attendance at a service school, attendance at a civilian institution or participation in a short, intensive military course would be an acceptable substitute. This would increase the diversity of skills, backgrounds, and experience in the armed forces.

The Question of Authority

The military must face openly and candidly the question of authority. The United States Marine Corps may be able, as its top commanders hope, to maintain its traditional organizational code of repressive basic training and formal ritual and protocol. This may be possible since the Marine Corps requires only a small number of men, and any advanced industrialized society produces sufficient young men who are attracted to the aggressive symbolism and "killer" imagery of its enlisted ranks. The United States Marine Corps is a carry-over from nineteenth-century gentlemen-type officers with an admixture of toughs in the ranks. The Marines will persist, but they are more and more incompatible with the emerging political and social values of the larger society—especially in a period in which United States foreign policy operates under the banner "no more Vietnams" or its equivalents, and the purpose of the military is to maintain a defensive posture of deterrent force, operating under the conception of a constabulary.

There is sufficient experience to show that a combat-ready force, fully sensitive to its "heroic" traditions and under the closest operational control, can be trained and maintained without brutality, personal degradation, or "Mickey Mouse" discipline. The armed forces must review their routines, for they do not fully realize the extent to which, in comparison with other highly effective forces, they maintain outmoded procedures. (Thus, for example; saluting on base serves no purpose but to degrade the act; saluting must be reserved for crucial and selected formations.) Military traditions, military ceremonies, and esprit de corps are essential—even more so—in an all-volunteer force. Moreover, these changes will have to be generated by the military itself within the context of standards set by the civilian society. In order to modify and modernize military discipline an all-service commission on these issues needs to be established and a comparison made with the experiences of our allies.

Relation to Civilian Life

The amenities supplied by the military base are essential for the well-being of the military officer and his family. The military establishment is more of a welfare state than civilian society, and these benefits are important for the retention of personnel. Nevertheless, there is considerable evidence that the military base tends to isolate the military professional from the larger civilian society. In recent years, the Department of Defense has sought to expand off-base housing under the assumption that such facilities are less expensive, or that they relieve the military of the complex of overhead activities associated with military community housing.

Yet there is no reason to believe that off-base housing enhances recruitment or effectively integrates the military into civilian society. Relocation of residence into a civilian community does not necessarily produce social integration into civilian society. It may, in fact, produce an off-base ghetto of military families. Off-base housing tends to separate military families from military base facilities, and exposes the family to disruptive pressures so long as high rates of rotation are maintained, especially under conditions where the male head of the household must frequently be away on duty assignments. A delicate balance needs to be maintained. The opportunity for base housing, in particular and appropriate areas, should be expanded. However, the essential issue is that military personnel should have some choice as between residence on or off base. But if the question is one of integration into civilian society, the issue of civic participation is more important than location of residence. What is involved is participation in the voluntary associations which are characteristic of the larger society.

The vitality of the military profession depends on a delicate balance between a special sense of inner-group loyalty and participation in the larger society. Rather than residence per se, the quality of integration in civilian society depends on personal initiative and membership in voluntary religious and community associations. Military regulations and practice encourage participation within the format of nonpartisanship, that is, without direct affiliation to political party groups. But rotation from one assignment to another limits the ability of a military man and his family to make contact with their community. Some research studies indicate that the level of community participation of military personnel is similar to that of persons in other occupations which have a high degree of job rotation. One would hope, therefore, that the introduction of a modified regimental system with less job rotation would increase the possibilities for more meaningful community integration.

However, new perspectives on civic participation are required if the military profession, under an all-volunteer force, is not to become socially isolated and if it is to maintain and enhance its self-respect. In West Germany the idea that an army man is a civilian in uniform has been pressed to the point at which regular personnel—both officer and enlisted—are permitted to stand for political elections while on active duty. In the American context, the need to avoid a political party affiliation probably is essential. However, military personnel should be permitted to serve on local school boards, run in nonpartisan local elections, and be members of government advisory boards and public panels wherever they have the essential qualifications, competencies, and interest.

But the issue goes deeper. It is not the responsibility of military personnel to defend and publicize the official military policies of the United States. This is the responsibility of the elected national officials who make policy. However, in the contemporary scene, as the volunteer service becomes more and more a reality, military personnel are highly sensitive to the charge that they are mere "mercenaries." Military personnel who wish to articulate the goals and purposes of the military in a democratic society cannot be deprived of participation in community and public affairs.

By law, and particularly by judicial decree, military personnel now exercise an element of free speech and citizen petition. In a truly pluralistic society, military personnel on active duty should be able to attend educational, community, and public affairs meetings and to state their definition of the legitimacy of their profession. In short, new definitions of civic participation need to emerge which are broader than the existing ones, but still compatible with the nonpartisan stance of American military law and traditions.

Redefining the Profession

Men select a profession or occupation for a variety of motives, and in part by accident or the sheer force of immediate circumstances. The military in the future, as in the past, will recruit from among the sons of military families—the same pattern also holds for other professions. But because of the overriding importance of the military, it is essential that there be no concentration of military families (difficult though it may be to define that level). In fact, it is doubtful whether the military could be managed without the particular input of the sons of military families.

The military has distinctive characteristics as to the style of life it offers. In the years ahead, under a volunteer force, some of this distinctiveness will no doubt be maintained. There is also an element of activism in the military life of movement and outdoor living. Even foreign travel attracts some, and leads them to remain. Yet the scope for travel and residence abroad will decline, and again the British experience indicates that this limitation operates to inhibit recruitment and retention.

The issues of professional morale and self-respect, of course, are vital and involve the background of prolonged hostilities in Indochina and their aftermath. First, there is the issue of atrocities: their origin and character, their extent, and their appropriate punishment. From the point of view of the military profession, the orderly process of military investigation and military justice constitutes the essential mechanism for coming to terms with these grave issues. But this problem is more complex; it involves an examination of the training and outlook of the United States military in Vietnam, including an understanding of the impact of that particular environment on the behavior of Americans under combat conditions. It is not an issue that can be avoided.

Second, the conduct of the war in Vietnam brings into question the role of military advice and the adequacy of military planning. In the post–Korean War period the military expressed the "never again" concept, and strongly resisted the idea of a land force commitment on the mainland of Asia. This strategic perspective was embodied in the person of General Matthew Ridgway, even though other views were found in the military. In Indochina, basic decision making was managed in all three Presidential administrations by the small group in the office of the President. Vietnam was a President's war. Whatever may have been the initial opposition (or more accurately, reluctance to become involved), it gave way and the military displayed their traditional dedication once the decision was made by civilians. However, many military issues and failures need to be clarified. Once it became engaged in the war, the United States military accepted the notion of "victory through air power"; the limitations of that doctrine which were evident in World War II and Korea were ignored. How does one explain this extraordinary shift in military doctrine, and why was it accepted by the Joint Chiefs? These are issues for professional self-clarification.

But it is the purpose and the goals of military institutions that are the key elements in the quality of an all-volunteer force. Much has been written about the changing role of the military in contemporary society. The military profession is divided and unclear as to how much of the emerging doctrines it will accept. The notion that the military is mainly in the "killing business" dies slowly. It is difficult for any profession and especially the military to see its function alter and change.

Toward a New Military Role

Basically, the goal of effective deterrence requires a break in military traditions for the United States, although important steps have already been taken in this direction. The military will face real organizational problems in attempting to maintain its viability. A variety of tailor-made suggestions supplies no realistic basis for change. For example, while there may be specific lessons to be learned from the Israeli model, differences both in military tasks and in political settings render such an approach irrelevant to the American context. The same can be said for the Swedish format. If analogies with foreign armies are to be drawn, it is the experience of Great Britain with its volunteer force that is the closest. Likewise, monumental schemes for giving the military new functions tend to be more ideological than practical. The tasks of the American military remain, in the first instance, military.

There is a second instance, however, and the military can and should have multiple functions. The deterrent force will have vast standby resources. To reconstruct the American military it will be necessary that these resources be utilized for a wide range of national emergency functions. A force-in-being of one and one-half million, with only a ground force element stationed in Western Europe for NATO, will present considerable available manpower. The basic issue is not (as traditionalists see it) one of diverting the military from its fundamental mission. In fact, the military has traditionally been engaged in a variety of tasks, but the nature and content of such work changes. Not to make use of its standby capacity would weaken the vitality of the military, unduly isolate it from civilian society, and represent a vast wastage of valuable resources.

Clearly, the military cannot engage in activities or programs which are better performed by civilian agencies. The armed forces cannot make up for the failure of civilian education and welfare, although they can and do make their contributions in these areas as a result of their routine activities. Moreover, in a democratic society the military must be removed from domestic police activities except in rare and grave crises. But a military committed to deterrence will have considerable ability to respond to emergencies, broadly defined, and to improvise. The armed forces are already involved in the control of natural disasters. Floods, hurricanes, and the like pose emergency situations which require the military's flexible resources. To natural disasters can be added the increasing number of "man-made" emergencies: oil spills, power failures, and chemical and atomic disasters. The armed forces are already indispensable in a vast array of air and sea rescue work, to which is being added, on an experimental basis, medical evacuation. But the major frontier facing the military in the years ahead rests in environmental control and in the handling of particular aspects of pollution and resources destruction.

The armed forces of the future will have to understand and participate in arms control arrangements. A case can be made for renaming them national emergency forces (as suggested by Albert Biderman) in order to emphasize their evolving character. I have made use of the term constabulary forces. But it makes little sense to argue about new labels. It is more important that civilian society assume an active role in directing the military to redefine its professional outlook so that it will understand that peace keeping through a military presence, deterrence, and participation in the control of national emergencies constitute the modern definition of the heroic role.

NOTE

1. President Nixon's Commission on an All-Volunteer Armed Force projected, after the end of the draft, an all-volunteer force of approximately 2.6 million, or slightly less than the total before the pre-Vietnam build-up. In retrospect this appears a major miscalculation, if not a form of self-deception. In the spring of 1971 civilian officials in the Department of Defense were speaking publicly of a post-Selective Service force of approximately 2.25 million, while privately they predicted a more realistic level of 2.0 million. However, it now seems likely that the total will be 1.75 million by 1975.

THE STATE-MANAGEMENT

Seymour Melman

In the name of defense, and without announcement or debate, a basic alteration has been effected in the governing institutions of the United States. An industrial management has been installed in the federal government, under the Secretary of Defense, to control the nation's largest network of industrial enterprises. With the characteristic managerial propensity for extending its power, limited only by its allocated share of the national product, the new state-management combines peak economic, political, and military decision-making. Hitherto, this combination of powers in the same hands has been a feature of statist societies—communist, fascist, and others—where individual rights cannot constrain central rule.

This new institution of state-managerial control has been the result of actions undertaken for the declared purposes of adding to military power and economic efficiency and of reinforcing civilian, rather than professional, military rule. Its main characteristics are institutionally specific and therefore substantially independent of its chief of the moment. The effects of its operations are independent of the intention of its architects, and may even have been unforeseen by them.

The creation of the state-management marked the transformation of President Dwight Eisenhower's "military-industrial complex," a loose callaboration, mainly through market relations, of senior military officers, industrial managers, and legislators. Robert McNamara, under the direction of President John Kennedy, organized a formal central-management office to administer the military-industrial empire. The market was replaced by a management. In place of the complex, there is now a defined administrative control center that regulates tens of thousands of subordinate managers. In 1968, they directed the production of $44 billion of goods and services for military use. By the measure of the scope and scale of its decision-power, the new state-management is by far the largest and most important single management in the United States. There are about fifteen thousand men who arrange work assignments to subordinate managers (contract negotiation), and forty thousand who oversee compliance of submanagers of subdivisions with the top management's rules. This is the largest industrial central administrative office in the United States—perhaps in the world.

The state-management has also become the most powerful decision-making unit in the United States government. Thereby, the federal government does not "serve" business or "regulate" business. For the new management is the largest of them all. Government *is* business. That is state capitalism.

The normal operation, including expansion, of the new state-management has been based upon preemption of a lion's share of federal tax revenue and of the nation's finite supply of technical manpower. This use of capital and skill has produced parasitic economic growth— military products which are not part of the level of living and which cannot be used for further production. All this, while the ability to defend the United States, to shield it from external attack, has diminished.

From 1946 to 1969, the United States government spent over $1,000 billion on the military, more than half of this under the Kennedy and Johnson administrations—the period during which the state-management was established as a formal institution. This sum of staggering size (try to visualize a billion of something) does not express the cost of the military establishment to the nation as a whole. The true cost is measured by what has been foregone, by the accumulated deterioration in many facets of life, by the inability to alleviate human wretchedness of long duration.

Here is part of the human inventory of depletion:

1. By 1968, there were six million grossly substandard dwellings, mainly in the cities.
2. Ten million Americans suffered from hunger in 1968-1969.
3. The United States ranked 18th at last report (1966) among nations in infant mortality rate (23.7 infant deaths in first year per 1,000 live births). In Sweden (1966) the rate was 12.6.
4. In 1967, 40.7 percent of the young men examined were disqualified for military service (28.5 percent for medical reasons).
5. In 1950, there were 109 physicians in the United States per 100,000 population. By 1966 there were 98.
6. About thirty million Americans are an economically underdeveloped sector of the society.

The human cost of military priority is paralleled by the industrial-technological depletion caused by the concentration of technical manpower and capital on military technology and in military industry. For example:

1. By 1968, United States industry operated the world's oldest stock of metal-working machinery; 64 percent was ten years old and over.
2. No United States railroad has anything in motion that compares with the Japanese and French fast trains.

3. The United States merchant fleet ranks 23rd in age of vessels. In 1966, world average-age of vessels was 17 years, United States 21, Japan 9.
4. While the United States uses the largest number of research scientists and engineers in the world, key United States industries, such as steel and machine tools, are in trouble in domestic markets: in 1967, for the first time, the United States imported more machine tools than it exported.

As civilian industrial technology deteriorates or fails to advance, productive employment opportunity for Americans diminishes.

All of this only begins to reckon the true cost to America of operating the state military machine. (The cost of the Vietnam war to the Vietnamese people has no reckoning.) Clearly, no mere ideology or desire for individual power can account for the colossal costs of the military machine. A lust for power has been at work here, but it is not explicable in terms of an individual's power drive. Rather, the state-management represents an institutionalized power-lust. A normal thirst for more managerial power within the largest management in the United States gives the new state-management an unprecedented ability and opportunity for building a military-industry empire at home and for using this as an instrument for building an empire abroad. This is the new imperialism.

The magnitude of the decision-power of the Pentagon management has reached that of a state. After all, the fiscal 1970 budget plan of the Department of Defense—*$83 billion*—exceeds the gross national product (GNP) of entire nations: in billions of dollars for 1966—Belgium, $18.1; Italy, $61.4; Sweden, $21.3. The state-management has become a para-state, a state within a state.

In its beginning, the government of the United States was a political entity. The managing of economic and industrial activity was to be the province of private persons. This division of function was the grand design for American government and society, within which personal and political freedom could flourish alongside of rapid economic growth and technological progress. After 1960, this design was transformed. In the name of ensuring civilian control over the Department of Defense and of obtaining efficiencies of modern management, Secretary of Defense Robert McNamara redesigned the organization of his department to include, within the office of the Secretary, a central administrative office. This was designed to control operations in thousands of subsidiary industrial enterprises undertaken on behalf of the Department of Defense. Modeled after the central administrative offices of multi-division industrial firms—such as the Ford Motor Company, the General Motors Corporation, and the General Electric Company—the new top management in the Department of Defense was designed to control the activities of subsidiary managements of firms producing, in 1968, $44 billion of goods and services for the Department of Defense.

By the measure of industrial activity governed from one central office, this new management in the Department of Defense is beyond compare the largest industrial management in the United States, perhaps in the world. Never before in American experience has there been such a combination of economic and political decision-power in the same hands. The senior officers of the new state-management are also senior political officers of the government of the United States. Thus, one consequence of the establishment of the new state-management has been the installation, within American society, of an institutional feature of a totalitarian system.

The original design of the American government was oriented toward safeguarding individual political freedom and economic liberties. These safeguards were abridged by the establishment of the new state-management in the Department of Defense. In order to perceive the abridgement of traditional liberties by the operation of the new managerial institution, one must focus on its functional performance. For the official titles of its units sound like just another government bureaucracy: Office of the Secretary of Defense, Defense Supply Agency, etcetera.

The new industrial management has been created in the name of defending America from its external enemies and preserving a way of life of a free society. It has long been understood, however, that one of the safeguards of individual liberty is the separation of roles of a citizen and of an employee. When an individual relates to the same person both as a citizen and as an employee, then the effect is such—regardless of intention—that the employer-government official has an unprecedented combination of decision-making power over the individual citizen-employee.

In the Soviet Union, the combination of top economic and political decision-power is a formal part of the organization and ideology of that society. In the United States, in contrast, the joining of the economic-managerial and top political power has been done in an unannounced and, in effect, covert fashion. In addition to the significance of the new state-management with respect to individual liberty in American society, the new organization is significant for its effects in preempting resources and committing the nation to the military operations that the new organization is designed to serve. Finally, the new power center is important because of the self-powered drive toward expansion that is built into the normal operation of an industrial management.

The preemption of resources takes place because of the sheer size of the funds that are wielded by the Department of Defense. Its budget, amounting to over $80 billion in 1969, gives this organization and its industrial-management arm unequalled decision-power over manpower, materials, and industrial production capacity in the United States and abroad. It is, therefore, predictable that this organization will be able to get the people and other resources that it needs whenever it needs them, even if this requires outbidding other industries and other organizations—including other agencies of the federal and other governments.

Regardless of the individual avowals and commitments of the principal officers of the new industrial machine, it is necessarily the case that the increased competence of this organization contributes to the competence of the parent body—the Department of Defense. This competence is a war-making capability. Hence, the very efficiency and success of the new industrial-management, unavoidably and regardless of intention, enhances the war-making capability of the government of the United States. As the war-making department accumulates diverse resources and planning capability, it is able to offer the President blue-print-stage options for responding to all manner of problem situations—while other government agencies look (and are) unready, understaffed, and under-equipped. This increases the likelihood of recourse to "solutions" based upon military power.

Finally, the new government management, insofar as it shares the usual characteristics of industrial management, has a built-in propensity for expanding the scope and intensity of its operations—for this expansion is the hallmark of success in management. The chiefs of the new state-management, in order to be successful in their own eyes, strive to maintain and extend their decision-power—by enlarging their activities, the number of their employees, the size of the capital investments which they control, and by gaining control over more and more subsidiary managements. By 1967–1968, the scope of the state-management's control over production had established it as the dominant decision-maker in United States industry. The industrial output of $44 billion of goods and services under state-management control in 1968 exceeded by far the reported net sales of American industry's leading firms (in billions of dollars for 1968): A.T.&T., $14.1; Du Pont, $3.4; General Electric, $8.4; General Motors, $22.8; U.S. Steel, $4.6. The giants of United States industry have become small- and medium-sized firms, compared with the new state-management—with its conglomerate industrial base.

The appearance of the new state-managerial machine marks a transformation in the character of the American government and requires us to reexamine our understanding of its behavior. Various classic theories of industrial capitalist society have described government as an essentially political entity, ideally impartial. Other theories depict government as justifiably favoring, or even identifying with, business management, while the theories in the Marxist tradition have depicted government as an arm of business. These theories require revision.

Development of the State-Management Concept

From 1965 to 1969, several developments converged to compel attention to the operations and efforts of a top industrial-management in the Department of Defense. There seemed to be no militarily rational explanation for certain major policies: the persistent pile-up of strategic overkill power, and the continuation and expansion of the war in Vietnam. The pile-up of nuclear overkill power (by 1968, 4,200 nuclear warheads in the largest missiles and planes, as compared to 156 Soviet cities of over 100,000 population) made no military sense whatsoever. It only made sense as a way of continuing far-flung mining and industrial productions and the expansion of the military organization. At the same time, the war in Vietnam was conducted at very high cost and without traceable offsetting returns. This, again, made no sense in terms of many conventional theories of the role of government and the relation of government to business.

Some critical comments in response to the ideas expressed in my book *Our Depleted Society,* published in 1965, included a skeptical view about its central thesis. The thesis is that priority given to military production and allied work was responsible for a shortage of skilled manpower in many other classes of work in the society. This thesis was not plausible to many people, because of their estimate that the United States is indefinitely rich, indefinitely productive. The development from 1965 to 1969, nevertheless, has supported the thesis of a depletion process with great force. Some people were also skeptical of the idea that priority given to the Pentagon could conceivably produce such a wide-ranging set of depletion effects in society. Has there been a plot to produce such a result? If so, who are the plotters? If not a plot, then is all this a result of the "military-industrial complex"? But the complex has no office, no defined executive; who is in charge?

At the same time it appeared that the Department of Defense was uninterested in and opposed to serious planning for conversion from a military to a civilian economy. This policy orientation was confirmed in my discussion with the Secretary of Defense and with members of his staff in the spring of 1965. The same policy was reflected in the report of the *Committee on the Economic Impact of Defense and Disarmament,* of July 1965. The Committee report recommended a continuation of a fragmented, uncoordinated, and altogether inadequate set of federal activities which might be relevant to problems of conversion from military to civilian industry. What was bad for the country, nevertheless, was helpful to somebody. Otherwise, how could one explain the firmness with which the problem was dismissed by the top officers of the Department of Defense? It later became clear to me that these men were protecting their management of the biggest industrial empire in the land. But recognizing this fact first required knowing about the existence and characteristics of the top management itself.

In 1961, at Columbia University, I began a series of studies on industrial conversion. These produced a considerable volume of data on the internal managerial characteristics of military-industry contractors. All this information converged on the estimation that the management criteria and decision processes of the military-industrial firm were markedly different from management operation of the ordinary civilian-industrial enterprise. It also became clear that the operation of the military-industrial enterprise was not managerially autonomous, for all these firms were required to function within the framework of rules set for them by their principal customer.

The studies at Columbia in 1965–1966 inquired into the details of decision-making in military-industrial firms working with the Department of Defense. These analyses explored the elaborately detailed regulations formulated in Washington, covering every major aspect of the managing of an industrial enterprise.

The next step was to inquire into the nature of the organization in the Department of Defense which produced this system of regulations. At this point, I could draw on prior studies that I had done on the operations and costs of industrial administration and, especially, on the organization and operation of central administrative offices of large multiplant firms.

The information that I gathered on organization in the Department of Defense fitted closely with the information that had been accumulated on the style of organization and operation of central administrative offices of major industrial firms. And so, apart from the fact that the names of the government administrative bodies were different from those of private organizations and that this new organization was located in a government office, it was quite clear that, on functional grounds, the groups operating under the office of the Secretary of Defense were a true central-administrative office performing the principal management functions characteristic of such offices elsewhere in American industry. This finding was the crucial clue to discovering the general characteristics of the new state-industrial-management, the creation and operation of which marks an essential alteration of American economy, government and society.

Characteristics of the State-Management

As in other major industrial managements, the state-management shows a propensity in problem-solving to select solutions that also serve to extend its decision-power. Furthermore, this selective preference is a built-in professional-occupational feature that operates with great regularity as a characteristic of people doing their jobs in management organizations. This may be illustrated by the policy preferences shown with respect to questions of the draft, overkill, and the gold reserve of the United States.

In considering the policy options that were selected, it is crucial to recall that the new industrial management is located in the Office of the Secretary of Defense, whose chief is the Secretary of Defense, and that he, in turn, is a Cabinet officer directly responsible to the President of the United States. Therefore, the basic policy decisions of the new state-industrial-management are also the decisions of the principal political officers of the federal government.

During the last years, many proposals have been offered for coping with the elimination of discrimination in the military draft. From the wide array of possibilities in this field, Robert McNamara put himself on record as preferring the idea of universal service. This policy would require every young man to give three years of national service, with military service being a major part of this three-year service period. Regardless of intention, this particular alternative, if implemented, would give the Secretary of Defense and his associates control over three years of the lives of about ten million young Americans. This policy preference, if implemented, would make available to the top military-political officers of the United States a pool of several million young men to be deployed at home or abroad in accordance with their policy orientations at the moment. The effect of this policy preference is greatly to extend the decision-power of the state-management over additional millions of man-years.

For several years, there has been a growing awareness of the irrationality of piling up nuclear overkill power. The United States armed forces can now deliver more than six tons of TNT for each person on our planet. Obviously, no one is about to discover how to destroy people or communities more than once. Furthermore, no one has found, or is likely to find, ways of converting this destructive-overkill power into a defensive shield. Nevertheless, the spending of as much as $22 billion a year for maintaining, enlarging, and operating the strategic overkill force continues. This military irrationality, particularly when practiced by a Secretary of Defense who proclaimed "cost effectiveness" principles, defies explanation by ordinary criteria.

Many policy options are conceivable: stop production of further overkill weaponry; stop production and also retire some significant parts of the available overkill stockpile; stop production and retire some of these weapons as part of an international agreement, with accompanying inspection; or, continue the research and development and production pile-up of further overkill power. The last option was preferred. This makes sense if we see the Secretary of Defense—functionally—as the Chairman of the Board of Directors of a state-management that accumulates decision-power as a priority end-in-view. For then the additional billions for overkill are sensible expenditures. These billions maintain control over a great network of subsidiary firms with millions of employees. And so, what is patently preposterous by the test of military rationality is altogether rational by the criteria of service to the decision-power requirements of the new state-management.

The declining gold reserves of the federal treasury, and the problems it portends for the value of the dollar at home and abroad, are a further illustration of the power-extending propensity of the new management. For several years, the annual reports of the Secretary of Defense to the House Armed Services Committee have disclosed the critical importance of military expenditures abroad as a dominant factor in the nation's payments deficit. The United States Treasury had $24 billion in gold in 1950; by 1968 the Treasury gold reserve had diminished to $10 billion. At the same time, claims in the form of dollars and other paper redeemable in gold, held abroad, amounted to more than twice the gold reserve held by the federal treasury. This development has threatened a crisis in the international value of the dollar and, by implication, a crisis of the value of currency at home. Inescapably, a decline in the value of the dollar relative to other currencies would affect every piece of paper with the dollar sign on it. Accordingly, the Secretary of Defense has given considerable attention to the role of military expenditures abroad in the balance of payments. In 1967, for example, the net adverse balance of military expenditures was $2.3 billion; this accounted for the lion's share of the nation's adverse balance of payments that year.

Since 1961, the federal government has been closely aware of the crisis potential that is implicit in the continuing adverse balance of payments of the United States, with a parallel loss of gold reserves and a threatened collapse in the relative value of the dollar. Among the various alternatives that could be utilized for correcting this chronic condition, however, there has been sustained avoidance of change in the cold war pattern of basing American international relations mainly on military power. Foreign policies that relied less on a military component would necessarily include a reduction in the size of armed forces and reductions in the military-industrial enterprise directed from the Department of Defense. As a result, pressure from the state-management has been to cope with the problem of balance of payments by a program of international arms sales, promoted by the Department of Defense itself. The state-management pretends thereby to help the international balance-of-payments position of the United States, but does so by the method that is uniquely suited to the maintenance and extension of its decision-power: an enlargement of military-industrial activity at home and abroad.

In connection with the value of dollar balance-of-payments gold problem of the United States, it is critically important to remember that private finance and private industry would be seriously affected by a collapse in the value of the dollar. Private industry and finance are involved in long-term investments and commitments, which include assumptions about a currency of reasonable value. These assumptions, however, are not essential for the managers of the new state-machine. Private managers must recoup invested money as a prime method for securing capital for further investment. This requirement does not apply to the new state-management. Its capital and operating funds do not depend on a currency of stable value, but rather on the proportion of the GNP given to it each year by the Congress of the United States.

Therefore, the managers of the state-management have a special view of the gold reserve problem, the balance-of-payments issue, and the significance of the value of the dollar—rather different from the attitude that is natural to productive economic organizations of every sort. The managers of the Pentagon hold firmly to their viewpoint and argue that their preferred approaches to the nation's balance-of-payments problem are also in the larger interest of the nation. They hold that maintaining and enlarging the military-industrial base of the United States is part of the economic growth at home and contributes to the military establishments of "free world" nations, while also linking these nations to United States sources of supply. The Department of Defense management extends control over the dependent military establishments because of their necessary reliance on American sources of supply to maintain and operate new weaponry produced in this country.

In the present case, the drive for improvement of their standing as managers requires them to maintain and enlarge the military-industry and military organizations of the United States; that is precisely what the state-management has done. From 1960 to 1970, the budget of the Department of Defense has been enlarged by 80 percent—from $45 to $83 billion. All large managerial organizations, whether private or governmental, carry on planning and calculate choices among alternatives. When confronted with an array of different ways to solve a particular problem, members of a managerial team are impelled by their particular professional-occupational requirements to select those options that will maintain and extend the decision-power of the managerial group and improve their own professional standing in the managerial hierarchy. This sort of selective preference by managers is operative in industrial management whether private or public.

An enterprise is private when its top decision-making group is not located in a government office. For this analysis of the Pentagon, what is crucial is whether the top decision-making group is a true management. A management is defined by the performance of a set of definable functions which give management its common character, whether the enterprise is private or public. A management accumulates capital for making investments. Management decides what to produce, how to carry on production, how much to produce, and where to dispose of the product at the acceptable price. It is the performance of these functions by the new organizations in the industrial directorate of the Department of Defense which defines it as a bona fide industrial management. In addition, the operating characteristics of this new management are comparable to those of other industrial managements. The special characteristics of the state-management are associated with its location in the government and its control over military production.

While the industrial-management in the Department of Defense actually owns only a minority part of the industrial capital that is used for military production, it exercises elaborate control over the use of *all* resources in thousands of enterprises. This differentiation between ownership and control is the classic one of the modern industrial corporation. Ever since Berle and Means did their classic study on *The Modern Corporation and Private Property,* it is well understood that the top managers of an industrial corporation do not necessarily wield property rights over the assets used in production, but do control the use of these assets. The differentiation between ownership and control is a central feature of the new state-management.

The Pentagon management also displays the other characteristic features of corporate organization. Management decision-making usually includes a hierarchical organization of the administration group and built-in pressures for expanding the decision-making sphere of the management. Hierarchical organization means the separation of decision-making on production matters from the performance of the work itself, and the investment of final decision-power in the men at the top of the management organization. This sort of organization structure is visible in the Pentagon's organization charts and in the key role played by the Secretary of Defense and his closest aides in controlling the enlargement of nuclear and conventional forces from 1961 to 1969.

Success of management is ordinarily shown by growth in decision-power, measured by size of investment, number of employees, volume of sales, or quality of goods produced. Such criteria indicate a true competitive gain only when they reflect a differential increase as against other management; thus, what is critical in defining the importance of a management at any one moment is not simply the absolute quantity of sales, but more importantly, the proportion of an industry's activity controlled by the management. Similarly, an increase in the volume of sales or the size of investment or the number of employees is significant only in terms of a proportional increase. In a military organization, for example, if everyone is promoted at the same time by one grade, then no one has been promoted. Similarly, promotion in a hierarchical organization must be relative promotion, and a gain in managerial position must be a relative gain. If we are competitors, then your gain must include my relative loss or you have not gained. This idea of relative gain in managerial position applies not only within a single managerial-hierarchical organization, but also applies *among* managerial organizations.

Within and among managements, the controlling criterion of managerial success is, therefore, competitive gain in decision-making position. From 1960 to 1970, the Defense Department budget rose from $45 to $83 billion, with industrial procurement roughly 50 percent of these amounts. No other management, private or public, has enjoyed such growth. The military-managerial machine is in a class by itself.

I have emphasized here the idea of enlarging decision-power as the occupational imperative, the operative end-in-view of modern corporate management— as against the more traditional idea that profit-making is the avowed central purpose of management. Profit-making, as a step in the recoupment of invested money, has diminished in importance as an independent measure of managerial performance. This stems from the fact that modern industrial operations increasingly involve classes of "fixed" or "regulated" costs, which are subject to substantial managerial control during a given accounting period. For example, a management must decide how it assigns the cost, year by year, of a new factory or a road that it has constructed. There is nothing in the nature of the factory that determines whether its capital investment shall be allocated to the costs of operations in one year, two years, or twenty years, or varied each year according to degree of use. This decision is an entirely arbitrary one, subject to the convenience of the management, within the limits allowed by the tax authorities. Since such assignment of costs is managerially controlled and has substantial effect on the size of profits that remain after costs, profits *per se* have a lessened importance as an autonomous indicator of managerial success. Moreover, there is accumulating evidence that some industrial costs, notably the costs of administration and of selling operations, are enlarged even where that involves reduction in the size of profits that would otherwise be available in a given accounting period. Such reductions in profit are ordinarily made and justified in the name of long-term maintenance or extension of the relative decision-power of the management and its enterprise.

One of the characteristic processes in industrial managements during the twentieth century has been an elaboration in the scope and intensity of managerial controlling. This has been accompanied by growing management costs and a growing ratio of managerial to production employees. All this has meant higher costs and, necessarily, diminished profits. But the choice of options in industrial management has systematically been toward enlarging the scope and intensity of managerial control, rather than toward management methods which would minimize costs and thereby enlarge profits or allow a reduction in prices. The state-management has also been piling on managerial controls, obviously giving priority to the consequent growth in its decision-power, as against possible economies that might be effected in its own central offices or in the operation of subsidiary enterprises of the Pentagon empire.

All this is no mere theoretical exercise for understanding the operation of the state-management. This organization skips over the customary processes of industrial capitalism for enlarging control via an intervening mechanism of investing and recouping money with a gain-profit, then reinvesting more money and, thereby, adding to decision-power. Instead, the state-management, drawing on its unique capital resource—an annual portion of the nation's product—applies this directly to increasing either the scope or the intensity of its decision-power. The usual processes of marketing products and recouping capital are leapfrogged by the state-management.

One of the characteristic features of private industrial management has been a sustained pressure to minimize costs in production. In modern industry, this effort is institutionalized by making it the special province of industrial engineers, cost accountants and others. The state-management includes various professional groups that are identified as acting to control costs. But that does not necessarily produce cost-minimization. For cost control can be focused mainly on controlling the people in various occupations.

The Pentagon record—before, during, and after Robert McNamara—includes obvious cost excesses. Before McNamara, average prices on major weapons systems were 3.2 times their initial cost estimates. Under McNamara, the famous F-111 airplane was costing $12.7 million per plane by December 1969, as compared to one first cost estimate of $3.9 million—or 3.25 times the initial estimate. Such performance under the well-advertised regime of the state-management's "cost effectiveness" programs was characteristic of this era as well. This pattern of cost excesses during the rule of "cost effectiveness" is explicable, not as aberrant behavior, but as a pattern that is normal to the state-management. The state-management's control system includes monitoring for so-called cost overruns as a regular function. Payment for the cost overruns by the Pentagon has been the functional equivalent of a grant of capital from a central office to a division of its firm, serving to enlarge the assets of the larger enterprise.

Owing to the basic difference between private industrial management and the state-management with respect to the role of conversion of capital through the marketplace, there is a parallel, distinguishing interest in the stability and instability of industrial operations. Stability means operating within predictable and acceptable limits of variation in output. For private industrial management, this is a highly desirable condition, because this makes possible predictability in the ongoing processes of conversion of money from investment funds to products sold on the marketplace and to new capital funds for further investment. Where costs, prices, and the value of the dollar in purchasing power are highly unstable, the investment-recoupment process of capital for private management is rendered extremely difficult to operate—it is put "out of control." These limiting conditions are not operative for the administrators of the state-management, for they deal directly with the conversion of capital funds into decision-orders on industrial operations. Also, their products need not be designed to be salable at a price producing a profit which they may accumulate for further investment. Their investment funds have been constantly acquired in the name of defense from a willing Congress and nation. Accordingly, instability in costs, prices, and profits are no major constraint for the managers of the state machine. And so, when military outlays at home and abroad become the traceable cause of danger to the value of the dollar relative to other currencies, it is not a source for alarm among the Pentagon managers. Some measures are taken to slow down the outflow of Treasury gold, but no major policy changes are introduced.

Scope of Operations of the State-Management

Since its formal organization after 1960 under Robert McNamara, the new state-industrial management has focused attention on military production, its organization and control. At the same time, many Americans, seeing the array of managerial and technical talent deployed in the state-management, have suggested that the same group could apply its talents to organize almost anything—housing, public health, and so forth. Some individuals in the state-management may very well choose to change their employment. Indeed, there has been a sustained turnover, especially in some of the more senior posts of the state-management. Such flexibility does not apply, however, to the organization as an institution. Military organization and military production have special value as a base for the power-extending operations of industrial management.

For a management seeking to enlarge its operations, the military sphere offers the unequaled opportunity to obtain virtually unlimited quantities of fresh capital from the Congress of the United States. This is so because of the "defense" use of this money; the name, Department of Defense, is itself helpful. (Would Congress and the public be equally compliant with a War Department?) Thereby, the state-industrial-management has an unmatched opportunity for extending its decision-power. This is illustrated in the case of the draft. There are alternative ways of organizing military operations with varying numbers of men being required. There are also alternative ways of obtaining the services of a given number of men. The draft is the one way which not only secures the required number of men, but also guarantees decision-power by the military managers over a fixed proportion of the young people of the society at any given time. This extension of decision-power, unprecedented in peacetime in American history, was made possible by the promise of the state-management to perform the service of defending the United States, a promise which cannot be fulfilled.

An important collateral feature of the military emphasis in the operation of the state machine is the substantially "untouchable" character of the entire military organization. Many people might otherwise want to be concerned with and have informed opinions about the operation of the largest organization in the nation. But they are constrained from doing this by the technological mystique that has been built up around military activity. The idea is that only persons with advanced technical training and access to secret information have the capability really to understand what is going on in this sphere. At the same time, because of the promise to defend the United States, the entire military establishment, including the affairs of the state-management, has been given a "sacred cow" quality. The Chamber of Commerce of the United States, for example, has a national committee which reviews budgets of various government departments and operations and makes recommendations, including those designed to achieve economies. The budget of the Department of Defense, which now comprises more than half the administrative budget of the United States, is excluded from this evaluation. This committee does not even make an effort to inquire into the operations of this Department. For all these reasons, the new management in the Department of Defense has an opportunity for extension of decision-power over defense-linked industry that is unequaled by any other management, public or private.

As a rule, industrial managements enlarge their decision-power by supplying a public with products that are acceptably serviceable in accordance with their understood purpose. In the case of the state-management in the Department of Defense, these ordinary tests of serviceability of performance are not operative. Scrapping old weapons and organizations, and multi-billion-dollar spending for the development, design, production, and purchase of new weapons of every kind—all this is independent of the particular military or political serviceability of the new weapons systems. Thus, the famous F-111 airplane project, for example: it was assigned to General Dynamics, which produced a defective plane at $12.7 million per unit compared with the anticipated cost of $3.9 million.

The presumed function of the Department, as the name implies, is that of a Department of Defense—hence, the service to be performed is that of shielding the United States from outside physical attack. However, since several countries have acquired nuclear weapons in quantity, defense—in the ordinarily understood sense of that word—is no longer possible. Instead, the United States is engaged in an operation called deterrence—an attempt to forestall a society-destroying war by sustained threat of nuclear counterattack. In September 1967, Secretary of Defense McNamara discussed the nature of the relationship between the United States and its principal military rival, the Soviet Union: "The blunt fact is then, that neither the United States nor the Soviet Union can attack the other without being destroyed in retaliation; nor can either of us obtain a first-strike capability in the foreseeable future." (From address to United Press International, San Francisco, September 18, 1967.)

Deterrence is not defense. Deterrence is not a shield. Deterrence is an experiment in applied psychology. There is no scientific basis from which to forecast the probability of the success or failure of this experiment. Just imagine the difference in the public and Congressional attitudes with respect to lavish granting of funds if the name were not Department of Defense but Department of Deterrence. In many public addresses and reports, McNamara elaborated on ideas like "deterrence" or "assured destruction capability." At no point did he, or the President of the United States, say plainly to the American people that the nation could no longer be defended. The pre-nuclear promise of defense has sustained reality only in the title of the Department.

Instead of defense, the managers of the Department sell weapons-improvement programs to Congress and to the public. It is constantly implied that as you improve the parts, you improve the whole. Thus, weapons-systems programs are formulated and sold to the appropriate committees of the Congress and to the public on the promise that they are, in each instance, better than what had existed before. The M-16 rifle is thereby better than the M-1 rifle, because it fires more than ten times as many shots per minute. Minuteman-3 is better than Minuteman-1, since it can carry a larger nuclear explosive and presumably have a greater capability for penetrating conceivable defensive systems. In nuclear as well as conventional weapons, technical improvement reaches a limit called over-kill—meaning that, try though they may, even the United States state-management is unlikely to be able to kill more than once. Thus, technical improvement in the overkill range is militarily meaningless, but absolutely vital for sustaining the rule of the state-management over its military-industry empire. That is given first priority, in the name of defense. Thereby the budget of the Department of Defense in 1968-1969 almost equaled the peak spending of World War II.

Veteran chiefs of the Air Force, for example, announced that a few weeks of bombing of North Vietnam would produce termination of the war in that area by surrender of the Viet Cong and the North Vietnamese, or peace negotiations. This result was not achieved after many months of intensive bombing during which the daily tonnage of explosives dropped in Vietnam was in excess of the daily tonnage of explosives dropped over Nazi-controlled Europe during the Second World War. Evidently, military rationality has not been the controlling consideration in decisions on the budgeting of research, development, and production of new bomber fleets. The rationality that compels this is rather the serviceability of these programs for maintaining or extending the decision-power of the state-management.

There is another result of the acquisition of nuclear weapons in quantity. The prospect of escalation from conventional to nuclear war makes it unfeasible for the major powers to attempt to win political victories against each other by the use of conventional weapons, because there is no way to exclude the possibility that a military conflict started with conventional weapons may escalate to the nuclear, hence society-destroying level. However, such limits of usefulness of military power do not restrain the process of selling "defense," which is used to justify obsolescence of particular weapons in the name of improvements in weapon performance.

Military industry has major attractiveness as an arena for extension of decision-power insofar as it is mainly non-competitive, in the marketing sense, with existing industries. Thus, the aerospace, electronics, and ordnance industries have developed primarily into suppliers of the military establishment. Hence, these new industries, and the managements that operate them, do not compete in the same markets as managements in already established civilian industries. The managers of the state machine appear as competitors of civilian industrial management only when the scale of operations reaches the point of intensity where a rationing of crucial and limited resources, such as technical talent, is required. At that point, the military industry managers utilize the political powers of the federal government and its unequaled capital supply to enforce rationing of critical resources—either by outbidding in the areas of price, wages, and salaries, or by formal rationing (classifying some civilian industries as "non-essential") giving priority to military industry. Civilian industries, even such vital ones as machine tools, have been deprived of the services of young engineers as a result of not being classified "essential" by the Department of Defense.

The importance of these considerations for the managers of the military-industrial establishment is also confirmed indirectly by the unwillingness of the state-management to plan for non-military utilization of the manpower and industrial resources which they control. Both the Kennedy and the Johnson administrations were firmly resistant to efforts to establish a National Economic Conversion Commission. Under both John F. Kennedy and Lyndon B. Johnson, the policy was to leave these matters in the hands of the military-industry managers, who were already in charge. It is also noteworthy that the industrial planners for new weapons-systems collaborate with the military chieftains in preparing and advocating new weapons, even though the evidence of field use indicates that the weapons simply do not serve their declared purposes.

Among many sophisticated Americans there is at least a suspicion of the limited capability of the Department of Defense to implement its official defense function. Nevertheless, there is widespread support for the managers of the Department of Defense, and especially for its industrial activity. Americans have believed that "cost-effectiveness" has ruled in military decisions—because McNamara and his aides said so. The growth of weapons orders has been supported on the assumption that this produces new economic growth, with the further mythology that this economic growth does not deplete anything else—that the United States can have both guns and butter.

Military planners and educated men in American society have generally been reluctant to confront the meaning of the concentration of energy release of nuclear weapons and its consequences for the meaning of warfare. It is now feasible, with ordinary nuclear weapons, to release at one time and at one place energy equivalent to the sum of explosives used during World War II in the entire European theater of operations. There is no present or conceivable shield against such concentrated explosive force. The word "defense" has come to have an increasingly ceremonial, rather than military, significance. None of this is altered by adding to or altering the characteristics of "offensive" and "defensive" missile systems. The search for military and strategic advantages through extensive sub-optimizing (improving subsystems and single weapons) is thus an exercise in futility. The sum of particular weaponry changes cannot produce either "defense" or military superiority in any ordinary meaning of these words. "Improvement" of overkill has no military value or human meaning. (The same reasoning applies, of course, to the U.S.S.R.)

Mythology that Supports the State-Management

The size of the United States Gross National Product, approaching $900 billion for 1969, makes it difficult to absorb the fact that while the nation is rich, it is not indefinitely rich. An important part of the nation's productive resources are being used for growth that is parasitic rather than productive. Parasitic growth refers to products which are not part of the current level of living and cannot be used for further production. Productive growth refers to products that are part of the current level of living, or that can be used for further production. The activities of producing for and operating the military establishment fall in the category of parasitic growth. This holds despite the fact that the people who do the work are paid wages and salaries, and that these are used, in turn, to supply their own level of living. The crucial point is that the product of the military-serving workers, technicians, and managers is a product that does not enter the marketplace, is not bought back, and cannot be used for current level of living or for future production. This economic differentiation is independent of the worth which may be assigned to military activity for other reasons. With $900 billion per year, a military budget of $83 billion appears as less than 10 percent of the GNP. Such arithmetic, however, conceals the fact that the lion's share of the nation's research and development manpower is used for military purposes, that this manpower is present in finite supply even in a rich society, and that this imposes severe constraints on what can be done in the many spheres of civilian life that require the services of this class of skilled manpower. The long-standing military priority for skilled manpower, financial and other resources was the final constraint on the ability of the Johnson administration to implement its "Great Society" programs. Many of the programs looked fine on paper. The preambles to the various laws of the Johnson administration's legislative program read as admirable descriptions of conditions in American society and as statements of intent. Only one thing was lacking: the commitment of men and money to make the work possible. This commitment was restrained by the fact that priority was given to military and related work.

This is not to say that the effects from giving priority to the military cannot be surmounted. This could be done in two ways: first, the drastic regrouping, under central control, of civilian production and other resources; or, second, changing the whole national priorities schedule away from military emphasis. Regrouping of industrial resources could mean, for example, the arbitrary conversion of two of the three major automobile firms, allowing the auto market to be supplied by the remaining firm. Thereby, an enormous block of industrial resources, manpower, and so forth, would be made available for other uses. This is technically conceivable, but it is not socially conceivable as long as the country wishes to have something other than a rigorously state-controlled economy and society. A garrrison society, in which the state is empowered to dispose of resources at will, would be able to make this sort of regrouping. But such a regrouping of industrial resources under state control has not been acceptable to the American people except in a war crisis. Within the present political-economic framework, fresh resources for productive economic growth could only be made available by a basic change in national priorities. In detail, that would mean utilizing the federal public-responsibility budget of the nation for other than military priority purposes, which would necessarily involve a major reduction in the decision-power of the state-management. This is why the managers and apologists for the state-management are vigorous in maintaining the mythology of unlimited wealth, unlimited growth, and the absence of a priorities problem in American society.

The American people and the Congress have accepted decision-making by the state-management in the belief that it possesses critical expertise, not only in military matters, but also in the management of industry and the economy. In its 1966 Report, the Joint Economic Committee of the Congress declared: "Let no one, at home or abroad, doubt the ability of the United States to support, if need be, simultaneous programs of military defense of freedom and economic and social progress for our people, or (2) our capacity and preference to live and grow economically without the stimulus of government spending on defense or a competitive arms race." Here the Committee affirmed that government spending for military purposes is an economic stimulus and that the country can afford guns and butter at the same time. This assurance among the members of the Joint Economic Committee of Congress reflects repeated assertions in a similar vein made by the President and by the Secretary of Defense, the two senior executives of the state-management. Accordingly, in the presentation of the federal budget, the accompanying analyses of economic growth characteristically show no differentiation between parasitic and productive growth.

Against this background, the mayors of principal American cities have formulated varying estimates of the capital investment needed to bring material conditions of life up to a reasonable standard. In 1966, the mayor of Detroit, Jerome P. Cavanaugh, estimated that $242 billion would be required to solve the plight of the cities. The chief officers and ideologists of the state-management respond to such proposals in two ways. First, they say, there is no reason why such money could not be made available, if the nation only had the will to do it. Second, they say, there is no reason why this cannot be done while maintaining military priority in the federal government's budget, the largest pool of tax funds in the land. In a similar vein, many editors have written during the last years on the theme that "Cities Cannot Wait" (for example, The New York Times, August 22, 1966). But these writers show no readiness to come to grips with the military budget and the scale of the military organization and management in the federal government, both of which preempt the money, men, and materials needed to establish decent conditions in many areas of civilian life. In a memorable address at the University of Connecticut, Senator Fulbright stated the contradiction: "There is a kind of madness in the facile assumption that we can raise the many billions of dollars necessary to rebuild our schools and cities and public transport and eliminate the pollution of air and water while also spending tens of billions to finance an open-ended war in Asia."

Even in the wealthiest economy, war expenditures change from economic stimulus to economic damage: first, when the military activity preempts production resources to a degree that limits the ability of the society to supply necessities such as shelter; second, when the military spending causes rapid price inflation, thereby depressing the level of living of all who live on limited incomes; and third, when price inflation disrupts the process of civilian capital investment which requires capability for predicting the worth of a nation's currency.

During the last years, there has been more than a beginning of an understanding that the nation does, in fact, have a priorities problem. But there has been hardly a beginning in preparing for the conversion of resources from military to civilian use. The official economic advisors of the federal government have repeatedly counseled that if there is sufficient advance planning, and the will in Washington to establish a clear set of priorities, then a transition from war to peace activity can be made without great upheaval (*The New York Times,* April 14, 1968). The point is precisely that until now, there has been no advance planning or a will in Washington to establish peace-time priorities, and the lack of will in this realm contrasts sharply with the clear will and the openhanded dedication of resources to the requirements of the state-managerial machine.

Many lines of evidence contribute to the conclusion that both recognition and denial of a national priorities problem cut across conventional political lines. Support of the state-management and its functioning in the name of defense is independent not only of party, but also of personalities. The Kennedy administration was formally Democratic, but the architect of the present military machine, and its operating chief from 1961 to 1968, was a Republican, Robert McNamara. Support for the plans and the budgets of the state-management have come from both major parties in the Congress. At the same time, there has been a fair amount of turnover in the persons holding key posts at the top of the state-management.

Indeed, the very openness of operations of the state machine is one of its great sources of strength. Thus, no conspiracy, in the ordinary sense of the word, was required to get the American people to accept the myth of the missile gap and the subsequent major capital outlays for an overkill nuclear war program. The American people were sold on the myth and thought they were buying defense. Nor is a conspiracy required to secure fresh capital funds of unprecedented size for further expansion of the state-management. This is agreed to by a Congress and a public that has been taught to believe that all this activity is for defense and that it stimulates the economy of a society that can enjoy both guns and butter. In all of this, the controlling factor is not a political party or a single political theory, not a personality, not a conspiracy: the existence and normal operation of the Pentagon's management-institution dominates and gives continuity of direction.

The government of the United States now includes a self-expanding war machine that uses military power for diverse political operations and is based upon an industrial management that has priority claims to virtually unlimited capital funds from the federal budget. The state-management is economically parasitic, hence exploitative, in its relation to American society at home. The military-political operations of the Pentagon chieftains abroad, following the pattern of the Vietnam war program, are parasitic there as well. To the older pattern of exploitative imperialism abroad, there is now added an institutional network that is parasitic at home. This combination is the new imperialism.

DOES THE U.S. ECONOMY REQUIRE MILITARY SPENDING?

Michael Reich

> It is, it seems, politically impossible for a capitalistic democracy to organize expenditure on the scale necessary to make the grand experiment which would prove my case—except in war conditions.
>
> *J. M. Keynes*

Since 1950 the U.S. government has spent well over a trillion dollars on the military, or about one-tenth of total economic output; in recent years $30 billion has been spent annually on destruction in Southeast Asia alone. Why does this murderous and seemingly irrational allocation of resources occur? Why give the Pentagon $80 billion per year in spending money when so many basic social needs go unmet both in the United States and in the rest of the world? What sorts of changes in our political-economic system are needed to reorder fundamentally the militaristic priorities of the United States?

I shall argue in this paper that a major shift in social and economic priorities would require a fundamental transformation of the U.S. capitalist economy. The growth and persistence of a high level of military spending is a natural outcome in an advanced capitalist society that both suffers from the problem of inadequate private aggregate demand and plays a leading role in the preservation and expansion of the international capitalist system.[1] In my view, barring a revolutionary change, militarism and military spending priorities are likely to persist for the foreseeable future.

In what follows, I shall present three principal propositions on the role of military spending in the U.S. economy. (1) In the period beginning in 1950, if not earlier, the U.S. economy was not sufficiently sustained by private aggregate demand; some form of government expenditure was needed to maintain expansion. Without such stimulus, the growth rate of the United States as well as the

Reprinted from *American Economic Review*, May, 1972. Used by permission.

international capitalist economy would have been substantially lower. (2) The U.S. government turned to military spending as the outlet for needed government expenditures precisely because it provides the most convenient such outlet; in a capitalist context, spending on the military is easily expandable and highly attractive to corporations. Military spending supplements rather than competes with private demand, more is always "needed" for adequate "defense," it is highly profitable to the firms that receive weapons contracts, and no interest group is explicitly against it. (3) Federal expenditures on socially useful needs on a scale comparable to the military budget are not a feasible substitute. Massive social expenditures would tend to undermine profitability in many sectors of the private economy, remove potential areas of profitmaking, interfere with work incentives in the labor market, and weaken the basic ideological premise of capitalism that social welfare is maximized by giving primary responsibility for the production of goods and services to profit-motivated private enterprises. In short, military spending is much more consistent than is social services spending with the maintenance and reproduction of the basic social relations of capitalism.

These propositions contrast sharply with the conventional wisdom. The dominant view among economists is that military spending is not necessary for the prosperity of the U.S. economy and should not be blamed on capitalism per se. To stimulate the economy any form of government spending is about as good as any other; the *aggregate* amount of demand is what matters and not its composition. Expenditures on social needs could easily replace military spending, provided demand is maintained by a proper mix of monetary and fiscal policies. The implication is that, apart from the difficulties of converting a few large military contractors and the retraining of specialized engineers and scientists, the problem of "conversion" is political rather than economic. Many economists have also argued from analogy with other capitalist nations: advanced capitalist economies in Europe and Japan have experienced fairly high rates of economic growth with considerably lower proportions of their *GNP* allocated to military expenditures. Finally, many economists point to the changing composition of government spending in the United States in recent years: while military spending has declined slightly as a percentage of *GNP*, the total of federal, state, and local nonmilitary expenditures has been increasing as a percentage of *GNP*. Thus, the United States seems to be moving away from dependence on military spending. None of these points is convincing, and in what follows I will try to answer each of them.

I. The Inadequacy of Private Demand

Let me turn now to my first proposition. Private investment and consumption demand have by themselves been insufficient to maintain low unemployment and an adequate rate of growth; some form of government expenditure has been necessary since at least the late 1940s to stimulate the U.S. economy and maintain expansion. This proposition has been amply verified by historical evidence and needs little substantiation here. For example, Hickman's elaborate econometric analysis of postwar investment demand showed that sluggish growth in the period 1948-1963 was caused by a *downward* trend in business fixed investment as well as a full employment surplus in the government budget. Without the stimulus that was provided by government spending, economic growth in this period would have been substantially lower. In other words, autonomous investment demand has not been constrained by the claims on economic resources induced by government expenditures.

The government stimulation that is necessary must include increased government expenditures as well as tax cuts. While the economy can be stimulated for a time without increased government expenditures by reducing taxes and running larger deficits, such tax cuts cannot be used indefinitely. As the tax rate approaches zero, a further decrease in taxes has very little leverage effect on the economy, and further stimulus will necessarily involve increasing government expenditures; a large budget with a small deficit can have as stimulating an effect on the economy as a small budget with a large deficit (see Musgrave, pp. 429-443). So expenditures can and must play a role in stimulating the economy. Since 1950, military expenditures, averaging about 10 percent of *GNP,* have played this stimulative role. And within the strategic capital goods-producing industry, the sector of the economy that is most subject to cyclical fluctuations and is most affected by secular declines in business fixed investment, military spending plays a stimulative role that is twice as great as in the economy as a whole (see Reich and Finkelhor).

Note that I am not asserting here that *every* capitalist economy must at all times be suffering from inadequate aggregate demand. Nor am I offering an explanation of *why* the private sector has been inadequate.[2] I am asserting *only* that the U.S. economy has been sick in this regard for the last several decades.

It may also be the case that the international capitalist system as a whole has been suffering the disease of inadequate demand in recent decades. By seeing each capitalist nation as part of a larger international system, we can explain the apparent ability of some developed capitalist countries within that system to prosper without leaning so heavily on military spending. Although I have not engaged in any quantitative calculations, it seems plausible to hypothesize that military spending by the United States in the postwar period has been not only a direct prop for the American economy but also an indirect prop for the economies of Europe and Japan as well. Certainly, the export performance of these economies would have been substantially less conducive to growth had the major U.S. market for imports been much softer. The prosperity of these capitalist economies is thus related to the growth of the U.S. market, partially caused by U.S. military expenditures.

II. The Attractions of Military Spending

My second proposition is that, given the necessity of some form of government expenditures, military spending provides the most convenient outlet for such expenditures. Military contracts are both easily expandable in the economy without confronting any corporate opposition and are highly attractive to the firms that receive them.

Military spending is easily expandable basically because it adds to rather than competes with private demand. The amenability of military spending to expand to fill the need can be outlined with desperate brevity as follows.

First, a convenient rationalization of the need for massive armaments expenditures exists. The ideology of anticommunism and the Cold War has been drummed into politicans and public alike for over twenty years. This is a powerful force behind military spending as well as a general legitimizer of capitalism. The U.S. government's role as global policeman for capitalism has reinforced this rationale for military expenditures.

Second, armaments are rapidly consumed or become obsolete very quickly. Bombers are shot down in Southeast Asia, ammunition is used up or captured, etcetera. The technology of advanced weapons systems becomes obsolete as fast as defense experts can think of "improvements" over existing weapons systems (or as soon as Soviet experts do). So the demand for weaponry is a bottomless pit. Moreover, the kind of machinery required for armament production is highly specific to particular armaments. So each time a new weapon is needed or a new process created, much existing production machinery must be scrapped. Extensive retooling at very great new outlays is required. Since the technologies involved tend to be highly complex and exotic, much gold-plating (or rather titanium-plating) can occur; only specialists know how superfluous a particular frill is, and whether a $1 billion missile would work as well as a $2 billion missile.

Third, there is no generally agreed upon yardstick for measuring how much defense we have. The public can't recognize waste here as it would in, say, education or public housing. How do we know when an adequate level of military security is achieved? National security managers can always claim that by some criteria what we have is not enough. Terms like missile gaps and nuclear parity and superiority are easily juggled. Military men always have access to new "secret intelligence reports" not available to the general public. Since few people are willing to gamble with national defense, the expertise of the managers is readily accepted. Politicians and the general public have little way of adequately questioning their judgment.

Fourth, military contracts are highly advantageous to the firms that receive them. Boondoggling and profiteering are endemic in the nature of the "product" and of the buyer-seller relationship in the military "market." While the structure and performance of the military "industry" has been analyzed in detail elsewhere (see Adams and Kaufman, 1970), a few summary comments here will indicate the inherent structural reasons for waste and profiteering.

Briefly, it has always been presumed that as much as possible and ideally all armaments production should be carried on by private profit-seeking corporations. Theoretically, the government, as sole buyer, would purchase from the most efficient, least-cost firms. But given the long lead times and the inherent cost and technological uncertainties in developing and producing complicated weapons systems, the government would find it difficult, to say the least, to identify in advance and reward the most efficient military contractors. In fact, of course, the Pentagon has rarely shown any interest in holding down costs or identifying efficient firms, since until recently, it has not faced a real budget constraint of its own. The reality is that contractors and Pentagon both follow the maxim of socialized risk, but private profits—in C. Wright Mills' words, "socialism for the rich."

The profit incentives in the military contracts reward boondoggling and waste.[3] The Pentagon provides without charge much of the fixed and working capital for major military contracts, underwrites and subsidizes the costs of technological research and development for firms that engage in civilian as well as military production, and negotiates (and when necessary, renegotiates) cost-plus contracts that virtually guarantee the contractors against any losses. It is thus not surprising that careful and objective studies of profit rates on investment in military contracts have found that such profits are significantly and substantially higher in military work than in comparable civilian work.

Nor is it surprising to find that most of the major corporations in the United States have become involved in military contracts. One hundred corporations receive two-thirds of the prime contract dollars, but among these top one hundred are twenty of the top twenty-five industrial firms in the United States.[4] The attraction of military spending to the major corporations is also apparent when one examines the impact of military contracts on sectoral growth and on the concentration of economic power. First, the rapidly growing industries of the postwar economy—aerospace, electronics, communications—owe a great deal to military dollars for research and development and final production. Second, in a typical year fifty firms get about 60 percent of the military procurement contract dollar, whereas in the economy as a whole, the top one hundred firms usually account for only 35 percent of manufacturing sales (see Reich and Finkelhor). So military procurement is much more concentrated than is the economy as a whole. Certainly, an expenditure program that benefits twenty of the top twenty-five corporations and contributes to the concentration of economic power among the corporate giants is going to enjoy a political power base that lies deep in the heart of the U.S. economy.

So military spending is easily expandable, is highly profitable and amenable to boondoggling, and benefits the major corporations in the economy. These factors combine so that military expenditures can be enormous and expandable almost without limit and not incur major corporate opposition. But the same cannot be said for the nonmilitary sector.

III. The Opposition to Social Service Expenditures

The last of my three major propositions was that federal spending on socially useful needs on a scale comparable to the military budget is not a feasible substitute. The contrast between government spending on the military and government spending on social services indicates how post-Keynesian macroeconomic theory has artificially separated economics from politics, that is, from power relation-ships. Social services spending is unlikely to be as profitable and expandable as is military spending. Social expenditures have never had the blank check that the military until recently have enjoyed.

Investments in social facilities are usually durable—they do not become obso-lete very quickly and are not rapidly consumed. Right now, of course, there are plenty of unmet needs in these areas. But once taxes have been increased and everyone is provided with a decent house, once there are new schools and health clinics stocked with materials, then what? They cannot be immediately torn down and built all over again.

The technology of social welfare facilities is not particularly exotic. Very con-ventional standards exist to tell us how much a house or a hospital should cost. The possibility for enormous padding to absorb funds is much less, since there are readily accessible yardsticks to ascertain how well social needs have been met. The public knows when adequate and convenient public transportation is avail-able. No one would want to extend it out to a suburb that did not exist.

In general, social spending beyond a certain point cannot be rapidly and wastefully expanded. The difference here is that investment in social services deals with people, not remote objects like weapons. People are resistant to allow-ing their lives to be dominated and their tax dollars used up by the priorities of waste—even if it does help to keep the economy running. For example, what would happen if a housing project or a school were built in the same way as a new missile? If a missile doesn't work, the company is excused and the planners go back to their drawing boards armed with another huge contract. Since it al-ready has the expertise, the same company is more than likely to get a new mis-sile contract. Imagine the political repercussions of an inadequate, but expensive, school or housing project? The community complains, a public scandal is de-clared, and all contracts with the offending company are cancelled. The school or housing bill has a rougher going the next time it comes up in the legislature.[5]

So social spending cannot provide the opportunities for waste that are pro-vided by military spending. But more important, massive social spending inevi-tably interferes with the existence and reproduction of the social relations of production under capitalism.[6]

First, many kinds of social spending put the government in direct competition with particular industries and with the private sector as a whole (see Baran and Sweezy, Chap. 6). This goes against the logic of a capitalist economy. For ex-ample, government production of low-cost housing in large amounts would sub-stantially reduce profits of private builders and landlords who own the existing housing stock. The supply of housing would be increased and land would be taken away from private developers who want to use it for commercial gain. Similarly, building *effective* mass public transportation would compete with the automobile interests.

Any one of these interests taken by itself might not be sufficient to put insur-mountable obstacles in the way of social spending. Most social service programs affect only one particular set of interests in the private economy. But there are so many forms of potential interference. All of the vested interests are aware of this problem explicitly or through their ideology and so work to help one another out. They adopt a general social ideology that says that too much social spending is dangerous and that governmental noninterference is good.

Furthermore, the capitalist system as a whole is threatened by massive governmental social spending because the very necessity of private ownership and control over production is thereby called into question. The basic assumption in any capitalist society, that goods and services should be produced by private enterprise according to criteria of market profitability, thus also fuels the general ideology limiting social spending. This limits the satisfaction of collective needs such as clean air and water, esthetic city planning, etcetera, that cannot be expressed in market terms as demand for individually saleable commodities.[7]

Massive social spending also tends to upset the labor market, one of the essential institutions of a capitalist economy. Public expenditures on an adequate welfare program would make it difficult for employers to get workers. If the government provided adequate nonwage income without social stigma to recipients, many workers would drop out of the labor force rather than take low-paying and unpleasant jobs. Those who stayed at jobs would be less likely to put up with demeaning working conditions. The whole basis of the capitalist labor market is that workers have no legitimate income source other than the sale of their labor power, and capitalist ideology has long made a cardinal rule that government should not interfere with this incentive to work. Powerful political forces thus operate to insure that direct income subsidization at adequate levels does not come into being.

Social service spending is also opposed because it threatens the class structure. Education, for example, is a crucial stratification mechanism, determining who gets to the top and legitimizing their position there (see Bowles, 1971). Good free universal education, extending through college, would undermine the transmission of inequality from one generation to the next. A truly open admissions system of higher education would undermine the labor market as well: workers would not settle so willingly for miserable, low-paying jobs (see Bowles, 1972). In general, many social service expenditures, because of their public good character, are consumed equally and so the distribution of their benefits is more equal than the overall distribution of income. For this reason, such expenditures are often opposed by the rich.

Finally, good social services, since they give people some security, comfort, and satisfaction—fulfill real needs—interfere with the market in consumer goods. Corporations can only sell people goods by playing on their unsatisfied needs and yearnings. New needs are constantly being artificially created: the need for status, security, sex appeal, etcetera. These needs are based on fears, anxieties, and dissatisfactions that people have and that are continually pandered to by the commercial world. But if people's needs were being more adequately fulfilled by the public sector, that is, if they had access to adequate housing, effective transportation, good schools, and good health care, they would be much less prey to the appeals of the commercial hucksters. These forms of collective consumption would have interfered with the demand for consumer products in the private market.

Military spending is acceptable to all corporate interests. It does not interfere with existing areas for profit making, it does not undermine the labor market, it does not challenge the class structure, and it does not produce income redistribution. Social spending does all these things, and thus faces obstacles for its own expansion.

I do not mean to imply by the above analysis that a capitalist economy has not and will not provide any basic social services through government expenditures. Some social overhead investment is obviously important and necessary for the smooth functioning of any economy, and the provision of local and national public goods has always been considered a proper activity for capitalist governments. For example, expenditures on education, highways, and transportation are obviously necessary for the production of workers and for getting them to the point of production; such expenditures are motivated by the needs of production, and only incidentally to fill human needs (see Gorz and O'Connor). In fact, most state and local government expenditures have been directed to these basic infrastructural needs.

In recent decades production has become, as Marx put it, more social in character: the economy has become much more complex, more interdependent, more urbanized, more in need of highly schooled labor. The recent increase in state and local expenditures can be explained by these increases in the social costs of production. Expenditures for such needs would be consistent with and are often necessary for private profitability.[8]

Moreover, state and local expenditures are not motivated by the need to stimulate aggregate demand, for only the federal government is concerned with maintaining aggregate demand.[9] But nonmilitary federal expenditures have increased barely, if at all, as a percentage of *GNP* since the 1930s. Nonmilitary federal purchases of goods and services were only 2.3 percent in 1970. By contrast, nonmilitary federal purchases as a percent of *GNP* were 4.6 percent in 1938 and 1.9 percent in 1954.[10] It thus cannot be said that the federal government has significantly turned to social services expenditures and away from military expenditures to meet the problem of inadequate aggregate demand.

This brings me to a final point regarding the meaning of the question, is military spending really necessary to capitalism? I have tried to frame the answer to this question in the following way. A capitalist economy with inadequate aggregate demand is much more *likely* to turn to military than to social spending because the former is more consistent with private profit and the social relations of production under capitalism. If this military outlet were cut off, say by massive public opposition, it is possible that a capitalist economy might accommodate and transform itself rather than commit suicide. But such reasoning misses the point. Military spending is favored by capitalists and is likely to be defended with considerable vigor, as recent years have shown. Perhaps a parallel with imperialism will clarify this point. It is not essential to a capitalist economy that it be imperialist, for growth can be domestically based. But so long as there are lands to be conquered and markets to be penetrated, it is natural to expect that capitalism will have an imperialist character. Similarly, so long as there is profit to be made in military spending, capitalists will turn to it.

NOTES

1. An important factor in the development of military spending has been the the assumption by the United States since World War II of the role of global policeman for capitalism. I shall not focus on this issue here because the importance of international operations to U.S. capitalism has been well sketched by others. See for example Harry Magdoff 1969, 1970, and Arthur MacEwan.
2. For a recent ambitious, though inadequate, attempt to explain theoretically the insufficiency of investment demand in the United States since 1929, see Baran and Sweezy.
3. For references see Reich and Finkelhor, Kaufman, 1970 and 1972.
4. Of the remaining five, one is the principal Atomic Energy Commission contractor, two are oil companies indirectly affected by military sales, and one is a steel company also indirectly affected. For a detailed analysis of the wide range of corporations and industries involved in military contracts, see Reich and Finkelhor.
5. This is not to deny that there is considerable waste and profiteering in civilian government contracts, for example in housing programs. But the potential magnitudes are much smaller.
6. Recall that capitalist relations of production are characterized by private ownership and control of production, with a hierarchical social division of labor between those who control, the capitalists and managers, and those who are controlled, the wage and salary workers.
7. For a discussion of the subordination of collective needs to private profit as well as a general Marxist analysis of civilian government expenditures under capitalism, see Andre Gorz.
8. Nonetheless, a relative impoverishment of living standards has taken place, as the destruction of the city and the environment has far outrun government provision of social goods. See Gorz and O'Connor.
9. Variations in state and local expenditures usually run counter to the stabilization needs of the aggregate economy.
10. Data from *The Statistical Abstract of the United States,* 1971.

REFERENCES

W. Adams, "The Military-Industrial Complex and the New Industrial State," *Amer. Econ. Rev.,* May 1968, *58,* 652–665.

P. Baran and P. Sweezy, *Monopoly Capital,* New York: Monthly Review Press, 1965.

S. Bowles, "Unequal Education and the Reproduction of the Social Division of Labor," *Rev. Radical Polit. Econ.*, Winter 1971, *3*, no. 4, reprinted in Edwards, Reich, and Weisskopf, 218–229.

_____, "Contradictions in Higher Education in the United States," in Edwards, Reich, and Weisskopf, 491–503.

R. Edwards, M. Reich, and T. Weisskopf, eds., *The Capitalist System,* Englewood Cliffs: Prentice-Hall, 1972.

A. Gorz, *A Strategy for Labor*, Boston, 1967.

B. Hickman, *Investment Demand and U.S. Economic Growth,* Washington, 1965.

Richard F. Kaufman, "MIRVing the Boondoggle," *Amer. Econ. Rev.,* May 1972.

_____, *The War Profiteers*, Indianapolis: Bobbs-Merrill, 1970.

J. M. Keynes, *New Republic*, July 29, 1940.

A. MacEwan, "Capitalist Expansion, Ideology and Intervention," in Edwards, Reich, and Weisskopf, 409–420.

H. Magdoff, *The Age of Imperialism,* New York: Monthly Review Press, 1969.

_____, "Is Imperialism Really Necessary?" *Monthly Rev.,* October and November 1970, *22*, nos. 5 and 6.

Richard A. Musgrave, *The Theory of Public Finance,* New York: McGraw-Hill, 1959.

J. O'Connor, "The Fiscal Crisis of the State," *Socialist Revolution,* Spring 1970, *1*, nos. 1 and 2.

M. Reich and D. Finkelhor, "Capitalism and the Military-Industrial Complex: The Obstacles to Conversion," *Rev. Radical Polit. Econ.,* Fall 1970, *2*, no. 4, 1–25; reprinted in Edwards, Reich, and Weisskopf, 392–406.

IS THERE
A MILITARY-INDUSTRIAL
COMPLEX
WHICH PREVENTS PEACE?

Marc Pilisuk and Tom Hayden

The term *military-industrial complex* appears often in popular books and in the newspapers today. If there exists an omnipotent elite committed to militarism, then there is simply no basis for hope that voices for peace have established, or can establish, an influential channel into inner policy circles. The purpose of this chapter is to examine the theory and evidence which help to clarify this issue.

The New Concern

Not since the thirties has there been such a rash of attention to military-industrial power as there is today. Then, as now, the president himself raised the specter of improper military influence. FDR, on the eve of a Senate investigation of the munitions industry, said flatly that the arms race was a "grave menace . . . due in no small measure to the uncontrolled activities of the manufacturers and merchants of the engines of destruction and it must be met by the concerted action of the people of all nations" (Raymond 1964, p. 262; also *Congressional Quarterly Weekly Report* 1964, 6, pp. 265-278). While Dwight Eisenhower did not sound so militant as Roosevelt, and while he never adopted FDR's 1932 campaign pledge to "take the profits out of war," he did resume a popular tradition with his warning against the "unwarranted influence" of the military-industrial complex. It may be a significant measure of the times that one president could make such warnings in his very first campaign for office, while the other couched it among several other farewell remarks.

Marc Pilisuk, *International Conflict and Social Policy,* © 1972. Reprinted by permission of Prentice-Hall, Inc., Englewood Cliffs, New Jersey. (An earlier version of this essay by Marc Pilisuk and Tom Hayden was published in the *Journal of Social Issues* 21, no. 3 [July 1965], pp. 67-117.)

The thirties are a prelude to the sixties, too, in the area of congressional investigation of militarism. Then Senator Gerald P. Nye investigated the fabulous World War I profits of United States Steel and Hercules Powder and discovered, with horror, the instrumental role of munitions makers and other commercial interests in beginning the war. Nye revealed, for example, that the American ambassador in London informed President Wilson in 1917 that probably "the only way of maintaining our preeminent trade position and averting a panic is by declaring war on Germany" (Raymond, p. 264). As Roosevelt was more aggressive than Eisenhower, so also were Nye, Borah, and other popular senators more aggressive than their counterparts in the sixties. Nevertheless, similar issues are now being raised in congressional committees. The most shocking of these issues may be found in the report of the hearings of Senator John McClellan's committee on government operations, *Pyramiding of Profits and Costs in the Missile Procurement Program.* This report pointed out the likely danger that the government "can be placed in the unenviable position of reluctant acquiescence to the demands and conditions set by the contractor," and that "profits were pyramided on other profits without any relationship at all to the effort being expended by those making the profit." In what might have been front page scandal in any area but national defense, the committee documented two mechanisms by which millions upon millions of dollars of excess profit have been reaped by the defense industries. The mechanisms are (a) claiming profits on work subcontracted to other firms (which in turn subcontract portions of their work to others and charge a profit on the subsubcontracted work, too), and (b) overestimating the subcontracting costs (on incentive type contracts), thereby reaping huge profits by undercutting the original estimates. However, the contrast with the thirties is clear. Senator McClellan only wanted to improve the efficiency of what he called "these necessary monopolies."[1] A more far-reaching investigation under the direction of Senator Clark dealt with the convertibility of the defense empire to civilian job-creating tasks. He claimed first that the new defense emphasis on electronics and on research and development, and the monopolization of defense by a few companies and geographic areas, considerably reduces the potential effect of defense as an economic stabilizer; and second that certain firms, especially those in the aerospace industry, suffer an overcapacity crisis that spurs them to insist on more missiles than the nation needs.[2] Senator Clark's hearings, too, were mild in contrast to those of the thirties. Even milder, however, was the 1962 survey report of Senator Hubert Humphrey, who said it was "nonsense" to believe that American industry is opposed to disarmament.[3]

Another measure of the interest in military-industrial power is the number of popular and technical books published dealing with the subject. In the thirties the widely read books were Davenport's *Zaharoff, High Priest of War,* Engelbrecht and Haneghen's *Merchants of Death,* and Seldes's *Iron, Blood and Profits.* Two decades passed before the work of C. Wright Mills began to attract broad attention to the subject of organized militarism. Including Mills's pioneering books, there have been at least twenty-one major books published on this subject during the period between Sputnik and the American escalation of the Vietnam war into North Vietnam. Many of them are by journalists (Cook, Coffin, Raymond, Swomley, Wise and Ross); some by economists (Benoit, Boulding, Melman, Peck, Perlo, Scherer); sociologists (Etzioni, Horowitz, Janowitz, Mills); political scientists (Meisel, Rogow); novelists (Bailey, Burdick, Knebel, Sutton); and at least one physical scientist (Lapp).

Whatever the objective referent, if any, of a "military-industrial complex," it is undeniable that the concept now plays an important role in the political consciousness of many persons, on a scale without precedent since the thirties. It is a telling fact that the new literature, with the exception of Mills, Cook, and Perlo, still lacks the bite of the old, and that the proposed solutions are very modest. In the thirties a popular idea, proposed by the Nye Committee but never implemented, was the nationalization of the munitions industries. By the sixties the reverse has happened; most military research, development, and production is done by private companies subsidized by the federal government. Military-political-industrial cooperation is so pervasive and frequent that it becomes a hair-splitting task to identify specifically any "merchants of death." Also, the scale of potential destruction has so increased, the nature of warfare strategy has so changed, and the existence of the military in peacetime is so accepted, that it seems quaint to imagine defense contractors with bloody hands. Furthermore, the assumed threat of communist expansion has become the ultimate justification of the postwar military buildup, whereas in the past such buildups could be attributed more clearly to industrial profit and power motives. Reasons such as these probably explain both the long silence and the modest character of the current resurgence in discussion of these matters.

But these reasons account partially for the inadequacy of analysis as well. The question, "Does there exist a military-industrial complex which prevents peace?" at first seems debatable in straightforward yes-or-no terms. Indeed, it might have been answerable in the twenties or thirties but not in the postwar period. When there is permanent intermingling and coordination among military, industrial, and government elites, and whenever greater war-preparedness can be justified by reference to the communist movement, the question becomes much stickier. Because of this, the easiest conclusion to support is that a "complex" simply does not exist as an omnipresent obstacle to policy change. Indeed, this belief has become the accepted norm for "informed" discussion of interests vested in the perpetuation of military preparedness. The next most easily supported conclusion would be that we have become trapped in the hell-fires of militarism by a sinister but concealed elite of military-industrial leaders, which through its puppets pulls the strings on every major policy decision. The latter theory is non-conformist, radical, and smacks too strongly of classical conspiracy theory to be palatable to most scholars. Indeed, the dominant attitude (explicit or tacit) in most of the literature of the early sixties was that there exists no military-industrial complex capable of preventing peace. It was claimed that the military-industrial complex operates as a subgroup within the limits of an essentially civilian society. This view sees the complex equating its own interests with those of the nation as a whole: but, it is argued, this tendency toward power aggrandizement is checked by countervailing interest blocs in society. Moreover, the complex is not seen as having a corrosive effect on democratic processes: even if it is conceded that military and technological expertise or well-financed public relations give the complex unusual privilege and visibility, it is argued that this is no different in principle from certain other influential groups, all of which are limited by the web of constraints that comprises a pluralist society. Usually it is added that the internal differences in the complex, such as differences among the separate services or between the military and the industrial procurement sectors, tend to restrict further its ability to impose a policy line on the United States. This point of view appears in scattered form throughout the literature.

Some important examples of this literature include *The Invisible Government* by Wise and Ross, *Power at the Pentagon* by Raymond, *Disarmament and the American Economy* edited by Benoit and Boulding, and *The Weapons Acquisition Process* by Peck and Scherer. Each points to a power bloc important in the determination of foreign policies, in the decision to move toward arms reduction or control, or in lobbying for increased defense expenditure. All acknowledge that some impediments to change are presented by the concentration of power in these groups, but none sees any one group sufficiently dominant to resist all forms of control or counter pressures from other segments of society.

None of these denials of irresponsible military–industrial power marshalls very significant evidence to support its views. Examples are given of specific conflicts between civilian and military groups in which the military lost (for example, the dismissal of General Walker for ultra-right-wing indoctrination of his troops, the refusal to be first to break the moratorium on nuclear weapons testing). Examples are given of heated divisions between the services over what military strategy should be pursued (the arguments over conventional warfare in the late fifties, and the more recent RS–70 controversy). Sociological studies reveal underlying diversities within single corporations, between competing corporations, and within the demographic and institutional character of each branch of the armed services.[4] And, throughout, American pluralism is cited as an automatic check against any elite group.[5]

At a more general level, these fragments of evidence point toward three grounds for denying that a military–industrial complex prevents peace:

1. It is held that the scope of decisions made by any interest group is quite narrow and cannot be said to govern anything so broad as foreign policy.
2. It is held that the complex is not monolithic, not self-conscious, and not coordinated, the presumed attributes of a ruling elite.
3. It is held that the military–industrial complex does not wield power if the term power is defined as the ability to realize one's will even against the resistance of others and regardless of external conditions.

These formulations, to repeat, are made neither explicitly nor consistently in the literature. But they crystallize the basic questions about definition which the literature raises. Moreover, they are quite definitely the major contentions of academic criticism of the power elite theory. The more widely read academic critics include Daniel Bell, Robert Dahl, and Talcott Parsons. Since their critiques are mainly directed at the work of C. Wright Mills, it is with Mills that we will begin to analyze the theories which claim that there *is* a military–industrial complex blocking peace.

The Thesis of Elite Control

Mills is by far the most formidable exponent of the theory of a power elite. In his view, the period since World War II has been dominated in America by the ascendance of corporate and military elites to positions of institutional power. These "commanding heights" allow them to control the trends of the business cycle and of international relations. The cold war set the conditions which legitimize their ascendance, and the decline and incorporation of significant left-liberal movements, such as the CIO, symbolize the end of opposition forces. The power elite monopolizes sovereignty, in that political initiative and control stem mainly from the top hierarchical levels of position and influence. Through the communications system the elite facilitates the growth of a politically indifferent mass society below the powerful institutions. This, according to Mills's argument, explains why an observer finds widespread apathy. Only a small minority of the people believe in actual participation in the larger decisions which affect their existence, and only the ritual forms of "popular democracy" are practiced by the vast majority. Mills's argument is addressed to the terms of the three basic issues we have designated, that is, scope of decision power, awareness of common interest, and definition of power exerted.

By scope, we mean the sphere of society over which an elite is presumed to exercise power. Mills argues that the scope of this military–industrial elite is general, embracing all the decisions which in any way could be called vital (slump and boom, peace and war, and so on). He does not argue that each decision is directly determined, but rather that the political alternatives from which the "deciders" choose are shaped and limited by the elite through its possession of all the large-scale institutions. By this kind of argument, Mills avoids the need to demonstrate how his elite works during each decision. He speaks instead in terms of institutions and resources. But his basic evidence is rather negative: no major decisions in twenty years have been contrary to the policies of anti-communism and corporate or military aggrandizement; therefore a power elite must be prevailing. Mills might have improved his claims about the scope of elite decisions by analyzing a series of actual decisions in terms of the premises which were *not* debated. Such analysis could point to the mechanisms (implicit or explicit) which led to the exclusion of these premises from debate. By this and other means he might have found more satisfying evidence of the common, though perhaps tacit, presuppositions of seemingly disparate institutions. He might then have developed a framework analyzing "scope" on different levels. The scope of the Joint Chiefs of Staff, for instance, could be seen as limited, while at the same time the Joint Chiefs could be included in a larger elite having larger scope. Whether this could be shown awaits research of this kind. Until then, however, Mills's theory of scope remains open to attack, but, conversely, is not subject to refutation.

Mills's theory also eludes the traditional requirements for inferring monolithic structure, that is, consciousness of elite status, and coordination. The modern tradition of viewing elites in this way began with Mosca's *The Ruling Class* in a period when family units and inheritance systems were the basic means of conferring power. Mills departs from this influential tradition precisely because of his emphasis on institutions as the basic elements of society. If the military, political, and economic institutional orders involve a high coincidence of interest, then the groups composing the institutional orders need not be monolithic, conscious, and coordinated, yet still they can exercise elite power.[6] This means specifically that a military–industrial complex could exist as an expression of a certain fixed ideology (reflecting common institutional needs), yet be composed of an endless shuffle of specific groups. For instance, eighty-two companies have dropped out of the list of one hundred top defense contractors and only thirty-six "durables" remained on the list from 1940 to 1960. In terms of industry, the percentage of contracts going to the automotive industry has dropped from 25 percent in World War II to 4 percent in the missile age. At the same time, the aircraft companies grew from 34 to 54 percent of all contracts, and the electronics industry from 9 to 28 percent (Peck and Scherer 1962). Mills's most central argument is that this ebb and flow is not necessarily evidence for the pluralists. He stresses the unities which underlie the procession of competition and change. The decision to change the technology of warfare enabled one group to "overcome" another in an overall system to which both are fundamentally committed. Moreover, the decision issued from the laboratories and planning boards of the defense establishment and only superficially involved public opinion. Case studies of weapons development by Peck and Scherer, in which politics is described as a marginal ritual, would certainly buttress Mills's point of view.

The institutional analysis enables Mills to make interesting comments on his human actors. The integration of institutions means that hundreds of individuals become familiar with several roles: general, politician, lobbyist, defense contractor. These men are the power elite, but they need not know it. They conspire, but conspiracy is not absolutely essential to their maintenance. They mix together easily, but can remain in power even if they are mostly anonymous to each other. They make decisions, large and small, sometimes with the knowledge of others and sometimes not, which ultimately control all the significant actions and resources of society.

Where Mills's approach tends to fall short is in its unclarity about how discontinuities arise. Is the military–industrial complex a feature of American society which can disappear and still leave the general social structure intact? Horst Brand has suggested a tension between financial companies and the defense industries because of the relatively few investment markets created by defense (1962). Others have challenged the traditional view that defense spending stimulates high demand and employment. They claim that the concentration of contracts in a few states, the monopolization of defense and space industry by the largest seventy-five or one hundred corporations, the low multiplier effect of the new weapons, the declining numbers of blue-collar workers required, and other factors make the defense economy more a drag than a stimulant (Melman 1963; Etzioni 1964). Certainly the rising unemployment of 1970 in the midst of expansion of the ABM system and extension of the Vietnam war to Laos and Cambodia show the flaws of relying on defense spending as an economic stimulant. Mills died before these trends became the subject of debate, but he might have pioneered in that debate if his analytic categories had differentiated more finely between various industries and interest groups in his power elite. His emphasis was almost entirely on the "need" for a "permanent war economy" just when that need was being questioned, even among his elite.

However, this failure does not necessarily undermine the rest of Mills's analysis. His institutional analysis is still the best means of identifying a complex without calling it monolithic, conscious, and coordinated. Had he differentiated more exactly he might have been able to describe various degrees of commitment to an arms race, a rightist ideology constricting the arena of meaningful debate, and other characteristics of a complex. More exact analysis has yet to be done. . . .

Mills's theory is most awkward in its assertion that the elite can, and does, make its decisions against the will of others and regardless of external conditions. This way of looking at power is inherited by Mills, and by much of modern sociology, directly from Max Weber. A rather fantastic quality is attributed to the elite: literal omnipotence. Conversely, any group that is not always able to realize its will even against the resistance of others is only "influential" but not an elite. Mills attempts to defend this viewpoint but, in essence, modifies it. He says he is describing a tendency, not a final state of affairs. This is a helpful device for explaining cracks in the monolith—for instance, the inability of the elite to establish a full corporate state against the will of small businessmen. However, it does not change the ultimate argument—that the power elite cannot become more than a tendency, cannot realize its actual self, unless it takes on the quality of omnipotence.

When power is defined as this kind of dominance, it is easily open to critical dispute. The conception of power depicts a vital and complex social system as essentially static, as having within it a set of stable governing components, with precharted interests which infiltrate and control every outpost of decision authority. Thereby, internal accommodation is made necessary and significant change, aside from growth, becomes impossible. This concept goes beyond the idea of social or economic determinism. In fact, it defines a "closed social system." A closed system may be a dramatic image, but it is a forced one as well. Its defender sees events such as the rise of the labor movement essentially as a means of rationalizing modern capitalism. True or false as this may be, did not the labor movement also constitute a "collective will" which the elite could not resist? An accommodation was reached, probably more on the side of capital than of labor, but the very term *accommodation* implies the existence of more than one independent will. On a world scale, this becomes even more obvious. Certainly the rise of communism has not been through the will of capitalists; Mills would be the first to agree to that. Nor does the elite fully control technological development; surely the process of invention has some independent, even if minor, place in the process of social change.

Mills's definition of power as dominance ironically serves the pluralist argument, rather than countering it. When power is defined so extremely, it becomes rather easy to claim that such power is curbed in the contemporary United States. The pluralists can say that Mills has conjured up a bogeyman to explain his own failure to realize his will. Indeed, they have said just that in review after review of Mills's writings. A leading pluralist thinker, Edward Shils, says that Mills was too much influenced by Trotsky and Kafka:

> Power, although concentrated, is not so concentrated, so powerful or so permeative as Professor Mills seems to believe. . . . There have been years in Western history, e.g., in Germany during the last years of the Weimar Republic and under the Nazis when reality approximated this picture more closely. . . . But as a picture of Western societies, and not just as an ideal type of extreme possibilities which might be realized if so much else that is vital were lacking, it will not do (Shils 1961).

But is Mills's definition of power the only suitable one here? If it is, then the pluralists have won the debate. But if there is a way to designate an irresponsible elite without giving it omnipotence, then the debate may at least be recast.

The fundamental question of the definition of power is not answered in the other major books which affirm the existence of a military–industrial complex. Cook's *The Warfare State,* Perlo's *Militarism and Industry,* and several more recent works are good examples of this literature which is theoretically inferior to Mills's perplexing account.

Cook's volume has been pilloried severely by deniers of the military–industrial complex. At least it has the merit of creating discussion by virtue of being one of the few dissenting books distributed widely on a commercial basis. It suffers, however, from many of the unclarities typical of the deniers. Its title assumes a warfare state while its evidence, although rich, is only a compilation of incidents, pronouncements, and trends, lacking any framework for weighing and measuring. From Cook's writing several hypotheses can be extracted about the "face of the Warfare State," all of them suggestive but none of them conclusive: (1) the Department of Defense owns more property than any other organization in the world;[7] (2) between 60 and 70 percent of the national budget is consistently allocated to defense or defense-related expenditures; (3) the military and big business have an inevitable meeting of minds over the billions of dollars in contracts the one has to order and the other to fulfill; (4) the one hundred top corporations monopolize three-fourths of the contracts, 85 percent of which are awarded without competition; (5) as much as one-third of all production and service indirectly depends on defense; and (6) business and other conservative groups, even though outside the defense establishment, benefit from the warfare emphasis because it subordinates the welfare state, which is an anathema to them (pp. 20–24, 162–202).

There is no doubt that Cook's data have held up during the years since his book was written. The federal budget of $154.9 billion for fiscal year 1971 assigns 64.8 cents of every tax dollar to the cost of past and present wars and war preparation. Vietnam war costs are concealed in the 48.4 cents per dollar for current military expenditures. Veterans' benefits and national debt interest are also sizeable items. The Nixon administration claims that 41 percent of its budget is for human resources. That figure, however, includes trust funds like social security (for which the government is merely a caretaker), veterans' benefits, and even the Selective Service System. The actual human resources figure is 17 percent, indicating that welfare is still being crushed by warfare (Senator Mark Hatfield, address, Feb. 10, 1970, Corvallis, Oregon).

Cook's work much more than Mills's is open to the counter-argument that no monolithic, semi-conspiratorial elite exists. Even Cook's definitions of vested interests are crude and presumed. Moreover, he suffers far more than Mills from a failure to differentiate between groups. For instance, there is nothing in his book (written in 1962) that would explain the economic drag of defense spending, which Cook perceptively observed in a 1963 *Nation* article, "The Coming Politics of Disarmament." In 1962 he wrote that big business was being fattened off war contracts, but the next year that the "prolonged arms race has started, at last, to commit a form of economic hara-kiri." Hara-kiri does not happen spontaneously; it is a culmination of long-developing abnormalities. That Cook could not diagnose them before they became common in congressional testimony illustrates the lack of refinement in his 1962 analysis. Cook's failure is that he visualizes a monolith, obscuring the strains that promote new trends and configurations.

It is because of his attention to strains that Perlo's book is useful. Perlo draws interesting connections between the largest industrial corporations and the defense economy, finding that defense accounts for 12 percent of the profits of the twenty-five largest firms. He adds that foreign investment creates a further propensity toward a large defense system, and he calculates that military business and foreign investments combined total 40 percent of the aggregate profits among the top twenty-five firms. He draws deeper connections between companies and the major financial groups controlling their assets.

Such an analysis begins to reveal important disunities within the business community. For instance, it can be seen that the Rockefellers are increasing their direct military investments while maintaining their largest foreign holdings in extremely volatile Middle Eastern and Latin American companies. The Morgans are involved in domestic industries of a rather easy-to-convert type, and their main foreign holdings are in the safer European countries, although they too have unsafe mining interests in Latin America and Africa. The First National City Bank, while it has large holdings in Latin American sugar and fruit, has a more technical relationship with its associated firms than the stockholder relationship. The Mellons have sizeable oil holdings in Kuwait, but on the whole they are less involved in defense than the other groups. The DuPonts, traditionally the major munitions makers, have "diversified" into the overextended aerospace and plutonium industries, but their overseas holdings are heavily in Europe. Certain other groups with financial holdings, such as Young and Eaton interests in Cleveland, have almost no profit stake in defense or foreign investments. On the other hand, some of the new wealth in Los Angeles is deeply committed to the aerospace industry.

Perlo makes several differentiations of this sort, including the use of foreign-policy statements by leading industrial groups. But he does not have a way to predict the conditions under which a given company would actively support economic shifts away from the arms race. These and other gaps, however, are not nearly as grave as his failure to analyze other components of the military-industrial complex.[8] He makes no attempt to include politicians, military groups, and other forces in a "map" of the military-industrial complex which he believes exists. Perhaps this is partly because of the book's intent, which is to document profiteering by arms contractors; nonetheless, his book is not theoretically enlightening about the question we are posing. Nor does it refute the pluralist case. In fact, it contains just the kind of evidence that pluralists currently employ to demonstrate the absence of a monolith.

The newer literature, written since 1965, gives a somewhat more penetrating glimpse into the extent of the merger of the military and the defense industry. Lapp, *The Weapons Culture,* Weidenbaum, "Arms and the American Economy," Galbraith, *The New Industrial State,* and Knoll and McFadden, *American Militarism 1970,* all show the heavy involvement of the Department of Defense with the corporate giants. The two most striking recent works which provide the most concrete detail on the operation of this military-industrial network are Seymour Melman's *Pentagon Capitalism* (1970) and Richard Barnet's *The Economy of Death* (1969). Both are well written and a must for any serious student of contemporary policy. *Pentagon Capitalism* describes the network as a giant enterprise controlled by the civilian defense establishment, or "state-management." Through the elaboration of government controls over the firms that carry out defense contracts, the Defense Department's role has changed from that of customer to that of administrator over a far-flung empire of defense production. The Pentagon is able to divert capital and scientific and technical manpower to its own purposes, drawing resources away from productive activity to what Melman calls economically parasitic activity. He holds that the prime goal of the "state-management" is to enlarge its decision power. Thus wars, once begun, tend to expand; "security gaps" are invented, causing weapons systems to grow in size and sophistication; and international arms sales increase.

Barnet (*The Economy of Death*) sees the military–industrial complex as more decentralized, like a machine with several separate parts that run together smoothly. Each institution that makes up the complex acts for its own purposes, and all contribute to justifying and maintaining the irrational and dangerous growth of military capability. Barnet documents the interchangeability of personnel between industry and the military. A major strength of Barnet's work is his willingness to be specific, to give the key names from those in his study of four hundred top decision-makers who come from a handful of law firms and executive suites "in shouting distance of one another in fifteen city blocks in New York, Washington, Detroit, Chicago and Boston." Many of the names are commonly known (although the extent of their financial-world connections is not)—Charles Wilson, Neil McElroy, Robert Anderson, George Humphrey, Douglas Dillon, John McCone, Adolphe Berle, Averell Harriman, William C. Foster, John McCloy, Robert McNamara, Roswell Gilpatric, James Douglas, William Rogers, and Nelson Rockefeller. Men such as these are systematically recruited into top cabinet posts and become "National Security Managers." Their common backgrounds, even to membership in the same elite social clubs, assure a measure of homogeneity for their task of defining who or what threatens this nation and what should be done about it. Their views on the national interest reflect their own success in judicious management of risk in the business world. Barnet's assumption about the homogeneity of this "club" is supported by Domhoff's "Who Made American Foreign Policy, 1945–1963?" It is clear that a man like William Rogers, with the right background but no particular knowledge or background in foreign affairs, can be made secretary of state while a civil rights leader, Martin Luther King, was admonished by official spokesmen for taking a position against the Vietnam war.

Barnet believes that the ongoing mechanisms of the system keep it moving in old paths. The evils are not incidental, he says, but built into the system. Military solutions to international problems seem more reliable and "tougher" than diplomatic solutions, and they are backed up by millions of dollars' worth of "scientific research"; so military solutions are preferred even by civilian defense officials. The military, the civilian defense establishment, and defense contractors constantly work together to develop new weapon systems to meet defense "needs"; they feed one another's ideologies, and costlier, more elaborate weapons result. It is difficult and expensive for military contractors to convert to peacetime production, so they have done virtually no planning for conversion, and many have abandoned all interest in such planning. Perhaps most important for Barnet, those in power see America's chief purpose as consolidating and extending American power around the world; military technology is an indispensable tool for that purpose. Whether this collection of civilian managers is really in control or whether it is merely serving a more powerful military bureaucracy is the point at issue; Barnet leans toward the view of the ascendance of the relatively smooth-working military hierarchy. Domhoff, using very similar evidence, places the aristocratic economic elite at the top of the pinnacle.

Melman, in particular, presents a strong case that militarism in the United States is no longer an example of civilian corporate interests dictating for the country a military role in order to produce hardware for profit from the government-consumer and to defend the outposts of capitalism. Instead, he feels that the system is led by the military managers for their own interests in power; it is a state socialism whose defense officials dictate the terms of policy, and of profits, to their subsidiary corporations. Melman supports his case by the observation that not only the personnel but also the actual operating procedures demonstrate that the Defense Department and the corporations that serve it have interpenetrated one another's operations—to such an extent that there is for all practical purposes really only one organization. The horrible example which comes to mind is that of the rise of Hitler, which was first backed and promoted by industrialists who later lost their measure of control over an uncontrollable military machine. Melman's thesis differs from both the pluralist doctrine, which sees various groups competing for power, and the Marxist doctrine, which sees the greed of the capitalists as the prime mover. In Melman's convincing analysis the military is fast becoming king.

Melman's analysis may yet prove true. For the present, however, corporate capitalism has fared too well to alleviate all suspicions of the hidden hand. The new interlocking industrial conglomerates like Litton, Textron, and General Dynamics, and the main financial houses of the United States, provide an inner core whose interests are permanently protected even as individual corporations prosper or falter. For such centers of elite power, which Barnett shows to be the main source of top Defense Department and other foreign policy-appointed officials, the terms of the military merger have been highly beneficial. The benefits must be seen not only in profits but in the retention of the entire profit-making system against the demands of a hungry and impatient world. Melman speaks of the drive of the new technocratic military bureaucracy to increase its power and control, but deemphasizes the interest this power is protecting. Barnet specifies the community of interest and outlook among the corporate decision managers who are recruited into the inner circles of foreign policy, but does not state explicitly that beliefs lie at the core of the practices which are thereby promoted.

Both Barnet and Melman believe that American militarism is a function of institutions directly involved with defense. It can be argued, on the other hand, that a description of something called a military–industrial complex should include all the power centers of American society. Directorates of the major defense contractors are not separable from those of industries geared primarily to the production of consumer goods. Neither are the consumer industries independent of military and diplomatic actions which protect international marketing advantages. Barnet himself notes that not only that faction of the labor movement directly employed in defense industries, but organized labor in general is a political supporter of military-industrial power. The universities are heavily involved in defense interests, as is the complex of oils, highways, and automotives. Even in education the armed services' Project 100,000 has inducted a large number of former draft rejects for resocialization and basic educational development (followed by two years of applied study abroad in Vietnam for the successful graduates) (Little 1968; Pilisuk 1968).

Barnet and Melman deal incompletely with the relationship of the sector they regard as the military-industrial complex to the rest of society. Both realize the tremendous power of the military, the civilian defense officials, and the defense industry combined. They are aware that the defense establishment has a powerful hold on public opinion through the public's fear of enemy attack and through defense control over a larger sector of the work force. Yet they seem to hope this power can be curbed by a loud enough public outcry. In the last analysis they too believe that the defense establishment has merely been allowed to grow out of hand, and that now the exercise of some countervailing power may bring sanity back into American policy and make peace possible.

Revising the Criteria for Inferring Power

We have found fault with so many books and divergent viewpoints that the most obvious conclusion is that current social theory is deficient in its explanation of power. We concur with one of Mills's severest critics, Daniel Bell, who at least agrees with Mills that most current analysis concentrates on the "intermediate sectors," for example, parties, interest groups, formal structures, without attempting to view the underlying system of "renewable power independent of any momentary group of actors" (Bell 1964). However, we have indicated that the only formidable analysis of the underlying system of renewable power, that of Mills, has profound shortcomings because of its definition of power. Therefore, before we can offer our own answer to the question, "Is there a military-industrial complex which blocks peace?" we must return to the question of power itself in American society.

We have agreed essentially with the pluralist claim that ruling-group models do not "fit" the American structure. We have classified Mills's model as that of a ruling group because of his Weberian definition of power, but we have noted also that Mills successfully escaped two traps common to elite theories, namely, that the elite is total in the scope of its decisions, and that the elite is a coordinated monolith.

But perhaps we have not stressed sufficiently that the alternative case supporting pluralism inadequately describes the historical dynamics of American society. The point of our dissent from pluralism is over the doctrine of "countervailing power." This is the modern version of Adam Smith's economics and of the Madisonian or Federalist theory of checks and balances, adapted to the new circumstances of large-scale organizations. The evidence for it is composed of self-serving incidents and a faith in semi-mystical resources. For instance, in the sphere of political economy, it is argued that oligopoly contains automatic checking mechanisms against undue corporate growth, and that the factors of public opinion and corporate conscience are additional built-in limiting forces.[9] We believe that evidence from the field, however, suggests that oligopoly is a means of stabilizing an industrial sphere either through tacit agreements to follow price leadership or through rigged agreements in the case of custom-made goods; that "public opinion" tends much more to be manipulated and apathetic than independently critical; that "corporate conscience" is less suitable as a description than is Reagan's term, *corporate arrogance.*

To take the more immediate example of the military sphere, the pluralist claim is that the military is subordinate to broader civilian interests. The first problem with that statement is the ambiguity of the term *civilian.* Is it clear that military men are more "militaristic" than civilians? To say so would be to deny the increasing trend of white-collar militarism. The top strategists in the Department of Defense, the Central Intelligence Agency, and key advisory positions are often Ph.D.'s. In fact, "civilians" including McGeorge Bundy, Robert Kennedy, James Rostow, and Robert McNamara are mainly responsible for the development of the only remaining "heroic" form of combat: counter-insurgency operations in the jungles of the underdeveloped countries. If "militarism"[10] has permeated this deeply into the "civilian" sphere, then the distinction between the terms becomes largely nominal.

The intrusion of civilian professors into the military arena has been most apparent in more than three hundred universities and non-profit research institutions which supply personnel to and rely upon contracts from the Department of Defense. About half these centers were created to do specialized strategic research. One of these, the RAND Corporation, was set up by Douglas Aviation and the Air Force to give "prestige type support for favored Air Force proposals" (Friedman 1963). When RAND strategy experts Wohlstetter and Dinerstein discovered a mythical "missile gap" and an equally unreal preemptive war strategy in Soviet post-Sputnik policy, they paved the way for the greatest military escalation of the cold war era, the missile race.

Civilian strategists have frequently retained an exasperating measure of autonomy from the services which support them. Such conflicts reached a peak when both the Skybolt and the RS-70 projects met their demise under the "cost effectiveness" program designed by Harvard economist Charles Hitch (then with RAND, later Defense Department comptroller, now president of the University of California). That the opinions of civilian and military planners of military policy sometimes differ does not detract from the argument. What must be stressed is that the apparent flourishing of such civilian agencies as RAND (it earned over twenty million dollars in 1962, with all the earnings going into expansion, and spawned the non-profit Systems Development Corporation whose annual earnings exceed fifty million dollars) is no reflection of countervailing power. The doctrine of controlled response, which dictated the end of the RS-70, served the general aspirations of each of the separate services, of the Polaris and

Minuteman stable deterrent factions, of the brush fire or limited war proponents, of the guerrilla war and paramilitary operations advocates, and of the counter-force adherents. It is a doctrine of versatility intended to leave the widest range of military options for retaliation and escalation in United States hands. It can hardly be claimed as victory against military thought. The in-fighting may have been intense, but the area of consensus between military and civilian factions was still great.

Consensus

Countervailing power is simply the relationship between groups which funda-mentally accept "the American system" but which compete for advantages within it. The corporate executive wants higher profits, the laborer a higher wage. The president wants the final word on military strategies, the chairman of the Joint Chiefs does not trust him with it. Boeing wants the contract, but General Dy-namics is closer at the time to the Navy secretary and the president, and so on. What is prevented by countervailing forces is the domination of society by a group, a clique, or a party. But this process suggests a profoundly important point: that *the constant pattern in American society is the rise and fall of tem-porarily irresponsible groups.* By temporary we mean that, except for the largest industrial conglomerates,[11] the groups that wield significant power to influence policy decisions are not guaranteed stability. By irresponsible we mean that many activities within their scope are essentially unaccountable in the demo-cratic process. These groups are too uneven to be described with the shorthand term *class.* Their personnel have many different characteristics (compare IBM executives with the Southern Dixiecrats), and their needs as groups are different enough to cause endless fights; for example, between small and big business. No one group or coalition of several groups can tyrannize the rest. This is demon-strated, for example, by the changing status of the major financial groups; for example, the Bank of America, which grew rapidly, built on the financial needs of the previously neglected small consumer.

However, these groups clearly exist within consensus relationships more gen-eral and durable than their conflict relationships. This is true, first of all, of their social characteristics. In an earlier version of this chapter we compiled tables using data from an exhaustive study of American elites contained in Warner et al., *The American Federal Executive* (1963) and from Suzanne Keller's compilation of military, economic, political, and diplomatic elite survey materials in *Beyond the Ruling Class* (1963). The relevant continuities demonstrated by the data suggest an educated elite with largely Protestant, business-oriented origins. Moreover, the data suggest inbreeding with the result that business orienta-tion has probably been at least maintained, if not augmented, by marriage. Domhoff, in *Who Rules America?,* has shown that elites generally attend the same exclusive prep schools and universities and belong to the same exclusive gentlemen's clubs. The consistencies suggest orientations not unlike those found

in an examination of the editorial content of major business newspapers and
weeklies, and in more directly sampled assessments of elite opinions.[12]

Other evidence for consensus relationships, besides attitude and background
data indicating a pro-business sympathy, would come from an examination of the
practice of decision making. By analyzing actual behavior we can understand
which consensus attitudes are reflected in decision making. Here, in retrospect,
it is possible to discover the values and assumptions which are recurrently defended. This is at least a rough means of finding the boundaries of consensus relationships. Often these boundaries are invisible because of the very infrequency
with which they are tested. What are visible most of the time are the parameters
of conflict relationships among different groups. These conflict relationships
constitute the ingredients of experience, which gives individuals or groups their
uniqueness and variety, while the consensus relationships constitute the common
underpinnings of behavior. Social scientists have tended to study decision making
in order to study group differences; we need to study decision making also to
understand group commonalities.

Were such studies done, our hypothesis would be that certain "core beliefs"
are never questioned. One of these beliefs, undoubtedly, would be that efficacy
is preferable to principle in foreign affairs. In practice, this means that violence is
preferable to nonviolence as a means of defense. A second belief is that private
property is preferable to collective property. A third assumption is that the particular form of constitutional government practiced within the United States is
preferable to any other system of government. We refer to that preferred mode
as limited parliamentary democracy, a system in which institutionalized forms of
direct representation are carefully retained, but with fundamental limitations on
the prerogatives of governing. Specifically included among the limitations are
many matters encroaching on corporation property and state hegemony. While
adherence to this form of government is conceivably the strongest of the domestic "core values," at least among business elites, it is probably the least strongly
held of the three on the international scene. American relations with, and assistance to, authoritarian and semi-feudal regimes indicate that the recipient regime
is evaluated primarily on the two former assumptions and given rather extensive
leeway on the latter one.

The implications of these "core beliefs" for the social system are immense, for
they justify the maintenance of our largest institutional structures: the military,
the corporate economy, and a system of partisan politics that protects the concept of limited democracy. These institutions, in turn, may be seen as current
agencies of the more basic social structure. The "renewable basis of power" in
America at the present time underlies those institutional orders linked in consensus relationships: military defense of private property and parliamentary democracy. These institutional orders are, by definition, not permanently secure.
Their maintenance involves a continuous coping with new conditions, such as
with technological innovation and with the inherent instabilities of a social struc-

ture which arbitrarily classifies persons by role, status, access to resources, and power. The myriad groups composing these orders are even less secure because of their weak ability to command "coping resources"; for example, the service branches are less stable than the institution of the military, particular companies are less stable than the institutions of corporate property, political parties are less stable than the institution of parliamentary government.

In the United States there is no ruling group. Nor is there any easily discernible ruling institutional order, so meshed have the separate sources of elite power become. But there is a social structure organized to create and protect power centers with only partial accountability. In our definition of power, we avoid the Weber-Mills meaning of *omnipotence* and the contrary pluralist definition of power as consistently *diffuse*. We are describing the current system as one of overall "minimal accountability" and "minimal consent." We mean that the role of democratic review, based on genuine popular consent, is made marginal and reactive. Elite groups are minimally accountable to publics and have a substantial, though by no means maximum, freedom to shape popular attitudes. The reverse of our system would be one in which democratic participation was the orienting demand around which the social structure was organized.

Some will counter this case by saying that we are measuring "reality" against an "ideal," a technique which permits the conclusion that the social structure is undemocratic according to its distance from our utopian values. This is a convenient apology for the present system, of course. We think it possible, at least in theory, to develop measures of the undemocratic in democratic conditions, and place given social structures at positions along a continuum. These measures, in rough form, might include such variables as economic security, education, legal guarantees, access to information, and participatory control over systems of economy, government, and jurisprudence.

The reasons why a chapter reviewing the power of a purported military-industrial complex should be concerned with democratic process are twofold. First, just as scientific method both legitimizes and promotes change in the world of knowledge, democratic method legitimizes and promotes change in the world of social institutions. Every society, regardless of how democratic it is, protects its core institutions in a web of widely shared values. But if the core institutions should be dictated by the requisites of military preparedness, then restrictions on the democratic process, that is, restrictions on mass opinion exchange (as by voluntary or imposed news management) or on decision-making bodies (as by selecting participants in a manner guaranteeing exclusion of certain positions), would be critical obstacles to peace.

Second, certain elements of democratic process are inimical to features of a military-oriented society, and the absence of these elements offers one type of evidence for the existence of a military-industrial complex even in the absence of a ruling elite. Secretary of Defense Robert McNamara made the point amply clear in his 1961 testimony before the Senate Armed Services Committee:

Why should we tell Russia that the Zeus development may not be satisfactory? What we ought to be saying is that we have the most per-
fect anti-ICBM system that the human mind will ever devise. Instead
the public domain is already full of statements that the Zeus may not
be satisfactory, that it has deficiencies. I think it is absurd to release
that level of information (Military Procurement Authorization,
Fiscal Year 1962).

Under subsequent questioning McNamara attempted to clarify his statement,
saying that he wished only to delude Russian, not American, citizens about
United States might. Exactly how this might be done was not explained.

A long established tradition of "executive privilege" permits the president to
refuse to release information when, in his opinion, its release would be damaging
to the national interest. Under modern conditions responsibility for handling
strategic information is shared among military, industrial, and executive agencies.
Discretion over when to withhold what information must also be shared. Moreover, the existence of a perpetual danger makes the justification, "in this time of
national crisis," suitable to every occasion in which secrecy must be justified.
McNamara's statement, cited above, referred not to a crisis in Cuba or Vietnam
but rather to the perpetual state of cold war crisis. Since the decision about what
is to be released and when is subject to just such management, the media have
become dependent on the agencies for timely leaks and major stories. This not
only gives an aura of omniscience to the agencies, but also gives them the power
to reward "good" journalists and punish critical ones.

The issues involved in the question of news management involve more than the
controls available to the president, the State Department, the Department of Defense, the Central Intelligence Agency, the Atomic Energy Commission, or any of
the major defense contractors. Outright control of news flow is probably less
pervasive than voluntary acquiescence to the objectives of these prominent institutions of our society. Nobody has to tell the wire services when to release a
story on the bearded dictator of our hemisphere, or the purported brutality of
Ho Chi Minh. The devil image of the enemy has become a press tradition. In addition to a sizeable quantity of radio and television programming and spot time
purchased directly by the Pentagon, an amount of service valued at $6 million by
Variety is donated annually by the networks and by public relations agencies for
various military shows (Swomley 1959). Again, the pluralistic shell of an independent press or broadcasting media is left hollow by the absence of a countervailing social force of any significant power.

We listed earlier several shared premises unquestioned by any potent locus of
institutionalized power:

1. Efficacy is preferable to principle in foreign affairs (thus military means are
   chosen over nonviolent means).
2. Private property is preferable to public property.

   3. Limited parliamentary democracy is preferable to any other system of government.

At issue is the question of whether an America protecting such assumptions can exist in a world of enduring peace. Three preconditions for enduring peace must be held up against these premises. The first is that enduring peace will first require or will soon generate disarmament. Offset programs, or plans for reallocation of the defense dollar, require a degree of coordinated planning for the change that is inconsistent with the working assumption that "private property is preferable to public property" in a corporate economy.

   The available projections regarding offset programs, especially regional and local offset programs, necessary to maintain economic well-being in the face of disarmament in this country highlight two important features. One is the lag time in industrial conversion. The second is the need for coordination in the timing and spacing of programs. One cannot reinvest in new home building in an area which has just been deserted by its major industry and left a ghost town. The short-term and long-term offset values of new hospitals and educational facilities will differ in the building and use stages, and regional offset programs have demonstrable interregional effects (Reiner 1964). Plans requiring large-scale worker mobility will require a central bank of job information and a smooth system for its dissemination. Such coordination will require a degree of centralization and control beyond that which our assumption regarding the primacy of private property would permit. Gross intransigence has already been seen even in contingency planning for non-defense work by single firms like Sperry Rand, which have already been severely hurt by project cutbacks. And the prospect of contingency planning will not be warmly welcomed by the new aeroframe industry (which is only 60 percent convertible to needs of a peacetime society) (McDonagh and Zimmerman 1964). Private planning by an individual firm for its own future does occur; however, without coordinated plans, the length of time ahead for which we can accurately forecast market conditions remains smaller than the lag time for major retooling. A lag time of six to ten years would not be atypical before plans of a somewhat overspecialized defense contractor could result in retooling for production in a peacetime market. In the meantime, technological innovations, government fiscal or regulatory policies, shifts in consumer preferences, or decisions by other firms to enter that same market could well make the market vanish. Moreover, the example of defense firms that have attempted even the smaller step toward diversification presents a picture which is not entirely promising (Fearon and Hook 1964). Indeed, one of several reasons for the failures in this endeavor has been that marketing skills necessary to compete in a private-enterprise economy have been lost by the industrial giants who have been managing with a sales force of one or two retired generals to deal with the firm's only customer. Even if successful conversion by some firms were to serve as the model for all individual attempts, the collective result would be poor.

To avoid a financially disastrous glutting of limited markets, some coordinated planning will be needed.

The intransigence regarding public or collaborative planning occurs against a backdrop of an increasing army of unemployed youth and aged, as well as of regional armies of unemployed victims of automation. Whether work is defined in traditional job market terms or as anything worthwhile that a person can do with his life, work (and some means of livelihood) will have to be found for these people. Much work needs to be done in community services, education, public health, and recreation, but this is people work, not product work. The lack of a countervailing force prevents the major reallocation of human and economic resources from the sector defined as preferable by the most potent institutions of society. One point must be stressed. We are *not* saying that limited planning to cushion the impact of arms reduction is impossible. Indeed, it is going on, and with the apparent blessing of the Department of Defense (Barber 1963). We are saying that accommodation to a cutback of $9 billion in research and development and $16 billion in military procurement requires a type of preparation not consistent with the three unchallenged assumptions.

Even the existence of facilities for coordinated planning does not, to be sure, guarantee the success of such planning. Bureaucratic institutions, designed as they may be for coordination and control, set up internal resistance to the very coordination they seek to achieve. The mechanisms for handling bureaucratic intransigency usually rely on such techniques as bringing participants into the process of formulating the decisions which will affect their own behavior. We can conceive of no system of coordinated conversion planning which could function without full and motivated cooperation from the major corporations, the larger unions, and representatives of smaller business and industry. Unfortunately, it is just as difficult to conceive of a system which would assure this necessary level of participation and cooperation. The same argument cuts deeper still when we speak of the millions of separate individuals in the "other America" whose lives would be increasingly "administered" by the centralized planning needed to offset a defense economy. Job assignments to distant geographical locations, vocational retraining programs, development of housing projects to meet minimal standards, educational enrichment programs—all of the programs conceived by middle-class white America for racially mixed low-income groups face the same difficulty in execution of their plans. Unless they can participate directly in the formulation of the programs, the target populations are less likely to participate in the programs and more likely to continue feeling alienated from the social system which views them as an unfortunate problem rather than as contributing members. Considering the need for active participation in real decisions, every step of coordinated planning carries with it the responsibility for an equal step in the direction of participatory democracy. This means that the voice of the unemployed urban worker may have to be heard, not only in city council meetings to discuss policy on rat control in his dwelling, but also in decisions about where a particular major corporation will be relocated and where the major resource allocations of the country will be invested. That such decision participation would run counter to the consensus on the items of limited parliamentary democracy and private property is exactly the point we wish to make.

Just as the theoretical offset plans can be traced to the sources of power with which they conflict, so too can the theoretical plans for international governing and peace-keeping operations be shown to conflict with the unquestioned beliefs. United States consent to international jurisdiction in the settlement of claims deriving from the nationalization of American overseas holdings or the removal of American military installations is almost inconceivable. Moreover, the mode of American relations to less developed countries is so much a part of the operations of those American institutions which base their existence on interminable conflict with communism that the contingency in which the United States might have to accept international jurisdiction in these areas seems unreal. For example, Mexican offers to mediate with Cuba are bluntly rejected. Acceptance of such offers would have called into question not one but all three of the assumptions in the core system. International jurisdictional authority might institutionalize a means to call the beliefs into question. For this reason (but perhaps most directly because of our preference for forceful means) America has been preoccupied, in negotiations regarding the extension of international control, almost exclusively with controls over weaponry and police operations and not at all with controls over political or social justice.[13]

The acceptance of complete international authority even in the area of weaponry poses certain inconsistencies with the preferred core beliefs. Nonviolent settlement of Asian–African area conflicts would be slow and ineffective in protecting American interests. The elimination, however, of military preparedness, both for projected crises and for their potential escalation, requires a faith in alternate means of conflict resolution. The phasing of the American plan for general and complete disarmament says in effect: prove that the alternatives are as efficient as our arms in protection of our interests and then we will disarm. In the short term, however, the effectiveness of force always looks greater.

The state of world peace is affected by people's comparison of themselves with persons who have more of the benefits of industrialization than they do. Such comparisons increase the demand for rapid change. While modern communications heighten the pressures imposed by such comparisons, the actual disparities revealed by comparison promote violence. Population growth rates, often as high as 3 percent, promise that population will double within a single generation in countries least able to provide for their people. The absolute number of illiterates as well as the absolute number of starving persons is greater now than ever before in history. Foreign aid barely offsets the disparity between declining prices paid for the underdeveloped countries' prime export commodities and rising prices paid for the finished products imported into these countries (Horowitz 1962). All schemes for tight centralized planning employed by these countries to rationally accrue and disperse scarce capital are blocked by the unchallenged assumptions on private property and limited parliamentary democracy. A restatement of the principle came in the report of General Lucius Clay's committee on foreign aid. The report stated that the United States should not assist foreign governments "in projects establishing government owned industrial and commercial enterprises which compete with existing private endeavors." When Congressman Broomfield's amendment on foreign aid resulted in the cancellation of a United States promise to India to build a steel mill in Bokaro, Broomfield stated the case succinctly: "The main issue is private enterprise vs. state socialism" (*Atlantic Monthly*, September 1964, p. 6). Moreover, preference for forceful solutions assures that the capital now invested in preparedness will not be allocated in a gross way to the needs of underdeveloped countries. Instead, the manifest crises periodically erupting in violence justify further the need for reliance upon military preparedness.

We agree fully with an analysis by Lowi (1964) distinguishing types of decisions over which elite-like forces seem to hold control (redistributive) from other types in which pluralist powers battle for their respective interests (distributive). In distributive decisions the pie is large and the fights are over who gets how much. Factional strife within and among military, industrial, and political forces in our country are largely of this nature. In redistributive decisions the factions coalesce, for the pie itself is threatened. We have been arguing that the transition to peace is a process of redistributive decision.

Is there, then, a military-industrial complex which prevents peace? The answer is inextricably embedded in American institutions and mores. Our concept is not that American society contains a ruling military-industrial complex. It is more nearly that American society *is* a military-industrial complex. The complex can accommodate a wide range of factional interests, from those concerned with the production or use of a particular weapon to those enraptured with the mystique of optimal global strategies. It can accommodate those who rabidly desire to advance toward the brink and into limitless intensification of the arms race. It can even accommodate those who wish either to prevent war or to limit the destructiveness of war through the gradual achievement of arms control and disarmament agreements. What it cannot accommodate is the type of radical departure needed to produce enduring peace.

NOTES

1. United States Senate, Committee on Government Operations, report of the Permanent Subcommittee on Investigations, *Pyramiding of Profits and Costs in the Missile Procurement Program*, March 31, 1964.
2. United States Senate, Committee on Labor and Public Welfare, report of the Subcommittee on Employment and Manpower, *Convertibility of Space and Defense Resources to Civilian Needs: A Search for New Employment Potentials*, 88th Congress, 2nd session, 1964.

3. United States Senate, Committee on Foreign Relations, Subcommittee on Disarmament, *The Economic Impact of Arms Control Agreements,* Congressional Record, October 5, 1962, pp. 2139-2194.

4. See Janowitz for a good sociological study of interservice differences.

5. For the thesis that a "peacefare state" counterweighs a "warfare state," see Klaus Knorr's review of Fred J. Cook in the *Journal of Conflict Resolution* 7, no. 4 (December 1963). The "pluralist position," which usually says that the social system has semi-automatic checking mechanisms against tyranny, is basic in discussions not only of the military, but of economics and politics as well. See Robert Dahl, *Who Governs?*; John Kenneth Galbraith, *American Capitalism*; Seymour Martin Lipset, *Political Man*; Talcott Parsons, *The Social System.*

6. See James H. Meisel, *The Myth of the Ruling Class,* for the best available discussion of this innovation in theorizing about elites. For evidence on this theory see Ben Seligman's *The Potentates* and William Domhoff's *The Inner Circles.*

7. Swomley (1964) accounts for Department of Defense holdings equivalent in size to eight states of the United States. Kenneth Boulding, using personnel as well as property criteria, calls the Department of Defense the world's third largest socialist state (personal discussion, 1963).

8. In an earlier book, *The Empire of High Finance* (1957), Perlo documented the close relations of the major financial groups and the political executive. He did not, however, extend this analysis to congressmen and senators, nor did he offer sufficient comparative evidence to demonstrate a long-term pattern.

9. For this argument, see A. A. Berle, *The Twentieth Century Capitalist Revolution,* and J. K. Galbraith, *American Capitalism.* For sound criticisms, but without sound alternatives, see Mills's and Perlo's books. Also see Michael Reagan, *The Managed Economy* (1963), and Bernard Nossiter, *The Mythmakers* (1964), for other refutations of the countervailing power thesis.

10. We are defining the term as "primary reliance on coercive means, particularly violence or the threat of violence, to deal with social problems."

11. The term refers to industrial organizations like Textron and Ling-Temco-Vought which have holdings in every major sector of American industry.

12. For some interesting work about the attitudes of business and military elites see Angell 1964; Bauer et al. 1963; Eells and Walton 1961; and Singer 1964.

13. An objective account of the major disarmament negotiations may be found in Frye (1963).

REFERENCES

Angell, Robert C.
   1964   "A Study of Social Values: Content Analysis of Elite Media." *Journal of Conflict Resolution* 8 (December): pp. 329–385.
Barber, Arthur
   1963   "Some Industrial Aspects of Arms Control." *Journal of Conflict Resolution* 7 (September): pp. 491–495.
Barnet, Richard
   1969   *The Economy of Death.* New York: Atheneum.

Bauer, Raymond A., I. Pool, and L. Dexter
   1963   *American Business and Public Policy.* New York: Alberton.
Bell, Daniel
   1964   *The End of Ideology.* Glencoe, Ill.: The Free Press.
Benoit, Emile, and K. E. Boulding, *eds.*
   1963   *Disarmament and the Economy.* New York: Harper & Row.
Berle, Adolph A.
   1954   *The Twentieth Century Capitalist Revolution.* New York: Harcourt.
Bluestone, Irving
   1963   "Problems of the Worker in Industrial Conversion." *Journal of Conflict Resolution* 7 (September): pp. 495–502.
Brand, Horst
   1962   "Disarmament and American Capitalism." *Dissent* 9 (Summer): pp. 236–251.
Burdick, Eugene, and H. Wheeler
   1962   *Fail-Safe.* New York: McGraw-Hill.
Burton, John
   1962   *Peace Theory.* New York: Knopf.
Cartwright, Dorwin
   1959   "Power: A Neglected Variable in Social Psychology," in Dorwin Cartwright, ed., *Studies in Social Power.* Ann Arbor, Mich.: Research Center for Group Dynamics.
Catton, Bruce
   1948   *The War Lords of Washington.* New York: Harcourt.
Coffin, Tristran
   1964   *The Passion of the Hawks.* New York: Macmillan.
Cohen, Bernard C.
   1963   *The Press and Foreign Policy.* Princeton, N.J.: Princeton University Press.
Cook, Fred J.
   1962   *The Warfare State.* New York: Macmillan.
   1963   "The Coming Politics of Disarmament." *The Nation* 196 (February 6): pp. 36–48.
Dahl, Robert A.
   1961   *Who Governs?* New Haven, Conn.: Yale University Press.
   1963   *A Modern Political Analysis.* Englewood Cliffs, N.J.: Prentice-Hall, Inc.
Dillon, W.
   1962   *Little Brother Is Watching.* Boston: Houghton Mifflin.
Domhoff, G. William
   1969   "Who Made American Foreign Policy, 1945–1963?" in David Horowitz, ed., *Corporations and the Cold War,* pp. 25–69. New York: Monthly Review Press.
Eells, Richard, and C. Walton
   1961   *Conceptual Foundations of Business.* Homewood, Ill.: Irwin Press.
Etzioni, Amitai
   1962   *The Hard Way to Peace.* New York: Collier.
   1964   *The Moon-Doggle.* Garden City, N.Y.: Doubleday & Co.

Fearon, H. E., and R. C. Hook, Jr.
   1964   "The Shift from Military to Industrial Markets." *Business Topics* 12
          (Winter): pp. 43–52.
Feingold, Eugene, and Thomas Hayden
   1964   "What Happened to Democracy?" *New University Thought* 4
          (Summer): pp. 39–48.
Fisher, Roger, *ed.*
   1964   *International Conflict and Behavioral Science.* New York: Basic
          Books.
Fishman, Leslie
   1962   "A Note on Disarmament and Effective Demand." *The Journal of
          Political Economy* 70 (June): pp. 183–186.
Freidman, S.
   1963   "The RAND Corporation and Our Policy Makers." *Atlantic Monthly*
          212 (September) : pp. 61–68.
Frye, William R.
   1963   "Characteristics of Recent Arms-control Proposals and Agreements,"
          in D. G. Brennan, ed., *Arms Control, Disarmament, and National
          Security.* New York: Braziller.
Galbraith, J. K.
   1956   *American Capitalism.* Boston: Houghton Mifflin.
   1962   "Poverty Among Nations." *Atlantic Monthly* 210 (October):
          pp. 47–53.
   1967   *The New Industrial State.* New York: Signet.
   1969   *How to Control the Military.* New York: Doubleday & Co.
Gans, Herbert J.
   1964   "Some Proposals for Government Policy in an Automating Society."
          The Correpondent 30 (Jan./Feb.): pp. 74–82.
Green, Philip
   1963   "Alternative to Overkill: Dream and Reality." *Bulletin of the
          Atomic Scientists* (November) : pp. 23–26.
Hayakawa, S. I.
   1960   "Formula for Peace: Listening." *New York Times Magazine*
          (July 31): pp. 10–12.
Heilbroner, Robert
   1970   "How the Pentagon Rules Us." *New York Review of Books* 15
          (July 23): p. 5.
Horowitz, David
   1962   *World Economic Disparities: The Haves and the Have-Nots.* Santa
          Barbara, Calif.: Center for the Study of Democratic Institutions.
Horowitz, I. L.
   1963   *The War Game: Studies of the New Civilian Militarists.* New York:
          Ballantine.
Humphrey, Hubert H.
   1962   "The Economic Impact of Arms Control Agreements." *Congres-
          sional Record* 108 (October 5) : pp. 2139–2194.
Isard, Walter, and E. W. Schooler
   1963   "An Economic Analysis of Local and Regional Impacts of Reduc-

tion of Military Expenditures." *Papers* I, Chicago Conference of the Peace Research Society International.

Janowitz, Morris
1957   "Military Elites and the Study of War." *The Journal of Conflict Resolution* 1 (March): pp. 9–18.
1960   *The Professional Soldier.* Glencoe, Ill.: The Free Press.

Keller, Suzanne
1963   *Beyond the Ruling Class.* New York: Random House.

Knebel, Fletcher, and C. Bailey
1962   *Seven Days in May.* New York: Harper & Row.

Knoll, Erwin, and Judith McFadden, eds.
1969   *American Militarism 1970.* New York: The Viking Press.

Knorr, Klaus
1963   "Warfare and Peacefare States and the Acts of Transition." *The Journal of Conflict Resolution* 7 (December) : pp. 754–762.

Lapp, Ralph E.
1962   *Kill and Overkill.* New York: Basic Books.
1968   *The Weapons Culture.* New York: Norton.

Larson, Arthur
1961   "The International Rule of Law." A report to the Committee on Research for Peace, Program of Research No. 3, Institute for International Order.

Lasswell, Harold
1958   *Politics: Who Gets What, When and How.* New York: Meridian.

Lipset, Seymour M.
1959   *Political Man.* Garden City, N.Y.: Doubleday & Co.

Little, Roger W.
1968   "Basic Education and Youth Socialization in the Armed Forces." *American Journal of Orthopsychiatry* 38 (October): pp. 869–876.

The Long Island Sunday Press
1964   February 23.

Lowi, Theodore J.
1964   "American Business, Public Policy, Case-Studies, and Political Theory." *World Politics* 16 (July) : pp. 676–715.

Lumer, Hyman
1954   *War Economy and Crisis.* New York: International Publishers.

Lynd, Robert S., and Helen Merrill
1959   *Middletown.* New York: Harcourt.

McDonagh, James J. and Steven M. Zimmerman
1964   "A Program for Civilian Diversifications of the Airplane Industry," in U.S. Senate Subcommittee on Employment and Manpower, *Convertibility of Space and Defense Resources to Civilian Needs.* Washington, D.C.: U.S. Government Printing Office.

McNamara, Robert S.
1963   "Remarks of the Secretary of Defense before the Economic Club of New York." Washington, D.C.: Department of Defense Office of Public Affairs.

Mannheim, Karl
    1956   *Freedom, Power and Democratic Planning.* London: Routledge and Kegan Paul.

Meisel, James H.
    1962   *The Fall of the Republic.* Ann Arbor, Mich.: University of Michigan Press.
    1962   *The Myth of the Ruling Class.* Ann Arbor, Mich.: University of Michigan Press.

Melman, Seymour, *ed.*
    1962   *The Peace Race.* New York: Braziller.
    1963   *A Strategy for American Security.* New York: Lee Offset, Inc.
    1970   *Pentagon Capitalism.* New York: McGraw-Hill.

Merbaum, R.
    1963   "RAND: Technocrats and Power." *New University Thought* 3 (December–January) : pp. 45–57.

Michael, Donald
    1962   *Cybernation: The Silent Conquest.* Santa Barbara, Calif.: Center for the Study of Democratic Institutions.

Milbrath, L. W.
    1963   *The Washington Lobbyists.* Chicago: Rand McNally.

Mills, C. Wright
    1958   *The Causes of World War III.* New York: Simon & Schuster.
    1959   *The Power Elite.* New York: Oxford University Press.

Minnis, Jack
    1946   "The Care and Feeding of Power Structures." *New University Thought* 5 (Summer) : pp. 73–79.

Mollenhoff, Clark R.
    1967   *The Pentagon: Politics, Profits, and Plunder.* New York: Putnam.

Nossiter, Bernard
    1964   *The Mythmakers: An Essay on Power and Wealth.* Boston: Houghton Mifflin.

Osgood, Charles E.
    1962   *An Alternative to War or Surrender.* Urbana, Ill.: University of Illinois Press.

Parsons, Talcott
    1951   *The Social System.* Glencoe, Ill.: The Free Press.
    1959   *Structure and Process in Modern Societies.* Glencoe, Ill.: The Free Press.

Paul, J., and J. Laulight
    1963   "Leaders' and Voters' Attitudes on Defense and Disarmament," in *In Your Opinion* 1. Clarkson, Ontario: Canadian Peace Research Institute.

Peck, M. J., and F. M. Scherer
    1962   *The Weapons Acquisition Process.* Cambridge, Mass.: Harvard University Press.

Perlo, Victor
    1963   *Militarism and Industry.* New York: International Publishers.

Piel, Gerard
1961 *Consumers of Abundance.* Santa Barbara, Calif.: Center for the Study of Democratic Institutions.
Pilisuk, Marc
1963 "Dominance of the Military." *Science* 139 (January 18) : pp. 247–248.
1965 "The Poor and the War on Poverty." *The Correspondent* 34 (Summer) : pp. 107–110.
1968 "A Reply to Roger Little: Basic Education and Youth Socialization Anywhere Else." *Americal Journal of Orthopsychiatry* 38 (October): pp. 877–881.
"The Power of the Pentagon"
1969 *The Progressive* 33 (June) : p. 6.
Rapoport, Anatol
1960 *Fights, Games, and Debates.* Ann Arbor, Mich.: University of Michigan Press.
1964 *Strategy and Conscience.* New York: Harper & Row.
Raymond, Jack
1964 *Power at the Pentagon.* New York: Harper & Row.
Reagan, Michael
1963 *The Managed Economy.* New York: Oxford University Press.
Reiner, Thomas
1964 "Spatial Criteria to Offset Military Cutbacks." Paper presented at the University of Chicago Peace Research Conference, November 18.
"Report on the World Today"
1964 *Atlantic Monthly* 214 (September) : pp. 4–8.
Rogow, Arnold A.
1963 *James Forrestal.* New York: Macmillan.
Scherer, Frederick
1964 *The Weapons Acquisition Process: Economic Incentives.* Cambridge, Mass.: Harvard University Business School.
Shils, Edward
1961 "Professor Mills on the Calling of Sociology." *World Politics* 13 (July) : pp. 600–621.
Singer, J. David
1962 *Deterrence, Arms Control and Disarmament.* Columbus, Ohio: Ohio State University Press.
1964 "A Study of Foreign Policy Attitudes." *Journal of Conflict Resolution* 8 (December) : pp. 424–485.
_____, ed.
1963 "Weapons Management in World Politics." *Journal of Conflict Resolution* 7 (September) : pp. 185–190 and *Journal of Arms Control* 1 (October) : pp. 279–284.
Stachey, John
1963 *On the Prevention of War.* New York: St. Martin's Press.
Strauss, Lewis L.
1962 *Men and Decisions.* Garden City, N.Y.: Doubleday & Co.

Sutton, Jefferson
   1963   *The Missile Lords.* New York: Dell.
Swomley, J. M., Jr.
   1959   "The Growing Power of the Military." *The Progressive* 23 (January):
          pp. 10–17.
   1964   *The Military Establishment.* Boston: Beacon Press.
U.S. Arms Control and Disarmament Agency
   1962   *Economic Impacts of Disarmament.* Economic Series 1. Washington,
          D.C.: U.S. Government Printing Office.
   1964   *Toward World Peace: A Summary of U.S. Disarmament Efforts Past
          and Present.* Publication 10. Washington, D.C.: U.S. Government
          Printing Office.
U.S. Congress
   1964   *Military Posture and Authorizing Appropriations for Aircraft, Missiles,
          and Naval Vessels.* Hearings No. 36, 88th Congress, 2nd session.
          Washington, D.C.: U.S. Government Printing Office.
   1964a   *Pyramiding of Profits and Costs in the Missile Procurement Program.*
          Report No. 970, 88th Congress, 2nd session. Washington, D.C.:
          U.S. Government Printing Office.
U.S. Congress, Committee on Banking and Currency
   1963   *Bank Holding Companies: Scope of Operations and Stock Owner-
          ship.* Washington, D.C.: U.S. Government Printing Office.
U.S. Congress, Committee on Foreign Affairs
   1964   *Foreign Assistance Act of 1964* (Parts 6 and 7). Hearings, 88th Con-
          gress, 2nd session. Washington, D.C.: U.S. Government Printing
          Office.
U.S. Congress, Committee on Government Operations
   ·1962   *Pyramiding of Profits and Costs in the Missile Procurement Program*
          (Parts 1, 2, and 3). Hearings, 87th Congress, 2nd session. Washing-
          ton, D.C.: U.S. Government Printing Office.
   1963   *Government Information Plans and Policies* (Parts 1–4). Hearings,
          88th Congress, 1st session. Washington, D.C.: U.S. Government
          Printing Office.
   1964   *Satellite Communications* (Part 1). Hearings, 88th Congress, 2nd
          session. Washington, D.C.: U.S. Government Printing Office.
U.S. Congress, Committee on Labor and Public Welfare
   1964   *Toward Full Employment: Proposals for a Comprehensive Em-
          ployment and Manpower Policy in the U.S.* Washington, D.C.:
          U.S. Government Printing Office.
U.S. Congress, Joint Economic Committee
   1963   *Impact of Military Supply and Service Activities on the Economy.*
          88th Congress, 2nd session. Washington, D.C.: U.S. Government
          Printing Office.
U.S. Congress, Senate Committee on Armed Services
   1961   *Military Procurement Authorization Fiscal Year 1962.* 87th Con-
          gress, 1st session. Washington, D.C.: U.S. Government Printing
          Office.

U.S. Congress, Subcommittee on Employment and Manpower
  1964   *Convertibility of Space and Defense Resources to Civilian Needs.*
          88th Congress, 2nd Session, vol. 2. Washington, D.C.: U.S. Government Printing Office.
Warner, William Lloyd, and J. D. Abegglen
  1955   *Big Business Leaders in America.* New York: Harper & Row.
Warner, William Lloyd, P. P. Van Riper, N. H. Martin,
and O. F. Collins
  1963   *The American Federal Executive.* New Haven, Conn.: Yale University Press.
Watson-Watt, Sir Robert
  1962   *Man's Means to His End.* London: Heinemann.
Weidenbaum, Murray L.
  1968   "Arms and the American Economy: A Domestic Emergence Hypothesis." *American Economic Review* 58 (May): pp. 625–629.
Westin, Alan
  1963   "Anti-communism and the Corporations." *Commentary* 36 (December): pp. 479–487.
Wise, David, and Thomas Ross
  1964   *The Invisible Government.* New York: Random House.
Wright, Quincy, William Evans, and Morton Deutsch, *eds.*
  1962   *Preventing World War III: Some Proposals.* New York: Simon & Schuster.

Part IV.
Science, Technology, and Health

Science is most often dealt with as a set of values and a procedure for "the discovery of new facts about the natural world and the biological and social environments, the systemization of knowledge into a coherent theoretical system, and the application of this knowledge to the solution of practical problems."[1] Although science developed in the West, its materialist values, rationalism, empiricism, skepticism, and belief that the universe is understandable through scientific investigation have spread throughout the world. Few oppose its progress and the lure of technology.

In earlier years scientists often came into conflict with other institutions. Galileo, for example, was persecuted by the church, and several scientists were put to death for their "heresy." But science has long since made its peace with the other institutions. Indeed, in the modern world, the scientific ethos has been largely absorbed by the general ideology. As the work of Thomas Kuhn and Nobel prize winner James D. Watson (see Suggested Readings) indicates, the public usually credits science with more progress and certainty—and less intuition—than is accurate. And scientists, like other mortals, do not rise in rank sheerly on their objective scientific merit: There is a star system (as in theater), and a buddy system that facilitates recognition and opens new research possibilities.

While the values and achievements of science are well known, the ways in which scientists are organized are probably less understood. Most are not employed in purely scientific organizations, but in the

---

[1] Gerard DeGré, *Science as a Social Institution* (New York: Random House, 1955), p. 22.

military, government, business, and education. Thus, science is a secondary or service institution. However, scientists are coordinated to some extent by crosscutting agencies, such as the National Science Foundation, and by voluntary professional associations. Due particularly to substantial financing of science by the federal government during the Cold War, it has become a major occupational category. Government financing, while boosting science as a career, has also steered it toward largely military ends. The boom years of scientific employment and expenditure, however, appear to be over, with federal research and development spending declining relative to total spending.

The federal government provides more than half of the funds for scientific research and development, but expenditure has dropped from $17.3 billion in 1968–1969. As Table 1 indicates, private industry gets the largest share of federal money and most business-financed research and development was performed by industry itself. Of the federal expenditures, $2.6 billion was used for basic research. Most of this went to universities and colleges ($1.42 billion added to the

Table 1
Estimated Expenditures for Research and Development, 1973
(dollars in millions)

Sources of Funds	Performers					Percent Distribution
	Government	Industry	Universities and Colleges	Other Nonprofit Institutions	Total	
Federal Government	4,500	8,100	2,660	725	15,985	53.1
Industry	—	12,200	83	110	12,393	41.1
Universities and Colleges	—	—	1,290[a]	—	1,290	4.3
Other Nonprofit Institutions	—	—	192	240	432	1.4
Total	4,500	20,300	4,225	1,075	30,100	
Percent Distribution, Performers	15.0	67.4	14.0	3.6		100.0

[a]Includes state and local government funds.
SOURCE: National Science Foundation, *National Patterns of Research and Development Resources, Funds and Manpower in the United States : 1953–1973*, p. 6.

$1.01 billion from their own sources and state and local governments). The expenditure for applied research was $3.63 billion ($1.6 spent within government, $1.05 by industry), and $9.75 billion for development ($6.9 billion to industry). The breakdown of industry funding was $0.64 billion for basic research, $2.8 billion for applied, and $8.95 billion for development.[2]

The growth of scientific employment in business is illustrated by Table 2. Note that total employment grew rapidly from 1958 to 1969, but has since declined, with some industries—for example, electrical and communication, and aircraft and missiles—leading the way. Many firms in these two industries were supported by federal funds (43.0 percent and 76.5 percent of their business respectively in 1972) and consequently they were the most affected by government cutbacks. In addition, approximately 47,000 scientists and engineers in universities and colleges (about 20 percent of their faculty in these fields) were engaged primarily in research and development; 11,000 scientists were at federally funded research and development centers; and 21,000 were in other nonprofit institutions. The government directly employs a further 44,800. These are categorized in Table 3, which shows that the largest numbers are assigned to the Department of Defense and NASA. This parallels the overall priorities of government research and development expenditures.

The National Science Foundation reported that in 1969 about 158,000 scientists and engineers held a doctorate degree, and three-fifths of them were employed in academia. At least in basic research, then, the universities are likely to remain entrenched in government funded research.

Theodore Roszak's article is concerned with science as a belief system. He finds it no longer *the* way of understanding reality, but only one "school of consciousness." But the hegemony of science over man's ideas is strong and is only beginning to be challenged. While science and technology have enriched the United States, claims Roszak, they have not enhanced spiritual well-being and they have generated their own devastating problems, which more technological "solutions" cannot cure. The dominant one-sided scientific outlook on life has led us into this "technocratic trap."

Since World War II, science has become a big bureaucratic business, spelling the doom of the individual genius, the free-thinking scientific

[2] National Science Foundation, *National Patterns of Research and Development Resources, Funds and Manpower in the United States:* 1953–73, pp. 6–7.

Table 2
Full-Time-Equivalent Number of Research and Development Scientists and Engineers, by Industry (in thousands).

Industry	1960	1962	1964	1966	1968	1969	1970	1971	1972
Total	292.0	312.0	340.2	353.2	376.7	387.1	384.1	370.6	356.1
Chemicals and allied products	36.1	36.5	35.3	38.6	38.9	40.3	40.2	42.8	41.4
Petroleum refining and extraction	9.2	9.1	8.1	8.9	9.2	10.0	9.9	9.2	8.2
Rubber products	5.3	5.6	6.0	5.7	6.1	6.3	6.8	5.9	5.9
Stone, clay, and glass products	—[a]	3.7	3.3	3.1	4.1	4.2	4.6	4.1	3.8
Primary metals	6.9	6.0	5.1	5.5	5.9	6.2	6.3	6.3	6.8
Fabricated metal products	7.4	7.4	7.0	6.3	5.6	6.6	5.9	6.9	6.0
Machinery	32.1	31.5	27.3	30.5	37.4	39.4	41.4	40.5	41.1
Electrical equipment and communication	72.1	82.3	89.5	92.0	98.4	101.6	102.4	95.2	87.7
Motor vehicles and other transportation equipment	17.8	20.8	23.3	24.8	24.3	25.0	25.1	27.8	29.5
Aircraft and missiles	72.4	79.4	101.1	99.3	101.1	99.9	92.6	78.3	72.7
Professional and scientific instruments	10.0	9.8	10.8	12.5	14.1	15.1	14.8	18.9	18.6
Other manufacturing industries	22.6[b]	11.7	13.6	14.3	16.5	17.4	17.8	19.1	18.5
Other nonmanufacturing industries		7.0	9.8	11.7	15.1	15.1	16.3	15.6	15.9

[a]Excludes social scientists. Data included in the "other manufacturing" group.
[b]For years 1958–1960, other manufacturing and nonmanufacturing combined. Other manufacturing industries include food and kindred products; textiles, apparel; lumber and wood products; paper and allied products; tobacco products; printing and publishing; leather products and miscellaneous manufacturing.
SOURCE: National Science Foundation, *National Patterns of Research and Development Resources, Funds and Manpower in the United States: 1953–1973*, p. 14.

Table 3

Distribution of Civilian Research and Development Scientists and Engineers in the Federal Government, by Agency and Occupation[a]

Agency	Total	Engineers	Physical scientists	Mathematicians and statisticians	Biological scientists	Social scientists
Total (number)[b]	44,800	21,300	14,200	2,800	4,500	2,000
			Percent distribution			
	100.0	100.0	100.0	100.0	100.0	100.0
Department of Defense	52.0	67.0	40.8	81.3	10.1	24.7
Department of Agriculture	8.8	2.2	7.2	3.2	41.2	27.1
Department of Health, Education, and Welfare	5.8	.4	7.3	2.2	24.8	13.7
Department of the Interior	7.3	3.2	14.5	1.7	8.8	4.2
National Aeronautics and Space Administration	15.1	21.4	15.2	.2	1.4	.5
Department of Commerce	5.1	1.9	9.5	5.6	7.4	2.9
Department of Transportation	1.5	2.1	.7	2.6	.4	2.7
Other agencies	4.3	1.9	4.9	3.2	5.8	24.1

[a]Refers to October 1971.
[b]Excludes uniformed military, scientists and engineers, and administration of research and development.
Note: Percents may not add up to 100 because of rounding.
SOURCE: National Science Foundation, National Patterns of Research and Development Resources, Funds and Manpower in the United States: 1953–1973, p. 17.

intellectual. Both physical and social scientists are swept along by
the "progress" of routine research and the scramble for government—
that is, taxpayers'—money. Public relations announcements flood
the market with "startling new discoveries," and scientists race to
keep abreast with "new findings." In the name of science, we have
raped our environment. We have gained knowledge but not wisdom.
What is needed, if we are to prevent self-suffocation, Roszak concludes, is nothing less than a new natural philosophy to guide our
civilization, for science is morally bankrupt.

The next article, by Harvey Brooks, is unconcerned with Roszak's
reservations and anxieties. Accepting science much as it is, Brooks
deals with the intricacies of its composition and direction. He sees
two major problems—how to organize scientific work for maximum
efficiency, and how to apply it to society's needs. Unlike Roszak,
Brooks is a believer in scientific progress, but he does not simply
equate it with social progress. He is hopeful that the newly developing political and ethical sensibilities of scientists will lead to socially
constructive rather than military and crass commercial science. He
discusses the applied–pure science dilemma, the costs and benefits of
centralized and decentralized organization of research, private corporate research, and the challenges now confronting science and technology. He maintains that science *could* solve the world's problems
if technical manpower and resources were channeled in the right directions. Although Brooks is optimistic on this score, it should be re-
membered that the main employers of scientists—the military and
business—are not primarily concerned with social service. Their moti-
vating goals are, respectively, assured destruction and profits.

Another major form of scientific employment is in what has been
called the medical–industrial complex. This includes the drug industry, insurance, and health care services. The latter is the domain of
the country's largest (270,000) and perhaps most influential group of
technicians—physicians. Most of them act as private businessmen
(although they have a club rule not to compete with each other in
pricing their services) but maintain loose ties to hospitals and clinics
where most of the other health workers—nurses, paramedics, managers, and menials—are employed.

Health care has been one of the fastest growing industries in money
terms. It has milked the population's sickness at massively rising cost,
as Table 4 indicates, and has consumed an ever greater proportion of
our GNP and public spending. Some of these increases, according to

Table 4

Expenditures for Health Care in the United States, 1950–1972

Year	Amount (in billions)	Percent of GNP	Percent by Public Funds
1950	$12.0	4.6	25.5
1960	25.9	5.2	24.7
1966	42.1	5.9	25.7
1972	83.4	7.6	39.4

SOURCE: Social Security Administration Figures reported by Herbert E. Klarman, "Major Public Issues in Health Care," *The Public Interest* 34 (Winter 1974): 106–123.

Klarman (see Table 4), have been induced by the government's Medicare and Medicaid programs. Management of such programs is a lucrative business, and the public may well pay more for its health if such programs are extended. Perhaps then more people will, for example, receive surgery that is unnecessary.[3] Unfortunately for the public, this industry expansion has *not* produced marked improvement, nor has it raised the country's low international ranking on several key indicators of public health. Escalating costs without improving service, however, is tarnishing the physicians' image. Perhaps more than any other scientific/technical worker, the physician's practice has been unquestioned. Indeed, his operation has been immersed in secrecy, seen as part unknowable science, part magic. Today, though, the modern "witch doctor's" practice is coming under increasing public scrutiny and assault by lawyers armed with malpractice suits.

Rick J. Carlson's article examines the health care industry. His diagnosis is that it is deficient in its service and will probably get worse. Service consists mainly of curing, not preventing, disease and is geared toward the needs of the affluent. Above all, health care is disorganized, with most of the country's one quarter million plus physicians acting privately. Increasing specialization has only magnified the problem. There is more to health care than costly medicine. Health care must deal with environment-induced ailments, alcoholism and dietary deficiencies, and the socially-induced problem of

[3] For a good discussion of this, see Godfrey Hodgson, "The Politics of American Health Care," *Atlantic*, October 1973, pp. 45–60; and Robert R. Alford, "The Political Economy of Health Care," *Politics and Society*, Winter 1972, pp. 127–164.

aging—we regard the aged as useless. The causes of these are not being
treated. Carlson concludes with a set of reordered priorities that
would rationalize health care. Before such a program could be implemented, however, there would have to be considerable outside (political) pressure—physicians are unlikely to tamper radically with a system that serves them so well.

Suggested Readings

Calder, Nigel. *Technopolis: Social Control of the Uses of Science.* New York:
    Simon and Schuster, 1970.
DeGré, Gerard. *Science as a Social Institution.* New York: Random House,
    1955.
Ehrenreich, Barbara, and Ehrenreich, John. *The American Health Empire.* New
    York: Random House, 1970.
Ferkiss, Victor C. *Technological Man.* New York: Mentor, 1969.
Friedson, Eliot. *The Profession of Medicine.* New York: Dodd, Mead, 1970.
Hirsch, Walter. *Scientists in American Society.* New York: Random House,
    1968.
Holton, Gerald, ed. *Science and Culture.* Boston: Beacon Press, 1967.
Kaplan, Norman, ed. *Science and Society.* Chicago: Rand McNally, 1965.
Krohn, Roger G. *The Social Shaping of Science.* Westport, Conn.: Greenwood,
    1971.
Kuhn, Thomas S. *The Structure of Scientific Revolutions.* 2nd ed. Chicago:
    University of Chicago Press, 1970.
Mullins, Nicholas C. *Science: Some Sociological Perspectives.* Indianapolis:
    Bobbs-Merrill, 1973.
Rose, Hilary, and Rose, Steven. *Science and Society.* Baltimore: Pelican, 1970.
Roszak, Theodore. *Where the Wasteland Ends.* New York: Doubleday, 1972.
Strickland, Stephen P. *Politics, Science, and Dread Disease.* Boston: Harvard
    University Press, 1972.
Waitzkin, Howard, and Waterman, Barbara. *The Exploitation of Illness in Capi-
    talist Society.* Indianapolis: Bobbs-Merrill, 1974.
Watson, James D. *The Double Helix.* New York: Signet, 1968.
Yablonsky, Lewis. *Robopaths: People as Machines.* Baltimore: Pelican, 1972.

SCIENCE:
A TECHNOCRATIC TRAP
Theodore Roszak

The day of the great lone wolves, embattled heretics, and outsiders—the Faradays, the Galileos, the Pasteurs, toiling away in
modest laboratories and private garrets with makeshift equipment is gone. Bigness, thickly structured professionalism, and
government-corporation subvention have become indispensable
to the progress of both research and development.

It is roughly a century since European art began to experience its first significant defections from the standards of painting and sculpture that we inherit from
the early Renaissance. Looking back now across a long succession of innovative
movements and stylistic revolutions, most of us have little trouble recognizing
that such aesthetic orthodoxies of the past as the representative convention, exact anatomy and optical perspective, the casement-window canvas, along with
the repertory of materials and subject matters we associate with the Old Masters—
that all this makes up not "art" itself in any absolute sense, but something like a
school of art, one great tradition among many. We acknowledge the excellence
which a Raphael or Rembrandt could achieve within the canons of that school;
but we have grown accustomed to the idea that there are other aesthetic visions
of equal validity. Indeed, innovation in the arts has become a convention in its
own right with us, a "tradition of the new," to such a degree that there are critics
to whom it seems to be intolerable that any two painters should paint alike. We
demand radical originality, and often confuse it with quality.

Yet what a jolt it was to our great-grandparents to see the certainties of the
academic tradition melt away before their eyes. How distressing, especially for
the academicians, who were the guardians of a classic heritage embodying time-
honored techniques and standards whose perfection had been the labor of genius.
Suddenly they found art as they understood it being rejected by upstarts who
were unwilling to let a single premise of the inherited wisdom stand unchallenged,

or so it seemed. Now, with a little hindsight, it is not difficult to discern continuities where our predecessors saw only ruthless disjunctions. To see, as well, that the artistic revolutionaries of the past were, at their best, only opening our minds to a more global conception of art which demanded a deeper experience of light, color, and form. Through their work, too, the art of our time has done much to salvage the values of the primitive and childlike, the dream, the immediate emotional response, the life of fantasy, and the transcendent symbol.

In our own day, much the same sort of turning point has been reached in the history of science. It is as if the aesthetic ground pioneered by the artists now unfolds before us as a new ontological awareness. We are at a moment when the reality to which scientists address themselves comes more and more to be recognized as but one segment of a far broader spectrum. Science, for so long regarded as our single valid picture of the world, now emerges as, also, a school: a *school of consciousness,* beside which alternative realities take their place.

There are, so far, only fragile and scattered beginnings of this perception. They are still the subterranean history of our time. How far they will carry toward liberating us from the orthodox world view of the technocratic establishment is still doubtful. These days, many gestures of rebellion are subtly denatured, adjusted, and converted into oaths of allegiance. In our society at large, little beyond submerged unease challenges the lingering authority of science and technique, that dull ache at the bottom of the soul we refer to when we speak (usually too glibly) of an "age of anxiety," an "age of longing." The disease is as yet largely unmentionable, like the cancer one would rather ignore than reveal for diagnosis. The political leadership, the experts and academicians, the publicists and opinion makers prefer for the most part to regard the condition of spiritual disintegration in which we live (if they admit that there is a problem at all) as no worse than a minor ailment for which some routine wonder drug will soon be found. Modern man—so runs the by now journalistic commonplace—is "in search of a soul." But this, like all the snags in the system, only attracts its quota of "problemsolvers," fair-haired young men with bright new techniques for filling "the meaning-and-purpose gap." Presidents summon together blue-ribbon committees on "national goals," and major corporations open up lunchtime "therapy tanks" for vaguely distraught employees. Specialists in "future shock" step forward to recommend strategies for adapting bedazzled millions to the mad pace of industrial progress. Always, always it is another dose of R&D, another appeal to expertise that will cure us.

Another point that helps to obscure the cultural crisis of our time: One need only glance beyond the boundaries of the high industrial heartland to see our science-based technics rolling across the globe like a mighty juggernaut, obliterating every alternative style of life. It is difficult not to be flattered by our billions of envious imitators. Though they revile the rich white West, we nonetheless know that we are the very incarnation of the "development" they long for. And if all the world wants what we have got, must we not then be *right?* Are we not the standard for all that progress and modernity mean?

But it is a pathetic self-deception to beguile the impotent and hungry with our power and opulence, and then to seek the validation of our existence by virtue of all that is most wretched in them . . . their dire need, their ignorance of where our standard of development leads, their desperate covetousness. Such easy self-congratulation has no proper place in a serious assessment of our condition. There are those of our fellows who still struggle to enter the twentieth century. Their search for human dignity sets them that task, perhaps as a necessary stage in cultural evolution. There are those of us who are now *in* the century (who have indeed *made* this century), and our task is another—possibly one which the underdeveloped will scarcely appreciate. They pin their highest hopes to science and technique, even as our ancestors did. Our job is to review the strange course that science and technique have traveled and the price we have paid for their cultural triumph.

We must consider the devolution of the scientific tradition, which is destined, I think, to be the most important cultural event of our generation. For many, the decline and fall of scientific orthodoxy may seem—if it is conceivable at all—like a despicable reversion to barbarism, a betrayal of reason that threatens a new dark age. But there is another way to view the matter. The barbarian may be at the gate because the empire has decayed from within. He may even come to voice well-justified grievances which, for the good of our souls, we dare not ignore.

If along the countercultural fringes of our society, science now loses its ability to shape the consciousness of people, I believe this is for reasons that emerge from within science itself. It is due to serious failures and limitations that can be traced to the heart of the scientific enterprise, but which only the achievement of cultural supremacy could make vividly apparent. These might be called the negative potentialities of the scientific world view, long hidden from sight but now unmistakably visible. Taken together, they explain why our unstinting commitment to single vision has led us not to the promised New Jerusalem but to the technocratic trap we find closing about us.

Science, like all things human, has its history. It too suffers the ironies of change, and probably in no respect more obviously than in its institutional development. Especially since the end of World War II, science, as a profession, has become big, official, capital intensive, and bureaucratic, which is to say, its heroic age has ended. The day of the great lone wolves, embattled heretics, and outsiders—the Faradays, the Galileos, the Pasteurs, toiling away in modest laboratories and private garrets with makeshift equipment—is at least two generations behind us and not only gone, but *never* to be recovered.

Bigness, thickly structured professionalism, and government-corporation subvention have become indispensable to the progress of both research and development. Science, being objective, is cumulative; its knowledge detaches from the knower (supposedly without loss) and piles up. Thus science exhausts intellectual terrain as it races forward. This is what "progress" means in the world of scientific research; this is the peculiar pride of the discipline. Metaphysicians may still dispute questions drawn from Plato or St. Thomas. Artists may recompose still lives as old as Vermeer. But in science, problems get solved; as Thomas Kuhn would put it, the paradigms get filled in and the profession moves on to occupy new ground. Each solution may, of course, raise new questions, so that the province of the unknown remains always there to challenge study. But the new questions are *further out;* they recede like an ever expanding frontier. Therefore, it requires more intensive specialization, more teamwork, more sophisticated equipment to catch hold of a piece of that traveling frontier. So, as time goes on, there must be *more* scientists, *more* money, *more* coordination of research, *more* administrative superstructure, and, all together, *more* political maneuvering within the scientific community, as well as between science and its society.

Just as the Church of the Renaissance Popes was a far cry from the Church of the martyrs in their catacombs, so the science of what Norbert Wiener once called "the science factories" is hardly that of Galileo in his workshop. It is a very different institution, and of necessity a far less appealing one. It has forfeited its human scale, and that is a grave loss. It means that science, too, joins in the ethos of impersonal giganticism, which is among the most oppressive features of our Kafkaesque modern world. When the layman views science today, he no longer finds there a community of self-actualizing men and women pursuing their chosen calling with style, daring, and simple passion. Such individuals may, of course, be there; but they are lost from sight within an establishment of baroque complexity, an acronymous labyrinth of official hierarchies and elite conferences, of bureaus and agencies filled with rich careers and mandarin status.

Already the world of Big Science has seen instances of opportunistic lobbying that reach the level of major scandal. The infamous Mohole Project of the midsixties which wasted nearly a hundred million dollars in a futile attempt to drill a hole through the earth's crust is but the most notable example of how willing scientists can be to bamboozle their way aboard the federal gravy train. Mohole was sanctimoniously justified as "pure research" at every appropriation along the way, but finally collapsed without result in the midst of several highly suspect subcontracting concessions. The purposeful obfuscation and special pleading that have long surrounded the AEC's extravagant nuclear-testing programs (overground and underground) and the unseemly competition of the universities for the federal funding of high-energy accelerators offer further melancholy examples of major scientific talent taking expensive advantage of the public gullibility.

Nor have the natural scientists been alone in their haste to gain official patronage. The several behavioral science professions have been every bit as eager (if less successful) to cut themselves in on the prestige of government sponsorship. They have long lobbied for a nicely endowed National Foundation for the Social Sciences to match the National Science Foundation. Meanwhile they have accepted the support of military and paramilitary agencies to finance high-cost, computerized research in counterinsurgency warfare or behavioral modeling. At times, their arguments have been as barefacedly nationalistic as that of any bomb physicist—as when Professor Kingsley Davis argued before Congress in

1967 that "the first nation which breaks through the barrier and manages to put social science on a footing at least as sound as that of the natural sciences will be way ahead of every other nation in the world. I would like to see the United States be that nation. . . ."

Obviously, clever minds continue to enter Big Science; we know they must be clever because their colleagues tell us so, and all the colleagues reward one another grandly. But it is as Daniel Greenberg, author of *The Politics of Pure Science,* observes:

> With the mechanization of much scientific research, it is now possible to function and thrive in scientific research without the sense of inspiration and commitment that characterized the community in its penurious days. Science was once a calling; today it is still a calling for many but for many others, it is simply a living, and an especially comfortable one. . . .

Unavoidably, this routinizing and collectivization of research deprive us of the element of sympathetic personality in science—the clear perception of outstanding, often eccentric individuality. More and more, those of us on the outside see Big Science (like Big Technics) as a featureless personnel—teams, groups, committees, staffs arranged around entrepreneurial leaders. But more important, such routinization selects a different breed of scientist, an organization man whose work is delicately geared to the technocratic imperatives: efficient group dynamics, submission to the powers, a proper respect for official channels and institutional procedures. As Michael Reagan, author of *Science and the Federal Patron,* observes, "Today, team research might even be said to *require* some unimaginative plodders," and therefore "some net loss in freewheeling imagination, some tendency to shy away from the high-risk projects because future support might be endangered by failure to achieve positive results."

Is there, in fact, anyone in our society who has a keener awareness than the scientist and technician of how incomparably *productive* the technocratic style can be—or of how richly rewarding "careerwise"? Of course the protest arises, "But contemporary science and technology are inconceivable without minute specialization, teamwork, sophisticated equipment, and much official patronage." Perhaps so. But *if* so, then the last place we must expect to look for an alternative to technocracy is among the scientists and technicians, for whom technocratic forms of organization and finance have become their professional life's blood.

Further, with the advent of Big Science and Big Technics, there is the growing congestion of discovery and invention. So much of everything . . . and too much to keep track of. Inevitability hangs over every breakthrough; if it had not come this year, then surely next. For with enough money and brains applied to the task, are not "positive results" bound to follow? So there is more and more the cloying sense that innovation has become routine, the spectacular ordinary. The excitement of the scientific enterprise cannot help diminishing with overstimulation. True, the public still gasps and blinks at the achievements unveiled before it; it has little else to expend its wonderment upon in the artificial environment. But even the admiration descends to cliché; the words "miracle" and "marvel" come too readily to the lips. One begins to *expect* the miraculous—an obvious contradiction—to such an extent that it takes a near disaster (like that of Apollo 13) to remind us that the wizards are yet fallible. Then, at the price of great risk, some touch of "human interest" is lent to the well-oiled project. And there is too much limelighted posturing by the astronauts and the research teams and the Nobel Prize laureates—all of them playing the same tiresome role over and again: the boyish modesty, the understatement, the winsome embarrassment at the applause. Meanwhile, on the other side, there are those of us who grow fatigued with endlessly applauding. One simply cannot send up a cheer for every last item that comes tumbling off the mass-production conveyor belt.

It is just this sense one has of intellectual impaction within the world of science that has led several observers (Eugene Wigner, Alvin Weinberg, Bentley Glass, Kenneth Boulding) to speculate that scientific research may fast be approaching the point of diminishing returns in its hyper-productivity. Perhaps there is an absolute limit of research, an "entropy trap," as Boulding calls it, where the difficulties of communication and data retrieval monopolize all available energy. "It is quite easy to visualize a situation, perhaps in one hundred years," Boulding remarks, "in which the stock of knowledge will be so large that the whole effort of the knowledge industry will have to be devoted to transmitting it from one generation to the next."

Already, Alvin Weinberg comments, it is nearly a full-time job for those at the top of their profession to keep up with the expansion of general theory in science. The standard journals can no longer process the glut; the use of semiprivate mailing lists, informal newsletters, conference abstracts, and preprint circuits increases by the year. By the time new knowledge has had the chance to be assimilated further down the hierarchy, it has often been undone or modified at the top. Accordingly, Weinberg has suggested the creation of "information centers" filled with "brokers" and "compacters of literature," whose role will be no more than to tally, file, and pass along the inflow of knowledge. There have been numerous proposals of the kind, a sure sign of overdevelopment.

Perhaps such conjectures about the limits of professional expansion—like the recurrent rumors one hears of entire fields of study such as high-energy physics being played out—are exaggerated. But the mass-production character of Big Science is real enough and lies heavy as a pall over its public image. Never a week goes by but another ingenious astonishment is launched out of the research mills and across the front pages. The scene begins to smell of press agentry and public relations. One cannot help wondering where the genuine research and development leave off and the journalistic grandstanding begins.

Our ecological troubles are now common knowledge and hot politics; they require no detailed review here. What does need emphasis is the critical relationship between our environmental bad habits and the devolution of the scientific tradition.

It might seem unfair to lay the blame for impending environmental disaster at the doorstep of the scientists. Granted, the rape of the environment has been carried out, not by scientists, but by profiteering industrialists and myopic developers, with the eager support of a burgeoning population greedy to consume more than nature can provide and to waste more than nature can clear away. But to absolve the scientific community from complicity in the matter is quite simply to ignore that science has been the only natural philosophy the Western world has known since the age of Newton. It is to ignore the key question: who provided us with the image of nature that invited the rape and with the sensibility that has licensed it? It is not, after all, the normal thing for people to ruin their environment. It is extraordinary and requires extraordinary incitement.

The scientific community cannot claim credit for our exponential economic and technical growth, and then beg off responsibility for what that impetuous growth has cost us in environmental stability. Nor can science, for all the good intentions that have motivated its labors, be excused for abetting the arrogance that still blinds so many to the values of alternative world views.

Because science has been linked (commendably) to a liberal political ethic in Western society, it is easy to overlook how systematically the scientific community has managed to disparage such alternatives over the past two centuries—until, at last, there is nowhere else our society has been able to look but to science for authoritative instruction about nature. To turn elsewhere has meant being written off as witlessly superstitious or inanely "Romantic." There are many subtle ways to enforce cultural orthodoxy; the scientists have done it by encouraging a smug airtight consensus around the power and plenty that flow from their kind of knowledge. What has fallen outside that consensus has been treated with cold neglect or crushing ridicule. For example, in one of the standard anthropology texts of the past generation, Alfred Kroeber without hesitation identifies the adoption of the scientific attitude as a prime criterion of cultural "progress." The alternative to science is "magic and superstition," and "in proportion as a culture disengages itself from reliance on these, it may be said to have registered an advance." Where deviation from scientific rationality occurs in our society, he observes, it is "chiefly among individuals whose social fortune is backward or who are psychotic, mentally deteriorated, or otherwise subnormal." Obviously, the views of "the most ignorant, warped and insane" among us are not to be taken seriously. "Or," Kroeber asks rhetorically, "are our discards, insane, and hypersuggestibles right and the rest of us wrong?"

It is just this stubborn prejudice in favor of single vision which has for so long closed our science off from that wise sense of natural harmony and wholeness, that knowledge of vital transaction between people and nature, which we now associate with the study of ecology. Surely the most remarkable fact about ecology is how late it arrived upon the scientific scene as a well-developed, publicly influential discipline. It was only in the very late nineteenth century that special studies of plant and animal ecology began to appear in biology, but without any great impact on science as a whole. No one, for example, has ever claimed for their fields the "revolutionary" importance granted to quantum theory, even though the ecological sensibility is a far sharper break with tradition.

As for the more critical, comprehensive study of Human Ecology (which is the style of ecology that now commands so much public attention), this does not emerge from the natural sciences at all. Rather, it traces back to a remarkable book published in 1864, *Man and Nature: Physical Geography as Modified by Human Action*. Its author, George Perkins Marsh, was not a scientist, but a diplomat and linguist; yet his work stands as the source of the modern conservation movement. His was the first significant study of how much damage human beings can do to their environment by "operations which, on a large scale, interfere with the spontaneous arrangements of the organic or the inorganic world," and the first prominent appeal to the industrial societies for "the restoration of disturbed harmonies" in nature. Closer to our own time, Human Ecology—both the name and the discipline—takes its origin from the writing of the offbeat sociologist Robert Ezra Park, who gave the study its vogue during the 1920s and 1930s. But after this brief, rather modish period of popularity, Human Ecology drifted to the margins of intellectual life, leaving little mark on the standard university curriculum. Only the recent panic reaction to the environmental crisis has ushered the ecologists, at last, into their proper, central place in the sciences.

At what point before the present eleventh hour did our natural philosophers step forward in creditable numbers to support the simple compassion of conservationists and nature lovers? From Bacon and Descartes to the present day, the same unhealthy images of the scientific project have been repeated with dismal insistence. Either we have the picture of the human being standing apart from nature as isolated spectator, or we have the picture of mankind aggressively asserting itself against nature as (in Descartes' phrase) "lords and possessors." One can easily imagine the protest: the task of the scientist is to tell us how nature works, not how it is to be used well. But is science then to be pardoned on the grounds that it has systematically taught our society to regard knowledge as a thing apart from wisdom? Surely, where our ecological debacle is concerned, that is not a defense, but a confession of guilt.

The Judeo-Christian estrangement from nature was absorbed into the psychology of scientific knowledge, there to find a new epistemological dignity. Objective knowing is alienated knowing; and alienated knowing is, sooner or later, ecologically disastrous knowing. Before the earth could become an industrial garbage can, it had first to become a research laboratory.

When Bacon first called upon mankind "to unite forces against the nature of things, to storm and occupy her castles and strongholds and extend the bounds of human empire," the ambition, though unbecoming, could be safely entertained. There was relatively little damage the human race could then do to its environment. The arrogance was as innocuous as it was exhilarating. But within the past few generations the scale of applied science has become global, and more than great enough to reveal the once negligible implications of the New Philosophy. Just as infinitesimal blemishes in a photograph may become prominent only when the picture is sufficiently enlarged, so the vastness of contemporary technical enterprise has magnified the innermost meaning of the scientific world view and revealed its full ecological ignorance.

We deal now in a technology that alters the climates of entire continents and threatens to murder the flora and fauna of whole oceans. Compulsively optimistic technicians may continue to talk of finding a quick technological fix for every problem; but does it not grow clearer by the day that they are woefully out of tune with the environment they claim to understand? They promise to feed the hungry by way of green revolutions and the harvest of the seas. But the World Health Organization reports that what most immediately results from the saturation use of DDT as part of green revolution technique (monocultures dependent on chemical fertilizers and heavy pesticidal treatment) is the ruinous contamination of mothers' milk. Perhaps in societies where nursing is common and prolonged this might be regarded as a grisly form of population control imposed surreptitiously by the demands of progress, a sort of developmental sleight of hand which increases the crops and poisons the babies. Meanwhile, the rising levels of oil, pesticides, nitrate runoff, and methyl mercury in the lakes and oceans threaten to eliminate fish from the diet of an underfed world long before the seas will be harvested.

The importance of the environmental crisis for the future of our culture is that it forces upon all of us in urban-industrialized society a terrible, inescapable awareness of how intolerably high the price is of our Baconian power-knowledge. At the very least, all of us must suffer the immediate discomforts of "development blight" (quaint phrase!), the noise, the foul smells, the corrosive anguish of the eyes and throat, the devastation of amenities. For most people, ecological politicking still seems to reach no further than such issues, taken up piecemeal as necessity dictates and always with the hope that minor adjustments will serve—like building the airport or freeway somewhere else. But even this superficial sense of the problem can be enough to raise bothersome doubts about the meaning of industrial progress. For once real issues are joined and the easy ecological platitudes evaporate, are not the government and the corporate spokesmen quick to castigate the comfort-and-amenity-conscious citizenry for being Luddites and to warn them that the clock must not be turned back? Suddenly, it becomes a subversion of progress to assert the commonsensible principle that communities exist for the health and enjoyment of those who live in them, not for the convenience of those who drive through them, fly over them, or exploit their real estate for profit. After all, the argument runs, the factories, freeways, and airports must be built somewhere, must they not? The economy *depends* on them. And so it does. Given the life-style demanded by the artificial environment, the economy is bound to be anti-environmental.

As that realization sinks into the general awareness, the great Western myth of progress and the science that is tied to it suffer skeptical examination. In what sense have we "progressed" if we now come to such a pass? By what right do we claim to possess a uniquely reliable knowledge of nature? Operational success has, supposedly, been the ultimate validation of scientific knowledge. Science is true, we have been told over and over again, because *"it works."* But now we discover that the scientific world view does *not* work. Not if our outlook is holistic. Not if we consider the long run—which, in the case of industrial society, seems to be about two centuries. More and more it looks as if the future were not destined to be an endless escalator of improvement. Rather, we may yet take our place in folk memory as the Age of the Great Sacrilege, which was smitten from on high for its wanton ways. And children will cringe to hear how vile in the sight of God was our existence.

Currently, the most ecologically involved young people in our society appear to be learning more about their proper place in nature from American Indian lore, Zen, and Tantra than from Western science. Science seems at best able to furnish them with many microscopic details that assume meaning only when assimilated into a primordial wisdom. This is a startling fact of our time. Surely it is a strange kind of progress, then, which brings us to the point where, under pressure of dire emergency, urban-industrial society must look beyond its own science to such primitive and exotic traditions for a life-enhancing natural philosophy.

KNOWLEDGE AND ACTION: THE DILEMMA OF SCIENCE POLICY IN THE '70s

Harvey Brooks

There are basically just two central questions regarding the organization and administration of science. These questions present themselves at many different levels of aggregate scientific activity, from the individual laboratory or university department, to multinational research institutes and collaborative programs, including research and development programs which are nationally funded.

The first question is how to organize, staff, and direct the search for knowledge so as to obtain the greatest rate of scientific progress for a given investment of human and material resources. The second question is how to couple the existing body of knowledge, as well as the search for new knowledge, to existing needs for policy or action, including those felt by education and technological innovation.

By scientific progress I mean not the mere accumulation of data and information, but rather the advancement of our codified understanding of the natural universe and of human behavior, social and individual. Such progress also embraces the conceptualization of knowledge about human artifacts, what Herbert Simon[1] terms the "science of the artificial," which is assuming greater relative importance as the conditions of life are increasingly determined by the man-made rather than the natural environment.

In practice, there are no simple objective measures of scientific progress external to the social processes of the scientific community which produces it. Thus, to evaluate scientific progress we are compelled to rely on a consensus of the scientific communities in each field. We are subject, of course, to uncertainties about which groups are competent to judge progress, and to the fallible fashions of any guild. Nevertheless, the highly structured system of mutual criticism; refereed publications; peer group evaluation of research projects; and personal recognition through prizes, fellowships, and academic appointments

Reprinted by permission of *Daedalus,* Journal of the American Academy of Arts and Sciences, Boston, Mass. Spring 1973, *The Search for Knowledge.*

constitute a kind of intellectual marketplace in which scientific contributions are valued in a more or less impersonal way. Available studies of this market, largely confined to the subject of physics, suggest that it is indeed reasonably objective in its operation.[2]

Modern nations devote substantial resources to the cultivation of science, not so much because they judge it worthwhile in itself as because they expect that scientific advance will foster some other social or national benefit. They assume that if scientists are encouraged, or at least permitted, to pursue their intellectual curiosity wherever it may lead, society will reap benefits in the most efficient and economical way. The autonomy of science is often defended by the scientific community in ideological terms, but viewed by others as a form of scientific arrogance which asserts that the scientist's own frame of reference is the only one appropriate for evaluating the output of science. What I am asserting is that the standards of the scientific community are indeed the proper measure of scientific progress, but not necessarily of the contribution of scientific progress to social progress. The latter must also be judged in other terms by other constituencies. I would maintain, however, that the most efficient scientific progress tends to make the greatest scientific contribution to society.

The second question, how to couple scientific knowledge and research to needs is subtler and harder to define. The potential social benefits of scientific progress cannot be realized unless the knowledge is either taken up by government decision-making bodies and industrial innovators, or contributes directly to educating the public and the next generation. Furthermore, knowledge by itself is always ambivalent; it has potential for evil as well as good. It can be used for purposes which many consider socially harmful, such as war, or it can put new tools into the hands of misguided or oppressive, but powerful men. More subtly and frequently, it is used with the best intentions for what are thought to be beneficial purposes, only to have it discovered afterwards that harmful secondary consequences are occurring. Frequently such secondary consequences increase faster than in proportion to the primary benefits as a technology becomes more widely diffused and used. It is these "non-linear" effects of technology which have often led to public reaction against technology, and even science, for the primary benefits are often forgotten in the light of the suddenness of the discovery of non-linear side-effects.

There are, in turn, two questions with regard to the utilization of scientific knowledge. The first is how to use knowledge which has been generated primarily for its own sake—fundamental research. How is this knowledge to be condensed, summarized, repackaged, and interpreted for use, and how is it to be communicated to those responsible for action—the decision-makers, the technological innovators, the service professionals, and the students who will fill all these roles in the future? The second question is how the needs of government policy, industrial technology, or professional service can and should influence the process of discovery itself. This is where the question arises of how human values and scientific knowledge interact with each other.

During most of the 1950s and 1960s discussions of national science policies and of research administration tended to focus on the first of these major questions, how best to promote progress in science itself, and in technological innovation generated directly by scientific research rather than by a previously perceived social need. Today the focus has shifted rather rapidly towards the second of the questions. Most contemporary criticism of scientific institutions is directed not at their effectiveness in advancing knowledge, which is almost taken for granted, but at their capacity to couple knowledge to action, and to the corollary question of what relevance the knowledge they generate has to the multiplicity of newly identified problems involved in economic and social progress, not only for national societies, but for humanity as a whole. Increasingly, the assumption that maximizing the rate of scientific progress as defined by scientists will in the long run automatically produce the insights most relevant to the solution of human problems is challenged, and attention focuses on the interfaces between scientists and their institutions on the one hand, and the rest of the social and political structure on the other. The movement of knowledge into decision and action, and the relationship between "objective" knowledge and the value structures of society has come to be a central concern.

This new climate of thinking, though most prevalent in the United States, is increasingly evident in Western Europe and Japan, and is beginning to be widespread in the Soviet Union.

Science and Political Decisions

In the past, science has been supported primarily because of the power it gives us to manipulate nature for human purposes. In the last few years, however, we have become more interested in another value of science, its capacity to provide the means for disciplining and channeling a technology which threatens to get out of control, or at least is so perceived by a growing public. Thus, in addition to providing the basis for technological innovation, science is becoming the basis of a new technological conscience which searches out the potential consequences of technology and questions its uncritical application.

In the United States this new function of science has projected scientists and scientific institutions into an unaccustomed political role, thereby generating a new set of public issues concerning the proper relationship of scientists to political decisions, particularly, but not exclusively, in the environmental field. Increasingly, scientists have been in demand as witnesses at hearings before congressional committees, administrative agencies, and even courts.

Both because of our general affluence and because of the absence of other forms of legitimation for social policy, there is probably a greater proliferation of such new social demands on science and scientists in the United States than elsewhere, but the same forces are present everywhere in advanced societies. The OECD report, *Science, Growth, and Society,* examined the new relationship between science and society; its enthusiastic reception by the OECD Science Ministers is indicative of its resonance for a broad spectrum of elite opinion in Europe and Japan.[3]

Historically both science and technological innovation have received much of their impetus from war or from political competition between nation-states. In most industrialized countries the largest fraction of technological effort goes into projects for national defense, space, and nuclear energy, and a large fraction also goes into supporting national competitiveness in international trade. It is estimated that 25 percent of the world's scientists and engineers are engaged in military research and development, and the great majority of the rest are engaged in industrial research. In these areas a fairly comprehensive system of innovation has evolved, so that knowledge does move into action, and work in research and development is coupled to end products—though perhaps least successfully when governments have subsidized R. and D. directed at products and services for the private market which, outside the socialist countries, they have done most extensively in Europe and the United Kingdom.

Today we are witnessing a broadly based worldwide movement, both within and outside the technical community, to utilize science and technology for less nationalistic purposes: for the alleviation of poverty on a global basis, for better management and protection of the world's resources with minimum detriment to economic development, for the achievement of greater social justice, for the more reasonable allocation of the resources of the biosphere toward sustaining a decent human life for all people. In these areas, however, we are faced with a massive deficiency of experience in coupling knowledge to action. We scarcely know how to translate what we know into tangible benefits or wise social restraints, and conventional wisdom, good intentions, and moral fervor are hardly adequate. The very successes of technology in some areas has generated expectations which make its inadequacies in others seem the more glaring and inexcusable. The "if we can land a man on the moon" syndrome has transformed what we expect from technology, but, in fact, American successes in space carry relatively few lessons applicable to problems, like virtually all of those mentioned above, where conflicting interests and values play a large part.

Intrinsic vs. Extrinsic Strategy of Science

There are two limitations on the coupling of science to its social utilization. On the one hand, knowledge is seldom used unless an individual or group recognizes a need, translates it into meaningful and manageable scientific questions, and then acts as an energetic advocate of concrete action. A "manageable scientific question" is one which is answerable either out of the existing body of scientific knowledge or through a search for new knowledge guided by existing understandings and involving only limited extensions of the current conceptual structure of science. Pure research, isolated from those who understand it sufficiently to know how to use it, cannot provide inspiration for innovation or better decisions. Such research may be very valuable, but it requires an incubation period before it can be appreciated in relation to its possible applications.

On the other hand, attempts to channel the search for knowledge narrowly on the basis of imagined social needs or other primarily non-scientific objectives usually result in frustration and expensive wasted effort. Such targeted research requires a critical mass of preexistent basic knowledge to be carried out efficiently. Until this critical mass is accumulated, the strategy of research is better governed by the internal logic of its subject than by our limited vision of what is likely to be relevant to a particular practical problem or impending policy decision. The questions we begin by asking are not those we end by answering, and an insight that initially appears to have little relevance may rather suddenly turn out to be the key to further progress towards a practical goal.

The best scientific strategy generally lies somewhere between isolation from practical problems and narrow channeling on the basis of practical needs, but to locate the balance point in any particular case requires the most experienced scientific and general judgment. There is no simple formula for resolving this dilemma, but certainly it is folly to drop all basic work when a pathway to a practical solution appears to be in sight. Studies of successful development programs show that important ingredients in a final technical solution frequently do not appear until the design of the end product is already supposedly frozen.[4] As a method to control fertility in poor countries, the IUD was so widely hailed a few years ago that some proponents were even recommending that basic studies of human reproduction be abandoned in favor of all-out action programs. Yet today there is such widespread disillusion with the IUD in parts of the underdeveloped world that they are accusing the developed countries of having foisted an impractical gimmick on them.

Centralization vs. Pluralism in Research

This issue occurs in two quite different contexts, first, in the organization and budgeting of science at the national level, in what is sometimes called "policy for science," and second, in the organization of efforts to achieve a given scientific objective. Is it better to gather together all the strands of research which might contribute to solving a given problem into a critical mass so that research can be channeled according to a grand strategy determined either centrally or by the consensus of a limited number of scientists interacting on a day-to-day basis? Or is it better to encourage a multiplicity of separate, even fragmented, approaches in many locations, with each scientist pursuing his own path, subject only to the indirect coordination provided by public scientific literature and by the informal communication networks which grow and dissolve within the scientific community?

At the level of national organization the question is whether all government scientific activities should be administered by one department, with its own organization and fiscal appropriation, or whether technical activities should be administered and budgeted as part of the total activity or mission of the specific department to which they relate. The latter departmental organization encourages the coupling of research to end uses, but at the price of autonomy and integrity in scientific planning.

In the United States, government science administration has a strongly pluralistic tradition, in which each government mission is responsible for its own research and development activities and budgets them in competition with its other operations. This provides, in theory at least, an orderly flow of ideas from basic research to the operational needs of the agency. Thus the Department of Agriculture is responsible both for agricultural research and for price supports. The Department of the Interior is responsible for geological research and for the management of natural resources. The Department of Health, Education, and Welfare is responsible for biomedical research and for the operation and financing of Medicare and Medicaid. The Defense Department is responsible for basic research relevant to military operations and also for operating the military services and procuring matériel.

In the United States, government support of science evolved piecemeal in response to a succession of opportunities and needs arising in separate historical epochs. Only after World War II did the federal government begin to consider the support of science on its own terms a legitimate responsibility of government, and to contract to an appreciable extent for research to be performed outside government laboratories.[5] A national commitment to the support of basic research was clearly institutionalized only in 1950 when the National Science Foundation was created. Even as late as 1972, however, the research budget of NSF accounted for only 2.5 percent of total federal R. and D. expenditures, or 5.2 percent of all non-military ones. The NSF supported less than 10 percent of basic research and less than 20 percent of all federally supported research in universities. All other federal R. and D. expenditures were budgeted and administered by the departments responsible for functions defined in social rather than scientific terms such as defense, health, agriculture, environmental services, housing, transportation, and social welfare. In this scheme the large expenditures of the Space Agency (NASA) and the Atomic Energy Commission (AEC) are something of a hybrid, for neither space nor atomic energy is a social function in the normal sense. Rather, each represents a defined range of technology supporting a variety of social and political objectives.

In contrast, the Department of Education and Science (DES) in the United Kingdom accounted in 1972 for 28.4 percent of all non-military R. and D. expenditures, almost six times as large a fraction as the 5.2 percent accounted for by the NSF, its nearest United States analogue. Most other industrial nations are closer to the British than the United States pattern.

There is, however, some trend towards convergence of the two patterns of R. and D. support. In the United States the fraction of government funds for R. and D. allocated by the NSF has steadily grown: for academic research, for example, it has grown from 15 percent to almost 20 percent. Furthermore, as its resources have grown, the NSF has gradually expanded its self-defined mission beyond that of supporting basic research in academic institutions. Although the legislation authorizing the NSF never prohibited it from engaging in applied research, a 1968 revision gave it an explicit charter to do so. During the past three years it has inaugurated a new program, Research Applied to National Needs

(RANN), which partially implements this legislation. Although RANN includes both basic and applied research, it is problem-oriented in the sense that it is organized according to socially rather than scientifically defined objectives. It now accounts for about 20 percent of NSF's research budget and for most of the recent growth in NSF program staff. Some of the NSF's experienced basic research program officers have been placed on the RANN program staff.

RANN has encouraged the academic scientific community to organize itself for systematic multidisciplinary attacks on problems of national energy policy, environmental management, urban planning, evaluation of large-scale social programs, and other national needs. It also deals with technological innovation; in addition, a new program, labeled "technological incentives," provides for joint industry-university teams to work on improving the productivity of technological innovation as well as of activities related to the public sector. Significantly, the success of the RANN program is to be evaluated in terms not only of the scientific quality of the work which it produces, but also of the effectiveness with which its results are coupled to policy and action, and hence of their acceptance by action-oriented agencies both in industry and in government.

It is not surprising that the RANN program has been controversial, especially within the academic community. Some fear it is eroding the standards of intellectual excellence previously upheld by the NSF as the main criteria for supporting research projects, and that second-rate research is being supported lavishly because it promises practical results, while first-rate pure science languishes on ever more constricted budgets. Others argue, however, that RANN is encouraging a long overdue reorientation and restructuring of the academic science community, breaking down often artificial and obsolete barriers between disciplinary departments. Still others, mostly from industry, consider RANN an expensive form of reeducation for university scientists. They say that if RANN's purpose were really to solve pressing social problems, the projects should have been assigned to teams in industry or to non-profit research institutes more accustomed to operating in a multidisciplinary, problem-focused context. Advocates of RANN point to the large number of new proposals generated from academic groups as an indication that the program meets a large previously unsatisfied need for support, and demonstrates the latent desire of many first-rate academic scientists to become more involved in action-related research with a potential social impact. Most academic scientists look upon RANN as applied research, though the officers of NSF are quick to point out that its projects actually include a good deal of interesting, challenging, and high quality basic research in a non-traditional, mission-oriented context. Debates rage as to whether discipline-oriented universities can or should be expected to organize themselves to perform policy-oriented research. Can academics ever be sufficiently connected to the point of ultimate use to produce important effects on action, or will their efforts result only in published papers of, perhaps, impeccable scientific quality, but with no real customer, reports that will be widely quoted, discussed, and duly referenced in other similar reports, but then gradually forgotten without attracting the attention of the decision-makers or achieving real credibility among those who are in a position to act on them?

All the arguments for and against RANN have some merit, especially when applied in isolation to particular projects. The program goals are ambitious, perhaps unrealistically so in relation to the resources and personnel available. In some cases, RANN has been oversold in terms of what practical results are realistically achievable within the time scale of a typical research project. On the other hand, the program has brought a fresh and innovative scientific and technical constituency into the attack on important national problems, much as a new constituency was brought to bear on military problems by OSRD early in World War II. The education and development of this constituency may well prove to be of much greater long-range importance than the results of specific projects. RANN should also help to provide new perspectives and formulations of what our problems really are. In this sense it could be viewed as a mechanism for translating broadly defined social problems into specific manageable technical problems and simultaneously for developing a constituency capable of attacking them. However, it is probably too early to judge the success of the program, which will ultimately depend more on the degree to which its results and people are put to use by other agencies than on the specific output of individual projects. The greatest dangers are that the public may be led to expect that the RANN program, or any other NSF program, can by itself resolve the problems to which it is addressing itself, and that it may have insufficient political influence to acquire the other ingredients it needs to succeed.

In a different kind of evolution, NSF is also turning with increasing frequency to non-academic performers not only to do applied research but to work in some of its basic programs as well, especially those in the environmental sciences that require large-scale collaborative effort. The RANN program uses non-profit research institutes and AEC national laboratories to a considerable extent, and the technological incentives program will use industry, although it gives preference to collaborative efforts of industry and university. Legislation now pending in the Senate would move NSF much further towards the support of industrial research and of technological programs to work on civilian problems such as those of housing and transportation. It would also provide for extensive retraining of space/defense-oriented scientists and engineers to participate in such civilian-oriented efforts. This augmenting of the power of NSF would be a clear move towards making it a department of science and technology, towards a centralization which, in my opinion, would be disastrous both to the health of basic research and to the successful application of technology. Through RANN the NSF can and has developed a new innovative and catalyst role in launching attacks on social problems through research. However, responsibility for their implementation, including most development and virtually all demonstration and testing activity, should continue to lie with the agencies most familiar with the environmental, political, and economic constraints within which new technological solutions will have to be applied.

No major country has ever collected *all* of its governmental scientific and technological activities into a single administration. In virtually all countries defense research and development have been separated from the rest of the government science structure and attached directly to the defense establishment. Nuclear energy has almost invariably enjoyed some form of special status whereby it reported directly to the chief of state. The U.S.S.R. has probably gone further than any Western nation in budgeting defense and nuclear research separately from corresponding research in other fields, but in view of the highly centralized control of Soviet society in general, it is not clear how much this budgetary separation reflects a separation in the administration of R. and D. activity in these areas.

In many countries, such as the United Kingdom and West Germany, a single cabinet department administers both science and higher education. In the United States a congressional committee recently recommended the consolidation of federal science activities "which are carried out in universities or similar institutions, and which are closely related to the total operations of higher education and advanced study" into a single "National Institute for Research and Advanced Studies" (NIRAS), modeled after the present National Institutes of Health within the Department of HEW. If this recommendation had been implemented, the new agency would have administered all federal support for activities in the indicated categories, as compared with about 19 percent currently administered by NSF.[6] On the other hand, it would have fallen far short of being a department of science and technology, for even the present NSF is less exclusively academically oriented than the proposed NIRAS.

While the United States has been evolving towards an autonomous science agency, Britain and Europe have been moving in the opposite direction, attempting to bring their science activities into closer relationship to other policies and objectives of government. In Britain the conservative government moved to take several Research Councils out of DES and place them directly under the appropriate cabinet ministries. When this proposal met with considerable resistance, the government asked Lord Rothschild to prepare a report on government science organization. Its central recommendation was a compromise.[7] The Research Councils were to remain within DES, but they were to derive an increasing fraction of their budgets from the relevant ministries. Thus the ministries would act as customers, purchasing research services from the Research Councils according to their own specifications and estimates of their needs for new knowledge. The Research Councils would no longer determine what the ministries ought to need. If the ministries did not like what they were getting, they would be free to withdraw support, and even to create their own separate activities.

The Rothschild recommendations departed sharply from the so-called "Haldane Doctrine," dating from World War I, which stated as a cardinal principle that all government scientific activities should be conducted in autonomous organizations administered by scientists rather than by civil service generalists. Despite this philosophical change, however, the recommendations would reduce the percentage of non-military R. and D. supported by DES only from 28.4 percent to 20.0 percent over a period of several years, leaving a percentage still four times that supported by NSF in the United States.[8] The purpose of the Rothschild recommendations was to insure that the work of the Research Councils, particularly their more applied activities, would be more responsive to the operational needs of the ministries, on the theory that he who paid the piper could call the tune.

It is interesting to observe that the present role of the British Research Councils within DES is somewhat analogous to the role which the RANN programs of NSF play in relation to the mission-oriented agencies. The advantage of such an autonomous agency is that it gives considerable policy initiative to a science-oriented agency. Such an agency is more likely to conceive and work on radically new approaches to problems than an operating agency bound by past experience and dependent on an external constituency for continuing political support in the annual budgetary process. On the other hand, its very freedom makes it vulnerable to the danger of reinventing the wheel or expending effort on approaches to problems which more experienced and knowledgeable hands know to be impractical. The NSF–RANN approach tries to avoid these dangers by closely coordinating general policy through interagency committees set up within the Office of Science and Technology directly under the President's Science Adviser. These committees include top-level representatives from the mission-oriented agencies most likely to be concerned and knowledgeable in particular problem areas to which RANN is addressing itself, such as energy and environmental protection.

On balance I feel that both RANN and the Rothschild recommendations are constructive, at least potentially so. No organizational changes can alone guarantee the solution of the interface problem between science and its applications, for this depends more upon individual personalities and motivations than on any kind of organization. On the other hand, organization can help to modify reward systems so as to change the nature of achievements. The RANN program does appear to fill an important gap between basic research and the civilian-oriented mission agencies which have limited experience in the sophisticated use of science to solve their problems. In the long run, however, RANN will succeed only if the contacts with the scientific community and the knowledgeable appreciation of scientific research characteristic of NSF in its administration of basic research can be infused into the mission-oriented agencies responsible for implementing results. Similarly, the recommendations of the Rothschild report will succeed only if the operational agencies develop their own scientific capabilities to the point where they are discriminating appraisers of the research they are obtaining from the Research Councils.

It may well be that, as the OECD report suggested, the best situation is one of dynamic tension between research in application-oriented agencies and research in science-oriented agencies. To quote the OECD report:

Not only do we consider an either-or choice undesirable; we also feel that some degree of shift, with time, towards each of the two models may have a positive value in keeping the overall scientific system both healthy in its own right and more adaptable.[9]

Fragmentation vs. Dispersion of Research Effort

The argument over centralization vs. pluralism in overall government organization is paralleled by an argument over concentration vs. dispersion in research efforts at the working level. In some basic research fields such as space science, elementary particle physics, astronomy, and nuclear structure physics, the increasing complexity and cost of instrumentation have forced scientists to concentrate in groups around the facilities, but even in these fields the United States has tended to favor the "user mode" of operation with a minimal staff attached to the facility itself and generous provisions for visiting scientists from universities and other research institutions.

The user mode is well illustrated by the situation in particle physics in the United States. Here the operation and staffing costs of eight major facilities, plus accelerator development, consumed 71 percent of federal funds going into this field in 1971, yet 76 percent of the Ph.D. personnel doing particle physics research were located in universities, and 77 percent of the publications in the field originated in universities.[10] Forecasts of future development in other fields such as nuclear structure physics indicate a similar concentration of funding in a few locations even when expansion in a field is assumed to be limited by manpower rather than money.[11]

For problem-solving research there are equal or greater pressures for concentration because of the advantages of bringing many different skills and disciplines into close communication. Counter to this, of course, run the strong egalitarian pressures of American politics, best illustrated by the existence of a federally supported agricultural experiment station in each of the fifty states.

The AEC national laboratories are currently making a very strong bid for a major part in newly developing environmental and other societal R. and D. programs in the United States.[12] Although a major motivation for this is simple bureaucratic self-preservation, their managers argue that they are in a better position than the universities to mount a tightly managed and at the same time diversified effort, particularly when it comes to coupling research to its potential uses. The universities argue, of course, that they are strong in the social sciences, while the large national laboratories are quite weak and would take a long time to develop comparable capabilities in these areas. Most of the AEC laboratories were created and organized by physical scientists, and it may prove difficult for them to create a climate sufficiently hospitable to social scientists to attract the highest quality people.

The large laboratories run into the dangers inherent in intellectual monopoly.

Their excessively close communication and management tend to exclude the most radical and innovative approaches as threatening, either because they are incompatible with official management doctrine and with the present hierarchical structure of the laboratory, or because they jeopardize its all-important relationship with its major sponsor. On the whole, I tend to favor a mixed strategy with a few major efforts as well as a definite and consciously protected margin of funds for the individual and less centralized projects which, as in basic research, have so frequently produced the most important new insights. Also in favor of considerable decentralization in research on societal problems is the fact that many of its applications have to be made in the context of a rather localized and specialized environment—in a particular city, or watershed, or local climatic situation. Thus regional research institutions are needed to adapt the generic findings of centralized institutions to the peculiarities of a local situation, and in return, their experience in doing so can give important guidance to the more generic research. This regional pattern appears to have been very successful in agricultural research, since it accommodated itself to the size of the United States and to its diversity of climate, soil, and hydrological conditions.[13]

Comparison of Government and Corporate Research Policy

Debate over the organization of science and technology at the national level is mirrored in discussion of the organization of R. and D. within large private corporations. A large corporation frequently creates a corporate laboratory as part of its central staff, supported by an assessment against the revenues of its various product or functional divisions. This laboratory is supposed to undertake research projects which are of general value to several product lines or functions, or which are so preliminary or so risky technically that an individual product division is unlikely to initiate them. Particularly important are projects likely to lead to new products or services which do not fit into any existing product division of the company. Even when an organization has a corporate laboratory, the product or functional divisions have laboratories of their own which undertake applied research clearly relevant to their own operational problems. These divisional laboratories help to make the divisions more sophisticated customers for the output of the corporate laboratory, but they can also be serious rivals to the corporate laboratory since, in the last analysis, they are competing for the same limited total corporate resources. The place of the NSF-RANN program in the federal government science structure is somewhat analogous to the place of the corporate laboratory in the structure of a large company, and it has some of the same problems and strengths.

Other large corporations do not have corporate laboratories as such, but have several strong divisional laboratories associated with various product lines, each reporting to the chief managing officer for the corresponding division. In such a corporation, however, the work of the strong divisional laboratories is coordinated by a vice president for research who reports directly to the top management of the company. These laboratories undertake on their own initiative some projects primarily related to the operational functions of the parent division, but they may also be assigned other projects aimed at developing new business or meeting a company-wide knowledge need, with the assignment governed primarily by the unique scientific capabilities of a particular laboratory. Thus, although they have no corporate laboratory as such, they may have, in addition to what amounts to a divisional research budget, a corporate research budget under the control of the vice president for research. The corporate research function is thus preserved as an overlay of the divisional structure. This model comes closest to that of the United States federal government, with the Office of Science and Technology in the Executive Office of the President playing the role of the vice president for research and his staff.

Probably the most fully developed example of the corporate laboratory model is that of the American Telephone and Telegraph Company, a private regulated monopoly. Here all research and development is centralized under the single management of the Bell Telephone Laboratories, supported half by the individual operating companies in proportion to their revenues.[14]

However, the Bell System found it essential to have, in addition to its central laboratory located near corporate headquarters in Murray Hill, New Jersey, a number of separate decentralized laboratories adjacent to various manufacturing operations and primarily supporting these operations, even though they remain under Bell Telephone Laboratories' administrative and budgetary control. The Bell System management believes that this system of administrative centralization combined with geographical decentralization achieves the best blend of a coherent technical management and a responsiveness to the operational needs of particular parts of the company. It provides for a single scientific and engineering career system within the corporation, allowing technical people with new skills developed in the central laboratory to move easily into the operating arms of the company. The Bell System represents the best example of a highly integrated technical structure in a high-technology industry and is widely regarded as the most successful and innovative technical organization in the world. It is often suggested as an appropriate model for what a federal scientific organization might become.

However, there are pitfalls in trying to carry too far the analogy between the governmental and corporate situations. In the first place almost all corporate research is carried out "in house"; corporations seldom give contracts or grants to independent outside organizations the way the government does. Of some $17 billion the United States spends on federal R. and D., only 14 percent goes to civil service laboratories manned by full-time government employees. Another 5 percent goes to research centers, either profit-making or non-profit, whose facilities are wholly government-owned, but which are operated by a contracting entity which hires its own employees to carry out the work and is frequently managed by a board of directors or trustees created solely for the purpose. Such "Federal Contract Research Centers," or "captive laboratories," as they are called, are a hybrid of government and private organization.

Even counting the captive laboratories as "in house," however, the federal government contracts most of its research out to organizations with different purposes and goals from those of its own agencies. Contracts or grants represent alliances for limited overlapping objectives. Thus they are not as responsive or as subject to close policy direction and to administrative and budgetary discipline as are the employees of a large corporation or its corporate laboratory. This is especially true in the case of universities and independent research institutes which together receive more than 15 percent of federal R. and D. expenditures. The program officers or contract monitors within government constitute a layer of technical management not present in the corporate analogy but required to couple the results of contract research to their final utilization in the decision-making or operations of an agency. The technical managers, in fact, identify in varying degrees with the goals of the contractor or the employing agency.

Extramural research has the advantage of access to a much wider variety of talents and ideas than the government could justify recruiting for its own purposes on a full-time basis. A corporate laboratory relies on the connections between its professionals and the general scientific community to provide a window on the whole potentially relevant world of science and technology outside the company. Contracted research provides a surer connection, but at a price of somewhat greater difficulty in coordination and coupling to end uses within an agency.

When applied or problem-centered research is administered by an agency such as NSF, the agency is really operating in the role of a corporate laboratory for the entire federal government. The kinds of research supported by NSF should be sufficiently generic and broad in scope to affect the mission needs of more than one federal agency or segment of industry. But support via NSF adds still another layer of management to complicate the coupling problem. Not only must NSF orchestrate, not too heavy-handedly, the efforts of many geographically dispersed and often fiercely independent grantees, keeping them aware of user needs, but it must channel all of their findings to potential users, and coordinate or reconcile the requirements of several different potential users. Much the same problem is faced by the Research Councils in the traditional British system of research management.

One of the questions that arises in this situation is how far NSF or Research Council research should be carried to insure a reasonable probability of its being picked up successfully by potential users and carried forward to final application. Unless there is considerable transfer of personnel, as occurs in the Bell System for example, the best research results may be lost due to the natural resistance of bureaucracies to new ideas, or to the "not invented here" syndrome. At the very least, considerable overlap in technical sophistication and perception of a problem is required between the producer and the user of new knowledge. The mere production of research documentation—published papers, reports, or lectures at professional meetings—is insufficient to insure its utilization even when it is demonstrably useful.

The second point on which the analogy between governmental and corporate research organization breaks down involves politics. All large organizations have bureaucratic politics, and governments and corporations are not too different in this respect. But in addition, government must cope with the politics of public opinion which have little parallel in the corporate world even in these days of large unions, active consumer groups, and public interest stockholder blocs. In the United States at least, the processes of government are increasingly conducted in a goldfish bowl. Recent legislation has opened up essentially all federal technical advisory activities to public and press observation, except when security classification or confidential personal information is involved. There is a serious question in my mind as to whether the scientific integrity of advice can be maintained under conditions where even tentative and subsequently discarded views may be subject to public scrutiny and the selective reporting of the media. The objectives of the new policy are, of course, to make decisions about science and technology responsive to the values and preferences of the public and to uncover and expose to public criticism the implicit value assumptions which often underlie ostensibly objective technical judgments. The difficulty with such procedures, however, is that they invite intervention by individuals and groups with very narrow interests, who bear no responsibility for the overall integrity of the resulting decisions or for the internal consistency of diverse governmental actions. The public exposure of the advisory process could easily result in a technical forum becoming a focus for contending political interests and conducting discussions with little relevance to the technical issues involved. Recent congressional hearings on issues with a strong technical component suggest the difficulty of obtaining scientifically sensible results from such a process. However, in fairness, it must be added that the confidential processes by which advice is given to the executive branch have not invariably produced a much better result.

These two unique features of governmental research—the use of external contracts and the potential politicization of the technical decision process—make it difficult to draw unambiguous lessons for government from the experience of successful industrial research. Nevertheless, I believe that government can learn more than it has from the corporate experience. Regardless of the conflict between centralization and pluralism, there should be greater mobility of technical people between agencies in government. It should be easier for large laboratories belonging to one agency to undertake research on behalf of another agency when their particular technical skills warrant it. Government research planning should allow for more technical activity in the area intermediate between basic research and final end-item or operational development, and for parallel exploratory investigations prior to the choice of a preferred technical path.

New Challenges to Science and Technology

Today all the advanced industrial nations are suffering from disillusionment with the failure of science in attacking what are perceived as the most urgent problems of the future. It is increasingly appreciated that the blame lies not so much with science itself as with a lack of mechanisms and institutions to couple science to its operational applications in the social sphere.

For example, less than 2 percent of global R. and D. expenditures can be said to support economic development of the less developed countries. If poverty is regarded as one of the major global problems, then a pitifully small proportion of the world's technical effort is aimed at its alleviation. On the other hand, with present institutional and political structures, even if a greater amount were spent on R. and D. relevant to economic development, the results might not find their way into use. The bottleneck may lie, not in the lack of requisite knowledge, but rather in the lack of mechanisms to utilize such knowledge and diffuse it widely among the people and organizations that could benefit from it. In fact, the present level of such research may already be in equilibrium with what present institutional arrangements are capable of putting to use.

The failure in most spheres of economic development is underlined by the spectacular success only recently achieved in agriculture in Asia. In the first half of the 1960s it was widely believed that the world's poor countries faced imminent famine. The crisis was emphasized by extensive crop failures in India, and by an alarming increase in the less developed countries' need for food aid from the developed countries. Yet within five years India and the Philippines had become self-sufficient in their production of grains, and an increase in food supplies was comfortably outpacing population growth in many parts of the underdeveloped world.[15] This so-called "green revolution" was the direct result of adaptive research and the diffusion of technology initiated at relatively modest cost by private foundations in the United States. The mechanics of this agricultural revolution include most of the factors commonly thought to be necessary for successful technological innovation: a basically sound technical idea based on an adequate background of basic scientific knowledge; good adaptive applied research in which potential users played an important part; receptive host governments and users, an organization for the diffusion of information closely coupled to the research organizations and designed to put knowledge into practice through the movement to the field of people closely involved in its original generation; and careful observation and feedback from the field of the results in operation.

However, this success did not spring full-blown from somebody's brain. It was based on long and successful experience in parallel circumstances: on the agricultural research and extension program in the United States, and on the twenty-five-year-old Rockefeller program in Mexico. It was a multinational effort which had continuity and stability, and was relatively free from political or "participatory" pressures.

Once such successes are achieved in a limited field, the probability that they can be imitated in other areas increases. Success can create a demand for more R. and D., in a way that researchers themselves cannot. Unfortunately, few governmental programs outside the defense/space field have had the continuity, stability of funding, political isolation, and opportunity for continuous organizational learning that seem to characterize the successful agricultural model and also the most successful innovations in the industrial field, including those of multinational corporations. The lack of political pressure for instant success has been one important factor in all of these successful innovations; at the same time, however, the pressure for long-term success created by the presence of eager and receptive users has also been important.

Conclusion

Everywhere in the developed world greater attention is being focused on the coupling of research to the needs of society, as opposed to the success of research on its own terms. The concern is especially with social problem areas in which past research efforts have been very modest and in which we have little experience to guide us as to the kinds of institutions and interface mechanisms which facilitate the successful application of new knowledge. In industrial manufacturing and in governmental military/space research, successful mechanisms for the translation of research into application have evolved gradually during an extended period. The spectacular success of developed countries at translating research into applications in agriculture has recently been transferred to less developed countries through the green revolution. It remains to be seen whether it will take as long to evolve patterns which will enable us to fulfill needs which have only recently moved to the center of the world stage: to alleviate poverty and unemployment, to manage the world's resources and to protect its environment, to achieve balance between human populations and the integrity of the biosphere, and to deliver efficient and effective public services equitably to all people.

The central problem of scientific organization is how to reconcile the scientific need for autonomy and integrity in its own internal processes of exploration and self-criticism with the demands of society that the fruits of science be guided into channels which society deems beneficial. This is a problem to which there is no single specifiable solution. Rather the situation is one of dynamic tension between science and society, a tension based on an equilibrium configuration that will change with time, resulting, perhaps, in somewhat different configurations in different political systems. Government scientific organization has evolved differently in the United States from the way it has in Europe and the United Kingdom. There now appears, however, to be some convergence of the two patterns, with Europe moving towards a closer coupling of science to the agencies responsible for its application, and the United States moving towards isolating more scientific initiative in a single science-oriented agency, the National Science Foundation, which is capable of undertaking not only basic but also exploratory applied research relevant to a wide range of social problems. There are some dangers inherent in both of these changes. In the United States the greater engagement of scientific institutions, including the NSF, in problems with high political visibility could lead to the politicization of all of science. In Europe the introduction of science into agencies not ready to accommodate it may have similar effects. There seems little question, however, that the challenges facing mankind as a whole call for a high degree of sophistication and wisdom in the application of science, not only in generating new technology, but also in guiding the evolution of old fields of technology and in selecting new directions for technology by processes more judicious and less random that those of the past.

If there is any single theme of this paper it is that there are no either-or answers to any of the issues I have raised. I think we are dealing with dynamic tensions in which the victory of any extreme view is likely to be unhealthy, for part of the creativeness of the scientific establishment emerges from these tensions and from the challenges which science and society throw down to each other.

NOTES

1. H. Simon, *The Science of the Artificial* (Cambridge: M.I.T. Press, 1968).
2. J. R. and C. Cole, "The Ortega Hypothesis," *Science,* Vol. CLXXVIII, October 27, 1972, pp. 368–374; H. Zuckerman and R. Merton, "Patterns of Evaluation in Science: Institutionalization, Structure, and Functions of the Referee System," *Minerva,* Vol. IX, No. 1 (January 1971), pp. 66–100.
3. OECD, *Science, Growth and Society: A New Perspective,* Report of the Secretary-General's Ad Hoc Group on New Concepts in Science Policy (Paris: 1971).
4. Office of the Director of Defense Research and Engineering, *Project Hind Sight Final Report* (Washington, D.C.: October 1969).
5. H. Brooks, "Impact of the Defense Establishment on Science and Education," *National Science Policy,* Hearings before the Subcommittee on Research and Development of the Committee on Science and Astronautics, U.S. House of Representatives, 91st Congress, 2nd Session (Washington, D.C.: U.S. Government Printing Office, 1969), pp. 931–963.
6. Science Policy Research Division, Legislative Reference Service, Library of Congress, "The National Institutes of Research and Advanced Studies: A Recommendation for Centralization of Federal Service Responsibilities," Report to the Subcommittee on Science, Research, and Development of HSAC, 91st Congress, 2nd Session, Serial No. 42–363–0 (Washington, D.C.: U.S. Government Printing Office, 1969).
7. British Government "Green Paper," *A Framework for Government Research and Development* (London: H.M. Stationery Office, Com. 4814, Nov. 24, 1971).
8. H. Brooks, "Rothschild's Recipe in the United States," *Nature,* 235:301 (1972).
9. OECD, *op. cit.,* page 68.
10. National Academy of Sciences/National Research Council, *Physics in Perspective,* ch. 9, p. 625. Report of Physics Survey Committee, National Academy of Sciences (Washington, D.C.: 1972).
11. J. Weneser *et al., Preliminary Report of the Nuclear Physics Panel of the Survey Committee,* National Academy of Sciences Report (Washington, D.C.: 1971), pp. 159–180.

12. A. M. Weinberg, "Social Problems and National Socio-Technical Institutes," *Applied Science and Technological Progress,* Report to the Committee on Science and Astronautics, U.S. House of Representatives, National Academy of Sciences Report (Washington, D.C.: June 1967), pp. 415–434.
13. NAS/NAE, D. Alpert, Chairman, "The Impact of Science and Technology on Regional Economic Development," National Academy of Sciences Report (Washington, D.C.: 1969).
14. H. Bode, *Synergy: Technical Integration and Technological Innovation in the Bell System* (Murray Hill, N.J.: privately printed by Bell Telephone Laboratories, 1971).
15. L. R. Brown, "The Social Impact of the Green Revolution," Carnegie Endowment for International Peace, *International Conciliation* (January 1971).

HEALTH IN AMERICA

Rick J. Carlson

Health care in the United States is deficient in many important respects and ineffective in others. And there is little likelihood that it will improve. Indeed, vis-à-vis various social trends and developments, our static, conservative, and unresponsive health care system may become more deficient and less effective than it is now.

Maldistribution of care and resources marks the present system:

Urban people receive better care than rural people. Thirty percent of the people live in rural areas, but only 12 percent of the physicians and 18 percent of the nurses practice there.

The rich receive better care than the poor. Poor people, whether urban or rural, are badly served; Medicaid has ameliorated but not solved the problem.

A disproportionate amount of resources is given to treating rather than preventing diseases.

A great amount of resources is lavished on costly equipment (e.g., coronary care units, kidney dialysis units) which saves a few lives but deprives many more people of either the medical treatment or the preventive care that might have saved their lives.

Most of our hospitals accommodate only the acutely ill or injured patient. The option for people whose health lies somewhere between well-being and severe morbidity is the physician's office.

It is estimated (by a U.S. public health official) that between fifty thousand and seventy-five thousand lives could be saved each year if our ambulances were better equipped and staffed with properly trained personnel. The National Research Council of the National Academy of Sciences says that trauma is the "neglected epidemic of modern society . . . the nation's most important environmental health problem."

Emergency-room treatment in our hospitals is uneven and in some cases poor. A recent study of 141 emergency room patients in Baltimore City Hospital revealed that 60 percent received ineffective care; 27 percent received effective care; and the remaining 13 percent received care that was neither effective nor ineffective.

Reprinted from the November/December 1972 issue of *The Center Magazine,* a publication of the Center for the Study of Democratic Institutions, Santa Barbara, California.

What are the reasons for this state of affairs?

For one, health care is a cottage industry which defies rational allocation and use of manpower and facilities. Most of the nation's 270,000 physicians practice independently of one another, communicating with each other informally and then usually only in connection with referral of patients. Also, a few physicians have entered into formal arrangements with hospitals. They do cooperate with hospitals in the delivery of health care services, but they are looked upon as independent contractors—private entrepreneurs—with all the discontinuities and uneven results that result from such a relationship.

Discontinuities are reflected, too, in the relationships between the remaining array of health service personnel and institutions. In addition to physicians and hospitals, there are hospital nurses, medical technicians, physical therapists, laboratories, clinics, nursing homes, visiting nurses, the pharmacies. The result is a fragmented and labor-intensive industry.

Increasing specialization among physicians aggravates the maldistribution problem; specialists prefer to practice in affluent urban areas in order to insure having enough patients.

Control of the performance of the health care system is in the hands of the providers. Although state laws, for example, grant the "right to practice" to physicians, this "licensure" process is vested, by statute, with physicians. When the quality of medical care is reviewed, it is done by physican and hospital committees. The size and distribution of health manpower, measured by specialty and geography, is largely determined by the availability of training and practice opportunities which are controlled by physicians and other health professionals.

We have paid, and continue to pay, an enormous price to perpetuate this system, most of which goes to support highly paid professionals and to amortize the mortgages on our hospitals. At the same time, we have let the system itself make the decisions about the allocation of its resources, and we make no attempt to judge the system's results because physicians insist on the right to monitor it by standards of their own making. In sum, it is a system that is formidable, fragmented, and complex at the point of entry; swathed in mystique during the treatment process; and haughty about the results of its performance. It is also a system whose impact on health status is far less significant than is generally assumed, less indeed than that of many socio-environmental factors. A review of recent books (by René Dubos, Allan Chase, Eli Ginzberg, and Victor Fuchs) indicates that while the physican does heal through such processes as reduction of fractures and surgical removal of pathenogenic organs, much disease is self-limiting and its virulence depends in great part not on the ministrations of the health care system, but upon social, economic, and cultural conditions.

Dr. Dubos has said:

> Without question, nutritional and infectious diseases account for the largest percentage of morbidity and mortality in most underprivileged countries, especially in those just becoming industrialized. Undernutrition, protein deficiency, malaria, tuberculosis, infestation with

worms, and a host of ill-defined gastrointestinal disorders are today the greatest killers in those countries, just as they used to be in the Western world one century ago. In contrast, the toll taken by malnutrition and infection decreases rapidly wherever and whenever the living standards improve, but other diseases then become more prevalent. In prosperous countries at the present time, heart diseases constitute the leading cause of death, with cancers in the second place, vascular lesions affecting the central nervous system in the third, and accidents in the fourth. Increasingly also, persons who are well fed and well sheltered suffer from a variety of chronic disorders, such as arthritis and allergies, that do not destroy life but often ruin it.

The quality and extent of one's education and the size of one's income correlate highly with good health status. The wealthier and more educated, the healthier. After examining a study of the National Bureau of Economic Research, Fuchs concluded that as large a reduction in mortality can be achieved by the expenditure of one more dollar for education as by an additional dollar for medical care.

And diet is crucial. Eli Ginzberg writes that "a diversified enriched diet will probably contribute more to the health of the population in the South than any specific addition to medical resources, such as an increase in the number of doctors or the number of hospital beds." And paradoxically the reverse is also true. According to Ginzberg, "For the first time in our history more people die prematurely because they eat too much rather than too little."

Little cost-benefit or cost-effective research has been focused on health care, but some studies find that money spent for preventive and disease-detection programs are efficacious, especially when compared with the cost of results of medical treatment. For example, fluoridation programs costing ten million dollars reduce caries in three hundred thousand children; the same money put into the treatment rather than the prevention of caries would affect something less than fifty thousand children.

There is little evidence of the impact of mental health services. There is, for example, no cure known for schizophrenia, the most prevalent psychosis. And while tranquilizers and shock therapy have reduced hospitalization time, rehospitalization rates are no better than with other therapies. However, there is some evidence that social-environmental factors do affect mental health. The Public Health Service reviews in its publication, *Mental Health,* a series of epidemiologic studies, covering such matters as poor housing, congestion, poverty, and malnutrition. About two of these studies, the authors conclude: "These two examples suggest strongly that improvement in the social environment probably does have a favorable effect on mental health."

Most cancers and heart diseases cannot presently be cured by medicine.

In sum, the delivery of medical care has a limited impact. It is most effective when applied to certain identifiable conditions of disease for which there is information as to efficacy. But, contrasted with all the socio-environmental factors which affect health status, medicine plays a minor role though it continues to be cast for the lead.

Things may get worse. Medicine may have less impact in the next two or three decades than it does now. If one looks to the future a number of social trends obviously affect health status; the question is whether and how our health care system will relate to these "social futures." They are:

Population skewing by age. Today, about 10 percent of our population, or twenty million people, are sixty-five or older. By the year 2000, based on current demographic projections, close to 15 percent, or thirty-five million people, will be sixty-five or older. Although there is such a thing as geriatric medicine, we do not produce geriatric specialists the way we produce, say, pediatricians. There are eighteen thousand pediatricians in the United States; but a current American Medical Association survey indicates that there may be no more than three hundred physicians who classify themselves as geriatricians.

Also, degenerative diseases associated with old age—atherosclerosis, heart disease, some cancers, and serious chronic disabling conditions like arthritis, rheumatism, and hypertension—are among those diseases on which the practice of medicine has had the least impact. Medicine has contributed to the preservation of life and human longevity but it is not able to do much more than maintain persons afflicted with the illnesses associated with aging.

Today, although the aged are 10 percent of the population, 27 percent of health care expenditures are made by them or on their behalf. And as they become a larger part of the total population, the aged will require an even larger share of health care resources simply to be maintained.

Medicine should not get all the blame for this. The medical care system has become the caretaker for countless older persons because society just cannot think what to do with them. A substantial number of patients in nursing homes and mental health institutions could be better—and possibly less expensively— placed elsewhere. An older person who is not fully capable of self-care should not be dumped automatically into a treatment center built for the helpless and nearly helpless.

Shift in disease patterns. We are experiencing almost exponential increases in stress-inducing environmental phenomena—e.g., noise, pace, rate of change, activity—which relate to the incidence of disease. Dr. Dubos has said it is justifiable to speak of "diseases of civilization" (cancer, heart disease, disorders of the cerebral system), and that the very use of that term is "tacit acknowledgment that our ways of life may have nefarious effects and that affluence, like poverty, can constitute a cause of disease."

Environmental stress is not likely to disappear. Stress is related to the pace of change, and although people apparently possess some inherent adaptability, there may be a limit to how much they can adapt to change. Dr. Dubos holds that "for the first time in the history of mankind, the biological and social experience of the father is almost useless to his son." It is likely that the diseases of civilization will exact an even higher toll in the future because medicine continues to be oriented to their cure rather than their prevention.

Accidents, self-inflicted morbidity, and mortality. As the world grows more congested and complicated, the incidence of accidents and resulting trauma increases. Auto accidents accounted for 27.5 percent of all deaths in 1968. If present auto-use patterns persist, eighty-six thousand people will die in auto accidents in 1980.

Also, what people take into their bodies can contribute to morbidity. Between 1940 and 1968, the annual consumption of liquor rose from 1.48 gallons per capita to 2.37 per capita; in that same period, beer consumption rose from 18.2 gallons to 23.8 gallons per capita. About nine million Americans are either alcoholics or nearly so. Alcoholism has been called the nation's "largest untreated treatable disease." Debilitative drug use has increased markedly in recent years. And although the link between smoking and lung cancer has been researched, the volume of cigarette sales has not gone down.

Unless the health care system improves its performance both at the scene of accidents and in emergency room treatment, and unless more resources—both general and specifically medical—are devoted to the prevention of accidents and self-inflicted morbidity, the incidence of health deterioration and mortality will grow apace with accidents.

Environmental pollution and degradation. Experts vary in their assessment of this phenomenon; while some view the earth as virtually inexhaustible, there are others who forecast inescapable disaster.

Experts also vary in their evaluation of the prospects of new technology to undo the ecological damage already done. In his book, *The Closing Circle,* Barry Commoner says that technological aims and methods are not responsive to ecological and environmental problems:

> "There is . . . a specific fault in our system of science and in the resultant understanding of the natural world which, I believe, helps to explain the ecological failure of technology. This fault is reductionism, the view that effective understanding of a complex system can be achieved by investigating the properties of its isolated parts. The reductionist methodology, which is so characteristic of much of modern research, is not an effective means of analyzing the vast natural systems that are threatened by degradation."

There is little likelihood that in the next thirty years we will stabilize growth and also develop technological methods to attack environmental degradation holistically rather than through our present piecemeal reductionism.

A powerful bloc of opinion and expertise now supports the proposition that, since socio-environmental factors are the single most important determinant of health status, a worsening of those conditions over the next thirty years will worsen our health status. And, environmentally induced debilitation is costly too. The National Institute of Environmental Health Sciences estimated that in 1970 the health cost of disease caused by environmental abuse was thirty-five billion dollars; ten billion for treatment, the remainder in lost wages and services.

The relationship of noise levels to psychiatric admissions, the relationship of air pollution to bronchitis, lung cancer, emphysema, various pulmonary maladies, and skin cancer; the effect of the ingestion of mercury, organic pesticides, and other contaminants; the incidence of rat bites and diseases associated with rat infestations—all of this evidence clearly points to the correlation of socio-environmental conditions and disease.

It also suggests that relatively small sums spent on cleaning up environmental conditions could sharply reduce disease, morbidity, and death. A recent article in *Science* by Lester Lave and Eugene Seskin makes this claim: it is likely that a 50 percent reduction in air pollution can reduce mortality from lung cancer by 25 percent; morbidity and mortality due to respiratory diseases by 25 percent; cardiovascular mortality by 20 percent; and reduction in the incidence of cancer by 15 percent.

Medicine as it is being practiced still focuses on repairs of the human machinery at a time when theoretical and empirical evidence indicates that health status is determined more by socio-environmental factors than by health care delivery services.

Mental and emotional disorder. Although various studies come up with conflicting evidence concerning the incidence and increase of mental illness, I am persuaded by the soundness of the theoretical arguments that mental illness is greater than we realize, and that it is increasing. Some of the conditions that probably lead to mental illness—stress, congestion, family divisiveness, delayed entry into the labor market—are being exacerbated, and so the incidence of mental and emotional disorders may grow.

Although various individuals claim to have been cured, there is little except anecdotes on which to base a judgment about the various therapies. Dr. Ginzberg counsels caution:

> Many articulate psychiatrists have repeatedly testified before Congress about significant therapeutic advances. But we must question whether there is solid evidence, reinforced by follow-up, to support such claims. Admittedly, state hospital census figures are down, not up; yet there has been an upward drift in patient admissions figures. But the total system has been changing and we now treat many patients in new kinds of settings. Are they included in the totals? Another reason for caution is the readmission rate. Still another is what happens to the patient who is discharged. Is his recovery maintained? Not much is known. To release a patient from the hospital is easier than to absorb him at home. And without adequate follow-up data, we remain in the dark.

If mental illness does increase in the years ahead, the uncertainty about whether the providing of medical services makes any difference will probably increase also. Amelioration in the social and environmental conditions would seem to be at least as likely to improve the mental health of the population.

Biomedical technology. Books and articles listing prospective biomedical "breakthroughs" abound. The claims include major reduction in hereditary and congenital defects; controlled super-effective relaxation and sleep; new and better drugs to control fatigue, alertness, mood, personality, perceptions, and fantasies; general and substantial increase in life expectancy; postponement of aging; limited rejuvenation; more extensive use of transplanted human organs, widespread use of cryogenics; improved chemical control of some mental illness and certain aspects of senility; organ regeneration; gene insertion and deletion; memory injection and memory editing.

It seems likely that some breakthroughs will occur. But the critical question is not what impact those breakthroughs will have on health status—generally it should be favorable—but what the impact will be on the existing health care delivery system. Physicians enjoy esoteric toys to play with. If the present orientation and focus of the system continues—i.e., concentration of resources and expensive equipment to the relatively few who can afford it at the expense of the many who lack adequate preventive and treatment care for the non-glamorous but no less fatal diseases—then biomedical breakthroughs in the years ahead can have no other effect than forcing the costs of medical care even higher, encouraging physicians to continue highly specialized practices, and effectively keeping preventive medical practice in the status of a neglected stepchild.

The new naturalism. This is variously known by various authors as the new culture, the counterculture, Consciousness III, new life-styles, the youth movement. However described and defined, it connotes a desire and a commitment to a more humane society that stresses community and cooperation rather than competitiveness, closeness to nature and to the land, a simplification of one's wants in material terms, participation in rather than observation of aesthetic and creative processes, putting a higher valuation on environment than on economic growth and technology or on the "conquest" of nature.

The health implications of this counter-cultural revolution are difficult to draw, but one of the effects of its discrediting growth for growth's sake may be an awakened determination to attack pollution, resource depletion, and other environmental degradations associated with growth and thus morbidity.

Also, consumer demand for more personalized medical care may increase. There may be a gradual return to the practice of folk medicine with the return of "community." And professionalism in health care, scrutinized by people who refuse to automatically accept the Olympian qualities and mystique of any class, may be enhanced.

What would be a design for a rational allocation of a nation's resources and a more comprehensive system of health care? The following would seem to be at least some of the features that should be included:

The current system should be stripped down and given responsibility for acute care, with more funds allocated to improve emergency care, and with all expenditures determined (competitively with other programs) on a cost-effective basis.

Physicians not involved in acute and emergency care should be redeployed and, if necessary, retrained to design and staff programs of prevention. They would be allowed to treat patients only in connection with preventive programs, or in residential complexes for the aged, or in outpatient facilities—all conditions not requiring hospitalization.

A new supply of practitioners, less intensively prepared than physicians, should be trained to provide initial detection and diagnostic services and some limited treatment for ambulatory patients.

An alternative to financing (which will undoubtedly be almost wholly public by the year 2000) should include the option of insuring payment to communities for their decisions as to how to provide the care they need.

The focus of regulation should be on the outcome of medical care, with full and open disclosure of information to the public.

Residential complexes should be built for those aged who cannot maintain a home. Medical care should be integrated into those complexes (as well as in private homes for those aged who prefer to live elsewhere).

Investment in biomedical research oriented to techniques of prevention in individual cases—to insure early detection of cancer, for example—should be expanded. A major focus of this program should be on the detection and cure of degenerative diseases of old age, and on the alleviation, if not the cure, of chronic conditions.

With the savings from a decreased investment in the personal health care system and in the training of physicians, and with such additional funding as is necessary, a substantial effort should be made to eliminate and mitigate the socio-environmental causes of illness through the development of aggregate prevention programs: rapid transit to reduce the pollution caused by motor vehicles; a new-towns program to create smaller, more human communities with less stress and congestion; comprehensive fluoridation programs; and accident prevention programs.

Part V.
Education in America

By law, everyone in the United States must have some contact with educational organizations, and students spend a good part of their lives in schools. The school is the first institution that the young experience directly, but they are taught little about its organization. The complexities of the adult part—the teachers, administrators, janitors—and the agencies that weld the separate units into the education industry—state and local boards of education, federal agencies, teachers' associations, and so on—are largely hidden from view. Although it has its own goals, including knowledge for its own sake, education is primarily a service institution serving political, military, and economic organizations. Thus, although the schools are run on a day-to-day basis by professionals, major decisions are made by politicians (especially in funding), semipolitical civic leaders, local business influentials, and, in the case of parochial schools, religious leaders. The Parent-Teacher Association (PTA), while it can shape life in the school, does not decide whether the budget for a school should be increased, whether a school should close down, which students should attend it, and what must be taught. Similarly, university and college faculty and administrators (much less students) do not have the ultimate say on budgets, enrollments, burdensome athletic programs, and so on. State universities are responsible to—that is, ultimately controlled by—government, while private colleges are directed by self-perpetuating governing boards made up, usually, of businessmen. Thus, even though there *is* considerable freedom and autonomy within universities (for example, often more nonconformity is permitted on a campus than at the telephone company), they do not control their own destinies. Neither government nor business will pay for higher education if it completely fails to turn out a useful product (good citizens, trained or trainable workers). They will not support the ivory tower just to keep some potential troublemakers off the streets.

Education is big business, in terms of the number of people involved, the operating expenditure, and the value of physical plant. According to U.S. Office of Education statistics, there were 45.9 million students enrolled in the public schools in 1970, 27.5 million in primary and 18.4 million in secondary schools. In 1970 there were also more than sixteen thousand private schools (65 percent Catholic) with enrollments of about 5.1 million (3.9 million in elementary, 1.2 million in secondary schools). The growth in total high school enrollment is shown in Table 1. High school attendance has become almost universal, with 78 percent of seventeen-year-olds graduating high school in 1970. According to the Office of Education,[1] these students are taught by almost 2.3 million full-time (equivalent) teachers: 1.3 million in primary schools (11.4 percent private) and 1 million in second-

Table 1

Enrollment in Grades 9–12 in Public and Nonpublic Schools Compared with Population 14–17 Years of Age: United States, 1889–1890 to Fall 1970

School Year	Enrollment, Grades 9–12 and Postgraduate			Population 14–17 Years of Age	Total Number Enrolled per 100 persons 14–17 Years of Age
	All Schools	Public Schools	Nonpublic Schools		
1889–90	359,949	202,963	94,931	5,354,653	6.7
1909–10	1,115,398	915,061	117,400	7,220,298	15.4
1929–30	4,804,255	4,399,422	341,158	9,341,221	51.4
1939–40	7,123,009	6,635,337	487,672	9,720,419	73.3
1949–50	6,453,009	5,757,810	695,199	8,404,768	76.8
1959–60	9,599,810	8,531,454	1,068,356	11,154,879	86.1
Fall 1970	14,840,000	13,400,000	1,440,000	15,816,000	93.8

SOURCE: U.S. Dept. of Health, Education, and Welfare, Office of Education, N.C.E.S., *Digest of Educational Statistics*, 1971; Washington, D.C.: Government Printing Office, 1972, p. 27.

[1] U.S. Office of Education, *Statistics of Public Schools*, Fall 1970 (Washington, D.C.: Government Printing Office, 1973).

ary schools (7.1 percent private). Teachers, then, compose the largest single industry work force.

The purposes of primary and secondary education are diverse. Formally they consist of socializing the young for useful participation in society. Students should learn basic citizenship, skill training, appreciation of high culture, and intellectual values, but often these goals are not achieved. Informally, the schools act as certification mills, as screening houses for future employers, as temporary detention centers for unemployables, and so on. They also provide an "objective" rationale for labeling some of the population "failures." Schools are sometimes a means of expressing civic pride. The buildings are often designed more as impressive showplaces than as learning centers. Many primary schools are too large—and too barren—for small children. High school bands and football teams, on which so much time and energy are spent, clearly have more civic than educational value. And the latent militarism of both would be quite alien, for example, to most European schools. Informal rewards to the student do not flow only from academic performance. Teachers often prefer obedient and dull students to those who are bright but troublesome, and popularity among the students is determined more by social activities (for girls) and sports ability (for boys) than by excellence in, say, biology.

There were 2,686 institutions of higher education operating in the United States in 1972–1973.[2] Of these, 1,193 were public and 1,493 private (696 independent, 797 religious affiliation). Nine hundred seventy were less than four-year colleges (most two-year junior colleges), 765 were baccalaureate-degree-only colleges. The remainder, 951, awarded bachelor's and professional, master's, or doctorate degrees. A survey of college enrollments compiled by Garland G. Parker[3] shows that there were more than 6.4 million students in 1,428 reporting four-year or more colleges and almost 1.7 million in 536 reporting two-year colleges. Since World War II enrollment in public universities has increased faster than in private schools, and the public sector has the two largest unified systems—the State University of New York and the University of California. The teachers that staff these colleges form a large professional grouping, about equal in size to the na-

[2] U.S. Department of Health, Education, and Welfare, *Education Directory 1972–1973: Higher Education* (Washington, D.C.: Government Printing Office, December 1972).
[3] Garland G. Parker, "College and University Enrollments in America, 1972–73, Statistics, Interpretations, and Trends." *Intellect,* vol. 101, nos. 2347 and 2349 (February and April 1973).

tion's supply of physicians. Thus, the American Association of College Professors lists 266,913 teachers in 1,242 institutions (this includes most major colleges) with professorial rank in 1972–1973. The cost of their compensation, although far short of that for physicians, was a substantial $4.38 billion.

The large universities are very complex organizational structures, and a special term, *multiversity*, has been used to describe them. As we saw in the previous chapter, they are the sites for large-scale government sponsored research. They are also expected to serve many public and business needs outside of teaching. They run agricultural extension services, forestry programs, business services, and they provide big-time mass entertainment. College football is a major item of television programming—it sells a lot of soft drinks, food, and deodorants, and it is the minor league for the National Football League.

There are often conflicts among the needs of graduate education, professional education, and undergraduate education. The latter often suffers, especially when professors are rewarded more for their nonteaching activities than for excellent undergraduate teaching.

Berenice M. Fisher sketches an overview of American education. She outlines three general interpretations that have shaped studies of education: the populist-socialist, the pragmatic-pluralist, and the developmental. She prefers a combination of the first two. The analysis focuses on conflicts of interest, and she asks three orienting questions: Who is involved in education? What are they attempting to do? What results from their differences? She sees three main categories of people in education: the sponsors (other institutions, social classes, and ethnic groups) who are concerned with their social standing; teaching groups who are partially committed to education; and students whose main concern is often survival. Resolution of conflicting interests is, she concludes, a central problem for future research in education.

Godfrey Hodgson's article looks at a related question—the degree to which education has promoted equality among Fisher's "sponsors." Recent research by James S. Coleman and analyses by Christopher Jencks have cast doubt on the capacity of education to transform society. The historic optimism has collapsed. Coleman and Jencks found that the quality of education—physical plant, teachers, curriculum—was less important in high academic achievement than family and that the achievements of minority students were not equal to those of whites even when minority students formally had equal opportunity. Genetic explanations for these differences were put forward by Jensen and Herrnstein. Liberals were shocked by what they perceived as open racism reasserted after decades of banishment from genteel academia. Thomas Pettigrew has claimed that desegregation, much less real integration, has not yet been achieved, so we cannot claim that it has failed. The article concludes with the different policy implications that have been drawn from this hot educational debate.

The two final articles deal with higher education in the United States. Martin Trow is concerned with the impact of enrollment increases as higher education becomes a universal need. This development parallels the changes that Trow described in an earlier paper, which outlines the changes in secondary education from college preparation for the elite around 1870 through vocational preparation for the masses around 1910 to mass (almost universal) college preparation today. Colleges are facing much wider responsibilities today than ever before. These include what used to be "outside" problems such as racism and urban regeneration. Although Trow is enamored with the traditions of scholarship and gentlemanly consensus, Robertson and Steele are clearly not. They are radicals who question the very basis of the university. They believe that higher education is an elitist institution that fails to educate—a caricature of a real center of learning, peopled by arrogant popes (professors) and humble ignorant peasants (students). While their argument has merit, their conclusions, I hope, are wrong.

Suggested Readings

Beck, Carlton E., et al. *Education for Relevance.* New York: Houghton Mifflin, 1968.

Carnoy, Martin, ed. *Schooling in a Corporate Society.* New York: McKay, 1972.

Coleman, James S., et al. *Equality of Educational Opportunity.* Washington, D.C.: U.S. Office of Education, 1966.

Francis, Roy G. *Crumbling Walls.* Cambridge, Mass.: Schenkman, 1970.

Goslin, David A. *The School in Contemporary Society.* Chicago: Scott, Foresman, 1965.

Henthoff, Nat. *Our Children Are Dying.* New York: Viking, 1966.

Holt, John. *How Children Fail.* New York: Delta-Dell, 1964.

Jencks, Christopher, et al. *Inequality: A Reassessment of the Effect of Family and Schooling in America.* New York: Basic, 1972.

Katz, Michael B. *Class, Bureaucracy and Schools.* New York: Praeger, 1971.

Kerr, Clark. *The Uses of the University.* Cambridge, Mass.: Harvard University Press, 1964.

Leonard, George B. *Education and Ecstasy.* New York: Delta-Dell, 1968.

Mayhew, Lewis B. *The Carnegie Commission on Higher Education.* San Francisco: Jossey-Bass, 1973.

Mosteller, F., and Moynihan, D. P., eds. *Equality of Educational Opportunity.* New York: Random House, 1971.

Renfield, Richard. *If Teachers Were Free.* Washington, D.C.: Acropolis, 1972.

Robertson, Don, and Steele, Marion. *The Halls of Yearning.* San Francisco: Canfield, 1971.

Sarason, Seymour B. *The Culture of the School and the Problem of Change.* Boston: Allyn and Bacon, 1971.

Woodring, Paul. *The Higher Learning in America: A Reassessment.* New York: McGraw-Hill, 1968.

EDUCATION IN
THE BIG PICTURE

Berenice M. Fisher

To the great disadvantage of those working in the sociology of education, the problem of the relation of education to the society as a whole has been out of fashion for about fifty years. Since the period when many social theorists abandoned their strong and explicit interest in social reform, the social analysis of education has appeared as either a marginal topic in the work of general sociologists or a vital but narrowed problem in research (by sociologists of education and others) on public schooling, higher education, and the few other educational areas to which public concern has directed attention.[1]

In the spirit of broadening argument and research, this paper offers a framework or series of questions for the sociological study of education—a way of analyzing how new kinds of formal education arise and how they acquire their particular characteristics. My approach is socio-historic, focusing on how long-term American social patterns have helped to shape American education. The notion of education which I employ is purposefully broad, although this particular discussion concentrates on formal education. I have not attempted a "complete" interpretation of American education. Rather, I have tried to point out questions which I think help to avoid the parochialism of conception and narrowness of subject matter from which even the best research in the sociology of education tends to suffer.

Moreover, although this discussion does not venture into cross-national comparisons, I believe that applying the questions I suggest to other countries would highlight new problems in comparative studies. At the same time, asking such questions of other educational settings should suggest ways in which we would need to modify, in order to generalize and correct, the framework presented here.

This paper, then, is offered in a critical spirit. But it also invites the reader to "try" these questions on the educational area or national educational context with which he is most familiar, to see where the framework I am suggesting fits and where it does not.

Reprinted from *Sociology of Education*, Vol. 45 (Summer 1972). Used by permission.

The Socio-Historic Study of American Education

Although I have just criticized the lack of broad, socio-historic studies of American education, such perspectives are not entirely lacking. In fact, one way of introducing my argument is to show how it is located in relation to other historical interpretations of education which American sociologists have forwarded. Viewed primarily with regard to their general approaches to education, these studies may be divided roughly into three types: 1) populist-socialist; 2) pragmatist or pluralist; and 3) developmental. Many studies, of course, fall somewhere in between the two groups. But, for now, I wish to emphasize neither the groupings *per se* nor the many factors in the occupational history of sociology which have led to the prominence of one or another interpretation. Instead, I want to stress the relation of these interpretations of education to interpretations of the social world in which the sociologist, as man and as professional, is rooted.[2]

From the early years of American sociology, continuing patterns of social conflict have given support to populist and socialist interpretations of education. In the latter part of the nineteenth century, the conflict, typically, was that between the railroads and the farmers or the rising financial interests and the common man; today the conflict is often cast in terms of the dominance of corporate institutions, or sometimes in terms of racial oppression. But, throughout, education seen from this general perspective tends to be interpreted in two ways: one, that education, basically, is an instrument of repression which is used by the ruling class or elites to rob the people of their livelihood and freedom, perhaps to mold them to the purposes of the dominant order; or, two, that education is the potential instrument for combating the ruling group, for establishing or reestablishing the rights of the common man. Theorists of this ilk often have stressed the corruption of education or the monopoly of knowledge by those in power—as, say, Veblen (1918) and Mills (1956) did with their biting analyses—but it is even more interesting that sociologists in both the populist and the socialist vein also have seen the public schools as a vehicle for bringing knowledge, and with it power, to the people. Ross (1922:174-182) argued for a public school system which would counteract the careers and values bred by business dominance, while Baran and Sweezy (1966:305-335) imply that American schools should at least match those of the U.S.S.R. in efficiency, as well as seek intellectual quality of the sort for which Robert Hutchins was striving.

The attempt to understand and respond to social conflict took another though related turn in the interpretations of the sociological pragmatists, from their end of the progressive tradition. They, too, focused on the injustice suffered by the working classes and criticized the business dominance of education—for instance, as in the efforts of businessmen to suit industrial education to their own purposes. But the pragmatists were concerned equally with the problems of the new immigrants and the growing conflict between them and the dominant Anglo-Saxons. In the interpretations of pragmatic theorists and allied reformers, the general social interest is served only through a continued quest for a common ground which transcends the current conflict. Communication and mutual education play crucial roles in finding this common ground, and for this reason such theorists usually insist on beginning with the actual positions of the conflicting parties, beginning education at whatever time or place seems appropriate to the parties involved, and seeking leadership from any group which might lead the way. Hence, Mead (1908) could implore labor leaders to help shape an industrial education which would serve the interests of all; Counts (1927, 1932) could envision school boards representing all elements of the community and see the school teachers themselves leading the way to a better society; and the settlement house intellectuals could picture the settlement as a place where all groups could argue for their views, with university students and professors contributing their special knowledge.[3]

The sociological studies of community life which began to bloom in the twenties drew on both the populist-socialist and pragmatic streams of social theory, which in turn were reflected in the ways that sociologists saw education's role in the community. The bridge between pragmatic theory and urban sociology was made through Robert Park (1950), whose work pointed to the problems of communication and education in the fractured modern community. Thus in Zorbaugh's (1929) classic study of the gold coast and slum, no less than Gans' (1962) more recent field work on the Italian ghetto, the themes of the settlement house movements echo—how diverse groups have their own goals and their own kinds of socialization and how difficult (though possibly desirable) it is to transcend them through education. On the other hand, community studies which have leaned heavily toward the populist-socialist stream tend to focus on the public schools (typically in a chapter on "education"). Some of this interest follows from the fact that, as Maurice Stein (1960:47ff.) has pointed out, among the crucial themes in community studies has been the price paid for industrialization, especially by the working class. Thus, when the Lynds (1929) include a chapter on the public schools or when Hollingshead (1949) makes this the subject of an entire volume, the implied question is: What has the school system done to redress this injustice?[4]

Finally, some of the interest in the public schools as a part of the community is based less on theories of conflict between social groups and more on interpretations which stress the need for developing the society. This developmental approach came into special prominence after the second world war, when, in line with America's national and international commitments to economic development (and the related national defense), many sociologists abandoned the more critical attitude toward urbanization and industrialization taken by earlier reformers. Instead, education was now seen as a series of pipelines which would feed trained manpower into areas of emerging need, according to the nation's stage of development. If the process worked properly, it would be a smooth one, embodying, as Parsons (1959) postulated, a congruity between the formal socialization of students and the requirements of the social structure. From this position it also follows that education, though of differing kinds of levels, might be relevant to many different parts of the social structure, depending on the stage of development: writers like Harbison and Meyers (1964) have pointed to various forms of technical training; others such as Shils (1965) have explored the function of higher education. And precisely because of their interest in how all parts of an evolving society fit together, such analysts also have had to cope with the "dysfunctional" consequences of education, the problem of over-educated intellectuals or technicians, of the young people who want more education than they are able to absorb.[5]

Indeed, not only those employing developmental theories, but socio-historic interpretations of education in general judge some kinds of education as functional, others dysfunctional—depending on the way the given analyst carves out the social world and on what kind of social ideal (no matter how vaguely articulated) is prized.

The approach for which I am going to argue here employs a kind of social analysis and involves a social ideal (*very* vaguely articulated) which falls somewhere between the populist-socialist and the pragmatist interpretations. This approach explicitly rejects evolutionary assumptions concerning industrial society and the assumptions concerning consensus on values which underlie developmental theory. On the other hand, I am not going to engage in elaborate criticism of this latter position. Such criticisms are now more frequent, and educational researchers can draw on them for their own critiques. Rather, I feel it is important to point out the particular contributions that have been made by the developmental approach. In its stress on macroscopic social theory it has reminded us of what the early social theorists saw so clearly, namely, that the social analysis of education must consider the nature of society as a whole. Moreover, because of their wide interests, the developmental theorists by and large have been the ones to underscore the diversity of educational institutions and to find such areas as adult or technical education worthy of serious sociological study.

My approach is far closer to the populist-socialist stream, especially to its basic insight into the way in which social groups climb to power, displacing established groups and molding those with less power to their—the climbers'—needs. However, in the actual application of this insight to education, it seems to me that populist and socialist critics have emphasized the manipulative use of education as an instrument for gaining and retaining power in a rather narrow sense, and to the exclusion of many other possible ways in which their criticism could flow. Like the mainstream of the labor movement, such critics have tended to settle for a critique of the public schools, with an underlying demand for increased individual mobility through a reformed public school system, or through private schooling which would perform a basically similar function. Many of the current arguments for "radical" alternatives in education are little more than a repetition of this critique. The irony, of course, is that such critics have tended, thereby, to abandon the very emphasis on the *social* nature of education which has characterized much radical theory and therefore also have tended to neglect those areas of education—education in the context of protest movements or of social movements in general, various kinds of adult, or utopian education—to which populist or perhaps especially socialist criticism would seem naturally to lead.[6]

Here, elements of the pragmatic tradition can be used as a valuable corrective, through a demand for open-endedness in analyzing the consequences of social conflict, an insistence on examining all the groups involved, and an emphasis on the symbolic as well as the structural dimension of behavior. That is, rather than begin with *assumptions* about the nature of education in a society which indeed may display certain structural characteristics or patterns of power, we need to begin with *questions* about what groups in fact are interested in education, how much they wish to and are able to control it, and what consequences therefore follow for the nature of education. By exploring rather than prejudging interest in education, we should be led to examine and compare groups which differ considerably in respect to their actual or desired positions in the social structure, their breadth or parochiality of social interests and aspirations for control—to ask how such differences are reflected in programs of and conflicts over education.

The following discussion, then, begins with a very simple typology of social groups, based on their general relation to education: 1) the social groups which sponsor education, 2) the teaching groups which make education their work, and 3) the students who presumably "get" the education. I am going to look at these kinds of groups in turn and to try to probe the relation between their structural characteristics, how they see education, and what activities they engage in regarding it. As already implied, I am not going to attempt an integrated analysis of the relationships between these groups as they have developed on the American scene. However, the discussion will seek to focus on conflicts of interest and of value which have arisen between such groups and will attempt some generalization about the consequences of these conflicts for the parties involved.

The Social Uses of Education

The primary questions which I wish to suggest for analyzing educational encounters as a part of the larger social scene are: 1) who is involved in the given educational encounter, 2) where are these parties going or seeking to go, and 3) what kinds of interaction result from the intersection of their worlds and interests?

This set of questions presupposes an emphasis on group membership and on individuals as group members.[7] In the case of education, the most obvious groups are *students, teachers* (including the other kinds of educational professionals who man educational programs), and *sponsors,* who support and often initiate or shape educational programs. Sponsors, teachers, or students variously may be in the foreground or background of given educational encounters; but the researcher's question always remains: who is (or is not) around, and why? Moreover, the distinction between sponsors, teachers, and students is not a hard and fast one. Rather, it is a way of typing the roles which groups (or individuals) play or seek to play in given kinds of educational encounters; and, in fact, one can find many examples of combining or switching such roles—the sponsors who want also to teach, the teachers who want to shape their own sponsorship, the students who teach each other or teach themselves. The point is that each combination we discover, like each new kind of educational encounter, should force us to ask "why?"

But, basically, this question cannot be answered without knowing where the groups or individuals are going or seeking to go, that is, the nature of their interests and their histories. Although group histories ultimately are composed of individual histories, the focus of this discussion is on the social mobility of those groups which come to be involved in educational encounters. In the case of sponsoring groups and teaching groups, the discussion primarily focuses on group histories—on the group or class aspirations of educational sponsors and on the quest for professional or occupational mobility on the part of teaching groups. It is important, however, to keep in mind that the careers of individual sponsors and teachers (who may or may not reflect the general trends of group movement) are an integral part of this story. In the case of students, the discussion emphasizes patterns of individual mobility vis-à-vis group membership, although it also gives attention to the problem of mobility for social groups *qua* groups by way of the student role. To a certain extent, this choice of emphasis regarding group or individual mobility is more the product of my current concern for the effect of organized educational efforts on individual careers than of the limitations of the framework itself.

Educational Sponsors

Who seeks to sponsor education? A tremendously wide array of social groups do so—economic groups, political groups, ethnic, racial or religious groups, social movements of every imaginable sort. However, such social groups do not always become educational sponsors. Indeed, in contrast to teaching groups, most social groups do not see education as their full-time business, and many do not see it as their business at all—which is to win out in the struggle to establish and maintain their respective interests, the positions they hold or covet on the social scene. To do this, groups sometimes, in effect, pick educational solutions as part of choosing a route for survival or success. The choice of education is not rational in any abstract sense, but a plausible solution to the particular problems the given groups face. To understand this choice of educational sponsorship, we need to view the mobility of such social groups as a complex phenomenon, with groups jostling to get to the top, competing or cooperating to stay there, trying to maintain control of others on whom their success depends, trying to build the cohesion they need to hold out against competitors or to strike out on some new social path.

Jostling to get to and stay at the top is, perhaps, the most striking pattern, and one often having, as Mills argued (1956), world-shaking consequences. But the consequences for education have been considerable too. For example, many of the changes in the universities and preparatory schools of the United States at the end of the nineteenth century reflected the jostling of competitive groups, especially in the attempts of newly emerging businessmen to protect their accumulated fortunes at the same time that they tried to garner the kind of legitimacy claimed by earlier arrivals. While the various new-rich established their own schools, they also invaded old-rich schools, the walls of which at least partly crumbled. Yet, ironically, some of the established social leadership was in almost the reverse bind from the newer climbers; that is, as their control over governing roles became more problematic, the education which they had assumed adequate for their sons (and which therefore, as Henry Adams' *Education* so brilliantly shows, was nothing but embellishment on the informal socialization to their class) was now itself becoming of doubtful use.

The other important aspect of this situation from our standpoint is the fact that many of the newly ascendant businessmen did not have the backgrounds to translate their educational visions into concrete or viable plans; it was at this point that the newly emerging breed of university leaders (together with other philanthropic entrepreneurs) stepped in—both to translate (or sometimes to midwife) the vision and to develop bargains which would accommodate rival social groups. Sometimes, as in the case of Andrew White's experience with Ezra Cornell, the problem was one of talking a self-made man into sponsoring a more "modern" kind of higher education. Sometimes, as in the case of Wilson at Princeton, the problem was one of transforming an institution geared to training gentlemen and scholars (including professionals) into one which trained leadership for an industrial society. In such bargains, social rivals often were accommodated to the extent that each got something—for instance, the older rich its ideal of responsible leadership preserved, the newer rich their need for legitimation met. But from their own standpoint, the university educators often got the most of all—that is, the opportunity to train the coming generation of national leaders. Indeed, the more seriously the university educators took their own role, the more possible it was for them to get into trouble with the various groups involved. Moreover, as Woodrow Wilson's academic career shows, not only might the sponsors begin to question education for leadership when its implications were pursued fully, but the students, over whose heads the deal was made, might begin to exert pressure. Wilson, said one disgruntled undergraduate, was trying to make Princeton into nothing but a "damned educational institution" (Bragdon, 1967:288).[8]

Sketchy though this example is, it raises a host of questions about the sponsorship of education and its payoffs. One wonders whether the new rich of various sorts would have been so enthusiastic if more direct routes for legitimation had been readily available. Why the universities? What was the relation between the goals which both the more established and emerging social groups had for themselves or their own generation vis-à-vis that of their sons, or the generation of their sons? In even more general terms, why does a given group look like a likely educational clientele in relation to the actual attributes of the group and the kind of symbolic value which various sponsors attach to education?

Although the relation of the symbolic value of education to the social structure is a complex question, two answers seem to be implied here. One is that education appeals to sponsors because of its use by some significant other group or groups, especially, perhaps, by the sponsors' own rivals. The use of education to counter rivals is essentially a form of coopting a social jurisdiction through socialization: the generational difference which may be a disadvantage in passing along business skills is converted into an advantage in crashing the upper social reaches ("Who will know his son from yours in the next generation?"); or, to take an example from American military strategy of the last few years, the same beseiged peasants who are recruited by enemy troops also become the objects of American efforts at political education ("If guerrillas and missionaries can gain loyalty through education, we can too!"). (See Rostow, 1961; Raskin, 1965; Luce and Sommer, 1969.)

Although such rivalry may well be the *sine qua non* of sponsors' willingness to adopt educational solutions (to repeat, this is usually after all not their business), the situation often seems to require another element in the form of intermediaries, that is, individuals and emerging groups who do make it their business to translate potential educational solutions into specific educational plans and ideologies, often to sell these ideas to sponsors.[9] Clearly, all social groups are not equally apt customers for such educational prescriptions, but our framework leads us to conjecture that they become apt customers when the kind of social mobility they are attempting to undergo, undergoing, or trying to avoid undergoing takes them into social territory and social worlds with which they are unfamiliar. Hence, in individual terms, Ezra Cornell on his way "up" and Henry Adams on his way "down" are both equally open to some kinds of educational entrepreneurship, whereas members of a tightly knit immigrant enclave or a settled upper-class community might not be.

In terms of the intermediaries' own aspirations, we can only note here that the job of selling education knits into their careers in a variety of ways.[10] But the more important point is the complexity of the job they cut out for themselves; it may require not only a sense of the potential for institution-building in relation to relevant changes in social structure, but a sense of how to use or create client groups out of the population changes which immigration, urbanization, war, and so on effect. Yet, despite the continued rise of intermediaries, it would be a mistake to assume this kind of calculation as necessarily professional, self-conscious, accurate, or moral, rather than, as it is, part of a groping through historical possibilities in the sponsors' own struggle for survival.

Finally, however, our discussion of this example has assumed a degree of awareness, cohesion, and consensus concerning the goals which sponsoring groups seek—any of which may, in fact, be lacking at any given period in a group's history. We cannot try to analyze the more general conditions under which such properties do become problems for social groups, but we can raise the question of under what conditions does the conscious struggle to build up a group, the effort to deal with the fragmenting of a group, or the problems of giving a group new form and a new goal lead to the employment of educational solutions.

Whether or not education is seen as an efficacious means of gaining or maintaining group cohesion seems to be related to factors such as the manner of recruitment, the heterogeneity of those to be recruited, and the success of group leadership in giving the members what it has promised—all factors which are particularly salient during the early and/or less secure moments of a social group or social movement's history. For instance, in the development of American business, it was only when business reached a certain complexity of organization plus heterogeneity of recruitment that education—of both businessmen and workers—became attractive; whereas, in the case of the labor movement of the same period the victory of the craft unions and their organizations along the lines of homogeneous groupings spelled the end for many education-oriented socialists, with their ideal of a broad and integrated labor movement.[11]

While union history suggests the generally familiar notion that the passion to gain converts wanes with institutionalization, the application of this notion to the use of formal education raises questions. For example, while on one hand machine politicians of the turn of the century had little use for education (it did not take much educating in the principle of exchange favors to recruit an immigrant constituency), the movement to uplift or liberate black Americans almost always has given to education a prominent role. Are not the relative difficulties involved in achieving long-run success for a movement and the relative accessibility of some kinds of educational niches which offer short-run success for individuals factors here? In the long struggle, education may be used not only to build up needed skills and morale, but to give members something to do and achieve while waiting out historical obstacles.

Moreover, education also may speak to the challenges which a relatively weak or threatened movement may suffer—from either rivals within or rivals without. Thus, Catholic America of the nineteenth century suffered both an internal struggle over leadership and a struggle with that part of Protestant America which was seeking assiduously to control it through such means as the public schools and similar philanthropic institutions. The mainstream Catholic answer, carved out by Bishop Spaulding and others, involved an educational route which in their eyes avoided the perils of ethnic isolationism, the threat of a too-liberal assimilationism, and the disaster of a Protestant takeover: a specifically Catholic education would train up new generations of good, Catholic, Americans. Only the rub was, as it almost always is, that the new generations then constituted a new social segment, promoting their own educational reforms.[12]

Teaching Groups

Teaching groups display many of the same historical patterns as social groups in general, but like other occupational groups, they also are characterized by the particular ways in which they seek to establish their occupational identities. As a type of service occupation, teaching seeks to establish its claim to do something for (or to) its clients; as teachers, such groups by definition are committed to some kind of education as the means.[13]

If we broaden the consideration of teaching groups to include any occupational group which claims some significant part of its work to be educational, many interesting questions are raised; for neither the meaning of education in such contexts nor its attractiveness as part of an occupational identity are self-evident. Some occupational groups do *not* want to be labeled as teachers or educators, while others fervidly aspire to such an identity. Both the occupational value and the meaning of education imply not only a social status but a kind of relationship to both sponsors and clients. For this reason, in addition to the struggle between rival occupational groups themselves, the attempt to establish or maintain such a status is fraught with problems. The nature of the group's sponsorship, its kind of occupational rivals, and the nature of its clientele, all shape how it attempts to solve these.

In contrast not only to the "free" professions but to many other kinds of occupations in industrial America, teaching groups have tended to begin as or quickly to become sponsored occupations. This has meant that the goals of the various teaching groups—the definitions of their work and their proper clienteles—have been laid out initially in terms of the sponsors' ideals for the social world. But, whom the sponsors seek and whom they actually can recruit as agents to carry out their desired educational tasks are often different matters. For example, the early nineteenth century public school crusaders in the United States began by looking for young men who would dedicate themselves to a lofty calling, and ended up with farm girls who were so barely literate that they themselves had to be educated in order to teach.[14]

Moreover, as teaching groups have developed, they have tended to produce subsequent generations whose relation to the sponsors, to the kind of work to be done, and, indeed, to the entire social world is different from that of the first generation. New generations of occupational leaders then attempt to carve out work prescriptions which follow the groups' emerging interests, which forward meanings for "education" and employ the appellation "teacher" in ways which fit these interests. Such efforts, in effect, involve new ideas and claims to occupational status which are based on some new form of expertise (one generation may claim inspiration, the next science, the next a new view of the social world) and which propose some kind of relationship to clients.

In developing such lines of action, teaching groups often not only encounter resistance from sponsors—who see their control of both agents and clients imperiled—but from occupational rivals who seek to do competitive things for the given clientele. The form such rivalry takes seems to be related closely to the social setting of the encounter. For example, in areas like school social work, which—following the pattern of many service occupations in quest of a secure work role—moved from philanthropic sponsorship into the public schools, one can see the story of an occupation straining for a clientele. In this case, the social workers (whose ideal was drawn from the social casework of the twenties) responded to their hostile or indifferent reception by attempting to "educate" the public school teachers to interpret student behavior in casework terms; that is, by styling themselves teachers, the social workers attempted both to secure greater control over the clients they desired—as the subjects of their clinical work—and to define the entire setting in educational terms of their professional choosing.[15]

This picture of occupational patterning suggests a number of parallels to our discussion of the rivalry of social groups in general, and raises a number of questions about the routes taken by teaching groups, especially in relation to their problems of control and legitimacy. Do such occupational groups seek to coopt social jurisdictions by adopting the educational rhetoric of their rivals? Do they always do so, or do factors such as the relative status of the different occupational groups influence the choice? Do such occupational groups choose or modify their educational rhetoric and educational activities when they have other means of claiming and controlling disputed clients? Is there some special virtue to education as a means of securing them?

To answer this, however, we must look at the characteristics of the given clientele itself, including such elements as whether or not being a client is voluntary, how many clients there are relative to the agent group, the kinds of mobility the agents expect or seek for their clients, and the relative status of the agent and client group.

Occupational groups with formally voluntary but unwilling clients seem likely to make part of their function educational as part of formalizing their efforts to persuade clients and shape their behavior. The matter of numbers also is crucial in institutions which deal with the poor and are poorly staffed themselves, where agents often stress teaching clients or inmates how to support or care for themselves. This pattern, too, is related closely to mobility expectations. Clients who never leave such an institution may have to be taught how to maintain themselves in it—a common concern of occupations that deal with the handicapped, chronically ill, or mentally retarded—while in situations in which agents expect their clients to be mobile, upwardly or downwardly, they tend to stress the teaching of general skills or principles which will be of use in any contingency—whether those met by a rising young engineer or a suddenly impoverished housewife. (See, for example, Board of Visitors, State of New York, 1948; Woodward, 1885–86; Bruere and Bruere, 1912.)

Also, the relative status of the occupational group and its clients is of great importance in the definition of educational work, but in subtler ways than usually assumed. It often is noted that ambitious occupational groups, as do career-minded individuals, try to avoid stigmatized clients; but it also is the case that emerging rivals build their own occupational identities by making these neglected clients their own. Thus, not only are the apparently unteachable problem children of the public schools claimed as students by the reform schools, but the incorrigibles of the reform schools become the students of the progressive prisons; likewise, the street waifs and the elderly whom the public schools ignore are courted as students by the settlement houses, while the unorganized workers whom the established unions ignore are sought as students by new labor movements.[16]

Finally, a close look at the ways in which such service groups seek to define their status vis-à-vis their clients reminds us that this effort to carve out a teaching role must be analyzed in terms of the particular ways in which given occupational groups are seeking to construct the social world, rather than as a function of some *a priori* drive for professionalization. The early settlement house movement suggests one variation on the meaning of relative status in its insistence that neighborhood people could teach the settlement workers as well as vice versa: the latter would contribute an education in leadership skills, the former an education in "life." Significantly, the settlement house pioneers eschewed a drive toward professionalization, seeing it as creating the very social distance which kept institutions like the public schools or relief agencies from really either teaching or learning. Whereas, the history of organized labor suggests what can happen to a group of educators operating on a similar theory when the movement of which they are themselves a part itself becomes professionalized: the educators, then reduced to human relations experts to keep the organization running, remain frustrated in what they take to be their real role and may long to convert the whole movement into a crusade which makes education its call to arms.[17]

Students

From the standpoint of students, both the educational strategies for survival which social groups employ and the educational commitments of occupational groups as they seek a place in the world of work stand merely as options, aids, or impediments in carving out individual careers. These careers, however, are enmeshed in the social worlds to which the student belongs or through which he is moving at given points in his life. Educational opportunities or blocks may or may not be an important part of relevant social worlds; and non-educational strategies or opportunities for informal education may be as important to the would-be student as anything sponsors or teachers might produce. Although we can only suggest the range of non-educational options here, it is crucial to keep their existence in mind.

The careers of students may be analyzed in relation to their own social mobility and in terms of the various ways they encounter teachers and sponsors. Such social mobility can be viewed as a property of groups having varying degrees of awareness and cohesion in their student roles, and of individuals whose relation to and type of membership in such groups will vary. There are still many questions to be asked about the relation to education of client groups. For despite the considerable amount of discussion about the ways in which social groups (primarily ethnic clienteles) value education, we still seem to know very little about the conditions under which groups *qua* groups develop and sustain educational interpretations. The experience of black Americans after the Civil War is often cited as a classic example of mass commitment to upward mobility through education, but this phenomenon still begs for a fuller explanation. Much less do we know about the ways in which education relates to other kinds of shared mobility; how, say, the downward mobility of housewives during a depression might generate conscious demand for domestic education.

But, given the interest of groups in gaining some kind of education, the question then becomes, To whom do students turn?—to each other or to some outside group. Students may turn to each other either as the natural outgrowth of other kinds of relationships or in default of accessible or credible teachers from outside the group. For example, penologists and others have long been aware of how mutual education in criminal techniques and outlooks is perpetuated in prisons—the efforts of penal reformers and educators notwithstanding. But such efforts not only reflect collective attempts to cope with and use such institutional situations in an immediate sense, but also may represent part of an effort for group mobility which goes beyond the given educational world. Hence, the efforts of the students who first founded black fraternities not only involved facilitating mutual education (in order to get through the white universities), but also implied the building of career routes by which upwardly mobile men like themselves could move into and shape black social and economic life. (See Yablonsky, 1965; Wesley, 1935; Drake and Cayton, 1962: vol. 2.)

How and why groups turn to outsiders is a puzzling matter even now: Why do some kinds of teaching groups rather than others seem credible sources of a desired education? How much do the promises which teaching groups make or the persuasive efforts in which they or sponsors engage affect such credibility? Are there members of given social groups who serve as intermediaries—by being a kind of avant garde that ventures into the outside world, discovers seemingly appropriate teachers, and then brings or sends educational interpretations back to their group of origin?

The situation of individual students who have left or taken flight from some group underlines this problem of seeking education outside a known social setting. Few mobile individuals can play the role of a Henry Adams, struggling to wrest their own definitions of education from the world itself, though some, because they are unable to find a willing teacher may end up, as machinists put it in the days of declining apprenticeship, "stealing a trade," that is, wresting an education from unwilling teachers. But, the ways in which most would-be students discover and come to define education is strongly patterned by the available and willing teachers they encounter.

However, simply discovering a teacher may not be sufficient. As we have seen, such teachers often operate in a world of educational rivalry, so that mobile students may be forced to choose which educational claim they credit—not merely as a way of learning given skills, but as part of the entire view of the world implied in the educational definition. This is frequently the case in the realm of occupational training, in which segmentation of occupational groups into competing schools or camps pushes the student to choose not only a temporary strategy for educational survival—how to get through a doctoral oral in sociology, how to get through a university nursing practicum conducted in a hospital—but the entire career route and even life-style which the given educational commitment may entail. (See Pupin, 1960; Glass, 1971.)

Though such students sometimes feel isolated in their decisions (even when they have company in making them), the more truly isolated student is the one whose mobility route and group membership is basically at odds with the educational setting in which he finds himself, or whose participation in that educational setting constitutes a threat to such group membership. Youths out of the socialist movement whose families still want them to have a college education, Catholic sisters who must go to a secular school to obtain their advanced degrees, black students who feel that their movement is in the ghetto but their ability to contribute to it in the universities, are all torn, all open to forms of educational seduction which have implications not only for individual mobility but for the various social enclaves and movements themselves. (See Peterson, 1941: vol. 2, 144.)

Finally, it is clear that such instances cannot be understood fully without also looking at the particular relationship of students to teachers and sponsors, especially with regard to whether being a student is voluntary and the relative status of students—where they are and in what directions they are going vis-à-vis teachers and sponsors.

Educational critics have long been interested in the problem of involuntary student status and the kinds of personal price and institutional subversion which follow from it. In consequence, there are numerous discussions of student strategies of avoidance—as well as student strategies of "learning the ropes"—the ways students get through educational institutions for whose lessons they have less than intense enthusiasm. Often, as one might suspect from our discussion of occupational rivalry, attention to such patterns, as well as the patterns themselves, are enmeshed in the efforts of some rival group to make the given students part of their own, the rival's, clientele instead. (See Covello, 1967; Qoyawayma, 1964; Rischin, 1970: 238–239; Becker et al., 1968.)

Perhaps partly because such situations pose less problems of social control or imply less noticeable rivalry, much less attention has been paid to situations in which students are voluntary and/or become engaged in education because they find through it something they really want. Under what conditions does this happen? Does it tend to happen more easily—as the history of some social movements might suggest—when mobility through the student to the teaching or sponsoring role is not only possible, but often desirable because of its being intertwined with mobility within the movement itself? (See Levens, 1971.) What of situations in which students move from the student role into worlds unlike those of their teachers or sponsors? Can we automatically assume that a difference between such worlds produces educational estrangement, or that when teachers and sponsors have careers similar to those of their students there is likely to be a better educational "fit"?

Educational Conflict and Its Consequences

In social theoretical terms most formal inquiry in the sociology of education stresses the classic problems of freedom and order—primarily the problems of institutional and interactional order—posed by the intersection of students and teaching groups, and the problems of personal and professional freedom generated by constraints on action and mobility in various institutional contexts. In contrast, the framework offered here emphasizes a third classic problem: how social groups strive through collective action for a redistribution of resources, prestige, and power. Thus, the type of analysis presented in this paper has focused on the histories of social groups and the conflicts in which they become involved because of their intersection.

One of the major consequences of the social patterning that I have sketched and, I believe, the major consequence for the development of formal education in relation to American social structure is the problematic character of formal socialization. That is, both change within the groups themselves and the regular presence of actual or potential social rivalry render problematic the character of socialization for a wide variety of emerging social groups.

By virtue of the well-known fact that in creating new social conditions each generation makes questionable the patterns of socialization which were utilized in its own education, group history alone is likely to render socialization patterns problematic. Self-made fathers—to recur to one of our examples—create (or help to create) the problem of how to educate their sons. But this kind of situation is given further shape by both the rivalry of parallel social groups and the interaction of sponsors, teachers, and students. That is, the fathers' notions of education are shaped partly by the conditions of competition between themselves and other groups—among these conditions the claims and goals they are forwarding regarding the social structure. Moreover, the teaching groups which the sponsoring generation creates or supports are likely to develop ideas in relation to their *own* potential or actual professional rivals—the other kinds of institutions which may be developing, or even the detractors who say that such education is not worth it all. For understandable reasons, the potential clients themselves often are among these detractors, for their interests and ambitions—in this example, the sons themselves—may well differ from those of any of the other parties.

Clearly the fact of group change, the difference of interests between different parties in a given educational encounter, and the rivalry or threat of rivalry between social groups with similar aims, all give birth to a set of mutual constraints on the educational ambitions of any given group. On the other hand, however, it is by no means clear how such constraints operate in relation to the interest of any given group—including the interests of students for whose sake most education in this social context is supposed, or at least claimed, to be undertaken. Sometimes the presence of rivals may result in patterns of accommodation or negotiation, in which the fate of both students and teachers is adjusted to the mutual interests of the sponsors involved. Sometimes—as is often the case in the realm of rivalry between occupational groups—competition will lead less toward the interests of the students involved than to occupational postures by which teachers can defend their territories.

Therefore, one of our major research problems must be to specify the conditions under which various kinds of educational interests are constrained and the results for the respective interests involved. When are given kinds of students able to carve out the kinds of careers they seek? When are given kinds of social movements able to develop effective educational prescriptions? How does this affect members of the movement? How and when are sponsors able to use education as an instrument of social control? When can given kinds of teaching groups forward what kinds of educational solutions?

Part of the burden of my argument in this paper is to challenge certain types of *a priori* answers to such questions as these. In addition, my discussion tries to suggest some of the ways in which converting answers into questions should result in payoffs for both substantive and theoretical inquiry concerning the nature of careers, of professionalization, and of the social structure itself. Sociologists of education cannot answer such questions by themselves, because questions about education are only one way of asking about the nature of society as a whole. It is, nevertheless, one fruitful and perhaps crucial way which may make a special contribution to social criticism and have something special to add to our understanding of the social conditions and the social ideals on which action is based.

NOTES

1. Although the topics of interest have varied, much of the basic pattern for this field was set in its early years. (See Richards, 1969.)
2. It should be clear from this discussion that I am not treating social theories of education *qua* theory, but rather, in Mannheim's and C. Wright Mills' sense, in terms of the sociology of knowledge. Richards (1969) discusses how interests in the sociology of education have been shaped by occupational concerns.
3. The stronger the socialist cast, the more figures like George Counts fall somewhere between this latter and the pragmatist group. Unfortunately, there has been little macroscopic work on education in this tradition since Counts' work of the twenties and thirties. (See Counts, 1928: Adams, 1910.)
4. Many studies combine the two kinds of questions, and the particular interpretation also varies with the structure of the community studied; for instance, in the well-known work of Seeley, Simm, and Loosley (1956) the price of progress for members of a well-to-do community has been mental

health, and education is viewed in its actual and desired relationship to that problem.

5. From Horace Mann on, notions of which kind of education is functional or dysfunctional from the standpoint of this kind of thought are geared to the particular image of cohesion and consensus held by the writer. (See Mann, 1851; Clark, 1960; Dreeben, 1968; Brim, 1968.)

6. How and why socialist thinking about education has become truncated in this way is intertwined with the fragmenting of American socialism, the history of the unions, and the relation of both to academia. Also on the fringes of academic respectability, those anarchist and adult educators who question the goal of individual mobility and the public school ideal seem to have done more to keep these questions alive. (Compare, for example, Walling, 1913; Hill, 1935; Goodman, 1951; Radical Teachers Group, 1970.) In addition to the relationship of socialism to academia, the lack of interest in social theory in general, plus the fact that studies in the sociology and history of education have by-and-large become rooted in schools of education and have *adopted many of their assumptions*—even their reformist assumptions—have reinforced this emphasis on the public schools. (See Richards, 1969.)

7. There is no attempt here to suggest that such groups comprise the only relevant factors, but that other elements (such as developments in technology) also are shaped in their application by the kinds of groups involved. (See Fisher, 1969; Friedman, 1970.)

8. The pattern I am suggesting here is certainly complex; it demands analysis in terms of a series of bargains, shaped in relation to regional and social structure and to the nature of agents available. (See Veysey, 1965; Baltzell, 1964; Link, 1947.)

9. The comparative success of educators in launching programs suggests something about the ways in which social or occupational skills were valued by potential clients. See, for example, the difficulties encountered by Harvard in its attempt to develop an elite business education (Copeland, 1958) and the kinds of mobility ideals of industrial educators (Fisher, 1967a). A more general discussion of mobility patterns, to which I am much indebted in discussing both individual and group mobility, is presented by Strauss (1971).

10. Adopting Howard S. Becker's term, Friedman has styled those looking around to make jobs for themselves in education educational entrepreneurs (Friedman, 1970). One of the interesting questions to be raised about such careers is not only how such men seek to make a place for themselves, but from where they have come—such as the higher education and foundation intermediaries who so often seem to come from religious institutions, bringing their predisposition for certain kinds of education with them. (See, for example, Storr, 1966.)

11. The later nineteenth century business pattern should be compared to notions of the factory as an educational institution current among the early corporation owners (Fisher, 1967a); while the response of mainstream labor to educational questions should be compared to the prescriptions of men as diverse as Powderly or Foster, who looked to education to overcome differ-

ences between workingmen (Curoe, 1926; Welter, 1962; Foster, 1947). The interweaving of these responses can be traced through industrial unionism and the various fragments of the labor movement.

12. For some of the many relevant discussions see Plunkitt (1905); Meier (1963); Cruse (1967); Seale (1970); Levens (1971); Spaulding (1895); and Cross (1958).

13. The distinction between doing to and doing for is stressed by Hughes (1958), while this kind of structural and ideological analysis of the professionalization process is pursued by Bucher and Strauss (1961), Schatzman and Strauss (1966), and Fisher (1969).

14. Some of the connection of teaching groups to sponsorship clearly stems from the roots of so many of the former in some kind of philanthropic enterprise; but I think the main issue runs deeper, raising questions about the relation of various occupations to the social structure. The early effort to upgrade teaching status in the U.S. is traced in Mattingly (1968), while the struggle to redefine the teacher's role can be seen in Counts (1928) and the various histories of the teacher's movement. Professors of education obviously played key roles as intermediaries in this process.

15. On school social work ideology see Fisher (1967b) and Richards (1969). This attempt to redefine the problems of a social setting in the educational terms of an aspiring occupational group can also be seen in such diverse areas as penal work (McKelvey, 1936; Barnes and Teeter, 1945) and community adult education (McNeil, 1970).

16. The definition of an educable clientele as part of the struggle to establish and define a division of labor between various institutions can be seen, for instance, in the worried warning in the 1900s of a state school for boys to its students that if they continued to run away the institution would begin to be labeled a reformatory instead of a school (Whittier, 1913). Also see the strong educational interest of the current Chicano movement as an example of this pattern of defining new educational clients (Steiner, 1970).

17. The settlement movement, of course, also made various accommodations to professionalization. (See Addams, 1910; Wald, 1912; Hawkins, 1937; Goldman, 1962; Wilensky, 1956.)

REFERENCES

Addams, Jane
    1910   *Twenty Years at Hull House.* New York: New American Library (1960).
Baltzell, E. Digby
    1964   *The Protestant Establishment: Aristocracy and Caste in America.*
            New York: Random House.
Baran, Paul A., and Paul M. Sweezy
    1966   *Monopoly Capital: An Essay on the American Economic and Social
            Order.* New York: Modern Reader.
Barnes, Harry Elmer, and Negley K. Teeters.
    1945   *New Horizons in Criminology: The American Crime Problem.* New
            York: Prentice-Hall. (Rev. ed.)

Becker, Howard S., Blanche Geer, and Everett Hughes.
  1968   *Making the Grade.* New York: John Wiley.
Bragdon, Henry Wilkinson
  1967   *Woodrow Wilson: The Academic Years.* Cambridge: Belknap
          (Harvard University).
Brim, Orville G., Jr.
  1968   "Adult Socialization." Pp. 182–226 in John A. Clausen (ed.), *Social-
          ization and Society.* Boston: Little, Brown.
Bruere, Martha Benseley and Robert W. Bruere
  1912   *Increasing Home Efficiency.* New York: Macmillan.
Bucher, Rue, and Anselm Strauss.
  1961   "Professions in Process." *American Journal of Sociology* 66 (Janu-
          ary): 225–234.
Clark, Burton R.
  1960   "The 'Cooling-out' Function in Higher Education." *American
          Journal of Sociology* 65 (May): 569–576.
Copeland, Melvin T.
  1958   *And Mark an Era: The Story of the Harvard Business School.* Bos-
          ton: Little, Brown.
Count, George S.
  1927   *The Social Composition of Boards of Education.* Chicago: Univer-
          sity of Chicago Press.
  1928   *School and Society in Chicago.* New York: Harcourt, Brace.
  1932   *Dare the Schools Build a New Social Order?* New York: John Day.
Corvello, Leonard
  1967   *The Social Background of the Italo-American School Child.* Leiden:
          E.J. Brill.
Cross, Robert D.
  1958   *The Emergence of Liberal Catholicism in America.* Cambridge:
          Harvard University.
Cruse, Harold
  1967   *The Crises of the Negro Intellectual.* New York: William Morrow.
Curoe, Philip R. V.
  1926   *Educational Attitudes and Policies of Organized Labor in the United
          States.* New York: Teachers College Press, Columbia University.
Drake, St. Clair, and Horace R. Cayton
  1926   *Black Metropolis: A Study of Negro Life in a Northern City.* New
          York: Harper Torchbooks. (Rev. ed.)
Dreeben, Robert
  1968   *On What Is Learned in School.* Reading, Mass.: Addison-Wesley.
Fisher, Berenice M.
  1967a   *Industrial Education.* Madison: University of Wisconsin.
  1967b   "Education and Philanthropy." *Teachers College Record* 68 (May):
          622–630.
  1969   "Claims and Credibility: A Discussion of Occupational Identity and
          the Agent-Client Relationship. *Social Problems* 16 (Spring): 423–433.

Foster, William Z.
  1947   *American Trade Unionism: Principles and Organization, Strategy and Tactics.* New York: International Publishers.
Friedman, Robert A.
  1970   "The Role of Technology and Occupation in Institutional Change: A Historical Case Study of American Public Education." (Unpublished manuscript.)
Gans, Herbert J.
  1962   *The Urban Villagers: Group and Class in the Life of Italian-Americans.* New York: The Free Press.
Glass, Helen P.
  1971   "Teaching Behavior in the Nursing Laboratory in Selected Baccalaureate Nursing Programs in Canada." Doctoral dissertation. New York: Teachers College Press.
Goldman, Freda H. (ed.)
  1955   *Universities and Unions in Workers' Education.* New York: Harper Bros.
Goodman, Paul
  1951   "From Inside an Anarchist School: An American View." (Excerpts from Parents Day.) Pp. 457–472 in Leonard I. Krimerman and Lewis Perry (eds.), *Patterns of Anarchy.* Garden City, New York: Anchor (Doubleday).
Harbison, Frederick, and Charles Myers
  1964   *Education, Manpower, and Economic Growth: Strategies of Human Resources Development.* New York: McGraw-Hill.
Hartmann, Edward George
  1948   *The Movement to Americanize the Immigrant.* New York: Columbia University.
Hawkins, Gaynell W.
  1937   *Educational Experiments in Social Settlements.* New York: American Association for Adult Education.
Hill, Frank Ernest
  1935   *School in the Camps: The Educational Program of the Civilian Conservation Corps.* New York: American Association for Adult Education.
Hollingshead, A. B.
  1949   *Elmtown's Youth: The Impact of Social Classes on Adolescents.* New York: John Wiley.
Hughes, Everett G.
  1958   *Men and Their Work.* New York: The Free Press.
Levens, Helene
  1971   "Bread and Justice: Participant Observer Study of Welfare Poor." Ph.D. dissertation. University of Wisconsin.
Link, Arthur S
  1947   *Wilson: The Road to the White House.* Princeton: Princeton University Press.

Luce, Don, and John Sommer
  1969   *Viet Nam: The Unheard Voices.* Ithaca: Cornell University Press.
Lynd, Robert S., and Helen Merrell Lynd
  1929   *Middletown: A Study in Contemporary American Culture.* New
           York: Harcourt, Brace.
McNeil, S. Teresa
  1970   "The Involvement of Nonmembers in Action Programs of Voluntary
           Groups: An Exploratory Study with Implications for Adult Educa-
           tion." Ph.D. dissertation. University of Wisconsin.
Mann, Horace
  1851   *Slavery: Letters and Speeches.* Boston: B. B. Mussey.
Mattingly, Paul H.
  1968   "Professional Strategies and New England Education, 1825–1860."
           Ph.D. dissertation. University of Wisconsin.
McKelvey, Blake
  1936   *American Prisons: A Study of American Social History Prior to 1915.*
           Chicago: University of Chicago Press.
Mead, George H.
  1908   "Educational Aspects of Trade Schools." Pp. 44–49 in James W.
           Petras (ed.), *George Herbert Mead: Essays on His Social Philosophy.*
           New York: Teachers College Press, Columbia University (1968).
Meier, August
  1963   *Negro Thought in America, 1880–1915: Racial Ideologies in the Age
           of Booker T. Washington.* Ann Arbor: University of Michigan.
Mills, C. Wright
  1956   *The Power Elite.* London: Oxford University Press.
New York Board of Visitors
  1948   *Life at Letchworth Village.* Fourteenth Annual Report, Department
           of Mental Health, State of New York.
Park, Robert Ezra
  1950   *Race and Culture.* Glencoe: Illinois Free Press.
Parsons, Talcott
  1959   "The School Class as a Social System: Some of Its Functions in
           American Society." *Harvard Educational Review* 29 (Fall): 297–318.
Peterson, Arnold
  1941   *Daniel DeLeon: Social Architect.* New York: New York Labor News.
Plunkitt, George Washington
  1905   "How to Get a Political Following." Pp. 154–158 in Edward C. Ban-
           field (ed.), *Urban Government: A Reader in Politics and Administra-
           tion.* New York: Free Press of Glencoe (1961).
Pupin, Michael
  1923   *From Immigrant to Inventor.* New York: Charles Scribner's Sons
           (1960).
Qoyawayma, Poligaysi
  1964   *No Turning Back: A True Account of a Hopi Girl's Struggle . . . As
           Told to Vada F. Carlson.* Albuquerque: University of New Mexico.

Radical Teachers Group
1970   *The Red Pencil,* 2 (December). Boston: The Radical Teachers Group.
Raskin, Marcus G.
1965   "A Citizen's White Paper on American Policy in Viet-Nam and
        Southeast Asia." Pp. 129–136 in Marcus G. Raskin and Bernard B.
        Fall, *The Viet-Nam Reader.* New York: Vintage (Random House).
Richards, Rosanda Rae
1969   "Perspectives on Sociological Inquiry in Education, 1917–1940."
        Ph.D. dissertation. University of Wisconsin.
Rischin, Moses
1962   *The Promised City: New York's Jews, 1870–1914.* New York: Har-
        per Torchbooks (1970).
Ross, Edward Alsworth
1922   *The Social Trend.* New York: Century Press.
Rostow, W. W.
1961   "Guerrilla Warfare in Underdeveloped Areas." Pp. 108–116 in Mar-
        cus G. Raskin and Bernard B. Fall, *The Viet-Nam Reader.* New
        York: Vintage (Random House) (1965).
Schatzman, Leonard, and Anselm Strauss
1966   "A Sociology for Psychiatry." *Social Problems* 14 (Summer): 3–16.
Seale, Bobby
1970   *Seize the Time.* New York: Vintage (Random House).
Seeley, John R., R. Alexander Sim, and Elizabeth W. Loosley
1965   *Crestwood Heights: A Study of the Culture of Suburban Life.* New
        York: John Wiley.
Shils, Edward A.
1965   "Toward a Modern Intellectual Community." Pp. 498–518 in James
        A. Coleman (ed.), *Education and Political Development.* Princeton:
        Princeton University Press.
Solomon, Barbara Miller
1956   *Ancestors and Immigrants: A Changing New England Tradition.*
        New York: John Wiley.
Spaulding, J. L.
1895   *The Means and Ends of Education.* Chicago: A. C. McClurg.
Stein, Maurice R.
1960   *The Eclipse of Community: An Interpretation of American Studies.*
        Princeton University Press.
Steiner, Stan
1968   *La Raza.* New York: Harper and Row.
Storr, Richard J.
1966   *Harper's University: The Beginnings.* Chicago: University of Chicago
        Press.
Strauss, Anselm L.
1971   *The Contexts of Social Mobility: Ideology and Theory.* Chicago:
        Aldine.
Veblen, Thorstein
1918   *The Higher Learning.* New York: Hill and Wang (1957).

Veysey, Laurence R.
1965   *The Emergence of the American University*. Chicago: University
       of Chicago Press.
Wald, Lillian
1912   "Qualifications and Training for Service with Children in a Crowded
       City Neighborhood." Pp. 244–256 in Sophonisba Breckinridge (ed.),
       The Child in the City. Chicago: Hollister.
Walling, William English
1913   *The Larger Aspects of Socialism*. New York: Macmillan.
Weinstein, James
1968   *The Corporate Ideal in the Liberal State, 1900–1918*. Boston: Bea-
       con Press.
Wesley, Charles H.
1935   *The History of Alpha Phi Alpha: A Development in Negro College
       Life*. Washington, D.C.: Howard University.
Whittier State School
1913   "A Somewhat Unusual Sort of Talk. . . ." P. 2 in *The Sentinel,*
       Whittier, California: Whittier State School.
Wilensky, Harold L.
1956   *Intellectuals in the Labor Unions: Organizational Pressure and Pro-
       fessional Roles*. Glencoe, Illinois: The Free Press.
Welter, Rush
1962   *Popular Education and Democratic Thought in America*. New York:
       Columbia University Press.
Woodward, Calvin M.
1885– "The Training of a Dynamic Engineer in Washington University,
1886   St. Louis." *Transactions of the American Society of Mechanical
       Engineering* 8:742–783.
Yablonsky, Lewis
1965   *The Tunnel Back: Synanon*. New York: Macmillan.
Zorbaugh, Harvey
1929   *The Gold Coast and the Slum*. Chicago: University of Chicago Press.

DO SCHOOLS
MAKE A DIFFERENCE?

Godfrey Hodgson

Since the days of Thomas Jefferson, we have believed that education is a means of achieving equality in our society. But in the last few years, social science has brought that assumption into question. The battle now rages; controversy surrounds the participants—Jencks, Moynihan, Coleman, Pettigrew, Jensen, Herrnstein, Armor; and where it all will end matters not just to the experts, but to all of us.

The day Daniel Patrick Moynihan arrived at Harvard in the spring of 1966, he met some of his new colleagues at the Faculty Club in Cambridge. One of those present that evening was Professor Seymour Martin Lipset of the Harvard government department. "Hello, Pat," said Lipset, "guess what Coleman's found?"

"Coleman" was James S. Coleman, professor of social relations at Johns Hopkins, who had been charged by the Johnson Administration with conducting an extensive survey of "the lack of availability of equal educational opportunities" by reason of race, religion, or national origin. And what the Coleman survey had found, as Lipset paraphrased its voluminous findings, could hardly have come as more of a surprise. He had found, as Lipset told Moynihan excitedly, that "schools make no difference; families make the difference."

Some six years later, Moynihan arrived a few minutes late for lunch with a friend at the same club, in a mood of jubilant intellectual pugnacity unusual even for him. Both the delay and the mood, he explained, resulted from a demonstration he had run into on his way across Harvard Yard from a class. Some students were handing out leaflets. It was their content which had produced Moynihan's mood of sardonic amusement. "Christopher Jencks," they said, "is a tool of reactionary American imperialist capitalism."

Christopher Jencks a tool of capitalism? In the dozen years since he graduated from the Harvard Graduate School of Education, where he is now an associate professor, Sandy Jencks (as he is called) had moved perceptibly from the liberal toward the radical position. While an editor of *The New Republic* he began working with the distinctly New Left Institute for Policy Studies in Washington. He got into the neighborhood community control thing, and he helped to found the Cambridge Institute, which looks for "alternative visions of the American future": decidedly one of the rising intellectual reputations on the American left. Now he has written a book, *Inequality,* in association with other researchers, working in large part from the same Coleman report data which, in Lipset's words, showed that "schools make no difference."

Pat Moynihan had started on the left, too. Trained as an orthodox social scientist, he grew up among liberals, and then discovered a most unorthodox flair for polemical prose and persuasive speech. After a political apprenticeship working for Governor Averell Harriman of New York, he took office as a liberal intellectual in good standing as an Assistant Secretary of Labor in the Kennedy Administration, and stayed on for a period under Johnson.

For some years now, however, he could hardly have been called a man of the left. His intellectual voyage can be dated from the publication of his report on the Negro family in 1965. Many liberals and blacks reacted with outrage to his dour assessment of the likelihood that orthodox liberal policies could eliminate the problems of the black under-class. He was outraged in turn by what he perceived as the liberals' dishonest and anti-intellectual refusal to follow where social science led. And by the time he returned to Washington in 1969 to serve Richard Nixon as a Cabinet-rank Counselor, he could no longer be called a man of the left at all. In recent years he has in fact established himself as the shrewdest strategist and most flamboyant impresario of an intellectual movement which can perhaps be called neo-conservative—though Moynihan maintains that it is radical. Whatever the label, it is almost contemptuously skeptical of the New Left and of conventional liberal shibboleths alike.

Moynihan's amusement at seeing his colleague Jencks leafleted in Harvard Yard was not due to malice or *Schadenfreude.* On the contrary, it seemed to him to confirm that the argument between him and his friends and the left was over: that he had won. "Jencks ends up," he told me, "where Richard Nixon was in 1969."

Christopher Jencks does not see it that way. In fact, it is a strange kind of argument: one in which the participants largely agree about the Coleman survey, greatly as it surprised them when they first grasped it, but disagree, sometimes vehemently, on what it implies. The fight calls into question certain propositions which, until the Coleman report, few social scientists and few liberals dreamed of doubting: principally, that one of the main causes of inequality in American life has been inequality in education; and that education could be used as a tool to reduce inequality in society. The crucial role which education has been assigned in the United States is under heavy challenge. Is there now to be a retreat from the traditional faith in education as a tool of social change in America?

Since the days of Horace Mann and John Dewey—indeed since the days of Thomas Jefferson, that child of the Enlightenment—education has occupied a

special place in the optimistic vision of American progressives, and of many
American conservatives, for that matter. As the historian David Potter pointed
out in *People of Plenty,* the American left, encouraged by the opportunities of
an unexhausted continent and by the experience of economic success, has always
differed sharply from the European left in that it has generally assumed that
social problems could be resolved out of incremental growth: that is, that the
life of the have-nots could be made tolerable without taking anything from the
haves. Education has always seemed one of the most acceptable ways of using
the national wealth to provide opportunity for the poor without offending the
comfortable. As a tool of reform, education had the advantage that it appealed
to the ideology of conservatives, to that ethic of self-improvement which stretches
back down the American tradition through Horatio Alger and McGuffey's
Readers to Benjamin Franklin himself. This was particularly true in the age of
the Great Migration. The public school systems of New York and other cities
with large immigrant populations really did provide a measure of equality of opportunity to the immigrant poor. By the time the New Deal coalition was
formed (and educators of one sort and another were to be a significant part of
that coalition), these assumptions were powerfully reinforced, and virtually certified with the authority of social science, by the Supreme Court's 1954 desegregation decision in *Brown* v. *The School Board of Topeka. Plessy* v. *Ferguson,* the
1896 Supreme Court decision by which statutory and customary segregation in
the South were reconciled with the Thirteenth, Fourteenth, and Fifteenth
Amendments, was not a school case. (As it happens, it concerned segregation on
a Lake Pontchartrain ferry steamer.) But when, in the late 1930s and the 1940s,
the NAACP, its lawyers, and its allies began to go to court to lay siege to segregation, they deliberately, and wisely, chose education as the field of attack. This
was not accidental; they well knew that education was so firmly associated with
equality in the public mind that it would be an easier point of attack than, say,
public accommodations or housing. Not coincidentally, they worked their way
up to the main citadel of the 1954 *Brown* decision by way of a series of law
school cases: lawyers would find it hard to deny that segregation in law school
was irrelevant to success in professional life.

In *Brown,* the NAACP's lawyers deployed social science evidence in support
of their contention that segregated education was inherently unequal, citing especially work done by psychologists Kenneth and Mamie Clark with black children and black and white dolls. The Clarks' conclusions were that segregation
inflicts psychological harm.

The historical accident of the circumstances in which school segregation came
to be overthrown by the Supreme Court contributed to the currency of what
turned out to be a shaky assumption. The great majority of American liberals,
and this included large numbers of judges, Democratic politicians, and educators,
came to suppose that there was incontrovertible evidence in the findings of social
science to prove not just that segregated education was unequal but that if you
wanted to achieve equality, education could do it for you. Or, to put the same
point in a slightly different way, the prominence given to footnote 11 in the

Brown judgment, which listed social science research showing that education could not be both separate and equal, had the effect of partially obscuring the real grounds for overthrowing segregation, which were constitutional, political, and moral.

Then a contemporary development put education right at the center of the political stage. President Johnson's "Great Society" was to be achieved without alienating the power structure and, above all, the Congress. Education was an important part of the Great Society strategy from the start, but as other approaches to reducing poverty and racial inequality, notably "community action," ran into political opposition, they fell apart, and so the proportional emphasis on educational programs in the Great Society scheme grew. In the end, the Johnson Administration, heavily committed to reducing inequality, was almost equally committed to education as one of the principal ways to do it.

Each of the events and historical developments sketched here increased the shock effect of the Coleman report—once its conclusions were understood. A handful of social scientists had indeed hinted, before Coleman, that the effect of schools on equality of opportunity might have been exaggerated. But such work had simply made no dent in the almost universal assumption to the contrary.

James Coleman himself has confessed he does not know exactly why Congress, in section 402 of the Civil Rights Act of 1964, ordered the Commissioner of Education to conduct a survey "concerning the lack of availability of equal educational opportunities for individuals by reason of race, color, religion or national origin." The most likely reason is that Congress thought it was setting out to document the obvious in order to arm the Administration with a public relations bludgeon to overcome opposition. Certainly James Coleman took it for granted that his survey would find gross differences in the quality of the schools that black and white children went to. "The study will show," he predicted in an interview more than halfway through the job, "the difference in the quality of schools that the average Negro child and the average white child are exposed to. You know yourself that the difference is going to be striking."

He was exactly wrong. Coleman was staggered—in the word of one of his associates—to find the *lack* of difference. When the results were in, from about 600,000 children and 60,000 teachers in roughly 4000 schools, when they had been collected and collated and computed, and sifted with regression analysis and all the other refinements of statistical science, they were astonishing. A writer in *Science* called them "a spear pointed at the heart of the cherished American belief that equality of educational opportunity will increase the equality of educational achievement."

What did the figures say? Christopher Jencks later picked out four major points:

(1) Most black and white Americans attended different schools.

(2) Despite popular impressions to the contrary, the physical facilities, the formal curricula, and most of the measurable characteristics of teachers in black and white schools were quite similar.

(3) Despite popular impressions to the contrary, measured differences in schools' physical facilities, formal curricula, and teacher characteristics had very little effect on either black or white students' performance on standardized tests.

(4) The one school characteristic that showed a consistent relationship to test performance was the one characteristic to which poor black children were denied access: classmates from affluent homes.

Here is how James Coleman himself summed up the 737 pages of his report (not to mention the additional 548 pages of statistical explanation):

> Children were tested at the beginning of grades 1, 3, 6, 9 and 12. Achievement of the average American Indian, Mexican American, Puerto Rican, and Negro (in this descending order)[1] was much lower than the average white or Oriental American, at all grade levels ... the differences are large to begin with, and they are even larger at higher grades. Two points, then, are clear: (1) these minority children have a serious educational deficiency at the start of school, which is obviously not a result of school, and (2) they have an even more serious deficiency at the end of school, which is obviously in part a result of school.

Coleman added that the survey showed that most of the variation in student achievement lay within the same school, and very little of it was between schools. Family background—whatever that might mean—must, he concluded, account for far more of the variation in achievement than differences between schools. Moreover, such differences as *could* be attributed to the schools seemed to result more from the social environment (Jenks's "affluent classmates," and also teachers) than from the quality of the school itself.

This was the most crucial point. For if quality were measured, as it had tended to be measured by administrators and educational reformers alike, in material terms, then the quality of the school, on Coleman's data, counted for virtually nothing.

When other things were equal, the report said, factors such as the amount of money spent per pupil, or the number of books in the library, or physical facilities such as gymnasiums or cafeterias or laboratories, or even differences in the curriculum, seemed to make no appreciable difference to the children's level of achievement. Nothing could have more flatly contradicted the assumptions on which the Administration in Washington, and urban school boards across the country, were pouring money into compensatory education programs.

As we shall see, the report exploded with immense force underground, sending seismic shocks through the academic and bureaucratic worlds of education. But on the surface the shock was not at first apparent. There were two main reasons for this. The first was that the report was, after all, long, tough, dry, and technical. It had been written in five months in order to comply with a congressional deadline, and it therefore made no attempt to point a moral or adorn a tale: it was essentially a mass of data. All of these characteristics militated against its being reported in detail by, for example, the Associated Press, the source from which most American newspapers get most of their out-of-town news.

The Office of Education, which realized all too clearly how explosive the report was, didn't exactly trumpet the news to the world. The report was released, by a hallowed bureaucratic stratagem, on the eve of July 4, 1966. Few reporters care to spend that holiday gutting 737 pages of regression analysis and standard deviations. And to head off those few who might have been tempted to make the effort if they had guessed that there was a good story at the end of it, the Office of Education put out a summary report which can only be described as misleading. "Nationally," it said, to take one example, "Negroes have fewer of some of the facilities that seem most related to academic achievement." That was true. But it was not the significant truth.

The point was that the gap was far smaller than anyone expected it to be. To take one of the summary report's own examples, it was true that Negro children had "less access" to chemistry labs than whites. But the difference was that only 94 percent of them, as compared to 98 percent of whites, went to schools with chemistry labs. That was hardly the kind of difference which could explain any large part of the gap between white and black achievements in school, let alone that larger gap, lurking in the back of every educational policy maker's mind, between the average status and income of blacks and whites in life after they leave school.

A few attempts were made to discredit the survey. But the Coleman findings were in greater danger of being ignored than of being controverted when, at the beginning of the academic year in the fall of 1966, Pat Moynihan began to apply his talents to make sure that the report should not be ignored. He and Professor Thomas Pettigrew of the Harvard School of Education organized a Seminar on the Equality of Educational Opportunity Report (SEEOR). The seminar met every week at the Harvard Faculty Club, and by the end more than eighty people had taken part.

Moynihan had taken the precaution of getting a grant for expenses from the Carnegie Corporation, some of which was laid out on refreshments stronger than coffee or cookies. "It was quite something, that seminar," says Jencks, reminiscing. "Pat always had the very best booze and the best cigars." But if Moynihan is a connoisseur of the good things in life, he also knows how to generate intellectual excitement, or to spot where it is welling up.

"When I was at the School of Education ten years ago," Jencks says, "almost nobody who was literate was interested in education. The educational sociologists and psychologists, the educational economists, they were all pretty near the bottom of the heap. Suddenly that's changed."

"That seminar taught me something about Harvard," Moynihan says. "People here are not interested in a problem when they think it's solved. There are no reputations to be made there. But when something which people think was locked up opens up, suddenly they all want to get involved." People started coming up to Moynihan in Harvard Yard and asking if they could take part:

statisticians, economists, pediatricians, Professor Abram Chayes from the Law School (and the Kennedy State Department). Education had become fashionable. Jason Epstein of Random House and Charles E. Silberman from *Fortune* magazine started coming up from New York.

Harvard had seen nothing quite like it since the arms control seminars of the late 1950s, at which the future strategic policies of the Kennedy Administration were forged and the nucleus of the elite that was to operate them in government was brought together. In the intervening decade, domestic social questions had reasserted their urgency. Education had emerged as the field where all the agonizing problems of race, poverty, and the cities seemed to intersect.

If schools, as Seymour Martin Lipset paraphrased Coleman, "make no difference," what could explain the inequalities of achievement in school and afterwards? One school of thought was ready and waiting in the wings with an answer. In the winter of 1969, the following words appeared in an article in the *Harvard Educational Review:*

> There is an increasing realization among students of the psychology of the disadvantaged that the discrepancy in their average performance cannot be completely or directly attributed to discrimination or inequalities in education. It seems not unreasonable, in view of the fact that intelligence variation has a large genetic component, to hypothesize that genetic factors may play a part in this picture.

The author was Professor Arthur Jensen, not a Harvard man, but an educational psychologist from Berkeley with a national reputation. He had jabbed his finger at the rawest, most sensitive spot in the entire system of liberal thinking about education and equality in America. For after more than a generation of widespread IQ testing, it is an experimental finding, beloved of racists and profoundly disconcerting to liberals, that while the average white IQ is 100, the average black IQ is 85. Racists have seen in this statistical finding confirmation of a theory of innate biological inferiority. Conservatives have seen in it an argument against heavy expenditures on education and against efforts to desegregate. And liberals have retorted that the lower average performance of blacks is due either to cultural bias in the tests used or to unfavorable environmental factors which require redoubled efforts on the part of social policy makers.

Jensen marched straight into the fiercest of this cross fire. He argued two propositions in particular in his article: that research findings suggest that heredity explains more of the differences in IQ between individuals than does environment, and that heredity accounts for the differences between the average IQs of groups as well as between those of individuals.

The article was scholarly in tone. In form it was largely a recital of research data. And it was tentative in its conclusion that perhaps more of the differential between blacks' and whites' average IQs was due to heredity than to environment. That did not stop it from causing a most formidable rumpus. It became a ninety days' wonder in the press and the news magazines. It was discussed at a Cabinet meeting. And Students for a Democratic Society rampaged around the Berkeley campus chanting "Fight racism! Fire Jensen!"

Two years later, a long article in *The Atlantic* by Professor Richard Herrnstein on the history and implications of IQ provoked a reaction which showed that the sensitivity of the issue had by no means subsided. Herrnstein touched only gingerly on the racial issue. "Although there are scraps of evidence for a genetic component in the black-white difference," he wrote, "the overwhelming case is for believing that American blacks have been at an environmental disadvantage . . . a neutral commentator (a rarity these days) would have to say that the case is simply not settled, given our present stage of knowledge."

Neutral commentators certainly proved rare among those who wrote in to the editor. Arthur Jensen wrote to say that Herrnstein's essay was "the most accurately informative psychological article I have ever read in the popular press"; while a professor from the University of Connecticut said: "This is not new. Hitler's propagandists used the same tactics in the thirties while his metal workers put the finishing touches on the gas ovens."

If Herrnstein—understandably enough—tiptoed cautiously around the outskirts of the black-white IQ argument, he charged boldly enough into another part of the field. The closer society came to its ideal of unimpeded upward social mobility, the closer he predicted it would come to "meritocracy," a visionary state of society described by the British sociologist Michael Young. A new upper class composed of the descendants of the most successful competitors with the highest IQs would defend its own advantage far more skillfully and successfully than did the old aristocracies. Herrnstein did not welcome this trend; he merely argued that it might be inevitable. "Our society may be sorting itself willy-nilly into inherited castes," he concluded gloomily. Or, as his Harvard colleague David K. Cohen neatly epigrammatized Herrnstein's long article in a rejoinder in *Commentary*, "His essay questioned the traditional liberal idea that stupidity results from the inheritance of poverty, contending instead that poverty results from the inheritance of stupidity."

Cohen went on to disagree with Herrnstein's prediction. "America is not a meritocracy," he wrote, "if by that we mean a society in which income, status, or power are heavily determined by IQ. . . . Being stupid is not what is responsible for being poor in America."

But that still left the original question open.

If differences in the quality of schools, as measured by money, facilities, and curricula, don't explain inequality, because the differences between the schools attended by children of different racial groups are simply not that great in those respects, then what does? Genetic differentials in IQ, perhaps, says Jensen. Nonsense, says a majority of the educational community; the explanation is more likely to be integration—or rather the lack of it.

"I'm a Southern liberal," says Tom Pettigrew. "There are only about thirty of us, and my wife says we all know each other." Pettigrew comes from Richmond, Virginia, but his father immigrated from Scotland, and there is something about him that strikes one as more typically Scots than Southern. He is a shy man with a passion for methodological precision: "I really believe that data can free us," he says. He also has a deceptive, because quiet, commitment to the liberal faith.

The Coleman report gave only three pages to the effects of desegregation, and Pettigrew didn't think that was enough. At Jim Coleman's explicit insistence, the data bank of the survey was to be made generally available for the cost of the computer tapes. Pettigrew persuaded the Civil Rights Commission to take advantage of this and to reanalyze the data to see what light it cast on the effects of desegregation. David Cohen and Pettigrew were the main authors of the resulting survey, which came out in 1967 as *Racial Isolation in the Public Schools* and gave the impression that the Coleman data supported desegregation. This was true up to a point. Coleman had concluded that desegregation did have an effect. But his report also showed that social class had a greater effect. Pettigrew is not much troubled by this, because of the close connection between race and social class in America. "Two-thirds of the whites are middle-class," he says, "and two-thirds of the blacks are working-class."

Pettigrew also draws a sharp distinction between desegregation and integration. By integration he means an atmosphere of genuine acceptance and friendly respect across racial lines, and he believes that mere desegregation won't help blacks to do better in school until this kind of atmosphere is achieved. He is impressed by the work of Professor Irwin Katz, who has found that black children do best in truly integrated situations, moderately well in all-black situations, and worst of all in "interracial situations characterized by stress and threat."

Pettigrew believes, in other words, that integration, as opposed to mere desegregation, will be needed to bring black children's achievement up to equality with whites'. And he argues that no one can say that integration hasn't worked, for the simple reason that it hasn't been tried.

"The U.S. is going through a period of self-flagellation," he said to me. "I dispute the argument that Moynihan is forever putting out. He says liberalism was tried and didn't work." This, as we shall see, misstates Moynihan's views. The difficulty is partly semantic. Moynihan believes that past policies, which can be called "liberal," have "worked" in the sense that they have produced a surprising degree of equality in terms of all the resources that go into schools, without, however, achieving equality of outcome. "I say liberalism hasn't been tried," Pettigrew goes on. "Racial integration has yet to be tried in this country." Desegregation proceeded so slowly, Pettigrew says, that the courts "got mad and started ruling for busing in 1969 and 1970." Until desegregation is achieved, he argues, we won't know whether integration works.

The Civil Rights Commission's report on racial isolation did recommend that the federal government set a national standard that no black children should go to a school that was more than 50 percent black. In practical terms, that meant busing. And, in fact, Pettigrew argues that some busing will be needed to achieve desegregation—and thus to produce the physical circumstances in which integration as he understands it can take place. He has been actively involved as a witness in several desegregation suits in which he has advocated busing.

It is, therefore, as Pettigrew himself wryly remarks, an irony that he should have suggested to one of his junior colleagues at the Harvard School of Education that he do a study on busing. The colleague's name was David Armor, and Pettigrew's idea was that it would be interesting to take a look at Project Metco, a scheme for busing children out of Roxbury, the main Boston ghetto, into nearby white suburban schools.

That was in 1969. Three years later, a paper by David Armor called "The Evidence on Busing" was published in *The Public Interest*. Armor said he had concentrated on the question of whether "induced integration"—that is, busing—"enhances black achievement, self-esteem, race relations, and opportunities for higher education." In a word, Armor maintained that it did not.

The article used data not only from Project Metco but from reports of four other Northern programs for induced integration: in White Plains, New York; Ann Arbor, Michigan; Riverside, California; and New Haven and Hartford, Connecticut. And on the basis of this data,[2] Armor maintained that "the available evidence . . . indicates that busing is *not* an effective policy instrument for raising the achievement of blacks or for increasing interracial harmony."

"None of the studies," said Armor, "were able to demonstrate conclusively that integration has had an effect on academic achievement as measured by standardized tests." Aspirations, indeed, were high among the black children in Project Metco. But they might be too high, in view of the fact that, while 80 percent of them started college, half of them dropped out. As for race relations, Armor found the bused students not only more militant but actually more hostile to integration than the study's "control group," which was not bused. Militancy, as measured, for example, by sympathy with the Black Panthers, seemed to be particularly rife among those children who had high aspirations (such as going to college) but were getting C grades or below in competitive suburban high schools.

But Armor did not limit himself to reporting the results of his own Metco study and the other four studies. His article was a sweeping, slashing attack on the whole tradition of liberal social science. He described what he called the "integration policy model," based on social science research going back to the time of John Dollard and Gunnar Myrdal. Though the "real goals of social science and public policy are not in opposition," Armor said, he claimed that almost all of the "major premises of the integration policy model are not supported by the data"—by which he meant the studies he quoted.

It was a frontal assault on the liberal tradition in the social sciences for a generation: on "forty years of studies," as one of his opponents put it. At one point Armor came close to accusing his opponents of deliberate dishonesty: "There is the danger that important research may be stopped when the desired results are not forthcoming. The current controversy over the busing of schoolchildren affords a prime example."

It was not likely that such an attack would go unanswered, and, in fact, the response was both swift and severe. Pettigrew and three colleagues fired back a critique which called Armor's article "a distorted and incomplete review." To back up their charge, they argued that the studies Armor had cited as "*the* evidence on busing" were highly selective. Armor had not discussed seven other studies which they said met his own methodological criteria—from New York, Buffalo, Rochester, Newark, Philadelphia, Sacramento, and North Carolina— surveys which had reported positive achievement results for bused blacks. The integrationists also found what they claimed were disastrous weaknesses in Armor's own Metco study. For one thing, they said, he compared the bused children with a control group which included children who were also attending desegregated schools, though not under Project Metco. "Incredible as it sounds," Pettigrew and his colleagues commented, "Dr. Armor compared children who were bused to desegregated schools with other children many of whom were also bused to desegregated schools. Not surprisingly he found few differences between them."

"We respect Dr. Armor's right to publish his views against mandatory busing," they said. "But we challenge his claim that those views are based on scientific evidence." (Armor is replying to the critique in *The Public Interest,* the journal which published his paper.)

If the tone of the public controversy sounds rough, it was positively courtly compared to the atmosphere inside William James Hall, the new Harvard high-rise where Pettigrew and Armor had their offices, two doors apart.

Armor, too, started out on the left. He was president of the student body at Berkeley in 1959–1960, and head of SLATE, a forerunner of the radical Free Speech Movement there. He was also a protégé of Pettigrew's at Harvard, and indeed a close friend. But by the spring of 1972, Pettigrew realized that Armor had become vehemently opposed to mandatory busing.

Both men became very bitter. Armor failed to get tenure at Harvard, and has now moved to a visiting professorship at UCLA. Armor accused one of Pettigrew's assistants of breaking into his office to steal his Metco data. Pettigrew wrote to the New York *Times*: "There is no evidence beyond the allegation itself for the charge, much less any link between the paper's critics and the alleged intrusion." Armor accused Pettigrew of suppressing his paper; Pettigrew does concede that he told Armor that he had done "incomparable harm" by publishing it.

Tempers, in short, were comprehensively lost over the Armor affair. Much of the bitterness, no doubt, must be put down to personal factors. But it would be wrong to dismiss the episode as a mere squabble between professors. For it shows just how traumatically a world where consensus reigned half a dozen years ago has been affected by the pressure to abandon certain cherished premises. And the issue, after all, is the interrelationship of education, race, and equality in America, which is not exactly a recondite academic quibble.

To an unbiased eye ("a rarity these days," as Richard Herrnstein might say), Armor's paper has been rather seriously impugned. It does not follow that his central thesis is entirely discredited. Even Pettigrew was quoted, at the height of the row, as saying that "nobody is claiming that integration has been a raving success." "That's not what they were saying before," says Moynihan. And Christopher Jencks, who can hardly be accused of conservative prejudice, has summed up the evidence in the most cautious and equivocal way. Blacks, he says, might do much better in "truly integrated schools, whatever they may be." Failing that consummation, devoutly to be wished, the benefits of desegregation appear to be spotty, and busing can be expected to yield contradictory results.

Jencks's position is easily misunderstood. In an interview, he drew some distinctions for me. He reminded me that he had himself written that the Coleman report "put the weight of social science behind integration." It was not until Armor's article was published, he said, that social scientists began to argue that desegregation itself might not work. Jencks personally feels that Armor's data were shaky, and that the effect of Armor's paper came from its review of other studies—a review which, as Pettigrew pointed out, does not refer to all the available studies. Jencks himself thinks that desegregation is probably necessary, simply in order to meet the constitutional requirements of the Fourteenth Amendment, in virtually every urban school district in the country. He does, however, have personal reservations about mandatory busing, on libertarian grounds. The furthest he would go was to say, "I think that a case can be made out that busing might be a useful part of an overall strategy of desegregation." That is not to say that he has any tenderness toward segregation. On the contrary, he rejects it as absolutely as any of the "integrationists." The difference is that Jencks does not think that segregation explains nearly as much of existing inequality as the integrationists think it does.

But with Armor's paper and its reception, we are getting ahead of the story. The Coleman report came out in 1966. It was not until 1972 that two major books appeared, each an attempt to reassess the whole question of the relationship between education and equality in America in the light of the Coleman data. Each was collaborative.

The first of these two books was the Random House collection of papers arising out of the SEEOR seminar, which was published as *On Equality of Educational Opportunity,* with Frederick Mosteller (professor of mathematical statistics at Harvard) and Daniel Patrick Moynihan as co-editors. Most of the leading participants in the debate contributed chapters: Pettigrew *and* Armor, Coleman, David Cohen, and Christopher Jencks among them. The introductory essay was signed jointly by Mosteller and Moynihan. If much of the technical analysis and of the drafting were Mosteller's, the essay's style and conclusions are vintage Moynihan.

Later in the year, Christopher Jencks and seven of his colleagues (two of whom, Marshall Smith and David Cohen, had also contributed to the Mosteller-Moynihan volume) published an only slightly less massive book: *Inequality: A Reassessment of the Effect of Family and Schooling in America.* This work displays considerably more intellectual cohesion than the Mosteller-Moynihan book, presumably because Jencks actually wrote his group's text himself from start to finish and, according to the preface, it "embodies his prejudices and obsessions, and these are not shared by all the authors." But again, though the book draws upon data from dozens of other large- and small-scale surveys, the data from the Coleman survey are the bedrock and foundation.

The enormous body of analysis and reinterpretation in these two books represents the completion of the first stage of the reaction to Coleman. I began by quoting Professor Lipset's hasty shorthand for Coleman's central discovery: "schools make no difference." Professor Pettigrew draws an important distinction. "Never once was it said that schools make no difference. The belief that Coleman hit was the belief that you could make a difference with money." (He added: "Americans are crazy in the head about money: they think you can do everything with money.") However that may be, the nub of the discovery that has set off the whole prolonged, disturbing, confusing, sometimes bitter debate can be expressed as a simple syllogism:

(1) The "quality" of the schools attended by black and white children in America was more nearly equal than anyone supposed. (2) The gap between the achievement of black and white children got wider, not narrower, over twelve years at school. (3) Therefore there was no reason to suppose that increasing the flow of resources into the schools would affect the outcome in terms of achievement, let alone eliminate inequality.

Among the social scientists, the central ground of debate about the meaning of those findings now lies between Jencks and Moynihan. It is a strange debate, for the two protagonists have much in common, even if one does have New Left loyalties, and the other served in Nixon's White House and now as Nixon's Ambassador to India. Both use the same data. Indeed, the spectacle of social scientists reaching into the same data bank for ammunition to fire at each other is sometimes reminiscent of war between two legs of the same octopus. Both agree on many of the implications of the data and on many of the conclusions to be drawn from them. Yet those who lump the two professors together, as many practical educators and civil rights lawyers do, as "Moynihan and Jencks and those people up at Harvard," could hardly be more wrong. The two men are divided by temperament and ideology in the preconceptions they bring to the data, and ultimately in the policy prescriptions they draw from that data.

Perhaps the very heart of their disagreement, after all, comes down to a matter of temperament. Is a glass half empty, or is it half full? A pessimist will say it is half empty when an optimist says it is half full. Pat Moynihan (and his co-author Mosteller—but I should be surprised if these particular thoughts were not Moynihan's contribution, since they coincide with so much that he has said and written elsewhere) looked at the Coleman data and made the very reasonable inference that if the differences in quality between the schools attended by different groups of children in the United States were so much smaller than everyone had expected to find them, then the United States had come much closer to realizing the goal of equality of educational opportunity than most people realized. He then chose to relate this to the general question of social optimism versus social pessimism. At the time of the Coleman report's publication, "a certain atmosphere of 'cultural despair' was gathering in the nation," they wrote, "and has since been more in evidence. Some would say more in order. We simply disagree with such despair."

One of the specific recommendations of the Mosteller-Moynihan essay is optimism. The electorate should maintain the pressure on government and school boards, the essay urges, "with an attitude that optimistically expects gains, but, knowing their rarity, appreciates them when they occur." Yet on examination this is a strange use of the word optimism. For optimism normally connotes an attitude toward the future. But the emotion that is being evoked here has more to do with the past: it is not optimism so much as pride. "The nation entered the middle third of the twentieth century bound to the mores of caste and class. The white race was dominant. . . . Education beyond a fairly rudimentary point was largely determined by social status. In a bare third of a century these circumstances have been extensively changed. *Changed!* Not merely a sequence of events drifting in one direction or another. To the contrary, events have been bent to the national will." True, the essay concedes, the period ended with racial tensions higher than ever before, and with dissatisfaction with the educational system approaching crisis. Nevertheless, say Moynihan and Mosteller, we should accentuate the positive. "It is simply extraordinary that so much has been done. . . . No small achievement! In truth, a splendid one. . . . It truly is not sinful to take modest satisfaction in our progress."

Swept along by the dithyrambic rhythm of these tributes to past policies, it would be easy to conclude that Moynihan thinks they should be pressed to the utmost. But he does not. When I asked him why not, he replied promptly, if cryptically: "Production functions." In an article in the fall 1972 issue of *The Public Interest,* he spells out what he means. The argument is characteristically simple, forceful, and provocative.

Proposition 1: "The most striking aspect of educational expenditure is how large it has become." It has now reached $1000 per pupil per annum, and it has been rising at 9.7 percent annually for the last ten years, while the GNP has risen 6.8 percent.

Proposition 2 (the Coleman point): Maybe not much learning takes place in a school without teachers or a roof. But "after a point school expenditure does not seem to have any notable influence on school achievement."

There are, Moynihan concedes, considerable regional, class, racial, and ethnic variations in achievement, and he would like to see them disappear. "But it is simply not clear that school expenditure is the heart of the matter."

This is where the production function, or what is more familiar to laymen as the law of diminishing returns, comes in, according to Moynihan. The liberal faith held that expenditure of resources on education would produce not merely a greater equality in scholastic achievement, but greater equality in society. On the contrary, says Moynihan, additional expenditure on education (and indeed on certain other social policies) is likely to produce greater *inequality,* at least of income.

The day the students leafleted Christopher Jencks in Harvard Yard, Moynihan said to me: "They're defending a class interest." What he meant was that as future teachers, or social workers, or administrators of education or social policies, left-wing students had a vested economic interest in the high-investment "liberal" policies they defended.

"Any increase in school expenditure," Moynihan wrote in *The Public Interest,* "will in the first instance accrue to teachers, who receive about 68 percent of the operating expenditure of elementary and secondary schools. That these are estimable and deserving persons none should doubt"—Brutus is an honorable man— "but neither should there be any illusion that they are deprived." With teachers earning some $10,000 a year on the average, he argues, and with many of them married women with well-paid husbands, "increasing educational expenditures will have the short-run effect of income inequality."

As a matter of statistical fact, that may be literally true. But it is a peculiar argument nonetheless, for several reasons. For, leaving aside the matter of their spouses' incomes, teachers are not, relatively, a highly paid group. Marginal increases in their salaries have an imperceptible effect on inequality in the national income distribution.

Whatever its merits, however, Moynihan's position is plain. But it is worth noting that this position fits oddly with an exhortation to optimism. There is indeed nothing sinful about taking satisfaction in past progress; but when this attitude is combined with skepticism about the benefits to be expected from future public expenditure, it is usually called not optimistic but conservative.

Like Moynihan, Christopher Jencks is concerned with equality, not only in the schools but also in the world after school. The essence, and the originality, of his thinking lie in the use he makes of two crucial, though in themselves unoriginal, distinctions.

The first distinction is between equality of opportunity and equality of condition. Most Americans say they are in favor of equality. But what most of them mean by this is equality of opportunity. What we have learned from the Coleman report, says Jencks, and from the fate of the reforms of the 1960s, is that contrary to the conventional wisdom, you cannot have equality of opportunity without a good deal of equality of condition—now and not in the hereafter.

This is where the second of Jencks's distinctions comes in. Where the Coleman survey, and most of the work published in the Mosteller-Moynihan volume, looked at the degree of equality between *groups,* Jencks is more interested in inequality between individuals. Coleman's conception of equality looked at the distribution of opportunity between two groups. For Coleman, as Marshall Smith puts it, if you laid the distribution curve of one group over the distribution curve of the other, and they coincided exactly, then you could say that the two groups were equal. And Coleman found that between white and black Americans, this was closer to being true than most people had suspected. "Sandy Jencks is saying that though this may apply as between groups, this approximate equality disappears when you look at individuals."

It is cause for shock, he says in the preface to his book, "that white workers earn 50 percent more than black workers." But it is a good deal more shocking "that the best-paid fifth of all white workers earns 600 percent more than the worst-paid fifth. From this point of view, racial inequality looks almost insignificant"—by comparison with economic inequality.

Is the glass half empty, or half full? If Moynihan's instinct is to emphasize the real progress that has been made toward reducing inequality in America, Jencks stresses how much inequality remains, not only in educational opportunity, in learning skills, and in educational credentials but also in job status, in job satisfaction, and in income.

The trouble is, he points out—and here I am summarizing an argument which is based, step by step, on mountains of statistical data—that whatever measure you take—income, socioeconomic status, or education—there is plenty of inequality among Americans. But the same people by no means always come out at the same point on each measure. In the social scientists' terms, these different kinds of inequality don't "correlate" very closely. It follows that school reform is not likely to effect much greater equality outside the school. The "factory model," which assumes that the school's outcome is the direct product of its inputs, must be abandoned, says Jencks. For him, a school is in reality more like a family than a factory.

This idea underlies a surprising strand in Jencks's thought. If there is no direct correlation between expenditure on schools and effects on society—for example, in producing greater equality between racial groups—some would draw the lesson that it is not worth spending more than a (possibly quite high) minimum on schools. (That is something like Moynihan's theoretical position, as we have seen.) No, says Jencks, spend more money; not because of the benefits it will bring in some sociological hereafter but simply because people spend something close to a fifth of their life in school, and it is better that they spend that time in a pleasant and comfortable environment.

"There is no evidence," Jencks writes, "that building a school playground will affect the students' chances of learning to read, getting into college, or earning $50,000 a year when they are fifty. Building a playground may, however, have a considerable effect on the students' chances of having a good time during recess when they are eight." And in a recent statement protesting the use of the conclusions which *Inequality* reaches "to justify limiting educational expenditures and abandoning efforts at desegregation," Jencks writes that "educators will have to keep struggling," and that "they need more help than they are currently getting." But he concludes that the egalitarian trend in American education over the last thirty years has not made the distribution of either income or status outside the schools much more equal. He writes: "As long as egalitarians assume that public policy cannot contribute to economic equality directly, but must proceed by ingenious manipulation of marginal institutions like the schools, progress will remain glacial."

"Marginal institutions like the schools"! The phrase sets Jencks every bit as far outside the old liberal orthodoxy as Moynihan's suggestion that spending money on schools may actually increase inequality. Fourteen words from the end of his book Jencks unfurls a word which startles many of his readers. "If we want to move beyond this tradition, we will have to establish political control over the economic institutions that shape our society. That is what other countries usually call socialism. Anything less will end in the same disappointment as the reforms of the 1960s."[3]

Norman Drachler was superintendent of the huge, tormented Detroit public school system from 1966 to 1971. When I talked to him recently, he was going through the anguish of liberal educators who had the intellectual honesty to try to reconcile the new teachings of the social scientists with the working assumptions of a lifetime of effort.

He showed me a headline from the New York *Times* of December 4, 1966, which perfectly summed up the pre-Coleman orthodoxy. WHEN SPENDING FOR EDUCATION IS LOW, it said, ARMY INTELLIGENCE TEST FAILURES ARE HIGH. And he showed me figures to prove that when federal money under Title I of the Elementary and Secondary Education Act of 1965 was concentrated on the schools with the greatest need in Detroit, reading scores improved by two months from 1965 to 1971, while the city-wide average declined by two months. "In the worst schools, Title I helped to arrest a disastrous fall," says Drachler. "Where we spent more money, we did do better."

How did he square this with the Coleman report?

"I think Coleman is basically correct. With better schools we can only make a small difference. But it is worth that investment."

The post-Coleman challenge to the case for spending money on education is beginning to echo through the halls of Congress, ominously for the supporters of federal aid to education, who include both Representative John Brademas, Democrat of Indiana, the chairman of the House Select Subcommittee on Education, and one of his Republican colleagues, Representative Albert Quie of Minnesota. In a recent speech Quie has made it plain that he remains to be convinced that compensatory education makes no difference. John Brademas is afraid that the social science findings, misunderstood or deliberately misrepresented, will be used to justify savage cuts in federal aid to elementary and secondary education and to make opposition to such programs respectable. He is deeply skeptical of the case against the efficacy of educational spending, pointing out not only that federal aid still amounts to only 7 percent of the cost of elementary and secondary schooling but also that in many cases funds intended under Title I for compensatory education for underprivileged children have been indiscriminately spent for political reasons on middle-class children, so that few valid conclusions can be drawn from the experience of Title I. He feels adrift without adequate information, while the opponents of educational spending are able to use the social scientists' evidence, often disingenuously. In his own reelection campaign in Indiana last fall he was amused, but not happy, to find his Republican opponent quoting what he called the "Colombo report" (meaning the Coleman report) at him.

Education lobbyists claim that the "Jencks report" has been freely cited by the Nixon Administration's Office of Management and Budget on Capitol Hill in justification of the cuts in the fiscal 1974 budget. And even in some of the more conservative governors' offices, one lobbyist for elementary and secondary education told me that there is a widespread feeling that "Coleman and Jencks" have the effect of giving education a low priority.

Money is one issue; integration is another. Although, as Christopher Jencks put it to me, "the impact both of Coleman and of the Moynihan–Mosteller book is to put the support of social science behind integration," and even though a majority of the social scientists who have spoken up remains integrationist, there is no mistaking the chill which the Armor paper, supported as it has been to some extent by various influential figures in the intellectual community, has sent down the spines of the integrationists. Last November, for example, Harold Howe, U.S. Commissioner for Education in the Johnson Administration (he is now with the Ford Foundation), conceded that "the lively researches of statistically oriented social scientists have cast some shadows on conventional assumptions about the benefits of integration, particularly in the schools."

The first place where those shadows would fall is in the courts, which are now jammed with cases arising from the tough desegregation orders made by federal judges in all parts of the country since 1969. Integrationists insist that the law requires school desegregation under the Fourteenth Amendment, wholly independent of social science data regarding its effect. As former Chief Justice Earl Warren put it in a recent interview with Dr. Abram Sachar of Brandeis, *Brown* was a race case, not an education case. And so far the judges have upheld the principle that the requirement of desegregation in the law is independent of evidence about its effect.

But already the courts have begun to hear social science evidence about the equality of achievement in schools. In *Keyes* (the Denver school desegregation case which the Supreme Court has already heard, but on which it has not yet handed down its opinion), Judge William Doyle, in the district court, asked for evidence about the achievement of seventeen schools which he found to be segregated, though not as a result of public policy. James Coleman himself was one of the witnesses, and he testified that while compensatory education had proved disappointing, desegregation might be helpful.

David Armor was a witness on the other side in one of the Detroit desegregation hearings. But in the Memphis case, where his paper was produced in evidence, the court of appeals gave it short shrift. Judge Anthony Celebrezze (a former Democratic Secretary of HEW) dismissed it as "a single piece of much criticized sociological research," and said "it would be presumptuous in the extreme for us to refuse to follow a Supreme Court decision on the basis of such meager evidence."

Judicial reaction generally, says Louis Lucas, a Memphis lawyer who appeared for plaintiffs in both the Detroit and Memphis cases, "has been to say 'a plague on both your houses' to the social scientists. They have noticed how much criticism of the new findings there has been, and they say in effect, 'We are not going to re-try *Brown.*'"

But that is exactly what less sanguine integrationists are afraid the Supreme Court will do, with respect to the most difficult Northern desegregation cases: not frontally, but by erosion. Norman Drachler, for example, told me he thought it very probable that the Burger Court would find some way to re-try *Brown* without seeming to do so. Nick Flannery, of the Harvard Center for Law and Education, told me that "the Burger Court will almost certainly be looking for distinctions to draw that will narrow the scope of *Brown.*"

Flannery suggested some possibilities. The Court could adopt Judge Doyle's argument (in the Denver case) that not all segregation results from public policy. Or it could adopt the Justice Department's contention that the wrong to be remedied is not segregation itself, but discrimination, so that the plaintiff can get relief only when he can show not merely generalized segregation but particular instances of discrimination. In the *Swann* case, in 1971, having to do with Charlotte, North Carolina, Chief Justice Warren Burger laid down the principle that the scope of the remedy need not exceed the scope of the violation. That might seem to lay the groundwork for limiting *Brown* in this way. Alternatively, the Court might reverse the integrationist doctrine that has been developing in the lower courts, by imposing burdens of proof on the plaintiffs which would make the process of bringing a school desegregation case even lengthier and more expensive than it is already.

Some years ago, the great historian of the South, C. Vann Woodward of Yale, compared the civil rights movement of the 1960s to the Reconstruction period after the Civil War and said that he thought this second Reconstruction was ending. There is a parallel in the intellectual world that Woodward did not draw. The 1870s—the years of "reunion and reaction," when the nation wearied of the political impasse created by white resistance to the Radicals' drive for Negro equality—were also the years when American intellectual life was swept by the ideas of Herbert Spencer and his followers, the Social Darwinists. Their enthusiasm for ruthless competition that would drive the weakest to the wall, for "anarchy with a policeman" as the type of society most likely to produce the highest evolution of man, did much to rationalize and to justify public indifference as white supremacy reasserted itself after Reconstruction. The skepticism about the efficacy of social reform which seems to be emerging from the social science of the Nixon era in itself, of course, bears no resemblance to the harsh

Social Darwinism of the age of the Robber Barons. The only parallel would lie in the danger that this new skepticism which is eroding the confident liberal assumptions could be distorted and used to rationalize a second period of indifference in a nation once again weary of the stress of reform.

What can be said, at the end of the first stage of the reception of the Coleman doctrine, is that—whether you believe with Daniel Patrick Moynihan that liberal education policies of the last few generations have succeeded so well that they have run into diminishing returns, or with Christopher Jencks that they have proved disappointing—those policies, and the intellectual assumptions on which they were built, are in bad trouble. They have lost support in the ranks of the social scientists who provided America, from Roosevelt to Johnson, with a major part of its operating ideology.

NOTES

1. Coleman oversimplified his own report slightly on this point: in the first grade blacks did better than Puerto Ricans, while in the twelfth grade Mexican Americans did better than American Indians.
2. Armor mentioned three other studies: one from Berkeley, California, one from Evanston, Illinois, and one from Rochester, New York.
3. In one sense, Moynihan is closer to Jencks than is generally supposed. When he went to work for President Nixon, both he and the President were fully aware of the Coleman conclusions. At that point, in February, 1969, two documents arrived on Moynihan's desk within seventy-two hours. The first was Arthur Jensen's article, which started from the proposition that compensatory education wasn't working. The second document, the Ohio Westinghouse report, was a gloomy appraisal of one major experiment with compensatory education, Project Headstart. Moynihan says that the conception of his Family Assistance Plan was directly influenced by the social science findings about education and equality. "The argument was put to the President," he says, "that enormous expectations had built up that you could achieve racial equality through compensatory education, and it was not working. Point two: a proposition had been put forward by Dr. Jensen which the democracy could not live with. Therefore, point three: you had to move directly to income redistribution." There is an ironic parallel here—if a distant one—to the way in which Christopher Jencks concludes his book *Inequality*.

REFLECTIONS ON THE TRANSITION FROM MASS TO UNIVERSAL HIGHER EDUCATION

Martin Trow

Autonomous and Popular Functions of American Higher Education

If we consider American higher education today with any degree of detachment, we are struck by a paradox. On the one hand, the system seems to be in serious trouble and perhaps even in crisis. Almost all major universities and many others as well have been the scene of student disturbances and even insurrections. Events at Berkeley and Columbia, at Harvard and San Francisco State, have become national news; on many other campuses militant blacks and whites and dissident faculty confront their university's authority with bold demands, threats, strikes, and sit-ins. On the other hand, if looked at from another perspective, and especially from a European perspective, American higher education is successful and thriving, and, indeed, provides the model for educational reformers in almost every European country. American research and scholarship make contributions to every field of learning and dominate many. In applied science and technology we are the envy of the world: As Servan-Schreiber has observed, the Americans have worked out "a close association between business, universities, and the government which has never been perfected nor successful in any European country." Our universities are deeply involved in the life of the society and contribute much to the efforts to solve its problems—from social medicine to the inner city. And finally, this sprawling system of some 2,500 colleges and universities enrolls over 40 percent of the age grade, over 50 percent of all high school graduates, and those proportions are steadily rising.[1] In some large states like California, where roughly 80 percent of high school graduates go on to some form of higher education, our system of mass higher education begins

Reprinted by permission of *Daedalus,* Journal of the American Academy of Arts and Sciences, Boston, Mass. Winter 1970, *The Embattled University.*

to be very nearly universal. Whatever one's assessment of those figures and their implications, they must be counted a considerable achievement.

But there must be too much irony in a celebration of the triumphs of American higher education just at present, when scarcely a day goes by without another report of a confrontation or disruption on a campus. There is perhaps more profit in considering its difficulties. I believe these, of which student unrest is only the most visible, can be better understood in light of the heightened tension between the autonomous and the popular functions of American colleges and universities, arising out of the movement from mass toward universal higher education.

American colleges and universities, almost from their beginnings, have performed these two sets of functions. The distinction is between those activities and purposes that the university defines for itself and those that it takes on in response to external needs and demands. The autonomous functions are intrinsic to the conception of the university and the academic role as these have evolved in Europe and America over the past 150 years, and are now shared with universities all over the world. The popular functions, most broadly developed in the United States, are best seen as services to other institutions of the society. The line between them is not hard and fast; ultimately, it can be argued, all university activities are in some sense responsive to societal interests. But the distinction is a useful one, perhaps most clearly to Europeans whose universities until recently have largely confined themselves to their traditional and autonomous functions and have resisted accepting tasks set for them by other parts of the society or the population at large.

At the heart of the traditional university is its commitment to the transmission of the high culture, the possession of which has been thought to make men truly civilized. This was really the only function that Cardinal Newman and more recently Robert Hutchins have thought appropriate to the university. Closely related to this, and certainly central to our conception of liberal education, is the shaping of mind and character: the cultivation of aesthetic sensibilities, broad human sympathies, and the capacity for critical and independent judgment. The second autonomous function of the American university is the creation of new knowledge through "pure" scholarship and basic scientific research. Third is the selection, formation, and certification of elite groups: the learned professions, the higher civil service, the politicians, and (though less in Britain than in the United States and on the Continent) the commercial and industrial leadership.[2] These functions involve values and standards that are institutionalized in the universities and elite private colleges, and are maintained by them autonomously and even in resistance to popular demands and sentiments.

The popular functions fall into two general categories. First, there is a commitment on the part of the American system as a whole to provide places somewhere for as many students as can be encouraged to continue their education beyond high school. For a very long time it has been believed in this country that talented youth of humble origins should go to college. But the extension of these expectations to all young men and women—that is, the transformation of a privilege into a right for all—dates no further back than World War II. In part, this notion is a reflection of the erosion of the legitimacy of class cultures and of the growing feeling in every industrial society, but most markedly in the United States, that it is right and proper for all men to claim the possession of the high culture of their own societies.[3] In school and through the mass media, ordinary people are encouraged to send their children to college to share in the high culture, for its own sake as well as for its instrumental value in gaining entrance to the old and emerging elite occupations. Higher education is assuming an increasingly important role in placing people in the occupational structure and, thus, in determining their adult class positions and life chances. Social mobility across generations now commonly takes the form of providing children with more education than their parents had, and the achievement of near-universal secondary education in America by World War II has provided the platform for the development of mass higher education since then. The tremendous growth of occupations demanding some form of higher education both reflects and further stimulates the increase in college and university enrollments. All this shows itself in yet another way, as a marked rise in the educational standard of living of the whole population. Throughout the class structure, already fully accomplished in the upper-middle but increasingly so in the lower-middle and working classes, "going to college" comes to be seen as not just appropriate for people of wealth or extraordinary talent or ambition, but as possible and desirable for youngsters of quite ordinary talent and ambition, and increasingly for people with little of either.[4] We are now seeing what was a privilege that became a right transformed into something very near to an obligation for growing numbers of young men and women.

If one popular function is the provision of mass higher education to nearly everybody who applies for it, the second is the provision of useful knowledge and service to nearly every group and institution that want it. The service orientation of American higher education is too well known to need discussion. But the demands on the universities for such service are increasing all the time. In part, they reflect the growth of the knowledge base created by the scientific explosion of the past few decades. Not only is much of this new knowledge of potential applied value to industry, agriculture, the military, the health professions, and so on, but also new areas of national life are coming to be seen as users of knowledge created in the university. We may know more about how to increase corn production than how to educate black children in our urban slums, but it is likely that the universities will shortly be as deeply involved in efforts to solve our urban and racial problems as ever they were in agriculture.

The Academic Division of Labor

How has American higher education been able to fulfill both its autonomous and its popular functions? Put differently, what have been the institutional mechanisms through which the colleges and universities have been able to contribute to the transmission and creation of knowledge, and also serve the variety of other demands the society has made on them?

The chief such mechanism has been the division of labor between and within institutions. A very large number of American colleges are essentially single-function institutions, either autonomous or popular. Swarthmore College, Haverford, and Reed are essentially preparatory colleges for graduate and professional schools. Their faculties for the most part are men who have taken a Ph.D. in distinguished universities, but who prefer a career in a teaching college rather than in a big university. In addition, there are the elite private universities which are highly selective in admissions and which subordinate service to basic research and the transmission of the high culture.

By contrast, a very large number of American colleges are essentially service institutions. The roughly two hundred teachers' colleges, the many small, weak denominational colleges, the less ambitious engineering schools, the over eight hundred junior colleges—these are serving primarily vocational ends, preparing youngsters from relatively modest backgrounds for technical, semiprofessional, and other white-collar jobs.

There is another group of institutions—most notably the big state universities—which performs the autonomous and popular functions within the same institution. On the one hand, these institutions, along with the state colleges and junior colleges, have taken the brunt of the enormous expansion in enrollments in recent decades. They are centers for community service of every kind; they train the teachers, the social workers, the probation officers, and market researchers, and the myriad other new and semiprofessionals required by this service-oriented post-industrial society. On the other hand, they are also centers of scholarship and basic research, and contribute to the advancement of knowledge in every academic subject. Moreover, they offer, in their undergraduate colleges of letters and sciences, the full range of academic subjects, some of which center on the transmission of the high culture and are concerned less with public service than with the cultivation of sensibility and independence of judgment, a sense of the past, of the uniqueness of the individual, of the varied forms of human experience and expression—in brief, all the desired outcomes of liberal education.

Within such universities, the popular and autonomous functions are insulated from one another in various ways that serve to protect the highly vulnerable autonomous functions of liberal education and basic research and scholarship from the direct impact of the larger society whose demands for vocational training, certification, service, and the like are reflected and met in the popular functions of universities. These insulations take various forms of a division of labor within the university. There is a division of labor between departments, as for example between a department of English or history and a department of education. There is a division of labor in the relatively unselective universities between the undergraduate and graduate schools, the former given over largely to mass higher education in the service of social mobility and occupational placement, entertainment, and custodial care, while the graduate departments in the same institutions are often able to maintain a climate in which scholarship and scientific research can be done to the highest standards. There is a familiar division of labor, though far from clear-cut, between graduate departments and professional schools. Among the faculty there is a division of labor, within many departments, between scientists and consultants, scholars and journalists, teachers and entertainers. More dangerously, there is a division of labor between regular faculty and a variety of fringe or marginal teachers—teaching assistants, visitors, and lecturers—who in some schools carry a disproportionate load of the mass teaching. Within the administration there is a division of labor between the dean of faculty and graduate dean, and the dean of students. And among the students there is a marked separation between the "collegiate" and "vocational" subcultures, on one hand, and academically or intellectually oriented subcultures, on the other.

Despite the strains that have developed around these divisions of function between and within American colleges and universities, they have worked surprisingly well, surprising especially to observers in European universities who have opposed the encroachment of popular functions on the universities as incompatible with their traditional commitments to increasing knowledge, transmitting the high culture, and shaping the character of the elite strata. American higher education, as a system, has been able to do those things and *also* to give a postsecondary education, often within the very same institutions, to millions of students, while serving every institution of society, every agency of government.

The enormous expansion of American higher education, both in its numbers and its range of activities, is putting great strains on these insulating mechanisms and thus is threatening the autonomous functions of the university.[5] The expansion of the university is involving it more directly in controversial issues and is therefore increasing the number and range of significant publics in the larger society that are attentive to what goes on in the university. This in turn is causing severe problems for boards of trustees and regents and for the overall governance of universities and the protection of their autonomy. These problems are reflected on campus, in the growing politicization both of the faculty and the student body (which also has other sources). The intrusion of politics onto the campus has many consequences, among them the threat to the procedures by which these institutions govern themselves. At the same time, the growth in enrollments brings to campus large numbers of students who do not accept the authority of the institution's traditional leadership to define the form and content of higher education: Some of these are disaffected middle-class whites, while increasing numbers are militant blacks. The progressive politicization of the campus threatens most the intellectual activities that require the suspension of commitment and an attitude of skepticism toward all received truth and conventional wisdoms. The central question for the American university is whether its indefinitely expanding popular functions are compatible with the survival of its autonomous functions of disinterested inquiry, whether in the classroom or through research and scholarship.

Governing Boards and Their Changing Publics

The role of trustees in American higher education is a peculiar one. They are, by law, the ultimate authority over these corporate bodies: They own the physical resources of the institution; they select its chief administrative officers; they possess the formal authority that is exercised by delegation by the administrative officers and faculty alike. And yet two parallel tendencies have been at work to reduce the actual importance of the trustees in recent decades. On the one hand, more and more power has been drained away from the trustees with the growth of major alternative sources of funds for academic programs over which the trustees have, in fact, had little or no control; and on the other, administrators and faculty have come increasingly to assert that powers that have over time been delegated to them are theirs by right. The growth of the contract grant system has enormously increased the power of the faculty in relation to administration as well as to trustees; and the tight competitive market for academic men, together with institutional ambitions for prestige in the academic league standings, have insured that trustees rarely exercise control over the funds granted to research professors. Trustees have been relatively ineffective in controlling even capital expansion, one remaining bastion of their power, when funds for new buildings come to support new research programs for which professors and administrators have jointly applied. Moreover, administrators are increasingly turning to outside funding agencies, especially to foundations, to support new academic programs, to set up experimental colleges, or to bring more minority-group students on campus. And again, trustees are really not consulted about these. External sources of funds mark a major diminution of the trustees' power to shape the character or guide the direction of "their" institution.

Second, the broad encompassing concept of "academic freedom" has meant that both administrators and faculty members come to feel that the powers they exercise over instruction, admissions, appointments, the internal allocation of resources, and even, increasingly, the physical design of the campus are all theirs by right. Some of the forces that have led to the extension and deepening of the concept of academic freedom have had to do with the enormous influence of the most distinguished American universities as models for all the others. Characteristically, it is in the most distinguished universities that the academic community has gained the widest autonomy, the broadest control over its own conditions of life and work. Many lesser institutions have come to see faculty power and institutional autonomy as a mark of institutional distinction, to be pursued as part of the strategy of institutional mobility to which so much of the energies and thought of academic men is devoted. The power of the faculties in the most distinguished universities flows precisely from their academic distinction, through the familiar academic transmutation of prestige into power. The faculties of weaker institutions see the relation, but endeavor to turn the causal connection on its head: They mean to gain the power and transmute it into prestige, for their institutions directly and themselves indirectly. Whatever its justification, the growth of faculty power has meant a diminution of the power of trustees and regents.

Boards of trustees traditionally have looked in two directions: inwardly to the government and direction of their universities; outwardly, to the groups and interests which provide the support for, and make claims for services on, the university. On the one hand, as I have suggested, trustees have been losing power over their own institutions: Many things are done and funded behind their backs, so to speak. At the same time (and this applies more to public than to private universities), their constituencies and their relation to their constituencies have been changing. Boards have traditionally dealt with very specific "relevant publics": legislative committees, wealthy donors, alumni organizations. In the leading universities, their job has been to get support from these publics while resisting inappropriate interference. And in this task trustees of public universities have not been so different from those of private universities: In most of their relationships, they have been dealing with people very much like themselves—in many cases graduates of the same state university, men of similar sentiments and values and prejudices. These relations could be, for the most part, cozy and private. Under these circumstances some of the leading state universities, such as the University of California, could until recently imagine themselves to be private universities operating largely on public funds, in a relationship to public authorities not unlike that of the British universities.

Today, the constituencies, the relevant publics, of state universities are much wider, more heterogeneous, and less familiar. In part, the growth of relevant publics has accompanied the simultaneous expansion of the universities and of their functions. For example, eleven years ago the University of California consisted of two major campuses, three small undergraduate colleges, and a medical school, with a total enrollment of about forty thousand, operating on a state budget of a little over one hundred million dollars. Today the university consists of nine campuses with over a hundred thousand students and a state budget of over three hundred million dollars, with nearly as much again from outside sources. The student body and faculty are not only bigger, but more heterogeneous, reflecting a variety of interests, many of which touch directly on sensitive and controversial issues. The schools of agriculture still do research on more fruitful crops and more effective pest control, but other students and faculty are active in support of the movement to organize migratory farm workers; the schools of education still produce schoolteachers and administrators, but also provide expert advice to school boards embarked on programs of total integration, while other faculty testify in defense of black militants and invite Black Panthers to give lectures on campus; administrative officers still define and defend academic criteria for admissions, while their colleagues press for the admission of larger numbers of minority-group students outside the ordinary procedures. And California, like many other universities, is now embarking on a major commitment to the solution of urban problems that inevitably will involve it in the most intense and passionate political controversies.

As a result of the expansion of the public universities, both in numbers and in the range of their activities, more and more people have come to take an interest in them and to feel that they have views on them that ought to be heard. In some uncertain sense, the constituency of the University of California, for example, has become the population of the state. But it is out of just this uncertainty about the nature and composition of the university's relevant publics that the Regents' anxieties arise. As the constituency of the trustees has grown, it has become less distinct. It is unclear just who the relevant publics are to which the Regents should attend. Moreover, with the disruption of the old cozy relations between the Regents and specific limited publics, they can no longer know their constituents' minds by consulting with them or by reading their own. And as the Regents lose touch with their constituents, so also they come to be less well known and trusted by their new constituents. To this new mass public, they are not people one can telephone or one has talked to; they are merely a remote part of the apparatus of government—the powerful people who need to be pressured. And some unrepresentative part of the anonymous public begins to write letters complaining about the university, and the Regents, for want of a genuine relation to these new publics, begin to read them and become anxious and worried. One important difference between the older specific and differentiated publics and the emerging mass undifferentiated public is that the former reflect specific interests that can be met, or compromised, or educated, or resisted. A mass public, by contrast, does not have interests so much as fears and angers—what it communicates to the trustees is "why can't you clean up that mess at the university—all those demonstrating students and unpatriotic faculty."

These two tendencies—the trustees' sense of a loss of control over "their" university and the emergence of a mass public of uncertain size and composition and temper with whom the trustees have no clear representative or communicating relationship—can undermine a board's conceptions of who they are and what their role is, and generate in them anger and anxiety. And out of that fear and anger, trustees appear to be more inclined to intervene directly in the academic life of the university: its curriculum, faculty appointments, and student discipline. In California where these developments are far advanced, these interventions are creating a serious crisis of authority within the university—what might be called a constitutional crisis—centering on who actually controls the curriculum and appointments of staff, which is not yet resolved. If it is not resolved, or if it leads to bitter struggles between the faculty and administrators and the Regents, or between the university and the state government, then the university's capacity to sustain a climate of intellectual excellence will be gravely threatened, and its ability to perform all its functions, but most especially its functions as an international center of learning, will be seriously weakened.

California is in many ways a populist democracy. The governor and legislature discuss and revise the university's annual operating budget in an atmosphere increasingly directly political and responsive to popular sentiments and indignation; and the whole electorate votes directly on proposed bond issues that are required for capital expansion. The Board of Regents, the majority of whose members are appointed to sixteen-year terms, was conceived precisely as a buffer between the university and popular or political pressures, to protect the necessary freedom of the university to explore issues and engage in educational innovations that might not have popular support at any given moment. But the board appears increasingly unable to perform that function. Instead of defending the university to its external publics, it begins to function as a conduit of popular sentiment and pressure on the university. And this, as I have suggested, places all the functions of the university in grave jeopardy.

But the problems I have been discussing are not confined to public state universities and populist societies. The emergence of a mass undifferentiated and angry public indeed poses a special threat to public universities. But the more general pattern in which university expansion creates new and easily neglected bodies of constituencies can be illustrated in the events at Columbia University two years ago. As Walter Metzger has noted, the physical expansion of Columbia, situated right at the edge of Harlem, made of that community a highly relevant and attentive public. Over many years Columbia has been expanding its operations into areas and buildings from which minority-group people have "necessarily" been evicted. But its board of trustees, and unfortunately also its administration, had not begun to see that Harlem was at least as relevent to Columbia's fate as were its alumni, its wealthy donors, and the great foundations. And it was the representatives of the black community, within the university as students, who precipitated the crisis that then was exploited by white radicals and greatly exacerbated by undisciplined police action.

Many of the popular functions of the universities in the past—mass education and public service—have indeed been popular in the other sense of the word and have gained the support or indifference of the general public. But it seems inescapable that the university in the future will be involved much more frequently in highly controversial issues and actions for which mass support cannot always be gained. The expansion of the universities, both in size and function, means that we will be living in an environment increasingly sensitive to what the university does, and especially to what it does that has direct effects outside the university. It is not generally recognized how much the university's freedom and autonomy were a function of popular indifference and of the management of special interest groups outside the arena of popular politics. But for various reasons the society is less and less indifferent, at the same time as trustees and regents are less able to perform their traditional function of defending the university through the forms of elite politics. And this is especially clear in the university's relations to the racial revolution.

Black Studies and Black Students

Almost every major college or university in the country is trying, in one way or another, to contribute to the enormous social movement that goes by the name of the "racial revolution." The first and most common response of universities is to increase the proportion of black students in their student bodies; the second is to develop programs or departments or colleges of black or ethnic studies; the third is to increase their commitment to the solution of urban problems.

The way a university responds to each of these challenges conditions the way it will or can respond to the others. How it goes about recruiting minority-group students heavily affects the character of a program or department of black or ethnic studies, and that in turn affects the ways in which an institution can try to approach a wider variety of urban problems. Moreover, how a university deals with all three of those programs will greatly influence how well its autonomous functions—of liberal education and basic research and scholarship—survive the current waves of populist sentiment and pressure.

But much of the discussion surrounding the need to increase the numbers of black students and faculty in our colleges and universities has focused on the mechanisms of black recruitment and the organization of a black curriculum. There has been little discussion of the characteristics and attitudes of black students and of differences among them. But the success of all these efforts may depend greatly on what black students in universities want from the institutions and the extent to which their hopes and desires are compatible with its basic values and processes.

We can usefully distinguish four positions among black students in colleges and universities today:

1. The revolutionaries, represented by but not confined to the Black Panthers, whose attention and energies are focused primarily on the black ghettos and the larger society, and who see the university chiefly as a base of operations and a pool of resources for revolutionary organization.

2. The radicals, who focus more on the university, but see it in its present form as a racist institution and in need of fundamental reorganization as a part of the radical transformation of society. They reject existing forms of university organization and governance: the way it selects its faculty, admits students, defines its curriculum, and awards credits and degrees. They demand "open enrollment," the abolition of "white" standards for appointments, admissions, and performance, and the full commitment of the institution, or a major part of it, to the racial revolution. They are likely to be separatists, demanding autonomous departments of black studies and special provisions for the recruitment and housing of black students. They differ from the revolutionaries chiefly in being less ideological, less interested in a world revolution along Maoist lines, and more in transforming the university. They are prepared to disrupt the university, to damage its buildings and close its classes, and indeed to destroy it, if necessary, to reconstruct it as an institution devoted to "the welfare of the people." Their hostility to the "racist" university as it exists is so great that they doubt that there is anything useful they can learn from it.

3. The militants, who also focus their attention on the university, but who accept, with some reservations, its basic character as a center for the creation and transmission of knowledge and values through free and objective inquiry. They push hard, however, in an active and organized way for a larger role for blacks in the university, both in numbers of students and faculty and in resources devoted to their special interests and problems. They may support departments or programs of black studies, but are prepared to see these integrated into the structure of the university, conforming (again with some reservations) to its academic norms and standards. They are prepared to demonstrate forcefully, but not (deliberately) in ways that threaten to destroy a university that they wish to reform. Most importantly, they differ from the radicals in having a greater interest in gaining an education for themselves in the university.

4. The moderates, who are largely committed to gaining skills and knowledge and training for careers in a multi-racial society. These people often support the demands of the militants, but draw back from confrontations and disruptions, and are little interested in, and indeed may oppose, separatist forms of education represented by departments of black studies. These students are often strongly committed to taking their skills back into the larger black community, where they may in fact be highly militant in relation to the white society and its institutions.

Individual students often straddle or combine two of these positions, shifting tone and emphasis on different issues and in different circumstances. Moreover, individuals will often use the rhetoric and arguments of one position while acting more consistently with another. In the general inflation of rhetoric, black militants often sound like radicals, making sweeping condemnations and demands when in fact their intention is to increase the numbers of black students and to gain somewhat larger resources for them in their institutions. Similarly, often under pressure and out of fear, moderates may sound like militants, expressing support for demonstrations when in fact they want nothing so much as to be allowed to get on with their studies. But this inflation of rhetoric is not merely a personal or group tactic; it has consequences for individuals and institutions. Students are captured by their own rhetoric, committed to positions and actions they may not have intended; the institution and the larger community often respond to the words and not the intentions, adopting either more submissive or more intransigent positions than are appropriate.

The inflation of black rhetoric, coupled with certain illusions and misconceptions among white faculty members and administrators, serves to obscure the actual character of black students on any given campus and the real distribution of sentiments and interests among them. The distortion is usually toward an exaggeration of the importance and influence of the radical and revolutionary blacks, as compared with the moderate and militant reformers. A case in point is provided by the events surrounding the strike called by the Third World Liberation Front at Berkeley during the winter of 1968-1969 in support of demands for an autonomous department of ethnic studies. The leadership of this organization and of its black component, the Afro-American Student Union, was predominantly radical. It had the support of black and white revolutionaries and also of many militants, though some of those opposed the more violent and destructive forms the strike took. It may be useful to sketch the background and context of this damaging strike.

At Berkeley, as at numbers of other major universities, the decision was made several years ago to increase the number of minority students in the student body. This was to be done both by encouraging black and Mexican-American students who qualified for admission in the ordinary way to apply to Berkeley and also by recruiting others whose high school records did not make them admissible through the ordinary procedures, but who might be admitted under a special rule which allows 2 (now 4) percent of the student body to be admitted outside the ordinary admissions criteria of the university. At Berkeley an Educational Opportunity Program was set up in 1966 to encourage youngsters from ethnic minorities to attend the university and specifically to admit some of them under this special 2, now 4, percent rule. The first director of this program, acting under the Chancellor's authority, was a man of great energy and commitment who developed relations with many of the black communities in the Bay Area and began to increase the numbers of students coming to Berkeley from those communities. In fall, 1966, the Berkeley EOP recruited and enrolled 130 students; in 1967, the number doubled to about 260, and in 1968 it doubled again. By January, 1969, there were over 800 EOP students at Berkeley, with the number still growing. His successor has continued this policy with similar energy and devotion. As a result of the efforts of this program and of other programs, and of the ordinary processes of admissions, there were in 1968-1969 some 1,200 black students at Berkeley.

I do not believe that anyone ever made a decision about the nature or characteristics of the black students to be recruited to Berkeley. The assumption was that the numbers were small and ought to be larger for many reasons, and that the way to do this was to go into the black neighborhoods and recruit students from substantially all-black high schools. Indeed, the Chancellor himself held the view that the university had a special responsibility to the most deprived black students. Increasing numbers of these youngsters have been going on to junior colleges, but, in his view, the university was richer and more powerful than these, and thus carried a larger responsibility to just those youngsters from the most handicapped and deprived backgrounds.

The resulting relationship between Berkeley and its growing numbers of minority students is conditioned by three factors: first, the characteristics of the minority students themselves, especially the values and attitudes that they bring with them to the university; second, the attitudes toward and perceptions of the minority students held by the faculty and especially by the administrators; and third, certain characteristics of the campus itself.

First, the black students recruited to Berkeley by and large have been militant and radical, clearly much more so than the black community as a whole. It may be that they reflect the attitudes of the average minority-group students of college age. It seems equally likely that there is a self-recruitment of more militant and radical blacks to the university, and a special interest in them on the part of the administrative officers who have headed the special program. There is, I think, a widely held belief that radicalism and militancy among young blacks is itself a sign of special energy and intelligence and, indeed, of potential leadership qualities. The youngsters with these characteristics recruited to the campus have brought their values with them and are indeed shaping the continued recruitment of black students to Berkeley.

Second, the romantic view of black militancy by white faculty and administrators is itself a factor of great importance in the present situation. It arises in part out of a generalized sense of guilt among liberal white men about the situation of Negroes in America—a sense that indeed blacks ought to be very angry, and that to be very angry and to express that anger in militant and radical forms are evidence of a certain freedom from older cultural constraints and a mark of being among the leaders of the emerging black community in America.

There is also the sheer ignorance of most white people regarding the distribution of attitudes and values among the black population, as a result of which young militant blacks are taken to be far more representative of their race than they in fact are. It was a source of great surprise and some embarrassment to members of the university community to discover that over 90 percent of black voters across the country voted for Hubert Humphrey in 1968, and that in California the Peace and Freedom Party, which carried the most radical and revolutionary racial slogans on its banners, gained very little support, even in the black ghettos.

The attitudes I am describing have affected the recruitment of black students to Berkeley and have exaggerated the significance of the black militants among the black students on the campus. For example, it was widely assumed that the Afro-American Student Union did, in fact, represent the black students on the Berkeley campus and express their views. It was also widely assumed that all black and other minority-group students supported the strike of the Third World Liberation Front during the winter quarter of 1969, and in their relations with the minority students on the campus the administration carefully dealt with the Third World Liberation Front as their legitimate leadership. But no one really knew how representative that body was, nor indeed how many black and minority-group students did not support the strike and even continued to attend class in the face of considerable fear and intimidation all during the strike. There has been, in general, a marked indifference in the university to the moderate or moderate-militant black and minority-group students, an indifference that in some cases has bordered on contempt.

There are two elements in this that are worth pointing to. The first is the invisibility of the Negro, which Ralph Ellison wrote about in his penetrating novel some years ago. In the university, both faculty and administrators are still inclined to deal with black students as group members, imputing to them a variety of characteristics and attitudes that reflect the guilt and wishes and assumptions of the whites themselves. The black students themselves, as individuals with unique characteristics, are largely invisible. It is in many ways more convenient to assimilate them into an Afro-American Student Union or Third World Liberation Front, where they comprise another political force which has to be accommodated in the university and with which one can negotiate and deal. Whatever the difficulties of that, it is still less difficult than to confront black students as people in all their uniqueness and individuality, differing sharply among themselves in their attitudes and orientation to the university.

In addition, there is the powerful ideological weapon of "Uncle Tomism." Uncle Tom, as an epithet, is assigned by radical and revolutionary blacks to any blacks less militant than they. It is a way of dismissing and discrediting the views of those who are still committed to an interracial and integrated society, and who do not in all cases support violent or other militant tactics. The term is reserved especially for moderate black students who want to use the university in traditional ways—to gain an education and increase their skills and opportunities in their future careers. Ironically, the university has accepted the black militants' definition of the nonmilitant Negro as an Uncle Tom, and has paid little attention to the interests of the very considerable number of black and other minority-group students who have not supported the Third World Liberation Front. This is, I think, in part because of the romantic apotheosis of black militancy among white liberal academics that I spoke of earlier, and in part because the militants can cause more trouble and are more powerful than the nonmilitants, who by the very fact of their not being organized can be safely ignored. And indeed they are ignored.

The black students recruited recently to the campus have brought their own values and culture with them. Many of them have had painful experiences throughout their school careers and have found schools and teachers unrewarding and punishing. They arrive at Berkeley and often begin to have the same kinds of unhappy and unsuccessful experiences in class that they have had before. Some very quickly cease going to class altogether, and for many the university, which so far as they can see is just another punishing kind of school which offers them little personal reward or psychological support, becomes the object of enormous anger and resentment. Berkeley, unlike some private and residential institutions, has never paid a great deal of attention to the emotional lives of its students, nor has it made any special effort to socialize them to the campus community. Nor has it been greatly concerned with the extent to which students hold the values which are essential to teaching and learning in the university. The university has traditionally concerned itself with the purely cognitive aspects of the student's life, and allowed his social and emotional life and moral development to take care of itself, or to find a home in the extracurricular forms of collegiate life. This was never very satisfactory, but it was not disastrous so long as the university recruited largely middle- and upper-middle-class students who already shared many of the views of themselves and the university that their teachers did, and whose attitudes, if not strictly academic, were at least not hostile to the university as it existed. These assumptions cannot be made about young militant blacks from the urban ghettos of the Bay Area,[6] but still nothing much has been done to socialize minority-group students to the university world after they are admitted. Indeed, even to suggest such an attempt is often seen as encouraging them to betray their identifications with their own ethnic communities.

Currently almost the whole of the attention of the university in this area is directed to problems of the curriculum and the organization of black studies. The issues have been autonomy, the recruitment of the faculty, the role of students in decision-making, and so forth. Those who have seen the report of the Harvard committee on black studies (the Rosovsky Report) will remember that the question of black studies there was embedded in a matrix of concern for the individual student and his sense of belonging, concerns that grew out of an awareness of his loneliness and anxieties on the campus. As much was said about the necessity for a black student union and for the integration of black students into the residential houses as about the curriculum of the black studies program.[7] In the Rosovsky Report, we see a sensitivity to the black student as an individual with special difficulties in adjusting to a university community. At Berkeley, as at many large public universities, there is no tradition for this kind of concern; instead, it deals with black students as an organized political force and bargains with them about the forms of a college of ethnic studies. The absence of a concern for the individual and his adjustment to the campus will have the most profound consequences for the relation between the university and minority-group students.

The decision at Berkeley to proceed with a College of Ethnic Studies will have consequences for the university, I suspect, as a source of continuing conflict and turmoil. It will also have consequences for the university's new broad commitment to urban problems. The proposed College of Ethnic Studies, at Berkeley as elsewhere, has in my view less to do with education than with politics. Some of the leaders of the Third World Liberation Front who are centrally involved in the creation of the new college see it primarily as a base for political action in the black ghettos and for the training of revolutionary cadres for the future. The real target, for them, is not the university, which is only incidental or instrumental, but rather the black community itself, which gave the bulk of its votes in the last election to Hubert Humphrey. For the radical and revolutionary Third World leaders, that is the real challenge—it is their brothers in the community who must be reached and shown the true nature of a racist society and the true nature of their own interests. And the disputes over the college, not all of which are yet resolved, have not centered on its academic character or curriculum, but on its degree of autonomy, its freedom from the ordinary constraints of the university which might inhibit its primary mission in the black community.

Chancellor Roger Heyns was aware of the problem. In a statement to the Academic Senate at Berkeley, in which he reaffirmed the necessity for the continued application of ordinary university procedures to the new college, he observed:

> I have a protective view about the proposition that the unit should engage in community service. I assume this does not mean service which is useful in the teaching and learning process as in field work or internships—to which there can be no objections. But I am very wary of any unit of the university becoming an instrument of community action.
>
> If the academic community chooses to use the University or any part of it as a base of political action, if it tries to identify the University with its causes, and mobilize the prestige and the resources of the University to goals which it chooses, then it has made the University an important piece of political real estate. And it will follow, inevitably, that others, outside the University, will then regard its control and management as important goals which *they select.*[8]

These are good and strong words. But I think they are illusory. I do not believe the Chancellor will be able to control events after the college has been established. The new college emerges out of a strike marked by many acts of violence and vandalism which the Chancellor himself has enumerated; it will grow and develop under the threat of renewed strikes and violence. The campus is desperate for peace; its faculty committees and its administration will be very reluctant to disrupt fragile agreements and ambiguous understandings by denying the college what it wants, especially if the college is prepared to get what it wants through regular university procedures. I believe the procedures will be defended (though they, too, have been attacked by faculty groups); but they can be operated with enough flexibility to demonstrate that they need not be "obstructive." My doubts on this score apply to staffing, curriculum, and admissions, but also, in the present context, to the college's role in the community. An active role in the ethnic communities is absolutely central to the concerns of many Third World faculty and students. The notion that their college will not be allowed to be "an instrument of community action," in the Chancellor's words, is, I believe, quite unrealistic. The further assumption—that such activity will not involve organizing and educating people and groups in that community for political action, but will be merely field work in connection with some course of study—is equally illusory. And, indeed, many of the Third World leaders and their supporters affirm in the strongest terms that the university should change its relation to the community, and precisely be an instrument for change in it. They point to the fact that the public land grant universities have long accepted their role as agents of social change, and merely demand that they broaden their conception of that role and of the forms of change it can effect in the community. The power of this strong tradition in American higher education, coupled with the moral and political power of the militant black movement itself, will make it extremely difficult for the Chancellor, or university presidents elsewhere, to try to prevent directly political activities in the community based in the new colleges of black or ethnic studies.

If my concerns are in fact realized, what are the consequences for the universities' new broad entry into the field of urban problems? The question is almost rhetorical. American universities have had some experience of service in public areas which involve political controversy. But surely the problems in this regard are likely to be greater in the area of urban affairs than in agriculture or medicine. The heart of the matter is whether the university can find a way to approach urban problems without being transformed into a political weapon or arena. I believe it can if the university can remember and respect its own unique qualities as a center for basic inquiry and rational discussion of issues, as a source of new ideas and critical examination of existing policy and practice, and as a training ground for the variety of professions and semiprofessions whose skills are in such short supply in the areas of urban problems. At best the university cannot avoid being drawn into areas of controversy, and its autonomy will be further strained by the appearance, if not the reality, of partisanship. Facts are, or quickly become, political weapons, and reports and recommendations, however firmly based on facts, have a tendency to support one position in a debate and not others. But if there is a continued concern for the quality of the knowledge base, a dedication to the effort to illuminate issues and to increase the number and variety of policy options, a scrupulous attention to negative evidence, and a sensitive avoidance of the technocratic contempt for the ordinary political processes, then the university may indeed survive its most ambitious program of service to the community.

But these are just the qualities that one can hope for, but not assume, in a college of ethnic studies. Some of its founders *know* what the problems are and know what must be done. "Enough of this endless study and discussion," they say. "After a hundred or two hundred or three hundred years of it, let us now do what needs to be done." However justified this may be for a radical political program, it cannot but complicate the university's broad involvement in the problems of the city, with which it inevitably will be associated in the public mind. As a result, it seems likely to me that the university will come to be seen as the source of direct and radical intervention in the politics of the minority communities themselves. The reaction to political action based in the university, as Chancellor Heyns observed, will be political reaction from the community and the state.

I have suggested that some of the problems at Berkeley have had their roots in the casual and almost unnoticed decision to increase the numbers of minority-group students by recruiting youngsters through special admission directly from the ghetto high schools. This decision has shaped succeeding events at Berkeley, including the strike and the ensuing proposals for a college of ethnic studies. But given a commitment to increase the numbers of minority students on campus, a commitment almost unanimously supported throughout the university, is there any alternative to the way Berkeley went about it? Was all this not inevitable, an inevitability embodying, as I have heard said, a kind of cosmic justice which visits on the university an appropriate suffering for its decades of neglect of the minority groups in the population? I do not believe it was inevitable, nor do I see a divine spirit at work in our current travail. I think there is another way to increase our service to minority groups in the state and nation—and that is by helping to strengthen and expand the strata of black and other minority-group professionals and semiprofessionals: teachers, lawyers, engineers, social workers, probation officers, professors, scientists, researchers, students of urban problems. Education in the freshman and sophomore years, after all, is not our strength at Berkeley, nor at many other big state universities; on the whole, we do it badly, and what success we have is with students who come to us already motivated and well educated, who can use the resources of the university in the service of their own self-education. Youngsters from local black high schools need much more than that. But we are ill equipped to give them the kinds of counseling and personal attention and patient concern that they need and deserve. Ironically we are much closer to being able to provide this kind of education to our juniors and seniors and graduate and professional students. And there, I think, is our special opportunity. The university can recognize and accept its unique qualities as a center for advanced undergraduate, graduate, and professional training, and for scholarship and research, and not use a program of special admissions to compete unreflectively with junior colleges and state colleges for youngsters just out of high school. We might, instead, come to be seen as a place where the minority-group draftsman and technician could return to school to become an engineer; the school aide, a teacher; the teacher, a trained administrator or educational specialist; the advanced undergraduate or graduate, a scientist or academic man. This would mean not a smaller, but a different commitment. It is true that many graduate departments and schools are also making special efforts at recruiting minority-group students. But what is required is a much fuller commitment by the university in this direction. For example, it may mean that we have to find ways of being more hospitable to older undergraduates with broken academic careers, and to use our special admissions programs for the man of thirty-five who left college ten or fifteen years ago, who does not meet the ordinary criteria for admission to the university, but who needs additional training to go beyond his dead-end white-collar job. And we might have to search out such people—in industry and politics, the civil service and community poverty programs and schools—with as much energy and initiative as we now use in looking for youngsters to come as freshmen. It may well be that one way to organize the education of many of them would be in a school of urban studies.

All this implies an effort to broaden and strengthen the black middle class. But somehow middle-class Negroes have a bad name among white academics— indeed, the name is Uncle Tom—and we have come to identify leadership in the minority community with radical militancy. That is not, I think, a service either to the minority communities or to the university.

The question, of course, is not whether public universities should or should not enroll more minority-group students, or develop programs of studies centering on their history and culture and experience and problems, or commit more of their resources and energies to such programs. There are many good reasons, moral and intellectual and pragmatic, for making those commitments. The question is the form such programs of special recruitment, ethnic studies, and the like should take: or, more precisely, what criteria we should use in making those decisions—decisions we are in danger of making either unreflectively, as with recruitment, or in direct response to confrontation as a way of gaining peace, as with ethnic studies. The answers lie in a clearer sense of the kinds of programs that are compatible with one's conception of the university. And here, of course, we come to what may be irreducible value preferences. Insofar as one sees the university as merely a political instrument, functioning at present chiefly to arm and legitimate a racist and utterly corrupt society, then indeed one need not worry overmuch about its survival; one may want to use it, or seize it, or, failing that, to unmask and then smash it. But if one sees the university as a vulnerable institution that in some respects can stand apart from politics and society and provide an arena for the critical examination of all views of man and society, then the survival of this function in the university is a matter of some consequence for the way in which the university performs its other, more directly service, functions.

"Compulsory" Higher Education

The growth of American higher education and the powerful wave of popular sentiment that accompanies that growth are affecting its relations to its environment, with trustees and regents, at the point of greatest strain. But the same forces, both within and outside the universities, are affecting the internal fabric of the universities: the character of their undergraduates and graduate students and faculty members, and their processes of governance. It begins to appear as if the expansion of American higher education, in numbers and functions, is transforming it from a system of mass higher education into one that will bear responsibility for nearly all of the college-age population—that is, into a system of universal higher education. That development, clear in trends and projections, is obscured by the fact that currently only about half of all high school graduates across the country go directly from high school to some form of higher education. But in the upper-middle classes and in states like California, the proportion of youngsters going on to some form of post-secondary education is already over 80 percent. For youngsters in those places and strata, universal higher education is here: Nearly everybody they know goes on to college. And those strata and areas are growing inexorably. Many of the difficulties now being experienced by American colleges and universities reflect the strains of this transformation from mass to universal higher education.

In the recent past, attendance in our system of mass higher education was voluntary—a privilege that had in some places become a right, but not yet for many an obligation. Whether seen as a privilege, as in certain selective, mostly private, institutions, or as a right, in unselective, mostly public, institutions, voluntary attendance carried with it an implicit acceptance of the character and purposes of the institution as defined by "the authorities." The authority of trustees or administrators or faculty to define the nature of the education and its requirements could be evaded, but was rarely challenged by students. With few exceptions students played little or no role in the government of the institution.

The growth of enrollments and the movement toward universal higher education has made enrollment in college increasingly obligatory for many students, and their presence there increasingly "involuntary." In this respect, in some strata and places, colleges begin to resemble elementary and secondary schools, where it has long been recognized that compulsory attendance increases problems of student motivation, boredom, and the maintenance of order. The coercions on college students take several forms. The most visible in recent years has been the draft, which has locked many young men into college who might otherwise be doing something else. But other pressures will outlive the reform or abolition of the draft: the unquestioned expectations of family and friends and the consequent sense of shame in not meeting those expectations; the scarcity of attractive alternatives for youngsters of eighteen and nineteen without college experience;[9] the strong and largely realistic anticipation that without some college credits they will be disqualified from most of the attractive and rewarding jobs in the society as adults. As more and more college-age youngsters go on to college, not to be or to have been a college student becomes increasingly a lasting stigma, a mark of some special failing of mind or character and a grave handicap in all the activities and pursuits of adult life.

The net effect of these forces and conditions is to make college attendance for many students nearly involuntary, a result of external pressures and constraints some of which do not even have the legitimacy of parental authority behind them. The result is that we are finding in our classrooms large numbers of students who really do not want to be in college, have not entered into willing contract with it, and do not accept the values or legitimacy of the institution.

In the past, the relative accessibility of higher education brought large numbers of students to American colleges and universities who had little interest in learning for its own sake, but who had strong ambitions to rise in the world and wanted the degree and sometimes the skills that would help them better their status. We are now seeing large numbers from more affluent homes who similarly enter college without much interest in bookish study, but who also are less interested in vocational preparation or social mobility— who either have little ambition for a middle-class career, or else take it completely for granted, or, as in many cases, both. These students also differ from the members of the old "collegiate culture" who took refuge from the higher learning in the "gentleman's C" and the distractions of college sport and social life. But these students, already securely lodged in the middle and upper-middle classes, were not inclined to challenge any authority, especially when the institution made its own relaxed compromises with their styles and evasions. For the members of the old collegiate culture, as for the vocationally oriented and the serious students with an interest in academic work, a willing contract with the college of their choice was implicit and, for the most part, honored.[10]

The entry of large numbers of "involuntary" students introduces into the university considerable resentment and hostility directed, among other things, to its conceptions of achievement and ambition. There have always been large numbers of people, in this as in other societies, whose ambitions were modest or who felt that the human price of striving and ambition was not worth the problematic gain. But these views are represented more strongly in the university today, where they assert their legitimacy in ways the institution seems peculiarly unable to counter. Part of the attack is on the *ends* of ambition and takes the form of the rejection of academic institutions and programs that threaten to fit people for jobs and careers in a "sick society." Part of the complaint is that academic or intellectual work is *intrinsically* dehumanizing, separating people from one an·other, destroying their human qualities, authenticity, and so forth. This sentiment sometimes takes the form: "Look, stop trying to put us on your treadmill; your own lives are spent running around doing pointless things. We just want to look at the flowers and love one another." This point of view, in its pure form, is clearly incompatible with any kind of consistent goal-directed effort. But many students, under the constraints to be enrolled in college, hold views close to this while continuing to attend classes and earn credits. Such students pose a special problem for the university. They are not only bored and resentful at having to be in college, but they are also quite vulnerable to the anti-rational or politically radical doctrines currently available in the university—and especially to those that explain and justify their distaste for formal academic work and their reluctance to get caught up in the patterns of striving and achievement.

There is no doubt that many student complaints have real objects—bad teaching, faculty indifference, and the impersonal people-processing of the big universities.[11] But it is sobering to learn that much the same anger is expressed by students in the most varied kinds of colleges and universities—in small liberal arts colleges as in multiversities, in innovative and permissive colleges and in conservative and traditional ones. Where does all the anger come from? Surely some of it comes from forcing youngsters into college who have no interest in bookish study, at least at this point in their lives. There may be other things for them to do now, and perhaps better times for them to be exposed to the disciplines and pleasures of formal study.

Problems of Graduate Education: A New Breed

There are interesting parallels between developments in undergraduate and in graduate schools. The rapid expansion of higher education, along with other developments in the larger society, has also brought into faculties and into departments young men whose commitments to academic values are weak or ambivalent. In part, this is because increasing numbers of students are entering graduate school who have little interest in the discipline and for whom graduate school is a chance to continue their liberal education, sometimes under more favorable conditions. There are visible among an increasing number of graduate students (and some of the ablest) a sharp recoil from professional training and, indeed, a rejection of that ambition to achieve distinction in one's field that we have always assumed to be a chief motive of our best graduate students, as of their teachers. For these students any ambition or striving, even for a successful academic or scientific career, involves the loss of personal authenticity and human qualities, and in social terms is a sellout to a basically corrupt and sick society. In these respects, it resembles the rejection of ambition and fear of success that are even more widespread among undergraduates. These new graduate students also reflect the enormous growth of higher education and of affluence that allow undergraduate interests to be pursued in graduate and professional schools. They cannot be said to be involuntary students, even in the metaphorical sense in which I have referred to a class of undergraduates. But insofar as their interests and motives are at odds with the purposes of graduate training and the values and expectations of the faculty, tensions and resentments develop among them that are not unlike those we find among the reluctant undergraduates.[12] For these students, graduate study has certain attractions that are quite independent of the department's central function of providing professional training for scholars and college teachers. The university is a pleasant, stimulating, and protected environment that affords the students the leisure to read in areas that interest them and, in a sense, to pursue the liberal education that many feel they did not really gain as undergraduates. It also provides the necessary conditions for the political activities in which some are involved.

Some of these students do in fact drop out of graduate work, especially from departments in vertebrate disciplines that have rigorous professional standards and do not allow themselves to be used as extensions of undergraduate liberal arts colleges. In many other departments, especially in the humanities and social sciences, professional training has always been tempered by the encouragement of the continued general intellectual growth of the graduate students. And, in some, the discipline and the faculty itself are divided on the relative importance of technical training, on one hand, and a broad general education and familiarity with the literature of other fields of study, on the other. This reflects an older struggle within universities between gentlemanly, aristocratic attitudes toward learning and the conception of the discipline as a body of knowledge that grows by patient systematic inquiry employing the technical apparatus of scholarly and scientific research. The disdain for "narrow technical studies" or professional training, as well as for the kinds of research that lead to a successful academic career, is common both to the gentlemanly conception of the university as well as to these graduate students, who would be horrified to be accused of behaving like gentlemen or aristocrats. (And indeed in other respects they do not resemble those older models.) Many professors of sociology and English, of history and anthropology, would argue that it is precisely the combination of professional skills and broad learning that is the best preparation for a life of scholarship and future work of high distinction. So the students of whom I am speaking often find encouragement from their teachers for studies that in their teachers' eyes are an appropriate part of their professional training, but to the student represent more accurately a rejection of the discipline and of the scholarly or scientific career.

The irony, of course, is that some of these students do in fact "succeed" in their graduate studies, sometimes with the help and sponsorship of faculty members who are themselves least in sympathy with the dominant professional and research orientations of their fields and departments. These students are rarely the most brilliant in their class (that usually requires a serious professional orientation as well as a general interest in ideas), but they are often very able and can meet the sometimes modest professional requirements of their department without too great an effort. These students often also hold teaching assistantships (though rarely research assistantships). And in some departments a very large part of undergraduate education is carried by TAs, many of whom are deeply hostile to their own departments and to the subject as it is taught there. In the sections of large undergraduate lecture courses that they teach, such TAs can effectively sabotage the design of the course, developing alliances with undergraduates who are similarly hostile to the institution in which they are studying. Increasingly these TAs, led or protected by sympathetic (often junior) faculty members, in fact create their own courses, which are explicitly designed to counteract the "conservative establishment" courses offered by the rest of the university. These courses, which as they multiply develop into a kind of shadow university, provide an academic base for dissident and politically active undergraduates.

Some of these students eventually pass their qualifying exams and, for want of an alternative, proceed on to college or university teaching, with or without a dissertation in hand. And some join our own ever-expanding departments as junior colleagues, in many cases with their own values—their sharp and painful ambivalence toward success and an academic career, their hostility to the discipline as a cumulative body of learning, to research, and to the organization of the academic departments, curriculum, and university—unchanged.

From another perspective these students and junior colleagues reflect a failure of graduate departments to socialize their students effectively or to gain from them a commitment to their purposes and values and conceptions of the discipline and the university. This is in part due to the values these students hold on entry to graduate school, values which are reinforced by currently fashionable cultural and political ideologies and sentiments, and by their peers. It also reflects the loss of confidence of the faculty in its own values and its inability or reluctance to communicate them with conviction. Perhaps most important, these departments are no longer (if they ever were) normative communities. And that, in turn, reflects the growth of the departments, the increasing specialization of knowledge, and the privatizing centrifugal pulls of research (as compared with the centripetal force of teaching and of curriculum design). The core values of a department may still be assumed, but they are not continuously reasserted, re-defined, and reinforced by men coming together and acting around them. The breakdown of a department as a moral community reflects these centrifugal forces, and then in turn reacts back on and contributes to them. Academic men are even less likely to interact around the shared work of a department when they discover deep divisions among them about the central purposes and conceptions of the subject and department. All this has marked consequences for each disci-pline, but it also contributes to the general weakening of academic authority and of the ability of graduate departments to socialize their graduate students to a common conception of the academic and scholarly role.

In short, we are steadily recruiting people to college and university faculties who are deeply hostile to the central values and functions of the department and institution they join. We see them increasingly at scholarly conventions and as supporters or leaders of student demonstrations. We are beginning to see them in growing numbers on departmental and university committees, where the old assumptions regarding the shared unspoken values of academic men, cutting across disciplinary lines, can no longer be sustained. And where these shared values are no longer shared, whether because of political students or dissident faculty, the old forms of university government by discussion and consensus be-gin to break down. The consequence is the steady politicization of government at every level and in every arena, attended by the withdrawal of men whose sense of obligation to university service does not extend to polemical politics.

The Management of Internal Conflict

This leads me to the impact of external pressures and student activism on the internal government and climate of universities. A number of forces work to limit the extent and intensity of disputes within the university; these forces tend to mute disputes and press toward compromise and accommodation between dif-fering points of view. One of these is the broad acceptance of the legitimacy of the multiple functions of the university. The practical effect of this conception of the university as multiversity is to remove from dispute the sharpest and fun-damentally irreconcilable issues; disputes then can take the form of arguments about the relative emphasis to be given to different views or the relative support to be allocated to different programs. And even those disputes are further di-luted in situations in which there is secular growth or expansion throughout the university, and where disputes then become merely questions of priority and time.

Disputes are also softened by a general agreement to conduct them within the regular academic and administrative machinery—the system of committees and meetings through which major universities govern themselves. They are still fur-ther softened by the institutional (and often also the geographical) insulation of conflicting views. For example, the humanistic scholars are typically centered in a university's college of letters and sciences, or its equivalent, the service orien-tations in the professional schools and some of the graduate departments. Historians and engineers may have different conceptions of the primary functions of the university, but they rarely have occasion to confront each other in argument.

Conflict between different conceptions of the university is also minimized by making the department, rather than a college or the university, the unit of effective educational decision. The departments, or most of them, are more homogeneous than the faculty as a whole, and they have their own strong mechanisms for compromise and accommodation, not least of which is to minimize the number and importance of issues involving collective decisions, allowing the privatization of intellectual life, a withdrawal to one's own classroom and research. On the graduate level, the university *is* for all practical purposes the aggregation of departments and professional schools, their satellite research centers and institutes, and the supporting infrastructure of libraries, labs, buildings, and administrative help. The departments effectively govern their own appointments and promotion of staff (subject to certain review procedures by extradepartmental committees), admit their own graduate students, and organize their instruction. On the undergraduate level (I am speaking here of the central liberal arts college), there is, of course, the necessity to organize some structure of education that is not confined to a single department. The form this takes at many institutions is a set of distribution requirements—so many units required in fields outside one's major, so many in a major field, the remainder in electives. This system, whatever its failings as education, has the substantial virtue of reducing the amount of academic decision-making that is necessary. This reduces the occasions for conflict involving educational values and philosophies, thus letting men get on with their own work. What we see there is a spirit of *laissez-faire*, within broad administrative constraints set by limitations of space, time, staff, and other resources, that mirrors the broader philosophy of the multiversity as a whole.[13]

This pattern may be seen as an institutional response to the problem of combining post-secondary education for large numbers of students of the most diverse character with the highest standards of scholarly and scientific work. But the events of the past few years have revealed basic weaknesses in the system which are in a sense the defects of its virtues. One of these is the lack of a central, widely shared sense of the nature of the institution and a weakness in its capacity to gain the loyalties and devotion of its participants. This means that the institution operates on a relatively thin margin of error. Closely related to this is its tendency to generate both among students and faculty somewhat diffuse resentments, feelings of frustration and alienation from an institution which provides services and facilities, but which seems singularly remote from the concerns of individuals, responsive only to pressures and problems that are organized and communicated through the regular channels, and not always even to those. It is this kind of institution marked by weak faculty loyalties, vague resentments, and complex administrative arrangements that is showing itself to be highly vulnerable to political attacks from without and within.

These attacks have other consequences than the disruptive demonstrations and sit-ins that are most widely publicized. The attacks, whether from a governor or a radical student group, work to politicize a campus, to polarize a faculty, and to force its members to make choices in an atmosphere of passion and partisanship. The differences that crystallize around the issues I have been describing differ from the ordinary issues of academic politics: For one thing, they involve the students more directly; for another, they are more stable, more closely linked to deep-rooted values and conceptions of the nature of the institution. Moreover, at many of the leading universities they are being institutionalized in the form of faculty caucuses and parties, which will persist as permanent elements in the governmental process, further contributing to the polarization of faculty out of which they arise. Perhaps most importantly, these tendencies threaten to disrupt the informal processes of consultation, negotiation, and compromise, among and between faculty and administrators, by which universities are ordinarily governed. And they threaten to break through all the devices for softening conflict that I was describing.

In their place are put forward two powerful democratic models for the government of institutions. One is the model of representative democracy, complete with the party system and judicial review. The other is the model of direct democracy in the self-governing small community. Both models, as well as a combination of the two involving the formalization of the governmental process in addition to the provision of a high degree of participatory democracy, have been advocated for the university. Such systems would require a relatively high and continuous level of faculty involvement in the issues and instruments of university government, as well as a basic decision regarding the extent of citizenship—that is, the role of the students in the decision-making machinery. And, indeed, both of these issues have been raised in a recent student-faculty report on university governance at Berkeley, which calls for a high level of participation by both faculty and students in units of government at every level, from the campus as a whole down to the individual departments.[14]

Many arguments can be made against such a proposal—its cumbersomeness; the impermanence of the student (they do not have to live very long with the consequences of their decisions on a campus); their incompetence to decide certain matters; and so forth. But, in my own view, more important than any of these is the absolute level of political activity and involvement required of teachers and students under these arrangements. The casual and rather informal methods by which faculty members and administrators govern a campus may have many failings, most clearly visible to those who are not part of such a government. But their chief virtue is that they have allowed students and teachers to get on with their work of teaching and learning. Some students and faculty who want to radically transform the universities are at least consistent in wanting to change the form of governance by making the process of government itself a central part and focus of a university education. But liberal education, scholarship, and research are not inherently political activities, even when they take politics as their subject. And they are threatened by a highly politicized environment, both by its partisanship and demand for loyalties and commitments, and also by its distractions, its encroachments on one's time and energies. The reactions of academic men who are not much interested in university governance is usually to withdraw their attention and let others govern. But this works only if those others, who *are* interested in politics, share the faculty's basic values and are concerned to create and protect an environment in which the old functions of teaching and research can go on without distraction or intimidation. That is an unlikely outcome of any arrangement that makes its own government a central activity of the university, insures that all disputes pass through its formal machinery, and brings students and faculty with a passion for politics to the center of the governing process. But that is the direction of much student and faculty sentiment at the moment, and of "reforms" on many campuses.

The demand for participatory democracy by those who see it as an instrument for radical change in the university involves a paradox that makes it suspect. Genuine participatory democracy, as those who have seen it at work in university departments or New England town meetings know, is an inherently conservative form of political organization. In these bodies there is a strong pressure for consensual decisions, arising largely out of the potential divisiveness of disputes unmediated by any representative machinery. The anticipation that one is going to have to continue to live and associate with one's colleagues or neighbors outside the political arena is a powerful inhibitor of actions or changes which some of them object to strongly.

But the forms of participatory democracy can be a vehicle for radical action when they involve large aggregates of people who do not comprise a genuine community, and whose relations with one another are not diffuse and continuous, but segmental and fleeting. Under those circumstances, participatory democracy becomes plebiscitary democracy, manipulated by small groups of activists who speak in the name of the passive masses. (And the demand for constant participation insures the passivity of most students and faculty, who have other things to do than govern themselves.) For a university government based on the forms of participatory democracy to be used for radical change, it must be captured and manipulated by political activists. The conditions making for this kind of manipulation grow as activist groups among faculty and students gain in strength, tactical experience, and ideological fervor. Those conditions are also strengthened by persistent and, in some universities, highly successful attacks on the legitimacy of existing forms of university governance.

The Quest for Legitimacy

It is widely recognized that events over the past decade, perhaps coinciding with other more fundamental and long-range developments in the society, have greatly weakened the legitimacy of institutional authority. The loss of authority and of confidence in that authority are nowhere more evident than in our colleges and universities. The constant attacks on the universities for their "irrelevance," their neglect of students, their "institutional racism," their implication in the war in Vietnam and in the "military-industrial complex" have deeply shaken the belief of many academic men in their own moral and intellectual authority. Many academic men no longer really believe they have a right to define a curriculum for their students or to set standards of performance, much less to prescribe the modes of thought and feeling appropriate to "an educated man." Indeed, the very notion that there are qualities of mind and sensibility to be gained from experience in a college or university is often treated with amusement or contempt, as merely a reactionary expression of middle-class prejudices.

This crisis of confidence is at the heart of the crisis of university governance. One common response in universities is to try to reestablish the legitimacy of institutional authority not on the older grounds of wisdom, technical competence, or certification, but on newer grounds of responsiveness to democratic political processes. And this coincides with demands from the student left for "more responsive machinery of government which will reflect the interests and sentiments of all the members of the university community," including, most particularly, the student body. And everywhere reforms and changes are under way to increase the role of students in university government—not merely in areas of traditional "student affairs," but directly within the faculty and departmental committees that deal with such matters as the curriculum, faculty recruitment, and student admissions. But this has not been done only to gain the perspectives and advice of students on academic issues. That could be done by co-opting students who are especially highly qualified or interested in a given area, and who would be likely to make the most thoughtful and helpful contribution to discussions. Changes currently proposed or being made reflect a greater interest in strengthening the legitimacy of academic decisions than in improving their quality. And that has meant borrowing the legitimacy of student government—its legitimacy as a democratically elected body—by assigning to it the authority for selecting the student representatives on academic committees. This effort to borrow legitimacy by university authorities helps account for the exaggerated importance that they attach to all organized groups and for their relative indifference to the majority of unorganized students, black and white.

One consequence, of course, is to increase greatly the political component in academic decisions; for the student governments in our major universities are primarily political, not academic, bodies. Their leading officers are now often nominated by political groups and parties, representing more or less elaborately articulated positions on general academic-political issues, and they are elected after heated and well-organized campaigns. To be nominated and elected, these students must themselves be highly political men who give to student politics a large part of their time and energy. They are consequently not likely to be students who are most deeply involved in their studies—in nineteenth-century history or solid state physics, for example—and in this important respect they are less likely to share the values and perspectives of the academic men whose committees they join. Moreover, on those committees they see themselves as representing constituencies with attitudes and interests, and this, coupled with the continuing fear of every student politician of being outflanked on the left, makes their position highly resistant, if not impervious, to change through reasoned argument in the ordinary give-and-take of committee discussion. By contrast, faculty members on committees have been more likely to represent no one but themselves and therefore can change their minds or views without concern for a constituency or for charges of "selling out." This may change with the institutionalization of parties and caucuses among the faculty, and that would similarly increase the purely political component of academic decisions.

In most discussions about student representation in university government two assumptions are made: first, that the student representatives do, in fact, reflect "student" views and perspectives; and, second, that while these may differ in certain respects from those of faculty and administrators (properly reflecting the special experience and age of students), they will arise out of fundamentally common values and conceptions of the university. Students are seen, in these discussions, as junior colleagues or apprentices in a common enterprise of teaching and learning. There is no doubt that many students do, in fact, have the character of junior colleagues, equally concerned from their own special perspectives with an environment in which teaching and learning can most fruitfully be carried on. And faculty members who have served on committees with able and serious students know just how valuable their perspectives can be on many issues, and how important they can be as a corrective to the administrative considerations and research orientations most strongly represented on those committees. But not all students are, in fact, junior colleagues: Some are indifferent timesavers, and still others are hostile antagonists. The nature of the political process surrounding student government in large universities these days makes it likely that student leaders will be far more political and almost certainly more radical than the average student. Moreover, they are likely to be more dogmatic and doctrinaire in rhetoric and action in their official positions than they might be in private. Nor can we safely assume that the leaders of student governments will share basic commitments to learning, scholarship, and academic freedom with the faculty members.[15]

Universities are fragile and vulnerable to disruption; in the face of bitter attacks, academic men and administrators lack confidence in their own authority and want to borrow that of elected student representatives. Both these facts help explain why academic men so rarely criticize student representatives and so commonly make them the objective of fulsome flattery. But by making student government the source of student representatives on faculty and administrative committees, universities may be shredding the very delicate procedures by which they govern themselves, procedures which depend on mutual trust, shared values, rational discussion, civility, and discretion. Insofar as important academic committees become arenas for ideological confrontation, short-run political maneuvers, and immediate exposure to publicity, they cannot function. Under those circumstances, serious scholars and students would refuse to serve on these committees,[16] and university government will be carried by political students, the

minority of academic men who enjoy polemical politics, and the hapless administrators who have no choice.[17]

Where Next?

The growth of numbers, functions, and political pressures within universities
takes many forms and has many consequences. I have touched on only a few of
those which I believe are especially serious threats to the university's core functions of liberal education, scholarship, and basic research. I have not spoken of
the crisis in undergraduate education arising out of the complete collapse of any
generally shared conception of what students ought to learn; nor of the role of
teaching assistants in the big state universities, who carry a great part of the undergraduate teaching, begin to see themselves as exploited employees, and organize in trade unions. Nor have I done more than touch on the changing character
of our undergraduates, on the boredom of some and the apparently unquench-
able anger of others, and on the meaning of their demands for "a relevant curriculum." Merely to point to these issues is to affirm that I do not judge the state
of our universities by the conventional measures of success that I mentioned in
my opening sentences. But I cannot close without at least acknowledging the
most pressing question of all: Given the inexorable movement toward universal
higher education in this country, what is likely to happen? How will American
colleges and universities respond to the enormous strains and dislocations already
visible within them?

I can see a number of possibilities, some of which have already begun to
emerge:

Progressively more repressive sanctions by public and private authorities may
be enacted against disruptions in the universities and colleges and against people
and activities perceived as "radical" or "subversive." These sanctions, if carried
very far, are likely to bring teachers and students into direct confrontation with
the state or the governing bodies, and result in further disturbances and loss of
autonomy, morale, and a measure of academic freedom.[18]

There may be an acceleration of the movement of academic men, especially
research scholars in the natural and physical and social sciences, out of the universities and into various public and private research centers which are (or seem
to be) better protected against attacks from left or right. Certainly there are
models for the separation of teaching and research in the continental and Soviet
systems of higher education. Although this shift would run sharply against
strongly held conceptions of the academic career in the United States, it is likely
to be present as one alternative for many academic men in the event of a deepening crisis in the university.

The system may develop an even sharper and more effectively insulated differentiation of character and function within and among institutions. Some
universities may self-consciously commit themselves to the primacy of disinterested inquiry in research and teaching, and select students, staff, and service
missions with that primary criterion in mind. Parts of other institutions—

departments, schools, research centers—may attempt to do the same. It is problematic, and will surely be variable, how effectively universities or parts of universities will be able to insulate themselves against the powerful populist forces afoot in higher education.[19]

There may evolve alternative forms of undergraduate education, breaking radically with the bookish and academic traditions that still link even the more "innovative" efforts at "relevance" with the high literary and scientific cultures. Much of the demand for "relevance" on the part of undergraduates is a revolt against formal learning and a wish to be involved immediately and directly in the society and its problems and opportunities. It is no use telling such students they should not be in college, but in the world and at work; the meaning of universal higher education is that these students have little choice but to be in some college, and that our system of higher education "owns" the years from eighteen to perhaps twenty or twenty-two of most of our youth. What may, perhaps must, emerge are various forms of nonacademic learning and service, organized by colleges and universities, allowing youngsters to define themselves as college students, earning credits for "degrees" and certificates, but off the campuses and free from classrooms, library, and laboratory disciplines. I believe we must reduce the involuntariness of college attendance for many who do not want to study if the college and universities are to survive in recognizable form for those who do. The creation of nonacademic forms of "higher education" off campus may be the most important innovation on the agenda for our colleges and universities.[20]

Finally, a word on the great state university. It is a matter of continual amazement that an institution so deeply involved in public service in so many ways has been able to preserve its autonomy and its critical and scholarly and research functions. The question is whether its new commitments to public service, on campus and off, will seriously endanger that autonomy and the disinterested and critical intellectual life that it allows. One answer, very tentatively is: that depends on *how* it performs these new services. The issue is very much in doubt. But if the autonomous functions of the great state universities are threatened and then crippled by the political pressures arising out of their commitments to service, then those functions, at their highest levels of performance, will be confined to the private universities or forced outside the university altogether. And if that happens, something very precious—the presence within institutions of popular democracy of the highest standards of intellectual life—will have been lost in America.

NOTES

1. *A Fact Book on Higher Education* (American Council on Education: Washington, D.C., 1969), p. 9048.
2. And in Europe the preparation of teachers for the selective secondary schools where the children of those elites are educated and prepared for their own accession to elite status.

3. This is now as much a scientific as a literary culture.

4. For discussion of the forces associated with the growth of mass higher education in the United States, see Martin Trow, "The Democratization of Higher Education in America," *European Journal of Sociology*, Vol. 3, No. 2 (1962).

5. This essay will focus on the problems of the great American "multiversities," public and private.

6. Nor can it be made about many white undergraduates today. On this, see below, on "compulsory" higher education.

7. *Report of the Faculty Committee on African and Afro-American Studies,* Faculty of Arts and Sciences, Harvard University (January 1969). The program of black studies recommended by the Rosovsky Committee and accepted by the Harvard faculty has been greatly modified under pressure, and is no longer a model for Berkeley or the country.

8. *Campus Report* (University of California, Berkeley), Vol. 3, No. 10 (March 6, 1969). Italics his.

9. And, of course, the "attractiveness of alternatives" is also defined by social norms held by family and friends.

10. The contracts and mutual understandings, of course, differed enormously for the great variety of students and the almost equally great variety of institutions.

11. Indeed, one function of political action on campus for many students is to introduce them to other students with similar values and attitudes, and to the pleasures of belonging to a community of like-minded people working together in a common task with common ideals and purposes. The euphoria in evidence in some demonstrations and sit-ins (for example, the occupation of Stanford's Applied Electronics Laboratory in the spring of 1969) is some indication of the deep intrinsic rewards for participants in political activism around issues whose moral content seems to be absolutely clear and simple. It is important that this kind of communal life and action does not seem to be possible within the framework of the university itself; it is difficult and dangerous *outside* the university (for example, in communes or community action programs); it is relatively easy and highly rewarding *inside* but *against* the university.

12. Of course, for undergraduates and graduate students alike who are locked into school by the draft, the term "involuntary" is not at all metaphorical.

13. For a fuller discussion of the triumph of *laissez-faire* over general education in American universities, see Martin Trow, "Bell, Book and Berkeley," *The American Behavioral Scientist* (May-June, 1968).

14. *The Culture of the University: Governance and Education,* Report of the Study Commission on University Governance (University of California: Berkeley, January 15, 1968). See also my "Conceptions of the University," *American Behavioral Scientist* (May-June, 1969).

15. An example of academic discussion (cant is perhaps too strong a word) on this issue is the following from the pen of the Chancellor of the Minnesota State College System: "Let us admit that, despite differences in age, experience, maturity, and background, our students should be viewed as col-

leagues-in-learning who must be actively and meaningfully involved in shaping all of the institutions of the campus—its curriculum, faculty, social life, administration, learning resources—its total image." G. Theodore Mitau, "Needed: Peacemakers and Social Engineers," *AAUP Bulletin* (Summer 1969), p. 157.

This statement shares with many others on this theme these characteristics: a) it imputes to all students the qualities of "a colleague-in-learning" possessed by only some; b) it recommends a larger role for students in college and university government without either specifying the forms, mechanisms, or possible limits of their participation, or anticipating the probable consequences for the institution; c) it encourages students to make unlimited demands on the faculty which, if (when) not met in full, will surely increase student feelings of frustration and anger.

16. There is already a noticeable withdrawal of participation by academic men from those areas of the university government which are most exposed to student attack. The withdrawal thus far is largely due to changes in the style of "debate," and to a distaste for threats and personal abuse in the gutter language sometimes employed by radical students to whom ordinary civility and rational discourse are contemptible middle-class evasions.

17. I am speaking here chiefly of undergraduates and campus-wide government. In the graduate departments and professional schools, a strong case can be made for participation of graduate students in at least some departmental decisions. But what kind of participation, in what kinds of decisions, will properly vary from department to department (depending on its size, the character of its students, and other factors), and should not be governed by any institution-wide formula or policy.

18. Continued campus disturbances may have even more serious consequences for the political climate of the larger society.

19. I suspect that, in the foreseeable future, institution-wide policies and standards in most multiversities will work more to dilute than to defend scholarship and academic freedom. Under great pressures, university administrators will be tempted to take popular positions on academic issues. For example, one of the few issues on which the New Left and the far right agree is that an overemphasis on research embodied in the doctrine of "publish or perish" is the prime enemy of good teaching in our big universities. University presidents can come out squarely on the side of virtue by instructing academic committees to give greater weight to "teaching effectiveness" in the appointment and promotion of faculty. Some will go a step further and instruct these committees that this is the appropriate place for student evaluations to enter the appointment and promotion procedures.

"Effective teaching" is notoriously hard to assess or even to define. In the present political climate, to stress it further in the assessment of faculty is to put even more pressure on teachers to seek the approval of their students, with subtle but serious implications for academic freedom and the fate of certain controversial subjects. A serious move toward the improvement of undergraduate teaching in the big public universities might start with an improvement in the ratio of teachers to students, which in turn would allow the institution to reduce the very large role of graduate teaching assistants in the undergraduate courses. But that would be expensive, and not nearly so popular.

20. We should also be able to increase the amount and legitimacy *within* the university of "expressive" activities—painting, music, the dance, the performing arts generally—for students prepared to submit themselves to these demanding, though less bookish, disciplines.

For another approach, the Swedes are just beginning to discuss the idea of an "education bank," under which all citizens would have a commitment from the state for one or two years of further (higher) education which they can take at any time during their lives if they choose to leave school during or on completion of their secondary schooling. The Swedes will very shortly also be bringing nearly all their youth to the point of university entrance; they anticipate mass but not universal higher education. An "education bank" would increase the voluntariness of university entrance and deserves consideration in the American context.

POPES AND PEASANTS: ASSUMPTIONS OF ELITIST EDUCATION

Don Robertson and Marion Steele

We would like, in this chapter, to take a look at two basic elitist assumptions upon which the present system is firmly planted. If these assumptions are false, and we believe they are demonstrably so, then the whole edifice of formal education is shaky beyond belief.

Look at the first assumption. Stated simply, the present structure of education assumes that there are qualified experts who "possess" a body of knowledge concerning various accepted academic subjects, and that these experts (teachers) transmit the knowledge to learners (students). While it might be put more elaborately, certainly few would doubt that this is indeed a basic assumption in almost all education in our society. Superficially, it is a truism. But it implies a total model of learning which has hidden consequences that actually undermine the education it purports to carry out.

For a start, it deeply implies that learning is a rather passive process. Of course, all educators routinely give lip service to the idea that education is not passive; but that is rhetoric again. We speak of someone "receiving an education," even of "giving" someone an education. It suggests that you can collect, so to speak, a learning experience by listening to and reading enough information about some subjects. Students are considered vessels to be filled up. And if they don't get filled up, it's their own fault. We flunk out students, not teachers. All of this is foreign to real learning, which can only be an active, dynamic involvement in pursuit of those things one is really interested in.

We're not finished with this first assumption, but it is closely interwoven with the second assumption—that is, that the members of the elite (the experts or teachers) know what should be learned, and have the responsibility not only of providing the knowledge but of arranging it and ordering it for the recipient.

Students are assumed to be incapable of directing their own education. The elite members say what is to be learned, when it is to be learned, how it is to be learned and at what point it is satisfactorily learned. Students are put through a "course" which teachers (and others) have set up. They are channeled through a sequence of "classes" their superiors have decided is the proper route of learning.

If this seems at first an overstatement, consider how we push students to select one of the prescribed routes as soon as possible. Students are urged to select a major, to get through their general educational requirements, to take courses in proper sequence, etcetera. Those who go to college just to hunt and peck for courses that interest them are deemed irresponsible. You are supposed to be pursuing an "educational goal" at all times, not just fooling around with the things that interest you. The upshot of this, however unintended by the benevolent dictators of education, is to make the narrowing down of options a major pressure within the "educational experience." How ridiculous; a learning environment should be a place which expands vistas of thought, opens up human possibilities, and broadens perspectives. People in such a setting must have maximum freedom to explore, to alter goals, and to make firsthand appraisals of the possible fields, goals, and experiences to which they might commit themselves. And we should not confuse this exploring with the traditional forced exposure to a required smattering of liberal arts and science courses. These courses are hopelessly fragmented and few students learn more than enough rhetoric to carry them out of the courses with acceptable grades. A year later, nothing remains but the old notes.

Taken together, these two assumptions provide a bastion of elitist education. Students arrive at college prepared to demonstrate appropriate deference to superiors at all times, to quietly go through their rounds of classes and exams, to suffer the trials and humiliations with the quiet determination of those who know what advantages will be theirs after they get the diploma. Students really can't expect much of themselves, generally, because the expertise, power, and prestige are the monopoly of the experts. And they know it. There are constant reminders. Not only are students inferiors, they are constantly on trial before the superiors in the knowledge factory, right up until the last bluebook is returned by the last instructor with paternalistic blessings.

Students must be patient and obey orders while their wise and benevolent masters fill them up with a "body of knowledge" which officially constitutes an "education." Actually, nobody gets filled up with a body of knowledge in college or graduate school. The whole idea is the purest fantasy—and the purest rhetoric. In truth, few people ever get a firm grasp on a very large proportion of the "subject matter" of even one academic course. Research has shown that 90 percent of course material is lost forever within two days after it is "successfully" completed. Then, too, there are countless special courses for each "discipline," adding up to a total of thousands of courses in large universities. Nobody has a chance of "mastering" even a fraction of the "body of knowledge" in a single academic field (even if there were a good reason for doing so). So it is obviously ridiculous to be constantly forcing people to answer questions about detailed knowledge in each professor's esoteric specialty.

It makes no sense at all, even within the traditional understanding of "liberal arts" education. The ideal of that tradition, supposedly the theoretical foundation of present-day liberal arts colleges, is that people can *select* widely from the various "branches of knowledge" in order to acquire what is useful to them in becoming free, responsible persons. Not a bad idea at all. But few professors have any understanding of the ideal or have any notion how it relates to their own behavior within their professional roles. They don't allow you to select whatever you feel is useful to you from *their* courses. They try to force you to cram into your head (or notebook—which is usually the same thing) all the dull stuff they think comprises the "material" in that "subject."

If you think it through, you will realize that "acquiring" a certain volume of particular bits of knowledge has nothing at all to do with education. (It doesn't really prepare you for a job either, but that's another point.) The vast majority of professors do, in fact, operate from this fallacious understanding of the purpose of education. They will inform you quite confidently that it is their task to transmit the concepts, ideas, facts, theories, etcetera, about a certain area of knowledge—say, Oriental Art History or the American Family System.

So, if you are taking Medieval History, you will be put on trial to show that you can remember the names of a few dozen very old Popes and emperors and wars. If you cannot come up with the "right" percentage of "correct" answers on the spot at one arbitrary time, then you didn't "get the material" and so you don't get credit. Or, if you're lucky, you'll get off with a low grade which will officially proclaim your mediocre performance for eternity. It doesn't matter one whit whether or not you were able to plug into your own perspective some insights or information that is of value—say, you gained a better understanding of some institution which has shaped your own life. It doesn't matter—in terms of the elitist "transmission of knowledge" model of education—how exposure to ideas in courses affects you as a human being.

If the body-of-knowledge nonsense were seriously applied, and professors had to demonstrate that they still "possess" their education (which is perfectly logical based on their own educational practices), probably hardly any of them could qualify for the B.A. degree. Perhaps 98 percent of today's Ph.D.'s would be disqualified if they had to demonstrate "competence" on one language exam again. Not many could "earn" high school diplomas. *Any* one of them could be flunked out in his own field, depending on which people in the field set up the test. So the whole assumption that education consists of the "transmission" of a certain body of knowledge to students is a gigantic bellylaugh. Yet the vast monstrosity of higher education today, including the crippling system of grading, sits firmly on this absurd assumption. Sometimes it hurts when we laugh.

We've already alluded to it briefly, but it must be stressed that one key manifestation of these elitist assumptions is the astounding powerlessness of students. Students have virtually no say in what their own education will consist of. And this they take for granted, for the most part. As usual, the oppressed are collaborators in their own oppression. Students are still openly grateful when you tell them what courses to take and who to see in order to have their programs approved.

A basic principle of any sound educational process (and this is doubly so at the college level) is that those who are "getting educated" be deeply involved in the decision-making about *their* education. There is no doubt in our minds that in any area of college curricula, a class of students, with no prof at all, would learn more and learn it more enjoyably than they do in a typical professor-dominated class. In a short time, they could decide where to go for the information, how to put it together, what experts they might call on for assistance. This would be a truer education because the students would be exploring a field themselves and they would have to determine what was relevant and important and interesting. All the studies on the matter have shown that students acquire at least as much knowledge without a teacher as with one—and they develop much more interest in the subject in the process.

As long as students are in the elitist trap, they learn simply to leave such thinking to the professor. Their job is to get down what he says and memorize what he seems to stress. Students can take scads of courses in a field and be ignorant of the basic perspectives, presuppositions, controversies and questions. Indeed, this is the typical case. You only learn well when you are making your *own* discoveries, never when you are jotting down someone else's stale discoveries.

Most professors literally quake at the thought of students sitting down as equals to work out a learning program—even in their own major fields. Few academic departments in the country allow students to share the power in directing their own educational experience. At Long Beach in 1968, in our department, a student association was formed and a proposal put forward to have students equally represented, with full voting rights in the department meetings. The proposal lost narrowly, and a compromise was effected in which the students would be guaranteed at least one representative for each two faculty members.

Despite the virtual meaninglessness of the student victory, the reactions of some of our colleagues indicated the deep-seated fear of what will happen when elitist monopoly is threatened. We were identified by some of our senior colleagues as "instigators" and a few have made it obvious that they will not even say hello, in passing, to such subversive types as us. With apparent seriousness, some of our colleagues even constructed an elaborate plot in which untenured faculty were said to be manipulating the students so as to gain votes within the department in order to alter the rules of tenure to assure preservation of their own jobs. Now, that is bizarre! We were half expecting to see a Communist conspiracy dredged up. The insult implied in this accusation has, we're sure, not been lost on the students, either. Elitist faculty members apparently do not even consider students capable of making *any* demands on their own behalf; somebody *must be* "manipulating" them.

Most departments and most colleges have never considered giving students a

serious voice in their own education. Most take refuge in bullshit about consultation with students. But we know what that really means in practice. The
course offerings, requirements, and sequences are designed according to the convenience and traditions of professors—not according to the interests of those
whom professors purportedly serve. This immense powerlessness is a direct
manifestation of elitist assumptions—and it is tragically out of tune with the
prerequisites of genuine learning. How can we pretend that colleges exist for
learners? How can we fail to expose such basic contradictions as these?

Another manifestation of these elitist assumptions about education is the unbelievable fragmentation and disunity of the learning situation. We have carved
education into tidy little bundles of units. It is assumed that the person who
fills his grab bag up with the right number of unit bundles has received an education. First, it is absurd to suppose that meaningful learning can take place when
knowledge is so fragmented and arbitrarily channeled. It comes right back to
the "smorgasbord" idea—that is, that profs have all these prepared dishes of educational goodies to be served to the procession of students continuously coming
through the line.

Learning doesn't happen that way. A learning environment must have a built-
in recognition that learners will explore in hundreds of different ways, follow
diversified paths, be influenced in their pursuits by world events, by personal
events, and by current friendships. These are simply not recognized in the "major
program." Seldom are students, in their course work, actually involved with the
questions which are most pressing for them at the time. We almost completely
dismiss the question of interest or motivation. There's little room for these vital
factors in our preprogrammed channels of education. So we erect artificial motivations, extrinsic rewards, which assure that students will keep going to classes
and visiting libraries, even though they do so with a sense of pure drudgery most
of the time.

This fragmentation and obstacle-course discipline effectively keep the lid on
most of the potential "community" of exploration that could emerge in a decent
learning environment. Students are individualized into their own separate set of
courses each semester; they are sent scurrying from class to class. How could
groups of students who deeply share and cooperate and find exhilaration together possibly develop in this routine? One of our top priorities in creating learning
environments would be to make it easy for small communities of learners who
share interests and commitments to find each other and be free to get totally involved in learning together. Instead, we make it impossible. Students are generally made to fear each other at the same time as they are made to fear their
superiors.

If learning environments were free to any significant extent, they would obviously "take off" in many different directions. No two schools would be alike,
no two years would be alike, no two "classes" would be alike. College would be
dynamic, like real learning is. But since the certified experts put their apprentices through a standard "course" of learning, with all of the subtle tendencies to

passivity, we have this amazing uniformity and quietude prevailing. The "image" of most colleges, to the larger public, is primarily in terms of athletic teams, which highlight the motifs of narrow parochialism and competition. Athletic events, significantly, are the main rallying points which provide a temporary, superficial "community" among students at most colleges.

Though he was speaking mainly of the schooling of younger children, the comments of *Look* magazine senior editor George Leonard are insightful:

> If human beings are unique, then any system of fixed scheduling and mass instruction must be insanely inefficient. It may seem tidy and convenient, but that is an illusion, maintained only by pretending that individual differences are not significant and that the human potential is incredibly low—only by giving up on education and concentrating on control. For an educator of courage and flexibility, the free learning situation is not only more educationally efficient but eventually easier to handle. . . . The conventional classroom is quiet and orderly on the surface. The noise and confusion are in the minds of the children.[1]

Leonard elsewhere, in a classic phrase, says, "What energy it takes to turn a torrent into a trickle. . . !" And we add, what an elaborate artifact is erected to channel and tame and control the energies of thousands of potentially creative young people on college campuses! What monstrously misused powers for communication and community go into running this unitized, sanitized pretense of education! What pitiful sincerity and commitment are wasted as professors and students trek through their scheduled rounds of boredom!

This system is as bewildering as it is stifling. Since there is little freedom to explore, little community and little honesty, students are seldom able to get an accurate picture of what is taking place in the college or in their own lives. The boggling array of segmented courses certainly does not contribute to clarity. Nor does the dividing up of one's time and classes and contacts into little parcels of administrative convenience.

Students seldom even get an accurate picture of what they will really be doing in the future work they are presumably preparing for. Most report later that they had no clue, in their academic years, of what they were going into or what the relationship was between the classroom and the world outside. And when it comes to bringing together the learning from the various academic "guilds" into some kind of larger perspective, well, forget it.

Implicit in this fragmented academic arrangement is the idea that synopsis is unimportant, that fitting together pieces of the confused puzzle is of no consequence. We make virtually no provision, in these places of "learning," for students to find shape and sense and unity in their learning. They end up with jumbled fragments of knowledge, most of them never to be used again. And when you challenge this nonsense, somebody pipes up about "adding a few interdisciplinary courses" to the curriculum. What can be expected when there is hardly any contact, except very formally, between faculty members from different departments?

At the very heart of this enslaving elitist system is the teacher-student myth, the notion that there really is a basic, categorical distinction between the repositories (students) and dispensers (teachers) of knowledge. As soon as one party in learning is defined as anything more than a fellow learner, as soon as one party becomes the "authority," education is corrupted. Pretense enters in a big way. The teachers must always project an image which supports their putative wisdom even when admission of their own uncertainty is the only path to learning. Students are continuously made dependent on the teacher's authority; and they don't get weaned. They seldom start hunting, selecting, and chewing for themselves. All they can do is suck. Students are put in awe (or fear) when they should be ridiculing and questioning persistently. And even when students see through the act and perceive the barrenness of a teacher, they know they must hide this revelation from the teacher. Teachers seldom have their ignorance put on display by students; the opposite, of course, is a deeply ingrained folkway of formal education. That, too, is pure elitism. The "masters" must be treated as masters, no matter what the reality is.

There are many more specific forms of dishonesty, such as cheating, which are invariably generated by this kind of structure. But what we are saying is that dishonesty is deeply woven into the very fabric of this system. It is manifested in many ways: in dishonest relationships between teachers and students, in dishonesty about what is actually taking place in classrooms, in dishonesty about the real priorities of the occupants of these buildings, and in dishonesty about the meaning of our prevalent symbols, from grades to diplomas.

The oppressive passivity that results in such an elitist system is reflected in "teachers" as well as "students." Teaching, communicating, inspiring: these should be the central goals of a professor, according to the rhetoric. Research is also a teaching vehicle, it is often said. College professors are paid fairly comfortable salaries—primarily to communicate with students. But what is the reality? The ability to communicate well with students bears almost no relation at all to an academic career. This is so preposterous it should plague the conscience of every college professor. How many good teachers does the average student encounter on his trek through school? Damn few, if any. Professors can be completely unprepared and uninteresting—it is just accepted with a few whimpers after class. Professors can monologue their students to sleep with obsolete lectures—it really makes no difference at all.

Good, creative, involved teaching is no prerequisite to academic advancement. There are as many worthless "full professors" as there are worthless "assistant professors." Graduate schools seldom make any provision for future professors to develop ways of communicating—they too know it just doesn't matter. Teachers never get fired for destroying students' appetites for a potentially exciting subject. We know of no profs who have been canned because they were completely closed to students or completely uninvolved in any learning themselves. In fact, that's precisely the way most profs in the system are.

In most of the "name" institutions, as everyone knows, it matters a hell of a lot to a prof whether he gets some pedantic paper in an arcane professional journal. And it matters everywhere how he plays the academic political games with his colleagues. But it just doesn't make any real difference how he teaches. Many of the big-name professors escape undergraduate teaching altogether; it is a mark of high academic status.[2]

In an elitist educational setting, the superiors get turned off, too. They keep busy moving the wheels of the unit-producing-machine, but they are seldom involved in any exciting relationships or pursuits. A caste system is destructive to everyone in it. What peripheral contact professors have with students outside the classroom is usually trivial and phony. We find that most of the time students come to our offices to find out about grades, or assignments, or deadlines, or some such trivia. It is enough to turn anyone off. Professors come to resent students—resent them for being the way they "have to be" in this kind of system. And students come to resent professors—resent them for being the way they "have to be" in this kind of system.

Passivity is written all over the standard classroom and all over the faces of those who feel obligated to be in it. How could learning possibly be encapsulated within such dull walls, in such short and arbitrary intervals, with such a predominance of uninterested people?

It is significant that, in academia, research and teaching are viewed as two separate areas of one's work. A great deal of verbal stress is put on the close interaction between the two, but you can disregard those words. The getting of knowledge and the giving of knowledge are separated, in mind and practice. Teaching is the "giving" part. Teachers do not see their classrooms as places where they, the teachers themselves, can learn. What if a professor entered a classroom and said, "This is a very confused subject, and I really don't have it worked out very well at all. But there are some interesting questions, and perhaps we can figure out a way to go into those questions together and get some answers"? Then learning might have a chance, depending on a lot of other things, of course.

Even when professors do condescend to describe themselves as something less than omniscient, it is clear that they expect to find further wisdom from other "experts," not from mere students. They do not ask students to help them resolve difficult, intriguing questions. Students get to spend their time answering the trivial exam questions which Professor Pope claims to have definite answers to. With few exceptions this is true, right through college and graduate school. It is directly connected with this permeating elitist model of the educational process. Since teachers do not regard classrooms as the settings in which they can make real learning discoveries, then they must either consider themselves something other than learners or else they know the classroom is not a place where you can really learn. Unfortunately, both are almost always the case. In addition, a higher caste member must always *appear* superior. It always follows that the master is a slave too.

NOTES

1. George B. Leonard, *Education and Ecstasy* (New York: Delta, 1968).
2. This point is documented in a survey made at the University of California at Berkeley, *Education at Berkeley* (Muscatine Report), 1968.

Part VI.
Religious Organization

There are more than two hundred fifty formally recognized religious organizations in the United States. One is Catholic, three are Jewish, and most of the remainder are Protestant. As an organization, the Catholic church is clearly the strongest. Its unified hierarchy (the church is the world's oldest successful bureaucracy), control of considerable (material) resources and its own school system, and its large membership and doctrinal control yield enormous political influence. Most of the other religious organizations are more loosely structured. Many of the Protestant denominations are only weakly coordinated by voluntary ecumenical ties. Some of the denominations as a matter of principle only minimally supervise their ministers, who are free to act more or less as independent, but licensed, professionals.

Religious organizations are seen as a secondary institution because they often act as servants to other institutions. Although there is no established church in America that is structurally linked to other institutions (such as the Anglican Church of England, whose head is the Monarch), the numerous established religious groups do seem to foster an ideology that is used by the major institutions. The state proclaims that we are "One nation under God," and "In God we Trust" is on all of our coins. More directly, ministers administer oaths of office to our politicians, thereby legitimizing them. Christian soldiers (rabbis too) march to real wars as chaplains and support anti-Communist *crusades*. Our "free enterprise system" is sanctified, universities are blessed, and invocations urge our football teams to righteous violence. Nonetheless, religious organizations are not centered about such legitimation, and though they are upsetting to bureaucratic stability, many maverick churchmen have appealed to

347

religious morality and ethics to castigate lay institutions for their in-sensitivity to human needs and social justice. This is often also done by small "radical," less established groups known as sects and cults. There is clearly, then, an ambivalence within religious groups about their legitimating tasks.

Religious orders do provide their followers with services not pro-vided by other institutions. First, they may provide the individual with religious solace and understanding, with a link to the past, fellow believers, and a timeless supernatural order. On the more mundane level, church membership may give purely social benefits—companion-ship, a sense of community belonging, some extracurricular fun and education for the children, low-cost psychotherapy, or a cut-rate country club range of activities. Like schools, churches are also mar-riage markets—people tend to marry coreligionists. Many religious groups have moved increasingly toward this type of social work task, and most have always reached outside their membership to provide welfare services to the disadvantaged, the poor, elderly, and sick.

Table 1 lists the number of members in the major religions. It must be kept in mind here that churches have differing criteria for membership.

Table 1
Church Membership, 1950–1970 (in millions)

	1950	1960	1970
Protestant	51.1	63.7	71.7
Roman Catholic	28.6	42.1	48.2
Jewish	5.0	5.4	5.9
All other Religions	2.1	3.2	5.2
Total	86.8	114.4	131.0

SOURCE: Yearbook of American Churches, 1962–1971.

While Protestants are by far the largest group, they are split organiza-tionally (as well as doctrinally). Even the largest subcategories—Baptist, Methodist, Lutheran, and Presbyterian—are not unitary churches. All have grown since 1950, but the percentage of the pop-ulation claimed as church members has not increased dramatically since 1950, as Table 2 indicates.

Table 2
Church Membership as Percentage of Total Population, 1880–1970

	Percentage		Percentage
1880	20	1940	49
1890	33	1950	57
1920	43	1960	64
1930	47	1970	63

SOURCE: *Yearbook of American Churches, 1962–1971.*

Nor, clearly, has America become *less* religious (in terms of membership) during the twentieth century. Attendance, however, has been declining in recent years. According to Gallup Polls, approximately 49 percent of adults surveyed in 1958 and 43 percent in 1968 claimed that they attended church each week. And many churches are struggling to retain or attract ministers.

The first article in this section, by Robert Bellah, examines what the author calls civil religion. This coexists with, but is separate from, the formal churches. It is made up of "common elements of religious orientation that the great majority of Americans share." References to God in the Kennedy inaugural were in the context of this civil religion, not his private religion, Catholicism. Bellah traces this civil religion back, and finds it clearly evident as a legitimation for the founding of the republic. The God is not Christian, but more of an Old Testament God, with Americans the chosen people in the Promised Land. Lincoln served as the symbolic Christ in the developing religion, and Thanksgiving and Memorial Day "provide an annual ritual calendar for the civil religion." This informal religious tradition, Bellah concludes, even though it can be abused, has been and will continue to be a source of strength for moral action.

Jeffrey K. Hadden deals with the political activity of men occupying formal religious offices. He reports here on the split between the ideology of clergymen—specifically in their support of civil rights—and the sentiments of their parishioners. The difference is an example of a formal organization becoming divorced from its constituency or clients, the people who provide both its finances and its primary reason for existence. This presumably could lead to a number of very damaging outcomes for the churches. Apart from financial losses, they could lose their sense of mission and morale. In addition, the institutional power of the churches would be decreased if the public came to believe that the clergy led no one but themselves.

Institutional decline can also take the form of bureaucratic formality. It is this, according to Edward Heenan, that makes established religion so moribund. He claims that a new religious revival among the young is taking place primarily outside the churches. Disillusionment over the immorality of the Vietnam War was a crowning blow to many idealistic young activists who cannot now support the other outsider—civil religion. Although the new religious movements are subverting formal religions and sanctified state values, Heenan concludes that it remains to be seen whether Jesus will be more than a top pop hit or will reach the narcissistic majority of young people. After all, didn't Judas and Herod have the best parts in *Super Star*?

Suggested Readings

Berger, Peter. *The Sacred Canopy.* New York: Doubleday, 1967.

Glock, Charles, and Stark, Rodney. *Religion and Society in Tension.* Chicago: Rand McNally, 1965.

Hadden, Jeffrey K. *The Gathering Storm in the Churches.* Garden City, N.Y.: Doubleday, 1969.

Heenan, Edward F., ed. *Mystery, Magic and Miracle.* Englewood Cliffs, N. J.: Prentice-Hall, 1973.

Lenski, Gerhard. *The Religious Factor.* Garden City, N. Y.: Doubleday, 1961.

Luckmann, Thomas. *The Invisible Religion.* New York: Macmillan, 1967.

Schneider, Louis, ed. *Religion, Culture and Society.* New York: John Wiley, 1964.

Wilson, Boyan. *Religion in Secular Society.* Baltimore: Penguin, 1969.

Yinger, Milton J. *The Scientific Study of Religion.* New York: Macmillan, 1970.

CIVIL RELIGION
IN AMERICA

Robert N. Bellah

While some have argued that Christianity is the national faith, and others that church and synagogue celebrate only the generalized religion of "the American Way of Life," few have realized that there actually exists alongside of and rather clearly differentiated from the churches an elaborate and well-institutionalized civil religion in America. This article argues not only that there is such a thing, but also that this religion—or perhaps better, this religious dimension—has its own seriousness and integrity and requires the same care in understanding that any other religion does.[1]

The Kennedy Inaugural

Kennedy's inaugural address of 20 January 1961 serves as an example and a clue with which to introduce this complex subject. That address began:

> We observe today not a victory of party but a celebration of free-dom—symbolizing an end as well as a beginning—signifying renewal as well as change. For I have sworn before you and Almighty God the same solemn oath our forebears prescribed nearly a century and three quarters ago.

> The world is very different now. For man holds in his mortal hands the power to abolish all forms of human poverty and to abolish all forms of human life. And yet the same revolutionary beliefs for which our forebears fought are still at issue around the globe—the belief that the rights of man come not from the generosity of the state but from the hand of God.

And it concluded:

> Finally, whether you are citizens of America or of the world, ask of us the same high standards of strength and sacrifice that we shall ask

Reprinted by permission of Robert N. Bellah and *Daedalus,* Journal of the American Academy of Arts and Sciences, Boston, Mass. Winter 1967, *Religion in America.*

of you. With a good conscience our only sure reward, with history
the final judge of our deeds, let us go forth to lead the land we love,
asking His blessing and His help, but knowing that here on earth
God's work must truly be our own.

These are the three places in this brief address in which Kennedy mentioned the
name of God. If we could understand why he mentioned God, the way in which
he did it, and what he meant to say in those three references, we would understand much about American civil religion. But this is not a simple or obvious
task, and American students of religion would probably differ widely in their
interpretation of these passages.

Let us consider first the placing of the three references. They occur in the
two opening paragraphs and in the closing paragraph, thus providing a sort of
frame for the more concrete remarks that form the middle part of the speech.
Looking beyond this particular speech, we would find that similar references to
God are almost invariably to be found in the pronouncements of American presidents on solemn occasions, though usually not in the working messages that the
president sends to Congress on various concrete issues. How, then, are we to interpret this placing of references to God?

It might be argued that the passages quoted reveal the essentially irrelevant
role of religion in the very secular society that is America. The placing of the
references in this speech as well as in public life generally indicates that religion
has "only a ceremonial significance"; it gets only a sentimental nod which serves
largely to placate the more unenlightened members of the community, before a
discussion of the really serious business with which religion has nothing whatever
to do. A cynical observer might even say that an American president has to mention God or risk losing votes. A semblance of piety is merely one of the unwrit-
ten qualifications for the office, a bit more traditional than but not essentially
different from the present-day requirement of a pleasing television personality.

But we know enough about the function of ceremonial and ritual in various
societies to make us suspicious of dismissing something as unimportant because
it is "only a ritual." What people say on solemn occasions need not be taken at
face value, but it is often indicative of deep-seated values and commitments that
are not made explicit in the course of everyday life. Following this line of argument, it is worth considering whether the very special placing of the references to
God in Kennedy's address may not reveal something rather important and serious
about religion in American life.

It might be countered that the very way in which Kennedy made his references
reveals the essentially vestigial place of religion today. He did not refer to any
religion in particular. He did not refer to Jesus Christ, or to Moses, or to the
Christian church; certainly he did not refer to the Catholic Church. In fact, his
only reference was to the concept of God, a word which almost all Americans
can accept but which means so many different things to so many different people
that it is almost an empty sign. Is this not just another indication that in Amer-

ica religion is considered vaguely to be a good thing, but that people care so little about it that it has lost any content whatever? Isn't Eisenhower reported to have said, "Our government makes no sense unless it is founded in a deeply felt religious faith—and I don't care what it is,"[2] and isn't that a complete negation of any real religion?

These questions are worth pursuing because they raise the issue of how civil religion relates to the political society, on the one hand, and to private religious organization, on the other. President Kennedy was a Christian, more specifically a Catholic Christian. Thus, his general references to God do not mean that he lacked a specific religious commitment. But why, then, did he not include some remark to the effect that Christ is the Lord of the world or some indication of respect for the Catholic Church? He did not because these are matters of his own private religious belief and of his relation to his own particular church; they are not matters relevant in any direct way to the conduct of his public office. Others with different religious views and commitments to different churches or denominations are equally qualified participants in the political process. The principle of separation of church and state guarantees the freedom of religious belief and association, but at the same time clearly segregates the religious sphere, which is considered to be essentially private, from the political one.

Considering the separation of church and state, how is a president justified in using the word *God* at all? The answer is that the separation of church and state has not denied the political realm a religious dimension. Although matters of personal religious belief, worship, and association are considered to be strictly private affairs, there are, at the same time, certain common elements of religious orientation that the great majority of Americans share. These have played a crucial role in the development of American institutions and still provide a religious dimension for the whole fabric of American life, including the political sphere. This public religious dimension is expressed in a set of beliefs, symbols, and rituals that I am calling the American civil religion. The inauguration of a president is an important ceremonial event in this religion. It reaffirms, among other things, the religious legitimation of the highest political authority.

Let us look more closely at what Kennedy actually said. First he said, "I have sworn before you and Almighty God the same solemn oath our forebears prescribed nearly a century and three quarters ago." The oath is the oath of office, including the acceptance of the obligation to uphold the Constitution. He swears it before the people (you) and God. Beyond the Constitution, then, the president's obligation extends not only to the people but to God. In American political theory, sovereignty rests, of course, with the people, but implicitly, and often explicitly, the ultimate sovereignty has been attributed to God. This is the meaning of the motto, "In God we trust," as well as the inclusion of the phrase "under God" in the pledge to the flag. What difference does it make that sovereignty belongs to God? Though the will of the people as expressed in majority vote is carefully institutionalized as the operative source of political authority, it is deprived of an ultimate significance. The will of the people is not itself the criterion

in terms of which this will can be judged; it is possible that the people may be
wrong. The president's obligation extends to the higher criterion.

When Kennedy says that "the rights of man come not from the generosity of
the state but from the hand of God," he is stressing this point again. It does not
matter whether the state is the expression of the will of an autocratic monarch
or of the "people"; the rights of man are more basic than any political structure
and provide a point of revolutionary leverage from which any state structure may
be radically altered. That is the basis for his reassertion of the revolutionary significance of America.

But the religious dimension in political life as recognized by Kennedy not only
provides a grounding for the rights of man which makes any form of political ab-
solutism illegitimate, it also provides a transcendent goal for the political process.
This is implied in his final words that "here on earth God's work must truly be
our own." What he means here is, I think, more clearly spelled out in a previous
paragraph, the wording of which, incidentally, has a distinctly Biblical ring:

> Now the trumpet summons us again—not as a call to bear arms,
> though arms we need—not as a call to battle, though embattled we
> are—but a call to bear the burden of a long twilight struggle, year in
> and year out, "rejoicing in hope, patient in tribulation"—a struggle
> against the common enemies of man: tyranny, poverty, disease and
> war itself.

The whole address can be understood as only the most recent statement of a
theme that lies very deep in the American tradition, namely the obligation, both
collective and individual, to carry out God's will on earth. This was the motiva-
ting spirit of those who founded America, and it has been present in every generation since. Just below the surface throughout Kennedy's inaugural address, it
becomes explicit in the closing statement that God's work must be our own.
That this very activist and non-contemplative conception of the fundamental religious obligation, which has been historically associated with the Protestant position, should be enunciated so clearly in the first major statement of the first
Catholic president seems to underline how deeply established it is in the American outlook. Let us now consider the form and history of the civil religious tradition in which Kennedy was speaking.

The Idea of a Civil Religion

The phrase *civil religion* is, of course, Rousseau's. In Chapter 8, Book 4, of
The Social Contract, he outlines the simple dogmas of the civil religion: the existence of God, the life to come, the reward of virtue and the punishment of vice,
and the exclusion of religious intolerance. All other religious opinions are outside the cognizance of the state and may be freely held by citizens. While the
phrase *civil religion* was not used, to the best of my knowledge, by the founding
fathers, and I am certainly not arguing for the particular influence of Rousseau,

it is clear that similar ideas, as part of the cultural climate of the late-eighteenth
century, were to be found among the Americans. For example, Franklin writes
in his autobiography,

> I never was without some religious principles. I never doubted, for
> instance, the existence of the Deity; that he made the world and
> govern'd it by his Providence; that the most acceptable service of God
> was the doing of good to men; that our souls are immortal; and that
> all crime will be punished, and virtue rewarded either here or hereafter.
> These I esteemed the essentials of every religion; and, being to be
> found in all the religions we had in our country, I respected them all,
> tho' with different degrees of respect, as I found them more or less
> mix'd with other articles, which, without any tendency to inspire,
> promote or confirm morality, serv'd principally to divide us, and
> make us unfriendly to one another.

It is easy to dispose of this sort of position as essentially utilitarian in relation to
religion. In Washington's Farewell Address (though the words may be Hamilton's) the utilitarian aspect is quite explicit:

> Of all the dispositions and habits which lead to political prosperity,
> Religion and Morality are indispensable supports. In vain would that
> man claim the tribute of Patriotism, who should labour to subvert
> these great Pillars of human happiness, these firmest props of the
> duties of men and citizens. The mere politician, equally with the
> pious man ought to respect and cherish them. A volume could not
> trace all their connections with private and public felicity. Let it
> simply be asked where is the security for property, for reputation,
> for life, if the sense of religious obligation *desert* the oaths, which are
> the instruments of investigation in Courts of Justice? And let us with
> caution indulge the supposition, that morality can be maintained
> without religion. Whatever may be conceded to the influence of re-
> fined education on minds of peculiar structure, reason and experi-
> ence both forbid us to expect that National morality can prevail in
> exclusion of religious principle.

But there is every reason to believe that religion, particularly the idea of God,
played a constitutive role in the thought of the early American statesmen.

Kennedy's inaugural pointed to the religious aspect of the Declaration of Independence, and it might be well to look at the document a bit more closely. There
are four references to God. The first speaks of the "Laws of Nature and of Nature's God" which entitle any people to be independent. The second is the famous statement that all men "are endowed by their Creator with certain inalien-
able Rights." Here Jefferson is locating the fundamental legitimacy of the new
nation in a conception of "higher law" that is itself based on both classical natural
law and Biblical religion. The third is an appeal to "the Supreme Judge of the

world for the rectitude of our intentions," and the last indicates "a firm reliance on the protection of divine Providence." In these last two references, a Biblical God of history who stands in judgment over the world is indicated.

The intimate relation of these religious notions with the self-conception of the new republic is indicated by the frequency of their appearance in early official documents. For example, we find in Washington's first inaugural address of 30 April 1789:

> It would be peculiarly improper to omit in this first official act my fervent supplications to that Almighty Being who rules over the universe, who presides in the councils of nations, and whose providential aids can supply every defect, that His benediction may consecrate to the liberties and happiness of the people of the United States a Government instituted by themselves for these essential purposes, and may enable every instrument employed in its administration to execute with success the functions allotted to his charge.

> No people can be bound to acknowledge and adore the Invisible Hand which conducts the affairs of man more than those of the United States. Every step by which we have advanced to the character of an independent nation seems to have been distinguished by some token of providential agency. . . .

> The propitious smiles of Heaven can never be expected in a nation that disregards the eternal rules of order and right which Heaven itself has ordained. . . . The preservation of the sacred fire of liberty and the destiny of the republican model of government are justly considered, perhaps, as *deeply*, as *finally*, staked on the experiment intrusted to the hands of the American people.

Nor did these religious sentiments remain merely the personal expression of the president. At the request of both Houses of Congress, Washington proclaimed on October 3 of that same first year as president that November 26 should be "a day of public thanksgiving and prayer," the first Thanksgiving Day under the Constitution.

The words and acts of the founding fathers, especially the first few presidents, shaped the form and tone of the civil religion as it has been maintained ever since. Though much is selectively derived from Christianity, this religion is clearly not itself Christianity. For one thing, neither Washington nor Adams nor Jefferson mentions Christ in his inaugural address; nor do any of the subsequent presidents, although not one of them fails to mention God.[3] The God of the civil religion is not only rather "unitarian," he is also on the austere side, much more related to order, law, and right than to salvation and love. Even though he is somewhat deist in cast, he is by no means simply a watchmaker God. He is actively interested and involved in history, with a special concern for America. Here the analogy has much less to do with natural law than with ancient Israel; the equation of America with Israel in the idea of the "American Israel" is not infrequent.[4] What was implicit in the words of Washington already quoted becomes explicit in Jefferson's second inaugural when he said: "I shall need, too, the favor of that Being in whose hands we are, who led our fathers, as Israel of old, from their native land and planted them in a country flowing with all the necessaries and comforts of life." Europe is Egypt; America, the promised land. God has led his people to establish a new sort of social order that shall be a light unto all the nations.[5]

This theme, too, has been a continuous one in the civil religion. We have already alluded to it in the case of the Kennedy inaugural. We find it again in President Johnson's inaugural address:

> They came here—the exile and the stranger, brave but frightened—to find a place where a man could be his own man. They made a covenant with this land. Conceived in justice, written in liberty, bound in union, it was meant one day to inspire the hopes of all mankind; and it binds us still. If we keep its terms, we shall flourish.

What we have, then, from the earliest years of the republic is a collection of beliefs, symbols, and rituals with respect to sacred things and institutionalized in a collectivity. This religion—there seems no other word for it—while not antithetical to and indeed sharing much in common with Christianity, was neither sectarian nor in any specific sense Christian. At a time when the society was overwhelmingly Christian, it seems unlikely that this lack of Christian reference was meant to spare the feelings of the tiny non-Christian minority. Rather, the civil religion expressed what those who set the precedents felt was appropriate under the circumstances. It reflected their private as well as public views. Nor was the civil religion simply "religion in general." While generality was undoubtedly seen as a virtue by some, as in the quotation from Franklin above, the civil religion was specific enough when it came to the topic of America. Precisely because of this specificity, the civil religion was saved from empty formalism and served as a genuine vehicle of national religious self-understanding.

But the civil religion was not, in the minds of Franklin, Washington, Jefferson, or other leaders, with the exception of a few radicals like Tom Paine, ever felt to be a substitute for Christianity. There was an implicit but quite clear division of function between the civil religion and Christianity. Under the doctrine of religious liberty, an exceptionally wide sphere of personal piety and voluntary social action was left to the churches. But the churches were neither to control the state nor to be controlled by it. The national magistrate, whatever his private religious views, operates under the rubrics of the civil religion as long as he is in his official capacity, as we have already seen in the case of Kennedy. This accommodation was undoubtedly the product of a particular historical moment and of a cultural background dominated by Protestantism of several varieties and by the Enlightenment, but it has survived despite subsequent changes in the cultural and religious climate.

Civil War and Civil Religion

Until the Civil War, the American civil religion focused above all on the event of the Revolution, which was seen as the final act of the Exodus from the old lands across the waters. The Declaration of Independence and the Constitution were the sacred scriptures and Washington the divinely appointed Moses who led his people out of the hands of tyranny. The Civil War, which Sidney Mead calls "the center of American history,"[6] was the second great event that involved the national self-understanding so deeply as to require expression in the civil religion. In 1835, de Tocqueville wrote that the American republic had never really been tried, that victory in the Revolutionary War was more the result of British preoccupation elsewhere and the presence of a powerful ally than of any great military success of the Americans. But in 1861 the time of testing had indeed come. Not only did the Civil War have the tragic intensity of fratricidal strife, but it was one of the bloodiest wars of the nineteenth century; the loss of life was far greater than any previously suffered by Americans.

The Civil War raised the deepest questions of national meaning. The man who not only formulated but in his own person embodied its meaning for Americans was Abraham Lincoln. For him the issue was not in the first instance slavery but "whether that nation, or any nation so conceived, and so dedicated, can long endure." He had said in Independence Hall in Philadelphia on 22 February 1861:

> All the political sentiments I entertain have been drawn, so far as I
> have been able to draw them, from the sentiments which originated
> in and were given to the world from this Hall. I have never had a feel-
> ing, politically, that did not spring from the sentiments embodied in
> the Declaration of Independence.[7]

The phrases of Jefferson constantly echo in Lincoln's speeches. His task was, first of all, to save the Union—not for America alone but for the meaning of America to the whole world so unforgettably etched in the last phrase of the Gettysburg Address.

But inevitably the issue of slavery as the deeper cause of the conflict had to be faced. In the second inaugural, Lincoln related slavery and the war in an ultimate perspective:

> If we shall suppose that American slavery is one of those offenses
> which, in the providence of God, must needs come, but which, hav-
> ing continued through His appointed time, He now wills to remove,
> and that He gives to both North and South this terrible war as the
> woe due to those by whom the offense came, shall we discern therein

any departure from those divine attributes which the believers in a living God always ascribe to Him? Fondly do we hope, fervently do we pray, that this mighty scourge of war may speedily pass away. Yet, if God wills that it continue until all the wealth piled by the bondsman's two hundred and fifty years of unrequited toil shall be sunk, and until every drop of blood drawn with the lash shall be paid by another drawn with the sword, as was said three thousand years ago, so still it must be said "the judgements of the Lord are true and righteous altogether."

But he closes on a note if not of redemption then of reconciliation—"With malice toward none, with charity for all."

With the Civil War, a new theme of death, sacrifice, and rebirth enters the civil religion. It is symbolized in the life and death of Lincoln. Nowhere is it stated more vividly than in the Gettysburg Address, itself part of the Lincolnian "New Testament" among the civil scriptures. Robert Lowell has recently pointed out the "insistent use of birth images" in this speech explicitly devoted to "these honored dead": "brought forth," "conceived," "created," "a new birth of freedom." He goes on to say:

> The Gettysburg Address is a symbolic and sacramental act. Its verbal quality is resonance combined with a logical, matter of fact, prosaic brevity. . . . In his words, Lincoln symbolically died, just as the Union soldiers really died—and as he himself was soon really to die. By his words, he gave the field of battle a symbolic significance that it had lacked. For us and our country, he left Jefferson's ideals of freedom and equality joined to the Christian sacrificial act of death and rebirth. I believe this is a meaning that goes beyond sect or religion and beyond peace and war, and is now part of our lives as a challenge, obstacle and hope.[8]

Lowell is certainly right in pointing out the Christian quality of the symbolism here, but he is also right in quickly disavowing any sectarian implication. The earlier symbolism of the civil religion had been Hebraic without being in any specific sense Jewish. The Gettysburg symbolism (". . . those who here gave their lives, that that nation might live") is Christian without having anything to do with the Christian church.

The symbolic equation of Lincoln with Jesus was made relatively early. Herndon, who had been Lincoln's law partner, wrote:

> For fifty years God rolled Abraham Lincoln through his fiery furnace. He did it to try Abraham and to purify him for his purposes. This made Mr. Lincoln humble, tender, forbearing, sympathetic to suffering, kind, sensitive, tolerant; broadening, deepening and widening his whole nature; making him the noblest and loveliest character since Jesus Christ. . . . I believe that Lincoln was God's chosen one.[9]

With the Christian archetype in the background, Lincoln, "our martyred president," was linked to the war dead, those who "gave the last full measure of devotion." The theme of sacrifice was indelibly written into the civil religion.

The new symbolism soon found both physical and ritualistic expression. The great number of the war dead required the establishment of a number of national cemeteries. Of these, the Gettysburg National Cemetery, which Lincoln's famous address served to dedicate, has been overshadowed only by the Arlington National Cemetery. Begun somewhat vindictively on the Lee estate across the river from Washington, partly with the end that the Lee family could never reclaim it,[10] it has subsequently become the most hallowed monument of the civil religion. Not only was a section set aside for the Confederate dead, but it has received the dead of each succeeding American war. It is the site of the one important new symbol to come out of World War I, the Tomb of the Unknown Soldier; more recently it has become the site of the tomb of another martyred president and its symbolic eternal flame.

Memorial Day, which grew out of the Civil War, gave ritual expression to the themes we have been discussing. As Lloyd Warner has so brilliantly analyzed it, the Memorial Day observance, especially in the towns and smaller cities of America, is a major event for the whole community involving a rededication to the martyred dead, to the spirit of sacrifice, and to the American vision.[11] Just as Thanksgiving Day, which incidentally was securely institutionalized as an annual national holiday only under the presidency of Lincoln, serves to integrate the family into the civil religion, so Memorial Day has acted to integrate the local community into the national cult. Together with the less overtly religious Fourth of July and the more minor celebrations of Veterans Day and the birthdays of Washington and Lincoln, these two holidays provide an annual ritual calendar for the civil religion. The public-school system serves as a particularly important context for the cultic celebration of the civil rituals.

The Civil Religion Today

In reifying and giving a name to something that, though pervasive enough when you look at it, has gone on only semiconsciously, there is risk of severely distorting the data. But the reification and the naming have already begun. The religious critics of "religion in general," or of the "religion of the 'American Way of Life,' " or of "American Shinto" have really been talking about the civil religion. As usual in religious polemic, they take as criteria the best in their own religious tradition and as typical the worst in the tradition of the civil religion. Against these critics, I would argue that the civil religion at its best is a genuine apprehension of universal and transcendent religious reality as seen in or, one could almost say, as revealed through the experience of the American people. Like all religions, it has suffered various deformations and demonic distortions. At its best, it has neither been so general that it has lacked incisive relevance to the American scene nor so particular that it has placed American society above universal human values. I am not at all convinced that the leaders of the churches have consistently represented a higher level of religious insight than the spokes-men of the civil religion. Reinhold Niebuhr has this to say of Lincoln, who never joined a church and who certainly represents civil religion at its best:

> An analysis of the religion of Abraham Lincoln in the context of the traditional religion of his time and place and of its polemical use on the slavery issue, which corrupted religious life in the days before and during the Civil War, must lead to the conclusion that Lincoln's reli-gious convictions were superior in depth and purity to those, not only of the political leaders of this day, but of the religious leaders of the era.[12]

Perhaps the real animus of the religious critics has been not so much against the civil religion in itself but against its pervasive and dominating influence within the sphere of church religion. As S. M. Lipset has recently shown, American reli-gion at least since the early-nineteenth century has been predominantly activist, moralistic, and social rather than contemplative, theological, or innerly spiritual.[13] De Tocqueville spoke of American church religion as "a political institution which powerfully contributes to the maintenance of a democratic republic among the Americans"[14] by supplying a strong moral consensus amidst continuous poli-tical change. Henry Bargy in 1902 spoke of American church religion as "la poésie du civisme."[15]

It is certainly true that the relation between religion and politics in America has been singularly smooth. This is in large part due to the dominant tradition. As de Tocqueville wrote:

> The greatest part of British America was peopled by men who, after having shaken off the authority of the Pope, acknowledged no other religious supremacy: they brought with them into the New World a form of Christianity which I cannot better describe than by styling it a democratic and republican religion.[16]

The churches opposed neither the Revolution nor the establishment of democra-tic institutions. Even when some of them opposed the full institutionalization of religious liberty, they accepted the final outcome with good grace and without nostalgia for an *ancien régime*. The American civil religion was never anticlerical or militantly secular. On the contrary, it borrowed selectively from the religious tradition in such a way that the average American saw no conflict between the two. In this way, the civil religion was able to build up without any bitter strug-gle with the church powerful symbols of national solidarity and to mobilize deep levels of personal motivation for the attainment of national goals.

Such an achievement is by no means to be taken for granted. It would seem that the way it is solved or not solved will have repercussions in many spheres. One needs only to think of France to see how differently things can go. The French Revolution was anticlerical to the core and attempted to set up an anti-

Christian civil religion. Throughout modern French history, the chasm between traditional Catholic symbols and the symbolism of 1789 has been immense.

American civil religion is still very much alive. Just three years ago we participated in a vivid reenactment of the sacrifice theme in connection with the funeral of our assassinated president. The American Israel theme is clearly behind both Kennedy's New Frontier and Johnson's Great Society. Let me give just one recent illustration of how the civil religion serves to mobilize support for the attainment of national goals. On 15 March 1965 President Johnson went before Congress to ask for a strong voting-rights bill. Early in the speech he said:

> Rarely are we met with the challenge, not to our growth or abundance, or our welfare or our security—but rather to the values and the purposes and the meaning of our beloved nation.

> The issue of equal rights for American Negroes is such an issue. And should we defeat every enemy, and should we double our wealth and conquer the stars and still be unequal to this issue, then we will have failed as a people and as a nation.

> For with a country as with a person, "What is a man profited, if he shall gain the whole world, and lose his own soul?"

And in conclusion he said:

> Above the pyramid on the great seal of the United States it says in Latin, "God has favored our undertaking."

> God will not favor everything that we do. It is rather our duty to divine his will. I cannot help but believe that He truly understands and that He really favors the undertaking that we begin here tonight.[17]

The civil religion has not always been invoked in favor of worthy causes. On the domestic scene, an American Legion type of ideology that fuses God, country, and flag has been used to attack nonconformist and liberal ideas and groups of all kinds. Still, it has been difficult to use the words of Jefferson and Lincoln to support special interests and undermine personal freedom. The defenders of slavery before the Civil War came to reject the thinking of the Declaration of Independence. Some of the most consistent of them turned against not only Jeffersonian democracy but Reformation religion; they dreamed of a South dominated by medieval chivalry and divine-right monarchy.[18] For all the overt religiosity of the radical right today, their relation to the civil religious consensus is tenuous, as when the John Birch Society attacks the central American symbol of Democracy itself.

With respect to America's role in the world, the dangers of distortion are greater and the built-in safeguards of the tradition weaker. The theme of the American Israel was used, almost from the beginning, as a justification for the shameful treatment of the Indians so characteristic of our history. It can be overtly or implicitly linked to the idea of manifest destiny which has been used to legitimate several adventures in imperialism since the early-nineteenth century. Never has the danger been greater than today. The issue is not so much one of imperial expansion, of which we are accused, as of the tendency to assimilate all governments or parties in the world which support our immediate policies or call upon our help by invoking the notion of free institutions and democratic values. Those nations that are for the moment "on our side" become "the free world." A repressive and unstable military dictatorship in South Viet-Nam becomes "the free people of South Viet-Nam and their government." It is then part of the role of America as the New Jerusalem and "the last hope of earth" to defend such governments with treasure and eventually with blood. When our soldiers are actually dying, it becomes possible to consecrate the struggle further by invoking the great theme of sacrifice. For the majority of the American people who are unable to judge whether the people in South Viet-Nam (or wherever) are "free like us," such arguments are convincing. Fortunately President Johnson has been less ready to assert that "God has favored our undertaking" in the case of Viet-Nam than with respect to civil rights. But others are not so hesitant. The civil religion has exercised long-term pressure for the humane solution of our greatest domestic problem, the treatment of the Negro American. It remains to be seen how relevant it can become for our role in the world at large, and whether we can effectually stand for "the revolutionary beliefs for which our forebears fought," in John F. Kennedy's words.

The civil religion is obviously involved in the most pressing moral and political issues of the day. But it is also caught in another kind of crisis, theoretical and theological, of which it is at the moment largely unaware. "God" has clearly been a central symbol in the civil religion from the beginning and remains so today. This symbol is just as central to the civil religion as it is to Judaism or Christianity. In the late-eighteenth century this posed no problem; even Tom Paine, contrary to his detractors, was not an atheist. From left to right and regardless of church or sect, all could accept the idea of God. But today, as even *Time* has recognized, the meaning of the word *God* is by no means so clear or so obvious. There is no formal creed in the civil religion. We have had a Catholic president; it is conceivable that we could have a Jewish one. But could we have an agnostic president? Could a man with conscientious scruples about using the word *God* the way Kennedy and Johnson have used it be elected chief magistrate of our country? If the whole God symbolism requires reformulation, there will be obvious consequences for the civil religion, consequences perhaps of liberal alienation and of fundamentalist ossification that have not so far been prominent in this realm. The civil religion has been a point of articulation between the profoundest commitments of the Western religious and philosophical tradition and the common beliefs of ordinary Americans. It is not too soon to consider how the deepening theological crisis may affect the future of this articulation.

The Third Time of Trial

In conclusion it may be worthwhile to relate the civil religion to the most serious situation that we as Americans now face, what I call the third time of trial. The first time of trial had to do with the question of independence, whether we should or could run our own affairs in our own way. The second time of trial was over the issue of slavery, which in turn was only the most salient aspect of the more general problem of the full institutionalization of democracy within our country. This second problem we are still far from solving though we have some notable successes to our credit. But we have been overtaken by a third great problem which has led to a third great crisis, in the midst of which we stand. This is the problem of responsible action in a revolutionary world, a world seeking to attain many of the things, material and spiritual, that we have already attained. Americans have, from the beginning, been aware of the responsibility and the significance our republican experiment has for the whole world. The first internal political polarization in the new nation had to do with our attitude toward the French Revolution. But we were small and weak then, and "foreign entanglements" seemed to threaten our very survival. During the last century, our relevance for the world was not forgotten, but our role was seen as purely exemplary. Our democratic republic rebuked tyranny by merely existing. Just after World War I we were on the brink of taking a different role in the world, but once again we turned our back.

Since World War II the old pattern has become impossible. Every president since Roosevelt has been groping toward a new pattern of action in the world, one that would be consonant with our power and our responsibilities. For Truman and for the period dominated by John Foster Dulles that pattern was seen to be the great Manichaean confrontation of East and West, the confrontation of democracy and "the false philosophy of Communism" that provided the structure of Truman's inaugural address. But with the last years of Eisenhower and with the successive two presidents, the pattern began to shift. The great problems came to be seen as caused not solely by the evil intent of any one group of men, but as stemming from much more complex and multiple sources. For Kennedy, it was not so much a struggle against particular men as against "the common enemies of man: tyranny, poverty, disease and war itself."

But in the midst of this trend toward a less primitive conception of ourselves and our world, we have somehow, without anyone really intending it, stumbled into a military confrontation where we have come to feel that our honor is at stake. We have in a moment of uncertainty been tempted to rely on our overwhelming physical power rather than on our intelligence, and we have, in part, succumbed to this temptation. Bewildered and unnerved when our terrible power fails to bring immediate success, we are at the edge of a chasm the depth of which no man knows.

I cannot help but think of Robinson Jeffers, whose poetry seems more apt now than when it was written, when he said:

> Unhappy country, what wings you have! . . .
> Weep (it is frequent in human affairs), weep for
>   the terrible magnificence of the means,
> The ridiculous incompetence of the reasons, the
>   bloody and shabby
> Pathos of the result.

But as so often before in similar times, we have a man of prophetic stature, without the bitterness or misanthropy of Jeffers, who, as Lincoln before him, calls this nation to its judgment:

> When a nation is very powerful but lacking in self-confidence, it is likely to behave in a manner that is dangerous both to itself and to others.

> Gradually but unmistakably, America is succumbing to that arrogance of power which has afflicted, weakened and in some cases destroyed great nations in the past.

> If the war goes on and expands, if that fatal process continues to accelerate until America becomes what it is not now and never has been, a seeker after unlimited power and empire, then Vietnam will have had a mighty and tragic fallout indeed.

> I do not believe that will happen. I am very apprehensive but I still remain hopeful, and even confident, that America, with its humane and democratic traditions, will find the wisdom to match its power.[19]

Without an awareness that our nation stands under higher judgment, the tradition of the civil religion would be dangerous indeed. Fortunately, the prophetic voices have never been lacking. Our present situation brings to mind the Mexican-American war that Lincoln, among so many others, opposed. The spirit of civil disobedience that is alive today in the civil rights movement and the opposition to the Viet-Nam war was already clearly outlined by Henry David Thoreau when he wrote, "If the law is of such a nature that it requires you to be an agent of injustice to another, then I say, break the law." Thoreau's words, "I would remind my countrymen that they are men first, and Americans at a late and convenient hour,"[20] provide an essential standard for any adequate thought and action in our third time of trial. As Americans, we have been well favored in the world, but it is as men that we will be judged.

Out of the first and second times of trial have come, as we have seen, the major symbols of the American civil religion. There seems little doubt that a successful negotiation of this third time of trial—the attainment of some kind of viable and coherent world order—would precipitate a major new set of symbolic forms. So far the flickering flame of the United Nations burns too low to be the focus of a cult, but the emergence of a genuine trans-national sovereignty would certainly change this. It would necessitate the incorporation of vital international symbolism into our civil religion, or, perhaps a better way of putting it, it would result in American civil religion becoming simply one part of a new civil religion of the world. It is useless to speculate on the form such a civil religion might take, though it obviously would draw on religious traditions beyond the sphere of Biblical religion alone. Fortunately, since the American civil religion is not the worship of the American nation but an understanding of the American experience in the light of ultimate and universal reality, the reorganization entailed by such a new situation need not disrupt the American civil religion's continuity. A world civil religion could be accepted as a fulfillment and not a denial of American civil religion. Indeed, such an outcome has been the eschatological hope of American civil religion from the beginning. To deny such an outcome would be to deny the meaning of America itself.

Behind the civil religion at every point lie Biblical archetypes: Exodus, Chosen People, Promised Land, New Jerusalem, Sacrificial Death and Rebirth. But it is also genuinely American and genuinely new. It has its own prophets and its own martyrs, its own sacred events and sacred places, its own solemn rituals and symbols. It is concerned that America be a society as perfectly in accord with the will of God as men can make it, and a light to all the nations.

It has often been used and is being used today as a cloak for petty interests and ugly passions. It is in need—as is any living faith—of continual reformation, of being measured by universal standards. But it is not evident that it is incapable of growth and new insight.

It does not make any decision for us. It does not remove us from moral ambiguity, from being, in Lincoln's fine phrase, an "almost chosen people." But it is a heritage of moral and religious experience from which we still have much to learn as we formulate the decisions that lie ahead.

NOTES

1. Why something so obvious should have escaped serious analytical attention is in itself an interesting problem. Part of the reason is probably the controversial nature of the subject. From the earliest years of the nineteenth century, conservative religious and political groups have argued that Christianity is, in fact, the national religion. Some of them have from time to time and as recently as the 1950s proposed constitutional amendments that would explicitly recognize the sovereignty of Christ. In defending the doctrine of separation of church and state, opponents of such groups have denied that the national polity has, intrinsically, anything to do with religion at all. The moderates on this issue have insisted that the American state has taken a permissive and indeed supportive attitude toward religious groups (tax exemption, et cetera), thus favoring religion but still missing the positive institutionalization with which I am concerned. But part of the reason this issue has been left in obscurity is certainly due to the peculiarly Western concept of "religion" as denoting a single type of collectivity of which an individual can be a member of one and only one at a time. The Durkheimian notion that every group has a religious dimension, which would be seen as obvious

in southern or eastern Asia, is foreign to us. This obscures the recognition of such dimensions in our society.

2. Quoted in Will Herberg, *Protestant-Catholic-Jew* (Garden City, N. Y.: Doubleday, 1956), p. 97.

3. God is mentioned or referred to in all inaugural addresses but Washington's second, which is a very brief (two paragraphs) and perfunctory acknowledgment. It is not without interest that the actual word *God* does not appear until Monroe's second inaugural, 5 March 1821. In his first inaugural, Washington refers to God as "that Almighty Being who rules the universe," "Great Author of every public and private good," "Invisible Hand," and "benign Parent of the Human Race." John Adams refers to God as "Providence," "Being who is supreme over all," "Patron of Order," "Fountain of Justice," and "Protector in all ages of the world of virtuous liberty." Jefferson speaks of "that Infinite Power which rules the destinies of the universe," and "that Being in whose hands we are." Madison speaks of "that Almighty Being whose power regulates the destiny of nations," and "Heaven." Monroe uses "Providence" and "the Almighty" in his first inaugural and finally "Almighty God" in his second. See, *Inaugural Addresses of the Presidents of the United States from George Washington 1789 to Harry S. Truman 1949,* 82d Congress, 2d Session, House Document No. 540, 1952.

4. For example, Abiel Abbot, pastor of the First Church in Haverhill, Massachusetts, delivered a Thanksgiving sermon in 1799, *Traits of Resemblance in the People of the United States of America to Ancient Israel,* in which he said, "It has been often remarked that the people of the United States come nearer to a parallel with Ancient Israel, than any other nation upon the globe. Hence OUR AMERICAN ISRAEL is a term frequently used; and common consent allows it apt and proper." Cited in Hans Kohn, *The Idea of Nationalism* (New York: Macmillan, 1944), p. 665.

5. That the Mosaic analogy was present in the minds of leaders at the very moment of the birth of the republic is indicated in the designs proposed by Franklin and Jefferson for a seal of the United States of America. Together with Adams, they formed a committee of three delegated by the Continental Congress on July 4, 1776, to draw up the new device. "Franklin proposed as the device Moses lifting up his wand and dividing the Red Sea while Pharaoh was overwhelmed by its waters, with the motto 'Rebellion to tyrants is obedience to God.' Jefferson proposed the children of Israel in the wilderness 'led by a cloud by day and a pillar of fire at night.' " Anson Phelps Stokes, *Church and State in the United States,* Vol. 1 (New York: Harper, 1950), pp. 467–468.

6. Sidney Mead, *The Lively Experiment* (New York, 1963), p. 12.

7. Quoted by Arthur Lehman Goodhart in Allan Nevins (ed.), *Lincoln and the Gettysburg Address* (Urbana, Ill.: University of Illinois, 1964), p. 39.

8. *Ibid.,* "On the Gettysburg Address," pp. 88–89.

9. Quoted in Sherwood Eddy, *The Kingdom of God and the American Dream* (New York, 1941), p. 162.

10. Karl Decker and Angus McSween, *Historic Arlington* (Washington, D.C.: Decker & McSween, 1892), pp. 60–67.

11. How extensive the activity associated with Memorial Day can be is indicated by Warner: "The sacred symbolic behavior of Memorial Day, in which

scores of the town's organizations are involved, is ordinarily divided into four periods. During the year separate rituals are held by many of the associations for their dead, and many of these activities are connected with later Memorial Day events. In the second phase, preparations are made during the last three or four weeks for the ceremony itself, and some of the associations perform public rituals. The third phase consists of scores of rituals held in all the cemeteries, churches, and halls of the associations. These rituals consist of speeches and highly ritualized behavior. They last for two days and are climaxed by the fourth and last phase, in which all the separate celebrants gather in the center of the business district on the afternoon of Memorial Day. The separate organizations, with their members in uniform or with fitting insignia, march through the town, visit the shrines and monuments of the hero dead, and, finally, enter the cemetery. Here dozens of ceremonies are held, most of them highly symbolic and formalized." During these various ceremonies Lincoln is continually referred to and the Gettysburg Address recited many times. W. Lloyd Warner, *American Life* (Chicago: University of Chicago Press, 1953), pp. 8–9.

12.   Reinhold Niebuhr, "The Religion of Abraham Lincoln," in Nevins (ed.), *op. cit.*, p. 72. William J. Wolfe of the Episcopal Theological School in Cambridge, Massachusetts, has written: "Lincoln is one of the greatest theologians of America—not in the technical meaning of producing a system of doctrine, certainly not as the defender of some one denomination, but in the sense of seeing the hand of God intimately in the affairs of nations. Just so the prophets of Israel criticized the events of their day from the perspective of the God who is concerned for history and who reveals His will within it. Lincoln now stands among God's latter-day prophets." *The Religion of Abraham Lincoln* (New York, 1963), p. 24.

13.   Seymour Martin Lipset, "Religion and American Values," Chapter 4, *The First New Nation* (New York: Basic Books, 1963).

14.   Alexis de Tocqueville, *Democracy in America*, Vol. 1 (New York, 1954), p. 310.

15.   Henry Bargy, *La Religion dans la Société aux États-Unis* (Paris, 1902), p. 31.

16.   De Tocqueville, *op. cit.*, p. 311. Later he says, "In the United States even the religion of most of the citizens is republican, since it submits the truths of the other world to private judgment, as in politics the care of their temporal interests is abandoned to the good sense of the people. Thus every man is allowed freely to take that road which he thinks will lead him to heaven, just as the law permits every citizen to have the right of choosing his own government" (p. 436).

17.   U. S., *Congressional Record*, House, 15 March 1965, pp. 4924, 4926.

18.   See Louis Hartz, "The Feudal Dream of the South," Part 4, Louis Hartz, *The Liberal Tradition in America* (New York: Harcourt Brace Jovanovich, Inc., 1955).

19.   Speech of Senator J. William Fulbright of 28 April 1966, as reported in *The New York Times*, 29 April 1966.

20.   Quoted in Yehoshua Arieli, *Individualism and Nationalism in American Ideology* (Cambridge, Mass.: Harvard University Press, 1964), p. 274.

CLERGY INVOLVEMENT
IN CIVIL RIGHTS

Jeffrey K. Hadden

The record of the American churches in the struggle to achieve civil rights is, at best, ambiguous. To deny, as some critics have, that the churches have played any positive role in the struggle for social justice in this country is demonstrably false and a significant distortion of history. However, the balance of evidence is much less on the side of the angels than many of those associated with the churches would like to believe. The late Robert Spike, who, in his role as Director of the National Council of Churches' Commission of Religion and Race, did much to draw the churches into the struggle, was not far from the truth when he wrote: "The outstanding fact about the churches is that with some major exceptions they have aided and abetted the Anglo-Saxon white conspiracy over the years."[1]

Among many kinds of evidence, one fact stands out as a compelling indictment of the churches' role in the struggle for social justice: those who are involved in religious institutions are no less prejudiced or racist than those who are uninvolved. In fact, those who are most involved in the institutional life of the church and personal expressions of pietism are somewhat more prejudiced than those who are less involved or not involved at all.[2] This is a reality that cannot be rationalized or defined away. The fact of the matter remains that religious leaders have not been very successful in convincing their constituency that the Gospel has something to do with brotherhood, love, and justice.

In juxtaposition to this reality is the Gospel's interpretation in the lives of some of the clergy themselves. The symbol of the clerical collar in the picket line or protest march became a central part of the imagery of the civil rights struggle during the 1960s. But just as certainly as there has been clergy involvement in the struggle for social justice during the past decade, so, too, has there been opposition to this involvement—so much so that the issue threatens to tear the churches apart during the coming decade.

Reprinted from "Clergy Involvement in Civil Rights" by Jeffrey K. Hadden in volume no. 387 of *The Annals of the American Academy of Political and Social Science.* ©1970, by The American Academy of Political and Social Science. Used by permission of the author and publisher.

All of this has not occurred in a vacuum or a sea of tranquility. Internally, the churches were facing the interlocking crises of meaning and purpose, belief and authority, long before the civil rights movement came along.[3] What the civil rights struggle did was to bring all of these things to a head.

Clergy have been in the process of recognizing a disparity between their doctrines and practices for a long time. For many clergymen, the civil rights issue emerged as a crystal-clear moral issue. They could no longer preach brotherhood and love while ignoring the plight of black Americans. At first, only a few strayed from their pulpits to join in the front ranks of the movement. But their numbers grew, and the institutional response increased with the creation of hundreds of commissions and committees on religion and race. Clergy were marching and organizing all over the country. The Selma march in 1965 drew several thousand clergy. Although less courageous than many acts of protest engaged in by clergy, this was, perhaps, the largest confession of guilt by professional leaders in the entire history of Christendom. But throughout the decade, church involvement in the civil rights struggle was coterminous with clergy involvement. With few exceptions, church laymen were not there.

Clergy involvement in the civil rights struggle has made dramatic journalism. Many were beaten by ugly mobs and Gestapolike police. Hundreds were hauled off to jail; a few gave their lives; and an indeterminate number lost their pulpits because their words and deeds were too strong for the members of their congregations who wished to occupy comfortable pews in a sanctuary which they had created in order to escape from the world.

Journalistic interest, however, was not matched by an equal enthusiasm among social scientists for studying the dynamics of this unprecedented involvement of clergy. By midway through the decade, only one team of social scientists had completed a systematic study of the role of clergy and the church in the civil rights struggle.[4]

My own interest in the involvement of clergy in the civil rights movement emerged in late 1964, shortly after I had agreed to work with the late Kenneth Underwood on the Danforth Study of Campus Ministries.[5] Unfortunately, many of my insights came too late to enable me to ask many of the right questions in the national survey that we sent to over ten thousand campus and parish clergymen in six major Protestant denominations in early 1965. Fortunately, however, Underwood's keen insight into the significance of these developments led him to permit me to utilize the study's resources, at his own personal sacrifice, in ways that were not central to the task that he was charged with completing for the Foundation. As a result, it was possible to move our understanding of the clergyman's role in the civil rights struggle beyond the speculations of journalism and, at the same time, to see this phenomenon in the context of the broader struggles that are taking place in the churches.

Attitudes

Clergy, as a group, are probably more deeply concerned about civil rights and social justice than any other group in our society—including students. In 1965 only 7 percent of the Protestant clergy in this country said that they basically disapproved of the civil rights movement. In sharp contrast, 44 percent of the adult Protestant population disapproved of the civil rights movement.[6] Two-thirds of the clergy indicated that they were sympathetic with Northern ministers and students who were going South to work for civil rights, while only one-third of their laity felt this way. More than four-fifths of the laity as compared with one-fifth of the clergy agreed with the stereotype of the Negro as carefree, lazy, and irresponsible. More than three years later, nearly half of the college seniors in America agreed with this blatant stereotype.[7]

In December 1966, Glenn Trimble asked delegates to the National Council of Churches Triennial Assembly how they felt about the rate of progress toward racial integration in the United States.[8] Only 6 percent of the clergy responded "too fast," and more than two-thirds said "not fast enough." A few weeks earlier, pollster Lou Harris had asked the same question to the American public. In dramatic contrast, 70 percent of the white sample said that racial integration was moving too fast, and only 4 percent felt that the progress was not fast enough.

These are but a few of many examples that show the attitudinal differences of clergy and lay populations of America on the civil rights issue. On every aspect, clergy express far more liberal views than laity. But the evidence also indicates that the distance between clergy and laity is very great on a whole variety of issues. For example, in 1968, Stanford political scientist Harold Quinley found dramatic differences between clergy and laity on the Vietnam war issue.[9] Quinley found 57 percent of the clergy in California favoring a halt to the bombing of North Vietnam, while only 21 percent of the public favored this position. Similarly, on a five-item hawk-dove scale, he found that the general public was two and a half times more hawkish than the clergy.

Although clergy have developed a social consciousness that will not permit them to compartmentalize their general views of social justice from specific applications in matters such as race, laity have not. Among clergy, age and theological orientation are important concomitants of attitudes on civil rights, as well as on other social issues. Younger clergy tend to be more liberal than their older colleagues. Clergy who describe themselves as theologically liberal or neo-orthodox are more sympathetic toward civil rights than are clergy whose theological orientation is conservative or fundamentalist. Younger clergy are more likely to be liberal or neo-orthodox in their theological outlook. When the relative impact of age and theological position were controlled, it was found that both do make a difference, but that theological position is the more important predictor.

Among laymen, we found that the younger tended to be more liberal on very general statements about civil rights, but as the statements became more specific in content, they tended to respond more like older age groups.[10] Using an index of biblical literalism, which, for clergy, correlated very highly with their own self-perception, we found essentially no relationship among laity between religious beliefs and attitudes toward civil rights. In other words, as clergy move away from a literalist theological orientation, there is a very strong tendency for them to become more liberal about civil rights and other social issues. However, this relationship does not hold for laity.

While laity affirm belief in the basic principles of the American Creed—freedom, justice, and equality of opportunity—they reject the applications of this creed to Negroes and other minority groups. Moreover, the large majority reject the legitimacy of the clergyman's role in the struggle for social justice. The following responses to a national survey that I conducted in 1967 illustrate the process of compartmentalization of *general* and *specific* views:

Item	*Agreeing (%)*
The best mark of a person's religiousness is the degree of his concern for others.	86
Clergymen have a responsibility to speak out as the moral conscience of this nation.	82
Clergymen who participate in demonstrations and picketing do more harm than good for the cause they support.	72
I would be upset if my (minister/priest/rabbi) were to participate in a picket line or demonstration.	72
Martin Luther King, Jr., is an outstanding example of making Christianity relevant and meaningful for our day.	29

The large majority indicate that they believe that concern for others is a good indicator of one's religiousness. Similarly, a large majority assent to the abstract idea that clergy should speak out as the moral conscience of this country. Yet, in their attitudes toward the civil rights movement and its leadership, and in their feelings about clergy involvement in civil rights, they seem, in large part, to contradict these general beliefs about the role of religion and the clergy in the achievement of a moral and just society.

So long as the cognitive processes of the mind can separate general values from the specific implications of these values, it is possible to profess belief in one thing and practice something quite different without experiencing any inner conflict or tension. The civil rights crisis has been approached in precisely this manner by the majority of American church-goers. General recognition of the deprivation of the American Creed of liberty and justice and the Gospel's creed of love and brotherhood to a minority of twenty million blacks does not, in itself, lead to the specific actions of remedy.

In spite of the liberal views of clergy, institutionalized religion has not confronted the civil rights issue in a way that has had much positive effect on the beliefs and practices of its membership. Rather, the church has permitted people

to sit in comfortable pews and reaffirm belief in brotherhood and love while escaping the implications and applications of this belief, the real issues of social
justice. Instead of heralding the challenge, and championing the cause, to re-
create the world as a place that is "good" and "life-giving," a place wherein all
men are seen as "created in his image and likeness," the churches have compromised their vision to more palatable charity bazaars and suppers for the far-away
pagans and orphans. As did El Gallo to the Girl in *The Fantastics,* the church
has offered its followers rose-colored glasses.

Part of the churches' failure must certainly result from the failure of many
clergy to face the issues head-on. Many have preached brotherhood, but failed to
underscore the brotherhood of *all* men. They have spoken in general or abstract
terms, hoping that those in the pews would understand the specific implications.
The implications, however, either remained mostly unperceived or, if recognized,
usually led to pressures, financial and otherwise, urging either different sermons
or a different clergyman.

But there is also some evidence to suggest that the church's failure in the civil
rights struggle is a function of its own belief system. A recent paper by Stark and
Glock postulates that underlying ideological assumptions of Christian doctrine
undergird and subtly support racial prejudice. They write:

> Underlying traditional Christian thought is an image of man as a
> free actor, as essentially unfettered by social circumstances, free to
> choose and thus free to effect his own salvation. This free-will con-
> ception of man has been central to the doctrines of sin and salvation.
> For only if man is totally free does it seem just to hold him respon-
> sible for his acts, to punish him for his sins, and to demand repent-
> ance. . . . The significance of this for prejudice is that radical and
> traditional Christian images of man prompt those who hold them to
> put the blame for disadvantage upon the individuals who are dis-
> advantaged. A radical free-will image of man makes for an inability
> to perceive the effect of those forces outside the individual which
> may utterly dominate his circumstances. . . . The simple fact seems
> to be that a great many church people, because they believe men are
> mainly in control of their own individual destinies, think that
> Negroes are largely to blame for their present misery.[11]

Stark and Glock report that this free-will image of man tends to be more prevalent among the more active church members in their studies. Moreover, the
free-willers are much more committed to conservative politics. In my own national survey of laymen, I found that 86 percent agreed that Negroes would be
better off if they would take advantage of the opportunities that have been made
available to them. Protestants were more likely than Catholics to agree with this
view, and Jews were much less willing to agree.

This theory is intriguing and has a certain compelling logic. Systematic examination of this proposition ought to rank high in the research priorities of social

scientists who are interested in prejudice. If further research should point toward the validity of the thesis, it will be one of social science's most important
findings.

While research data are yet insufficient to verify this theoretical proposition,
there can be no escaping the conclusion that the churches have not succeeded in
reducing prejudice among laymen. Moreover, it is becoming increasingly clear
that clergymen's efforts to communicate their understanding of the implications
of the Christian faith for race relations are encountering resistance. Whatever the
underlying reasons, laity do not see the same implications. The more the clergymen urge these ideas, the greater the conflict. The critical question is how much
urging clergymen are doing.

Behavior

Granted that clergy express deep concern for blacks and have quite liberal attitudes about issues of civil rights and social justice, how much have they been willing to do in order to match their words with deeds? This is not an easy question
to answer because (1) the data available are much less systematic and (2) ambi-
guities accrue in measuring involvement. Is the clergyman who marches anonymously in a large group more involved than the minister who would not dream of
carrying a picket sign, but is not afraid to hit civil rights issues head-on from the
pulpit? The answer to the question is not at all obvious.

However, it does seem clear from the data available that clergy involvement in
overt actions of protest for the cause of social justice is much greater than is generally believed by the American public. The average American thinks of the social actionist clergy in terms of a very small minority of "nuts" or "kooks."
There are reasons for this misperception of reality. One important dimension is
the fact that many clergy participate anonymously—sans collar or other clerical
identification and without the knowledge of their constituency. But a second
important reason is that the image of a clergyman involved in protest is so foreign that the average person simply refuses to believe it.

I encountered firsthand experience of this selective perception very early in
my studies of clergy involvement in protest. Picking up a newspaper, I commented to a desk clerk in the hotel where I was staying, "I see there were some
ministers arrested in the demonstration yesterday." "Yeah," he replied, "I saw
it on the news last night. They arrested Father X. They ought to lock him in the
can and throw away the key." I then asked him if he was aware that there were
thirty-nine clergymen arrested during the demonstration. Surprised, he replied,
"You're kidding. There might be a few more nuts in the world like that Father
X, but not right here in this town." This man watched the television news report
of that event. At least ten of the arrested clergy wore clerical collars.

Although systematic samples of clergy participation are not available, numerous case studies offer information on the extent of clergy involvement in civil
rights activities. Since 1963 there have been three events in which large numbers
of clergy have participated. The first was the 1963 Civil Rights March on Wash-

ington. The second was the Selma march in the spring of 1965. Because no records exist, it is impossible to determine just how many clergy were involved in each of these marches. Newspaper accounts vary widely, ranging from two thousand to more than ten thousand clergy participating in each of these marches. In the spring of 1967, approximately 2,600 clergymen and seminary students participated in a Clergy Mobilization March on Washington to protest the Vietnam war.

Local conflict situations are perhaps more revealing of the uneasiness of clergy about the civil rights crisis in this nation and of the extent of their mobilization in moments of crisis. In Cleveland, 221 clergymen (40 percent of the metropolitan area's white Protestant clergy) became involved in the Emergency Committee of Clergy for Civil Rights during the educational crisis in that city in 1964. An indeterminate but not insignificant number of this group participated in picketing. Sixty percent of the group signed a statement released to the press demanding the resignation of the Board of Education. During the summer of 1965, 444 civil rights demonstrators were arrested in two days of protesting in Chicago. One quarter of this group were clergymen and nuns. In 1966, 132 Detroit clergymen signed a statement pledging civil disobedience and submission to arrest if Mayor Jerome Cavanagh did not respond to housing demands of the poor.

These are but examples. The evidence seems clear that involvement of clergy is considerably more extensive than "a very small minority." The nature of involvement, of course, varies enormously. Similarly, activists do not emerge at random from the ranks of the clergy. We have already noted that younger and theologically liberal clergy tend to have more liberal views about civil rights. Hence, we would expect them to be more involved in activist roles, and, indeed, this is the case. Social-structural variables, however, seem to be more important in determining whether or not a clergyman will play an activist role. In my case studies, I was able to isolate three critical factors.

The first is the stance taken by his denomination, or in the case of a Catholic priest, the position of his bishop. The stronger the denominational position, the greater the probability of a clergyman's involvement. The second, and most critical, structural factor is the type of position the clergyman occupies. Nonparish clergy are much more involved in direct protest action and militant strategies than those clergymen who serve a congregation. The third factor is the presence of group support. Group interaction serves to reinforce the members' sense of the legitimacy of the concern and also tends to raise the level of the commitment of individual members. In several cases that I observed, clergy initially joined together for the purpose of discussing a problem without any intention of taking action. But the group reinforcement and the perception of the problem as critical then led to collective action.

Involvement, of course, may not be the result of interaction with other clergy. In many cases, the involvement emerges through efforts to minister to persons or groups of minority status. For example, the inner-city clergyman who is attempting to relate to a gang may find that his credibility with the group is dependent upon getting involved. Protest is a symbolic gesture of his commitment and concern for their problems. But, even here, the group process is the same. The group reinforces the legitimacy of the cause—supports, and indeed encourages, what they perceive as appropriate behavior. Having identified with the group, the clergyman must act in accordance with the group's expectations or be rejected.

In the attitudinal data above, we saw that three-quarters of the laity say that they would be upset if their minister became involved in social protest. Dozens of case studies indicate that they frequently become upset enough to dismiss the minister. But just as selective perception takes place in viewing the media's reporting of clergy involvement in civil rights protests, so, too, does this happen in interpreting conflict in the local congregation. For every minister who has been dismissed because his stance on issues of social justice was too bold, there are several others who were dismissed for "neglecting their parish duties" or some similar charge. Also, in some denominations, built-in expectations of relatively frequent pulpit changes have obviously quenched many a brewing fire.

The Years Ahead

The civil rights movement, as it was symbolized and personified by Dr. Martin Luther King, Jr., is now dead. For the moment, at least, blacks are largely committed to going it alone. These developments had the immediate effect of taking the pressure off clergymen to find overt expression for their consciences. But the lull did not last long. While blacks were busy working out their own thing, clergy began to heed the call of students to resist the war effort in Vietnam.

Virtually every war in history has been fought in the name of a deity. This nation has never experienced more than token resistance to its military efforts from the clergy. But all this is now prologue. Although clergy are much more divided on the war issue than they are about civil rights, there is a growing sentiment among them that the war is morally wrong, and consequently, they have become an important part of the war-resistance movement.

Quinley's California data again provide evidence that clergy involvement in the antiwar movement is not an isolated development by a very small minority.[12] Twenty-nine percent of the clergy in his sample were classified as hawks. The theologically conservative Southern Baptists and Missouri Synod Lutherans, who represented only 18 percent of the sample, accounted for more than half the hawks. Among the theological liberals, only 8 percent were hawks.

Of those who are most dovish (about 35 percent of the total sample), 85 percent believe it is appropriate to express one's convictions by participating in an antiwar protest march. Moreover, almost three-quarters approve of civil disobedience. Nineteen percent have actually participated in an antiwar protest, and 7 percent have committed acts of civil disobedience. These are the most extreme forms of protest behavior. A substantial number have engaged in "lesser" forms. More than a third have joined peace organizations. Almost half have attended a protest meeting. The same proportion have organized study groups. Four-fifths have delivered sermons on the war. More than half have signed a petition, and almost the same percentage have written a public official.

These figures certainly indicate a fairly high level of participation. Quinley does not report differences in participation by place of residence. It is clear, however, that clergy residing in metropolitan areas were more involved than clergy from smaller communities. One can only speculate, but the participation rate among clergy in the San Francisco Bay area must have been very high.

The Vietnam war is much more complex than the civil rights issue. Ideologically, it is much more an unsettled issue. The cross-pressures have resulted in laity's expressing somewhat greater tolerance of clergy involvement than has been the case with civil rights. Nonetheless, Quinley reports that local parishioners were more than twice as likely to discourage a minister's antiwar activities as they were to encourage him. One-quarter of the doves report losses in financial contributions to their churches, and approximately the same proportion report some loss of membership. About one in ten indicated that there had been an organized effort to have him removed from his pulpit.

These data lend support to my thesis that the civil rights movement of the late 1950s and early 1960s unleashed a deep sense of social consciousness among clergy that must find expression in social action and an ongoing commitment to the creation of a more just world. The data also reaffirm the layman's uneasiness about the widening gap between his perceptions and those of the clergy on the meaning and purpose of the church.

In the spring of 1969, the churches faced a new crisis—perhaps with more far-reaching implications than any development of a decade that was already unprecedented in turmoil for religious institutions. On April 26, James Forman presented a "Black Manifesto" to the National Black Economic Development Conference (NBEDC). The assembled voted to adopt the Manifesto by a 3 to 1 margin. The following week, Mr. Forman presented the Manifesto to the General Board of the National Council of Churches. The core of the Manifesto: a demand that the churches of America pay $500 million in reparations to blacks for injustices resulting from slavery.

The American public responded to the Black Manifesto as though it were a sick joke. The NCC's General Board responded in deadly earnest:

> The General Board records its deep appreciation to Mr. James Forman for his presentation of an explanation concerning the Black Manifesto and shares the aspirations of the Black people of this country from which it sprang. . . . The Board urges that the communions [denominations] give serious study to the Manifesto, expecting that each communion will act on the matter in its own way.

In the months that followed, Forman and the NBEDC did not collect very much of the demanded reparations—which were raised to $3 billion—but the

churches were trembling at their foundations. Again and again, as the denominations held their annual meetings, the Black Manifesto was the key item on the
agenda. The schisms cut in several directions, but, again, the deepest rift was
between clergy and laity.

In August, the *New York Times* reported the results of its own study of
church finances, showing that the national programs of the major Protestant denominations are suffering their first cutback in funds since the Depression.[13]
Hardest hit are the social-action programs. Perhaps even more significant is the
fact that these cutbacks largely occurred *before* the appearance of the Black
Manifesto. Denominational offices are being flooded with mail from laymen
who are enraged that their church could even consider responding to Forman.

As the 1960s come to a close, the stage is set for the unfolding drama of the
1970s. There seems to be little hope for altering the course of conflict. The
average church layman in America is not much different in his social views from
the average John Q. Public. The large majority of Americans believe that black
militants and college demonstrators have been treated too leniently. Nearly two-
thirds believe that police should have more power and that constitutional rights
should be denied those who are accused of criminal acts.[14] Although we do not
have an end-of-decade study of clergymen's views on these subjects, all the evidence indicates that they are largely at variance with these views. Clergy did
much in the 1960s to aid institutional and legislative change in the area of human
rights. If the churches are to survive the 1970s, the clergy must devote much
more of their energies toward changing men's hearts.

NOTES

1. Robert W. Spike, *The Freedom Revolution and the Churches* (New York: Association Press, 1965), p. 69.
2. Rodney Stark and Charles Y. Gₛⱼck, "Prejudice and the Churches," in Charles Y. Glock and Ellen Siₗgelman, eds., *Prejudice U.S.A.* (New York: Frederick A. Praeger, 1969).
3. These themes are developed in Jeffrey K. Hadden, *The Gathering Storm in the Churches* (Garden City, N.Y.: Doubleday, 1969).
4. Ernest Q. Campbell and Thomas F. Pettigrew, *Christians in Racial Crisis* (Washington, D.C.: Public Affairs Press, 1959). Obviously, a major obstacle to studying the role of clergy has been the scarcity of research monies for "controversial" issues. Indeed, for much the same reason, the unfolding drama of the civil rights movement has not been studied nearly so system-atically as it should have been.
5. Kenneth Underwood, *The Church, the University, and Social Policy*, 2 vols. (Middletown, Conn.: Wesleyan University Press, 1969).
6. Details of my own investigation appear in Hadden, *The Gathering Storm in the Churches.*
7. Jeffrey K. Hadden, "The Private Generation," *Psychology Today* (October 1969).

8. Results of the Trimble study were reported in "A Study Report on the Miami Assembly," *Information Service*, May 6, 1967. A reanalysis of these data appear in Hadden, *The Gathering Storm in the Churches*, pp. 198–205.

9. Harold Quinley, "Hawks and Doves among the Clergy: Protestant Reaction to the War in Vietnam," *Ministry Studies*, vol. 3, no. 3, 1969.

10. An interpretation of this is developed in some detail in *The Gathering Storm in the Churches*, chap. 4: "Clergy and Laity View the Civil Rights Issue."

11. Stark and Glock, "Prejudice and the Churches," pp. 80–82.

12. Quinley, "Hawks and Doves among the Clergy."

13. *New York Times*, August 10, 1969.

14. *Newsweek*, vol. 74, no 14, October 6, 1969.

THE JESUS GENERATION

Edward F. Heenan

It has been almost ten years since the announcement of the "death of God" by theologians Altizer, Van Buren, and Hamilton.[1] We were told that his death was not "unexpected" and that he died "during major surgery to correct a massive diminishing influence."[2] The news was traumatic to those who had believed in him so strongly. Others were less affected, recognizing in this startling proclamation a profound need not to eliminate the concept of God, but simply to change his image. Still others, whose credentials are unquestioned but whose investment in religion was minimal, found evidence for the dawn of a post-Christian era.[3]

With the aid of hindsight, it would seem that these predictions were, for the most part, premature. Unless one is extremely selective about what he admits as evidence, it seems clear that the concepts of God and religion are still alive in the minds of the majority of Americans. It seems equally clear, however, that the packaging of the image of God has changed in the last decade. Rather than focusing on a God "out there," the emphasis recently has been on the incarnate or immanent deity. In the Western religious tradition this means Jesus.

Jesus began his rise from association with a moribund God figure in a most improbable place—in the underground establishment and in the headshops that have emerged as the Sears Roebuck of the youth counter-culture. Posters proliferated, advertising Jesus as a hippie, capitalizing on the length of his hair, and marketing his radical political ideologies. The youth counter-culture was sold on Jesus.

After a period of a few years, Jesus settled in as the traditional American antihero. The antihero tends to be a figure who (1) is opposed to the law, which is seen as the corrupt tool of those who wish to protect vested interests, (2) is a friend to the poor and gives generously to them out of a sense of justice, (3) is inclined to subscribe to orthodox religion, (4) adopts the role of a "trickster" vis-à-vis the authorities, and (5) tends to be subject to betrayal by friends.[4] Conformity to these characteristics placed the historical Jesus at the center of the

From Edward F. Heenan, ed., *Mystery, Magic, and Miracle*, ©1973, Prentice-Hall, Inc., Englewood Cliffs, New Jersey. Reprinted by permission of the author.

youth counter-culture. As with most cult heroes, Jesus was called upon both to symbolize and to legitimize the emerging youth counter-culture.

Jesus' rise to prominence among the young in such a short span of time surely qualifies him for the label that Andy Warhol reserved for cult heroes—a Superstar. Looking back, it is ironic that John Lennon's assertion about the Beatles was reversed in so short a time. Jesus is again more popular than the Beatles.

Like the Beatles, Jesus' appeal has not been restricted to the youth counter-culture. The movement has developed corollary expressions with the emergence of "Jesus people," with a strong fundamentalist ideology, and of "Jesus freaks," who have a strong antidrug ideology.

Although each of these movements is characteristically located among the young, they differ in their levels of intensity and commitment to Jesus and their ideology regarding him. "Jesus people" believe him to be clearly the deity who acts in their daily existence through miracles, while "Jesus freaks" see him as one of the first and purest examples of the antihero—the hero as loser or the hero as a regular guy, just like all of us. The point is that all the young who have turned on to Jesus have not done so for the same reasons.

Why the Movement at This Time:
The Concomitant Conditions

Social scientists have found evidence for a religious revival having occurred in the 1950s.[5] The current interest in Jesus, however, differs from the revival of the '50s, and the major difference seems to be that the present revival is taking place primarily outside the churches.

The current revival differs from that of the '50s as much as a Brahms symphony differs from a rock festival, or as the Four Freshmen differ from the Grateful Dead. The religious revival of the '50s was a revival of institutional religion, whereas the recent "Jesus revival" is contrary to institutional religion and perhaps even antagonistic toward it. The Jesus generation holds beliefs similar to those of other Christians, but they practice these beliefs and experience the person of Jesus more enthusiastically and ecstatically than members of the traditional churches. The depth of their antagonism is, therefore, not related to the dogma of mainline denominations but to their bureaucratic organization. The churches in America have become outstanding examples of bureaucracy,[6] and the values of bureaucracy are diametrically opposed to the primary values of these young people.

However, the relationship between youth and the traditional churches is more complex. Both religious revivals coincide with particular points in the life cycle of these young people. Nash and Berger[7] suggest that the swelling of the church rolls in the '50s was due to an influx of children of primary-school age. Parents became affiliated with the institutional church for a variety of reasons. Some desired to see their children receive moral training; some wanted to escape the problems of urban public schools; others wished to see their children get a higher quality, parochial-school education. In effect, a large group of postwar babies led their parents to church.

If the first of the recent religious revivals was due to children "dropping in" to the churches, the most recent revival began at the time the same statistical cohort of children began to "drop out" of bureaucratic religion and to "turn on" to alternate interpretive schemes. The ideals of organized religion and many of its concepts and values gave impetus to this search for meaning.

The antagonism of youth toward bureaucracy and their impact on demographic changes are not causal factors, however, but rather concomitant conditions of the development of the Jesus generation. Ironically, still another conditioning factor in the movement toward new religious interpretations is the church-initiated ecumenical movement. The ecumenical movement's explicit purpose is to unify the churches. Instead, ecumenism has tacitly given all religious movements equal claim to legitimation. It has resulted in an expanded religious "marketplace," with new religious expressions taken as seriously as traditional religious forms.

The consequences of increasing bureaucratization and demographic changes on an expanded religious marketplace were felt not only in denominational religion but also in civil religion in the United States. According to Robert Bellah civil religion in the United States is a well-institutionalized set of public beliefs and rituals that are held in common by most Americans.[8] In this consensual religion, George Washington is revered as our Moses, the man who finally led us out of captivity and established us as a people with a manifest destiny. The civil religion had its scriptures concretized in the Bill of Rights and the Constitution. It had its scribes in the members of the Supreme Court. It had its savior—the man who died to preserve its integrity and to redeem it with his blood—in the person of Abraham Lincoln. Consequently, civil religion, or the religion of democracy, led this nation to carry out its foreign policy with missionary zeal. Beyond their denominational affiliations, this was the syncretic but common religion that held Americans together, that integrated American society, and that over a period of four centuries inextricably bound American religion with the democratic state.

The first indication of the breakdown of civil religion occurred early in the last decade, when many young people severed ties with their churches in order to invest their energies in the Southern civil rights movement. Perhaps most characteristic of the civil rights movement in the South was the religious motif of redemptive suffering. It was expressed in the strategy of nonviolence. Closely allied with nonviolence were two other religious themes, communalism and asceticism. The final religious themes that attracted young people to the civil rights movement were the ideas of prophetic authority and transcendence. These themes are, of course, intertwined with and derived from the concept of redemptive suffering. Those who suffer unjustly will ultimately transcend this suffering and be rewarded with victory. However, the movement that began as a sacred movement in the South secularized when it came North and finally died in the ashes of Watts.

Yet out of the civil rights experience a new, radical white movement based on the college campus arose. The ties between the leadership of SDS and the civil rights movements, especially SNCC, are clear. However, this movement offered the young not an expressly sacred movement but a movement based on secular morality. Newfield suggests that when SDSers are posed with a possible strategy they ask themselves not, "Is it workable?" or "How much support can we get on this from the liberals?" They ask themselves, "Is it right to do this?"[9] It was this moral idealism, especially when it was tied to the war in Vietnam, that held appeal to many middle-class, white young people. Nevertheless, that appeal was lost when it became obvious that SDS offered only a free-floating morality, with no sense of transcendent mission.

These movements, which attracted the energy of many young people, were merely the precursors of the breakdown of civil religion. The final bifurcation of civil religion occurred more dramatically as the Vietnam War became an increasingly divisive force. The consensual values of American civil religion were created in the context of two wars, but they broke down during the third. The Vietnam War fragmented them so that rationally stated religious views about identity, destiny, and nation were not to be found. Nevertheless, the need for religious views still prevailed among the young. They had dropped out of denominational religion (or at least were not committed to it), had seen the civil religion that President Kennedy had spoken so eloquently for in his Inaugural Address shattered in Dallas and DaNang, and so turned to alternate schemes of meaning, symbols, and rituals in an effort to achieve a sense of transcendence.

The young were greatly in need of some unifying experience, some deeply felt focus for their lives. As a result, many turned to drugs and rock music. These experiences were sought by the young because they added new dimensions to their lives and put ordinary experience in a different perspective. Yet the drug ethos—the shared symbols, rituals, communal feelings—was a religious phenomenon without reference to a super-empirical deity. It sought transcendence in the inner dimensions of the self.

Rock music supplies the occasion for the ritualistic celebration of this expression of the inner-self as well as for a new social ethos. A rock festival is a celebration of a communal life and epitomizes egalitarianism. Drugs and rock music supply a means of identification, a vehicle for finding meaning, and an impetus for living out a transcendent sense of reality.

While each of these movements wanders further away from traditional religion, it has been left to the Jesus movement to fashion the values of each of these alternative schemes into a quasi-traditional religious movement. Having examined some of the sources of the Jesus movement, let us now turn to its dimensions.

Who Joins the Movement: The Religious Youth Culture

There are a large number of young people both in the churches and outside of them who endorse religious values or endorse values of the youth culture that are religious in nature. They use religious values as symbols, respond to them in their music, and think of these values as part of the discovery being made by young people.

Berger's discussion of the "youth movement" is particularly useful in analyzing this religious movement. He distinguishes between three related but distinct concepts—youth culture, youth movement, and radical movements.[10] These concepts can be thought of as concentric circles, each smaller than the preceding one.

Youth culture is the broadest of these phenomena. It is found in all advanced industrial societies and has its roots in the composition of the populations of these societies. It finds its most consistent expressions in music, the media, clothes, and the use of soft drugs such as marijuana.

The second entity, that of youth movements, represents an ad hoc activation of the youth culture around certain issues or values that are salient to some of its members. Youth movements require more of a commitment on the part of their members. They are goal oriented, but use legitimate means, and are characteristically political in nature, although politics is not endemic to such movements. The "Children's Crusade" of Senator McCarthy in 1968 would be an example of the youth movement.

The third entity, that of radical movements, is at the moment in a state of tenuous symbiosis with the broader youth context. It of course demands a higher level of commitment than the other levels of the youth movement, involves fewer individuals, and is goal oriented, but its tactics are considered less than legitimate by most of those in the broader youth context. The Weathermen faction of SDS would be an example of the radical youth movement.

The Religious Youth Culture

The extent of the religious motif in the youth culture is evidenced by the number of rock musicians who have incorporated faith rock in their recordings. The list includes: Judy Collins (*Amazing Grace*); Spirit in the Flesh (*Spirit in the Flesh*); Cat Stevens (*Tea for the Tillerman*); The Who (*Tommy*); Moody Blues (all albums); Country Joe McDonald (*Hold On It's Coming*); Kris Kristofferson (*The Silver Tongued Devil and I*); Bob Dylan (*New Morning*); Jethro Tull (*Aqualung*); George Harrison (*All Things Must Pass*); Donovan (*Wear Your Love Like Heaven*); Johnny Cash (*The Holy Land*); and the Beatles (*Sergeant Pepper* and *Magical Mystery Tour*). Eastern religious rock is represented by George Harrison, Swami Satchidananda, Pharoah Sanders (*Karma*), and the Radha Krishna Temple. Occult rock is represented by La Lupe, Mick Jagger, and Black Sabbath.

It is difficult to discern whether this music created a culture responsive to religious themes or whether the religious interests of the culture enabled the groups to express these themes in the most significant medium of youth—their music. However, this music does reveal the values placed on ecstasy in youth culture and correspondingly the devaluation of science, technology, rationality, totalistic theories, and bureaucracy.[11]

The religious values of the youth culture have also been demonstrated in two New York stage productions, *Jesus Christ Superstar* and *Godspell*—both musicals, both centered about the gospel narratives of the life of Jesus, and both enormous successes. This, of course, is not the first time God has starred on Broadway (*Green Pastures,* 1930; *J.B.,* 1956; and *Gideon,* 1961), but previously He had been cast in fairly traditional Godly roles.

In his most recent appearances Jesus takes on other dimensions. *Godspell* represents the fun-and-games interpretation of religion. It features a clown in patchwork overalls (Harvey Cox—*Feast of Fools*) who bears little resemblance to the Jesus portrayed in the gospel. Nevertheless, He and His followers remind one of Ken Kesey and his Merry Pranksters (*The Electric Kool Aid Acid Test*) and they do entertain, with their pratfalls, pure energy, and vaudevillean charm.

The second coming on Broadway (the best-publicized ever) was *Jesus Christ Superstar.* Here, with the help of Tom O'Horgan (*Hair*), we have God at his gaudiest, making his entrance in a monumental silver cape, singing saccharine songs of peace and love.

But in the end, questions of aesthetic merit and theological verity do not explain the importance or success of these musicals. The explanation is found in understanding their social purpose. The composition of the audiences seems to indicate that these productions are a means of reducing the chasm between the young and the middle-aged. No doubt both groups filter the experience through their own perspectives while hoping it is something to be shared. Parents feel that toying with religion is at least less noxious an opiate than methamphetamine. In addition, these productions provide for the possibility of a ritualistic celebration (an indoor Woodstock Festival) of the values of the Woodstock Nation. They affirm the solidarity of the young, legitimize their values, and serve as a means of recruitment to these values.

The values that these musicals espouse are humanistic and personalistic ones such as sensitivity, responsiveness, openness, sensualism, ecstacy, communal solidarity, peace, antimaterialism, and radical egalitarianism (which explains their emphasis on the humanity of Jesus). All of those values were nascent in previous youth movements and emerged in response to the continuing problem of bureaucratic rationalism— an ethos of emphatic impersonality. However, the recent trend in music and the stage productions involving Jesus have provided a context for the articulation of the values of the new humanism as well as a context within which young people may become seriously interested in religious transcendence. They precipitate, or at least facilitate, the development of religious movements. The broad youth culture has permitted a quiet interest in Jesus, yoga, meditation, Hare Krishna, Meher Baba, astrology, and the use of drugs for the purpose of transcendent experience.

The Religious Youth Movement

The second entity, which draws its membership from the first, is that of religious youth movements. The religious youth movements centered on the person of Jesus can be somewhat arbitrarily divided into those of "Jesus people" and those of "Jesus freaks." Jesus people are the current members of campus organizations whose existence predates the renewed interest of the Jesus generation.

Such organizations as the Campus Crusade for Christ and Navigators, whose membership files were embarrassingly empty only five years ago, are now exhibiting new vigor. The revival of such organizations seems to indicate a symbiotic or possibly parasitical relationship between them and the media exposure of the Jesus freaks. In contrast to "Jesus people," "Jesus freaks" are more allied with the values of the youth culture and less allied with the values of the mainline churches.

However, "Jesus freaks" do not totally endorse all the values of the youth culture. What distinguishes this group is that the individual member has committed himself to the goal of the movement but usually has not done so on a full-time basis or has not organized around that goal.

Some aspects of the "Jesus freak" movement illustrate this level of analysis. It is an amorphous movement with its own symbols (One Way!), rituals (free concerts, with an invitation to accept Jesus), newspaper (*Hollywood Free Paper*) and musicians (J. C. Power Outlet and Love Song). It is composed of two age groups. The first is a fringe group of "Jesus boppers"—white, middle-class teenagers who perhaps find the movement a temporary solution to problems of the psychosexual identity crisis characteristic of early adolescence.[12] The second group is a smaller, more intense group of young adults who reportedly have extensive experience in the drug culture. For these the Jesus movement is often a ritual of reentry into the system from which they previously dropped out. Both groups are fundamentalist, authoritarian, revivalistic, antiintellectual, antirational, and politically conservative. Their values are similar to those of the youth cultures in some respects, but differ in other respects. "Jesus freaks" espouse personalistic values, ecstasy, sensitivity, responsiveness, openness, communal solidarity, and anti-materialism, which they have channeled into a religious movement. On the other hand, they reject the values of sensualism and radical egalitarianism that the youth culture has adopted.

Radical Religious Movements

The final level of the Jesus generation is that of the radical religious movements. The distinguishing characteristics of these movements are the intensity of their option for "other-worldly" values and their commitment to organize around these values. This level is comprised of autonomous religious communes, which are often not visible because they are located in rural areas and their members live an ascetic, pastoral existence that does not include proselytizing. The members are not employed outside of the commune and do not participate in the cultic aspects of the Jesus movement. Their values are similar to the personalistic values of the movement, except that they are more ascetic, disciplined, and antimaterialistic and emphasize communal solidarity to a greater extent. They also differ from the youth culture over the question of egalitarianism. At very least, they maintain the hierarchy between themselves and God.

Conclusion

The last decade has seen a number of youth movements, of which the Jesus generation is a partial product. Throughout this period young people have gradually fashioned a set of values that differ from those of the preceding generation. They have been engaged in a "bargaining process" between their culture and the larger society—a bargaining process that sees the young increasingly successful in achieving acceptance of their definition of reality. At this point, whether Jesus will have a meaningful place in this definition of reality or whether the majority of young people will continue to worship only themselves remains to be seen.

NOTES

1. Harvey Cox, "The Death of God and the Future of Theology," in William Robert Miller, ed., *The New Christianity* (New York: Delacorte Press, 1967), pp. 377–389.
2. Anthony Towne, "God is Dead in Georgia," *Motive*, February 1966.
3. Rodney Stark and Charles Y. Glock, *American Piety: The Nature of Religious Commitment* (Berkeley: University of California Press, 1968).
4. Kent L. Steckmesser, "Robin Hood and the American Outlaw," in *Journal of American Folklore*, 79, 348–354.
5. Charles Y. Glock, "The Religious Revival in America," in *Religion and the Face of America* (Berkeley: University of California Press, 1959); Seymour M. Lipset, "What Religious Revival?" in *Columbia University Forum*, 2 (1959), 17–21.
6. Gibson Winter, "Religious Organization," in W. Lloyd Warner, ed., *The Emergent American Society*, I: *Large-Scale Organizations* (New Haven: Yale University Press, 1967).
7. Dennison Nash and Peter Berger, "The Child, the Family, and the 'Religious Revival' in Suburbia," in *Journal for the Scientific Study of Religion*, 1 (1962), 85–93. See also Dennison Nash, "A Little Child Shall Lead Them: A Statistical Test of an Hypothesis that Children Were the Source of the American Religious Revival," in *Journal for the Scientific Study of Religion*, vol. 7, no. 2 (1968), 238–240.
8. Robert N. Bellah, "Civil Religion in America," in *Daedalus*, vol. 96, no. 1 (1967), 1–22.
9. Jack Newfield, *A Prophetic Minority* (New York: Signet Books, 1966). See also Harvey Cox, "The New Breed in American Churches: Sources of Social Activism in American Religion," in *Daedalus*, vol. 96, no. 1 (1967), 135–150.
10. Peter L. Berger and Richard J. Neuhaus, *Movement and Revolution* (Garden City, New York: Anchor Books, 1970).
11. Theodore Roszak, *The Making of the Counter Culture* (New York: Doubleday, 1969); Charles Reich, *The Greening of America* (New York: Random House, Inc., 1970); and Philip Slater, *In Pursuit of Loneliness: American Culture at the Breaking Point* (Boston: The Beacon Press, 1970).
12. Robert Adams and Robert Fox, "Mainlining Jesus," in *Transaction*, vol. 9, no. 4 (February 1972), 50–56.

Epilogue

This book has examined six major sets of organizations, or institutions, in American society. They do not fully define our society, nor are many of our problems found in them. Everyday life is too rich to be captured in full by simply looking at these six institutions. Our lives are shaped by many other interactions and involvements outside of them, in the family, friendship groups, voluntary associations, in spontaneous crowds, and in front of a TV set. Nonetheless, these large scale organizations set many limits on the way we live and either directly or indirectly cause many of our problems. They are the backbone of the society as well as the source of seemingly irresolvable contradictions.

Science has come to dominate our thought patterns, with perhaps dangerous results. But science is not well coordinated, nor are there powerful independent scientific organizations. Instead, most scientists are employed by organizations whose first interests are *not* the discovery of new knowledge for public benefit. Science, then, is not self-ordered. Its priorities and the uses of its resources are set by political, economic, and military policy-makers. Whether science can meet the challenges of the future is an open question. Clearly, in the fields of food and energy, science will have a hard task. In medicine it is in crisis already. Health care in America takes place in an economic setting—health for profit. In this system, physicians carve out lucrative careers selling their knowledge. Real advances in medicine, however, come from less wealthy researchers, many of them medical doctors working in hospitals and laboratories. Meanwhile, the public is confronted with expensive care, slipshod public services, and degenerating hospitals that are more expensive than luxury hotels. America's basic health statistics often place us well below the world's leading countries.

Education is another institution that is hard pressed to meet the demands thrust upon it. At all levels, education is short of funds, and there is inequality between schools and educational systems characterized by lack of coordination. Our schools have been unable to provide equally valued educations for all their students, and many schools are battlegrounds for the struggles of the outside world. Perhaps more than anything, schools suffer from uncertainty. We do not know fully what skills the graduate of tomorrow will need, nor even whether the other institutions can employ all of the future students that will be certified as "educated." Cultured minds will be of little value if their bodies cannot be fed. In consequence, the educational process all too often becomes a rat race, and schools become certification mills that determine who shall live well and who shall live in poverty.

Religious organizations, at least the old established ones, are in crisis in America. Their leadership is often not in tune with lay followers, their goals are often unclear, and recruitment is difficult. New organizations and movements, however, are constantly springing up, and powerful new spiritual organizations may well grow to prominence as other institutions lose their magic.

The three big institutions—the economy, polity, and military—and the power balance among them account for a large portion of the society's character. They also cause many of its problems. Military organizations have used a colossal share of resources, and while they guarantee civilian order, they are always a threat to it. In the United States, the military and their business contractors have had inordinate political influence. Toward the end of the Southeast Asian war the armed forces showed signs of internal decay, but they still wield massive organizational strength. Their struggle for resources in the name of national defense is far from over, and the question "How much is enough?" is not yet resolved.

Political institutions are similarly unstable. The government bureaucracies are large and often lack direction. At the state level they approach bankruptcy. Elected politicians lack a strong organizational base and are remote from their constituents, the public. Elections, rather than mobilizing a politically knowledgeable public, are more often popularity polls based on media campaigns. We may in the future continue the trend to buy our politicians like soap powder. Alternatively, we may form strong new political organizations and parties, or act more spontaneously through social movements. In one way or another, politics is likely to change.

Economic organizations, by and large, dominate life in America. The economy is controlled not by the self-employed individualistic capitalist but by the giant corporations. They are often very active overseas, and together they shape economic life—wages, prices, types of goods marketed, forms of entertainment, even in part the way we think. Their power is not absolute, but it is very extensive. The economy determines much of our physical lives, our status and self-images. Success is measured in dollars. Corporations create "needs" through advertising and sell their products in an unstable spiral of consumption. The largest corporations and banks, it is argued, should bear much responsibility for the unequal chances of some minority groups, the aged, and women, and for the constant troubles of the permanently poor. Many changes will have to be made in economic organization if the social tensions and depravity of poverty in America are to be healed, and the deprived will not rest content until they have economic justice.